STUDIES IN HISTORY, ECONOMICS AND PUBLIC LAW

Edited by the
FACULTY OF POLITICAL SCIENCE
OF COLUMBIA UNIVERSITY

NUMBER 392

THE ELECTION OF 1868

BY

CHARLES H. COLEMAN

THE ELECTION OF 1868

THE DEMOCRATIC EFFORT
TO REGAIN CONTROL

BY

CHARLES H. COLEMAN

1971

OCTAGON BOOKS
New York

Reprinted 1971

by special arrangement with Columbia University Press

OCTAGON BOOKS

A DIVISION OF FARRAR, STRAUS & GIROUX, INC.

19 Union Square West

New York, N. Y. 10003

LIBRARY OF CONGRESS CATALOG CARD NUMBER: 73-159242

ISBN-0-374-91848-1

Printed in U.S.A. by

NOBLE OFFSET PRINTERS, INC.

NEW YORK 3, N. Y.

To

HENRY JOHNSON

TEACHER AND FRIEND
WHO TAUGHT ME AN APPRECIATION
OF THE DIGNITIES AND DUTIES
OF SCHOLARSHIP

PREFACE

THE deficiencies of this study are in part due to certain gaps in the sources which the writer was unable to bridge. No collections of the papers of a number of important figures in this investigation were located. Of greatest significance was the absence of the papers of August Belmont, Francis Preston Blair, Jr., George Hunt Pendleton and Winfield Scott Hancock. The Blair family papers in the Library of Congress were barren for the purpose of this investigation. The August Belmont papers were destroyed by fire. The papers of Samuel Jones Tilden are in the New York Public Library but are not open to investigators. The printed Bigelow collection of Tilden letters is from these papers, and this printed collection has been used.

Acknowledgment should be made of the helpful courtesies extended by the staffs of various libraries in which material was examined. These were: The New York City Public Library, Manuscripts Division; The New York State Historical Library at Albany; the Library of Congress, Manuscripts Division; the Library of the New York Historical Society in New York City; and the Library of the Pennsylvania Historical Society in Philadelphia.

A portion of the manuscript, bearing on Horatio Seymour, was read by Mr. Alexander J. Wall of the New York Historical Society. Mr. Wall is in no way responsible for errors that may exist in the discussion of Seymour.

Mr. S. E. Thomas, head of the History Department of the Eastern Illinois State Teachers College, very kindly read the entire manuscript. His valuable and frank criticism prevented the inclusion of a number of errors of fact and of

7

judgment. He is in no way responsible for those that remain.

Mr. Howard De F. Widger, of the English Department of the Eastern Illinois State Teachers College, very kindly read a large portion of the manuscript and offered many helpful suggestions regarding style.

Mr. Allan Nevins, of the History Department of Columbia University, provided the inspiration for this investigation. The general form of this study assumed shape in a seminar under him during the year 1929-1930. He read the manuscript in the original and subsequent forms and assisted materially in its revision. The author feels under deep obligation to Mr. Nevins for the more than generous amount of time and effort he expended in improving the style and form of this study. If the completed work even remotely approximates the high standard he constantly held up, the author will be content.

Charleston, Illinois,
March, 1933.

TABLE OF CONTENTS

ERRATA

P. 51n, for *Nayes* read *Hayes*.

P. 52n, *Infra*, p. ——, read 144.

P. 53, l. 11, for *us* read *use*; last line, for *condidate*, read *candidate*.

P. 94, l. 5, for *Edwards* read *Edmonds*.

P. 101n, *Infra*, pp. ——, read 155-157.

P. 153, for *Frèmont* read *Frémont*.

P. 154, l. 23, for *momevent*, read *movement*.

P. 173, l. 22, after *feel*, add the word *as*.

P. 177, last line, for *show* read *shown*.

P. 181, l. 10, for *condition* read *circumstance*.

P. 211, l. 22, for *underway*, read *under way*.

P. 216, l. 21, for *began*, read *begun*.

P. 217, l. 7, for *nor*, read *or*.

CHAPTER I

THE ISSUES BEFORE THE COUNTRY

I. RECONSTRUCTION

THE background of the political struggle with which we are concerned was the process of reconstructing the nation after four years of war. The story of reconstruction has been told by so many authors that we need not pause for more than a brief statement of those phases of reconstruction which had the greatest influence in determining the position of the two parties in 1868.

The three elements of reconstruction which were of greatest significance at this time were the fourteenth amendment, the efforts to impose dictated constitutions on the Southern States, and negro suffrage. This last we shall consider separately. Southern " outrages " against the negro and his Northern advisers on the one hand, and Southern protests against "negro domination" on the other received wide attention in the press of the time, and were discussed with exceptional vehemence during the campaign. We shall consider them in the discussion of that phase of the campaign.

The purpose of the fourteenth amendment was to give vitality and stability to Southern constitutions written under Radical Republican inspiration; in other words, to secure and preserve Republican ascendancy in the late Confederate States. That it was not considered sufficient for the purpose is shown by the fact that it was soon followed by the fifteenth amendment, which attempted to make an outright grant of negro suffrage.

The fourteenth amendment attempted to penalize those States which denied suffrage to the negro and to place a political handicap on the former Confederates who remained obnoxious to the Radical Republicans.   The amendment was submitted to the States on June 13, 1866.[1]   The Southern States were clubbed into accepting it by a refusal to admit their representatives to Congress until it had been ratified by them, and had become a part of the Constitution.[2] At first the "insurrectionary States," except Tennessee, rejected the amendment by decisive majorities but seven had reversed this action in time to be included in the ratifying States. Arkansas, Florida, North Carolina, Louisiana, South Carolina, Alabama and Georgia.[3] Of the twenty-seven States whose action was not coerced, twenty-three adopted the amendment and four (Delaware, Maryland, Kentucky, and California) rejected it.

Following the ratifications in New Jersey and Ohio, the legislatures of these two States became Democratic and a gesture of withdrawal of ratification was made by both; in Ohio on January 13, 1868, and in New Jersey (over the Governor's veto) on March 5, 1868.[4]   When Secretary Seward, on July 20, proclaimed the adoption of the amendment, he did so with the proviso that the rescinding action of Ohio and New Jersey must be disregarded if the adoption was to hold.   On July 21 Congress attempted to resolve all doubts on the matter by a concurrent resolution proclaiming the adoption of the amendment.[5]   In October, 1868, after the amendment had been proclaimed, the Democratic

---

[1] McPherson, *Reconstruction* (Washington, 1875), p. 353.

[2] Act of June 25, 1868, *ibid.*, p. 353.

[3] July 20, 1868, *ibid.*, p. 352. Burgess, *Reconstruction and the Constitution* (N. Y. 1902), pp. 204, 205.

[4] *Ibid.*, p. 353.

[5] *Ibid.*, p. 380.

legislature of Oregon also rescinded its ratification [6]—a step which was without legal effect.

It was generally understood when the fourteenth amendment was submitted to the States in 1866 that it embodied the conditions upon which the Southern States would be restored to their full constitutional place in the Union and in Congress.[7] The refusal of the Southern States to accept this amendment when first offered to them was considered an evidence of their recalcitrancy, and was used as an excuse for the imposition of military rule, which followed in 1867. The leading spirit in this insistence on more severe measures was Thaddeus Stevens, who eventually carried his party with him.[8] Rhodes attaches the blame for the failure of the South to accept the amendment to President Johnson.[9] Neither the South nor President Johnson was able to foresee the programme of military coercion, and it was only natural that a people who had accepted their defeat in the field with resignation but good faith should rebel at accepting conditions so repugnant to their self-respect. If the Republicans wanted to impose the programme of the amendment on the South, they held, let them do so by main force and bear the responsibility. The Southerners refused to be a party to their own shame.

The significance of reconstruction as an issue in the approaching Presidential campaign would be slight, according to the Springfield *Republican* in January, 1868, if Congress should manage the matter with ordinary tact and discretion. However, "If any Southern States should continue excluded because their constitutions are so proscriptive

[6] *Oregon Historical Society Quarterly*, vol. ii, no. 4, p. 355 (1901), article by Fenton.

[7] Rhodes, *History of the United States* (New York, 1906), vol. vi, p. 4.

[8] *Ibid.*, pp. 14, 15.

[9] *Ibid.*, pp. 4-9.

and unjust that Congress can not approve them, it will not damage Congress or the Republican party, but quite the contrary." [10]   But *Harper's Weekly* believed that reconstruction would be the one paramount issue before the country. The Republican party stood for the formation of new governments in the Southern States by the whole body of the people, except those disfranchised as rebels, while the Democrats insisted that the late rebels should have the exclusive power of reorganization.[11]

The Democratic attitude towards the reconstruction issue in the early part of 1868 is shown by a letter from Samuel J. Tilden of New York to Ex-Governor William Bigler of Pennsylvania, dated February 28. " Our position must be condemnation and reversal of negro supremacy in the ten States (added to that in Tennessee) created by the measures of the Federal government." He added that this issue would be a strong one before the people because of racial feeling and because the policy of Congress was costing the country, directly and indirectly, one hundred million dollars annually.[12]

On March 2, 1867, the unhappy reconstruction act was passed which divided the South into five military districts, and required that the Southern States provide for negro suffrage and ratify the Fourteenth Amendment before readmission to Congress. There shortly followed the famous supplementary acts which dealt with the qualifications for voters, the machinery of elections, and the manner of adopting the new constitutions.[13]   These acts made it impossible for the Southern whites to block adoption by refraining

[10] January 3, 1868.

[11] January 18, 1868.

[12] Bigelow, *Letters, etc. of Tilden* (N. Y., 1885), vol. i, pp. 220-221; erroneously attributed to R. C. Root instead of Bigler.

[13] McPherson, *op. cit.*, pp. 191-194.

from voting. Members of Congress were to be voted on at the same time as the new constitutions.

While the qualifications of Southern voters were under consideration in the Senate, Doolittle of Wisconsin proposed an amendment to limit the suffrage to negroes who were either Union veterans, literates, or possessed of $250 worth of property. This was voted down thirty-three to three, only Senators Dixon of Connecticut and Hendricks of Indiana supporting Doolittle.[14]

In June, 1868, seven Southern States were readmitted to Congress, on condition that they ratify the Fourteenth Amendment and that they never change their constitutions to exclude negroes from the ballot. Arkansas was admitted first on June 22,[15] and North Carolina, South Carolina, Louisiana, Georgia, Alabama, and Florida were brought in by the "Omnibus Bill" of June 25.[16] On May 14, while this bill was being debated in the House, Thaddeus Stevens showed its real purpose when he said that he trusted the Almighty would "never permit the Democratic party to gain the ascendancy."[17] The bill, an assisting measure for the Almighty, was to secure the Southern electoral votes for Grant.[18] The New York *Tribune* voiced the Republican attitude when it said it wanted to see all the Southern States admitted with complete self-government and military rule, and the Freedman's Bureau withdrawn, before Congress adjourned. Thus the fang of the Copperhead would be drawn and he could only hiss.[19]

---

[14] February 25, 1868; *ibid.*, p. 338.

[15] McPherson, *op. cit.*, p. 337.

[16] *Ibid.*, pp. 337-338.

[17] Rhodes, *op. cit.*, vol. vi, p. 176.

[18] T. C. Smith in *Cambridge Modern History* (N. Y., 1903), vol. vii, p. 632.

[19] May 28, 1868.

The Acts of Admission in June left three Southern States —Virginia, Mississippi, and Texas—still unrepresented in Congress. In order to safeguard the Republican electoral majority in November, on July 20 a joint resolution was passed which excluded the vote of these States from the Electoral College.[20]

2. NEGRO SUFFRAGE

An important phase of the general question of reconstruction after the war was the problem of negro suffrage, a problem faced in both the North and the South. In 1865, the negro was permitted to vote in all the New England States except Connecticut, and under a special tax qualification ($250 freehold) in New York.[21] In the next three years, the negro was granted the vote in Nebraska, Iowa, Minnesota, and Wisconsin, so that by the end of 1868 ten Northern States had admitted the negro to the franchise. During this period efforts in other Northern States to give the negro the ballot were defeated. In 1865, Connecticut, Minnesota, Wisconsin and Colorado Territory voted the proposal down, while at the same time the voters were electing Republican State officers.[22] In 1867 Ohio and Kansas—and Minnesota by a reduced majority—rejected negro suffrage.[23] In New Jersey, it was thrust aside as an issue in a legislative campaign.[24] In 1868 the advocates of negro suffrage carried Iowa, Minnesota, and Wisconsin, but lost in Missouri and Michigan.[25]

This summary shows that, while the Republicans were

[20] McPherson, *op. cit.*, pp. 378-379.

[21] *Tribune Almanac*, 1866, pp. 46-48.

[22] *Ibid., passim.*

[23] *Democratic Almanac*, 1868, p. 5.

[24] Knapp, *New Jersey Politics During the Period of the Civil War and Reconstruction* (Geneva, N. Y., 1924), p. 168.

[25] *American Annual Cyclopedia*, 1868, *passim.*

forcing their bitter medicine upon the former Confederate States and providing bayonets to keep it there, the Northern people themselves were very reluctant to greet their few colored neighbors as political equals. Gideon Welles, as early as May, 1865, expressed a natural query: " Is it politic, and wise, or right even . . . to elevate the ignorant negro . . . to the discharge of the highest duties of citizenship, especially when our Free States will not permit the few negroes to vote? " [26] The most famous attack on the inconsistency of this position was that of President Johnson in his " Swing Around the Circle," when at Cleveland he taunted the Republicans for demanding that negroes vote in the South while denying them the suffrage in such Northern States as Ohio.[27] This inconsistency appeared in the Republican platform of 1868, where negro suffrage was proclaimed optional in " loyal " states, while it was insisted upon for the South.

It might have been expected that the Democratic party in its national platform for 1868 would come out flatly in opposition to negro suffrage. But the plank was limited to stating that suffrage was purely a State question. Everyone knew that this doctrine held no hope for negro suffrage in States under Democratic control, but it was not so offensive as outright opposition to Northern humanitarians and former abolitionists and others who, though opposed to the excesses of Congressional reconstruction, were skeptical of the Democrats' Southern policy.

A good many Republicans, especially the Radicals, wished their party to make a bold pronouncement for universal manhood suffrage in all States. Charles Sumner stated in April, 1867, that the question should be settled before the Presidential election. The Southern negroes were already voters.

[26] *The Diary of Gideon Welles* (Boston, 1911), vol. ii, p. 302, May 9, 1865.

[27] In Bowers, *The Tragic Era* (Boston, 1929), p. 136.

" But why should they vote at the South and not at the North? The rule of justice is the same for both. Their votes are needed at the North as well as at the South. There are Northern States where their votes can make the good cause safe beyond question." Enfranchisement, according to Sumner, should be national " proceeding from the national government and applicable to all the States." [28]   In November, 1867, the New York *Tribune* considered the Democratic successes a punishment for Republican cowardice on the negro suffrage question.[29]   Among other Republicans who thought their party should take a national manhood suffrage position were R. B. Hayes of Ohio and G. W. Julian of Indiana. Hayes wrote in his diary in January, 1866, " Universal suffrage is sound in principle. The Radical element is right." On April 15, 1866, he added that his preference was for suffrage for all in the South, and sooner or later in the North, to be achieved gradually by requiring a literacy test without regard to color for all new voters.[30]

One of the best answers to Democratic charges that political equality would lead to social equality was made by Julian in a speech at Indianapolis on November 17, 1865. " Nor has negro voting ever led to social equality or miscegenation, to my knowledge. If my Democratic friends, however, feel in danger of marrying negro women, I am in favor of a law for their protection." [31]

On one point the Republicans had been consistent enough. In January, 1866, unrestricted negro suffrage was finally

[28] In Gillett, *Democracy in the United States* (N. Y., 1868), p. 375; said to be from letter written by Sumner, April 20, 1867.

[29] November 6, 1867, cited by Alexander, *Political History of New York* (N. Y., 1909), vol. iii, p. 188.

[30] Williams, *Rutherford Birchard Hayes* (Boston, 1914), vol. i, p. 279.

[31] Clarke, *George W. Julian* (Indianapolis, 1923), p. 288.

fixed upon the District of Columbia in spite of the President's veto and of Democratic efforts to have a literacy test included.[32] The election troubles which resulted [33] brought about the elimination of the ballot in the District in 1874 and were a factor in the development of a Northern opinion which condoned Southern efforts to keep the negroes from the polls. In the capital, visitors from all parts of the Union saw at first hand how negro suffrage operated in a community with a large colored population.

There were some Democrats who perceived at an early date that negro suffrage, or at any rate the removal of legal discriminations against colored voters, was inevitable. The Democratic party before the War had championed the widest possible extension of the suffrage. It had been the friend of the foreigner and the poor man. Was it now to turn its back on an entire race of freedmen? The answer was—Yes. The liberal suffrage principle of the Democracy was in conflict with another and more sacred principle, that of " State Rights." The combination of State Rights and racial feeling determined the policy of the party. As Seymour of New York said: " It is not a proposition whether we will or will not give to the African freedman the right to vote. It is an attempt on the part of the general government to assert the power to determine the right of suffrage in the different States." [34]

Yet in the summer of 1865, John A. Reagan, former Postmaster-General of the Confederacy, while imprisoned in Fort Warren in Boston harbor, warned his Texas friends that the North would demand at least a qualified negro suf-

[32] *Democratic Almanac*, 1867, p. 5; Welles, *op. cit.*, vol. ii, p. 637, vol. iii, pp. 3-8; New York *World*, January 19, 1866.

[33] Welles, *op. cit.*, vol. iii, p. 102.

[34] Speech, Buffalo, October 21, 1865; Cook and Knox: *The Public Record* (etc.) of Horatio Seymour (N. Y., 1868), p. 270.

frage, and that the South had better yield to avoid military government and universal negro suffrage. He suggested that the qualifications for voting by negroes include a literacy test, tax-paying, and absence of criminal conviction.[35]   In November, 1866, after the Republican successes in the Congressional elections, the Chicago *Times,* edited by Democratic National Committeeman Wilbur Storey, called upon the South to concede negro suffrage as being inevitable.[36] In 1868 the *Times* returned to the attack, and asked for an impartial suffrage plank in the Democratic National platform.   It stated that had the Southern whites conceded impartial suffrage two years before, they would have been in control of their section by 1868.[37]

On April 4, 1868, a Democratic Convention in Charleston, S. C., adopted a resolution recognizing the colored population as an " integral element of the body politic " entitled to equal protection under the laws, and declaring " our willingness when we have the power to grant them, under proper qualifications as to property and intelligence, the right of suffrage." [38]   This was stated by the Washington *Express* to represent an attempt, which would probably be successful, to divide the negro vote and thus prevent the dangerous consequences of a united Radical negro vote.[39]   This action in South Carolina did not meet with the approval of all the Democrats in the State, however, for on June 8 another Convention at Columbia went on record as being opposed to negro suffrage.[40]   Both the April and June conventions

[35] Letter August 11, 1865, John A. Reagan, *Memories* (N. Y., 1906), pp. 240, 291.

[36] November 12, 1866, in Chicago *Republican* of August 21, 1868.

[37] June 20, 1868, in New York *Times* of June 25, 1868.

[38] New York *World*, April 10, 1868.

[39] April 20, 1868.

[40] Cincinnati *Commercial,* June 15, 1868.

appointed delegates to the National Convention, the earlier group let by Wade Hampton and the later group by B. F. Perry. Each was seated, and they divided the vote of the State.

The attitude of the South Carolina leaders who favored granting a limited franchise to the negroes is shown by statements of Generals James Chestnut, J. B. Kershaw, and Wade Hampton during 1868. Chestnut considered "negro suffrage the legal sequence of the action of the people of South Carolina in accepting emancipation." To secure to the negro qualified suffrage in the wisest possible way would not interfere with the whites, and it would make him a good citizen and a firm ally.[41] Kershaw in a public letter wrote that as a matter of policy the negro should be admitted to a qualified franchise.[42] General Hampton stated that for more than a year he had advocated giving the negro qualified suffrage.[43] In May the Charleston *Courier* said that the negroes were at last beginning to find out " that their truest friends are the white race of their own soil." [44]

The traditional States Rights attitude of the Democratic Party towards suffrage was taken by the New York *World*. On June 19, it remarked that the Democratic party could neither prevent the negroes from voting nor control their votes. This would have to be done by the white citizens of the States. " The mission of the national Democratic party is . . . to render *white* [45] voting less mischievous than it has been for the last eight years." This position was precisely that ultimately taken in the national platform.

But this manner of disposing of the issue did not meet

[41] *Ibid.*, April 11, 1868.
[42] Camden, S. C. *Journal*, in New York *Times* of July 8, 1868.
[43] Charleston *Daily News*, in New York *Tribune* of October 22, 1868.
[44] *National Intelligencer* of May 9, 1868.
[45] Italics not in original.

with the approval of all portions of the Democracy. For
example, the Delaware State Convention in June wanted the
party to take a forthright stand, and resolved that negro
suffrage was the issue of the campaign.[46]   The Pendleton,
or Western element in the party, was also opposed to compromise on the negro suffrage issue.   The Cincinnati
Enquirer, Washington McLean's organ, asserted that the
Democracy was a unit in holding that none but white men
should vote or hold office and that the imposition of negro
suffrage upon the Southern States was a Federal usurpation.[47]   Pendleton, in an interview on June 8, declared his
opposition to Congressional enfranchisement of the Southern negroes.   He thought that if the negroes were committed to the care of their white fellow-citizens in the South
they would be subjected to no more injustice than the women
of the North, who were without a vote and yet were secure
in all their rights.[48]

After the nominations had been made by both parties and
the campaign had reached its full stride, the Democrats for
two reasons found little opportunity to capitalize the suffrage
issue.   They were trying to attract the Conservative vote,
and they were kept busy defending themselves from Republican attacks based on " Southern Outrages " and on
imputations that they intended a revolution.

3. FINANCIAL ISSUES

Of the various issues before the country those concerning
the national finances came nearest to being bi-partisan.   The
financial questions were these: Should the Civil War bonds
be repaid, when due, in gold or in greenbacks?   Should the
bonds of the national government be taxed?   Should the

---

[46] New York *World* of June 23, 1868; *American Annual Cyclopedia,*
1868, p. 212.

[47] In New York *Times,* June 30, 1868.

[48] New York *Herald,* June 11, 1868.

volume of greenbacks, or United States notes, be contracted? Should national banks be permitted to retain their issue privilege, or should the national bank notes be replaced by greenbacks? To what extent should war taxes be eliminated or reduced? And finally, should the tariff on imports be reduced?

The " Greenback " proposal, or " Ohio Idea," [49] was in brief that the obligations of the national government should be paid in United States notes, in all cases except where the laws authorizing the issues specifically provided for repayment in gold. The fact that in 1868 one dollar in gold was equal in value to $1.40 in greenbacks made the question one of more than academic interest. The public debt of the United States on November 1, 1867, was $2,491,504,450 and on November 1, 1868, $2,527,129,552, the increase being accounted for by the issue of $24,000,000 in bonds in aid of the Pacific railroads, and the $7,200,000 paid for Alaska. Of the amount owed in 1868, $2,107,577,950 was in bonds, with the interest payable in coin.[50] The principal issues represented by this two billion dollars and more of bonded indebtedness were as follows:

July 17, 1861	$250,000,000	7% — 20 years
February 25, 1862	$500,000,000	6% — 5 to 20 years (the " 5/20's ")
March 3, 1864	$200,000,000	6% — 10 to 40 years (the " 10/40's ")
June 30, 1864............	$400,000,000	6% — 5 to 30 years
March 3, 1865	$600,000,000	6% (coin) 5 to 40 years, or 7% (United States notes) 5 to 40 years [51]

[49] For a general discussion, see Max Leroy Shipley: *The Greenback Issue in the Old Northwest* (abstract of Ph.D. thesis, University of Illinois, 1930).

[50] *American Annual Cyclopedia*, 1868, p. 251.

[51] *Ibid.*, pp. 254-255, Dewey, *Financial History of the United States* (N. Y., 1924), p. 344. The " 5/20's " were callable by the government in not less than five years, and were payable in twenty years.

Of these issues, $1,600,000,000 were either in 5/20's or in outstanding bonds convertible to that denomination. About $500,000,000 had become redeemable in 1867, and most of the balance could be redeemed within five years.[52] Those advocating the repayment of the bonds in paper particularly relied upon the circumstances under which the legal tender act of 1862 was passed. The notes were convertible into bonds and were a legal tender for all debts, except duties on imports and interest on bonds. It was urged that the absence of any explicit prohibition upon their use in payment of the principal of national bonds indicated the intent that they should be so used in order that the government should be able to take up its obligations in the same currency for which they were issued.[53]

Rhodes says that " according to some of the best lawyers in the country," the proposal to pay the principal of the five to twenty year bonds in greenbacks " was well-taken ". It was argued that " it would be a foolish excess of generosity and discrimination in favor of the rich to pay the obligations of the government in the most valuable medium, when it was not required by the letter of the law." [54]

It was pointed out that the privilege of redemption in five years, a feature of the 5/20's, was included in order that the government might not only take up its obligations in the same depreciated paper for which it issued them, but also refund the loans under the improved credit which would result from the restoration of the national authority.[55]

The point of contention in the dispute over the payment of the 5/20's was whether or not the absence of a direct stipulation for repayment of the principal in gold meant it

---

[52] Rhodes, *op. cit.*, vol. vi, p. 161.

[53] Dewey, *op. cit.*, p. 345.

[54] Rhodes, *op. cit.*, vol. vi, p. 161.

[55] *American Annual Cyclopedia*, 1868, p. 253.

was intended that paper be used. During the early years of the war the possibility of the payment of bonds in anything but coin was hardly raised, and repayment in coin was understood in Congress in 1862. The Bond Issue Act of 1863 included a gold provision for the principal, which was inserted from "abundant caution". Secretary Chase advertised that both principal and interest of the 5/20's would be paid in coin. The 6% loan which matured in January, 1863, was paid in gold, and on November 15, 1866, Secretary McCulloch announced that the 5/20 bonds of 1862 would either be called in at the end of five years from that date and paid in coin, or would remain outstanding until the government was prepared to pay them in coin.[56]

Advertisements by Jay Cooke & Co., who acted as the Treasury Department's agent in floating the 5/20 loan, stated that the principal as well as the interest would be met in gold.[57] When the 5/20's were sold by the Treasury Agent, Jay Cooke, it was understood and plainly declared in Congress, in the newspapers, and by the sellers that they were gold bonds with both principal and interest payable in gold. It was on this understanding that the issues were distributed to the people.[58]

In March, 1868, while the agitation was at its height, Jay Cooke wrote a public letter in which he defended the theory of gold payment. He declared of the 5/20 bonds that (1) there was nothing contrary to this theory in the Act creating the loan, (2) gold payment of bonds is an accepted American and international custom, (3) the debate in Congress at this time disclosed that understanding, (4)

[56] Dewey, *op. cit.*, pp. 346-347.

[57] Oberholtzer, *Jay Cooke, Financier of the Civil War* (Philadelphia, 1907), vol. i, pp. 235, 239-240, 256, 340.

[58] Oberholtzer, *A History of the United States Since the Civil War* (in progress), vol. ii, p. 160.

a gold sinking fund for their retirement was included in the Act,[59] (5) all the Secretaries of the Treasury since their issue had declared for gold payment, (6) the bonds were sold with that understanding, and (7) an attempt in Congress, at the time of issue, to make the 5/20's payable in paper was suppressed. Cooke offered as a solution of this problem an immediate return to specie payment, which he believed both desirable and possible.[60]

The Republican press of New York City was opposed to the " greenback idea ". Dana, of the *Sun,* said: " If we mean to be honest at all, there is no escaping payment in specie. Anything else is repudiation, disguise it as we may." [61] Horace Greeley of the *Tribune* was even more outspoken when he wrote, in October, 1867, in reply to an advocate of the " Ohio Idea ": " Should I ever consent to argue the propriety and policy of wholesale swindling, I shall take your proposal into consideration." [62]

The movement for the payment of the principal of the 5/20 bonds in greenbacks was launched in Ohio in 1867. It was " conceived in the womb of economic discontent that followed the Civil War. It was born in Ohio, and mothered by the Democratic party of that State." [63]

George Hunt Pendleton of Ohio, former member of Congress and candidate for Vice-President with McClellan in 1864, was a leading exponent of the doctrine and its chief formulator—if not originator. In a speech at St. Paul,

[59] The gold sinking fund provided in the Act of February 25, 1862, was repealed July 25, 1868, *American Annual Cyclopedia,* 1868, p. 254.

[60] Philadelphia *Evening Star,* March 21, 1868.

[61] Wilson, *Life of Chas. A. Dana* (N. Y., 1907), p. 384.

[62] To Henry Clay Dean of Iowa, *Annals of Iowa,* 3rd series, vol. xii, p. 618.

[63] *Mississippi Valley Historical Review,* vol. xi, March, 1925, by R. C. McGrane.

Minnesota, on July 11, 1867, Pendleton first proclaimed the " Greenback Idea." [64]

Pendleton stated his position at Milwaukee on November 2, 1867. The national debt, he asserted, in large measure grew out of the fraud and maladministration of the Republican party. All government bonds issued before the Legal Tender Act of 1862 were gold bonds, payable in coin, and since 1862, by a special provision, a gold-payable bond had been issued, the 10/40's. Other than these, he contended, every government bond was payable as to principal in greenbacks. Pendleton was also opposed to the national bank notes, and advocated replacing them with greenbacks by redeeming the 5/20 bond collateral of the banks in greenbacks. He advocated taxing government bonds on the same basis as other property and, if this were not done, he predicted " worse consequences will follow, involving perhaps the violation of national honor and plighted faith." [65]

An interview with Pendleton appeared in the New York *Herald* for June 11, 1868. He charged that the existing financial system was to be made an important part of the Republican party's program of consolidation and centralization; the enormous debt should be paid, principal and interest, when due; and he thought the country could pay it off in five years and that it should be paid as soon as possible. Pendleton opposed the whole national bank system and believed the law authorizing it should be repealed, the bank notes retired, and the collateral bonds purchased at their face value in greenbacks. He attributed the depreciation of the currency to " the redundancy of paper money, the lack of faith on the part of the community, and the consequent impairment of public credit." While Pendleton did not think any attempt should be made to pay the national debt by

[64] Bloss, *Life of Pendleton* (Cincinnati, 1868), p. 100.
[65] Speech in pamphlet, New York Public Library.

further issues of greenbacks, he was equally opposed to a sudden contraction of the currency. The public interest required " that any step in this direction should be of a most deliberate and gradual kind." [66]

This last point indicates the essential weakness of the greenback scheme. The billion and a half or more of 5/20's which Pendleton said should be paid in greenbacks could be paid only by greenbacks in addition to those in circulation. This addition would in itself reduce the gold value of all greenbacks. Pendleton said the redemption of the bonds should be made as speedily as possible, yet he stated that he was opposed to inflation. The two ideas were not compatible—as his critics were quick to point out. The Cincicinnati *Enquirer* proposed to redeem the bonds in greenbacks, and prevent inflation by eliminating the National Bank notes.[67] This was begging the question, as both notes and bonds were obligations of the government. The dangers of the inflation involved in the greenback scheme were pointed out frequently. For example, on May 11, 1868, the Springfield *Republican* said that if more greenbacks were issued in order to use them to pay off the 5/20's " the end will be made very speedily of the debt, but it will also make an end of the whole structure of credit, finance and industry—it may be of law and order."

In his opposition to a contraction in the amount of greenbacks outstanding, Pendleton was on popular ground. In February 1868, Congress repealed the Contraction Act of April 12, 1866, which had provided for retiring greenbacks at the rate of not over four millions a month.[68]

[66] New York *Herald*, June 11, 1868.

[67] *Ohio Archaeological and Historical Quarterly*, vol. xxxvii (1928), pp. 250-251, article by Moore.

[68] Oberholtzer, *op. cit.*, vol. ii, p. 160 (The amount of non-gold currency outstanding in November, 1868, was: U. S. notes—356 million dollars;

Naturally Pendleton's greenback ideas were criticised as inconsistent with the traditional Democratic "hard money" position, maintained since the time of Benton. However, in 1862, when the Greenback Act was under discussion in Congress, he had led in criticising it as contrary to sound money principles. He prophesied that as a result of this Act "the currency will be expanded, prices will be inflated, fixed values will deteriorate. . . . The day of reckoning must come. Contraction will follow. Private ruin and public bankruptcy either with or without repudiation will inevitably follow." [69]

National bank notes—295 million dollars; fractional currency—33 million dollars; total 685 million dollars—*American Annual Cyclopedia*, 1868, p. 256).

[69] *Congressional Globe*, 37th Cong., 2nd Sess., pp. 549-551. On February 6, 1862, the day the Legal Tender Act passed the House, Pendleton had expressed his views at length in a private letter to an unnamed addressee. "The House today passed the United States Note bill authorizing the issue of $150,000,000 payable at no specified time, bearing no interest, and declaring that they are 'lawful money' and a legal tender in discharge of all obligations private and public, as well as the interest in United States bonds, as State bonds. If this bill is effective, and the views and prophecies of its advocates are sound, there ought to be no trouble about taxes, for if a legislative enactment can make paper promises in fact money, there is nothing to do but to keep on passing laws, and to keep the paper mill at work, and money in any quantity is made to hand. This bill will be followed by the Banking scheme of Chase and the riot will commence—the carnival of speculation, fraud, robbery in every shape—to end only in the bankruptcy of fortune, as it will have progressed in the utter ruin of morals—and yet, the toadies of the administration were today jubilant over their success, and predicted a career of credit in the government hitherto unequalled—that the notes would never depreciate but would make a sounder, safer currency than even gold and silver. Taxes will be laid pretty heavily—and real estate come in for its share, the lion's share for New England, blating about her patriotism and readiness to spend the last dollar, etc., etc., takes devilish good care that she shall not spend the first as long as she can avoid it, and in avoiding it she is as sharp as in everything else. For when a western man says one word about the inequality of taxes, she raises such a shout of shame!! On the parsimony which would refuse to pay for

Pendleton's answer to the charge of inconsistency was that, though opposed to a paper currency on principle, now that one existed he was even more opposed to using it to pay most obligations, while giving to a favored class—the bondholders—the right to exact gold in payment of government debts. His opposition to the national banks was certainly in line with the Jacksonian tradition. A Michigan paper, in August, 1868, gave a clear statement of the position of the greenback element of the Democracy on this issue. It argued that the Democrats had always preferred hard money to soft, and had always opposed national bank notes. They opposed the Legal Tender Act of 1862 and were in favor of a speedy return to specie payment, but they believed that as long as greenbacks remained the currency of the country and a legal tender they should be used for all obligations, including bond payments.[70]

While the New York *World* did not believe in Pendleton's policy, it defended him against misrepresentation. He had merely made " a logical deduction from the Republican principles of finance." If it was right to pay off private creditors in a depreciated currency, it was equally right to discharge public obligations in the same way. If it was right to pay the funded debt in greenbacks and if it should be paid soon, it would be difficult to devise " a plan better calculated than this of Mr. Pendleton's to prevent great and sudden disturbance of values." [71]   Yet in spite of the *World's* sympathetic

the pleasure of carrying on this glorious war, that if the poor fellow is not frightened his hearers and sympathisers are, and his prospect falls like lead. Nevertheless we will keep a sharp lookout in that quarter and endeavor to keep them from taking all our rents to pay the taxes. Truly your friend, George H. Pendleton." New York Historical Society Library, Misc. Mss. P.

[70] Ann Arbor, Mich. *Argus*, August 21, 1868, in Dilla, *The Politics of Michigan* (New York, 1912), p. 96.

[71] January 30, 1868; February 1, 1868.

attitude, Pendleton's Greenback program estranged him from the Eastern party leaders, and contributed largely to his defeat for the Democratic nomination. At one time in the Convention, New York supported Senator Thomas A. Henricks of Indiana, as preferable to Pendleton.

Horatio Seymour, who was a " hard money " Democrat, had a more consistent record than Pendleton upon the currency and bond issue. In 1864, while Governor of New York, he had advised the New York legislature to safeguard the gold-interest feature of State bonds,[72] which the Republican press declared to be a covert attack on the national government.[73] Although opposed to the greenback theory, Seymour was not himself a bondholder, as he made clear on more than one occasion.[74]

During the spring of 1868, Seymour adroitly combined attacks on the Republican financial policy with rejection of the Ohio Idea. On March 11, 1868, at the State Democratic Convention at Albany he said: " If we come into power there will be no discredit in our currency, no speculation in paying our bonds in paper." " We are not trying to give paper to the bond holders but gold and silver to the people." He attacked the tax-exempt feature of the bond issues as a " stupid folly " which was largely responsible for " a distrust that a measure so odious would endanger their payment." He reminded his hearers that the bondholders were not all capitalists. Many of the bonds were owned by children and widows. The large amounts held by insurance companies and savings banks were in fact " held in trust for the great body of active business and laboring men and

[72] Speech October 3, 1867, in Cook and Knox, *op. cit.*, p. 303.

[73] Fulton, *History of the Democratic Party, etc.* (New York, 1892), p. 464.

[74] Speech, Albany, October 3, 1867; Letter, July 21, 1868, *Public Record*, pp. 305, 347.

women, or of widows and orphans." The interests of the landholders and the tax payers were not antagonistic and if the bondholder should be given a debased paper " we must bring upon ourselves disaster and dishonor. . . . We can not afford to speculate upon the nation's honor at so fearful a cost." But though opposed to the greenback theory, he warned the Democracy against allowing the currency issue to cause distraction among its members.[75]

The New York *World,* commenting on this speech, emphasized this last point. " He justly thinks that the ways and means of payment (of the 5/20 bonds) is not an immediate question." [76] John Quincy Adams (son of Charles Francis Adams), the lone Democrat among the Adams family, wrote to Seymour congratulating him on his " noble speech." He wondered if the people were " to be led astray by a thinly veiled repudiation, preferring disgraceful bankruptcy to a painful and honest retrenchment and payment," and was thankful that Seymour had "sounded a key note so high and clear." [77] Seymour's deprecatory attitude towards the agitation of the currency question corresponded with the position of the Washington *Express,* which on January 15, 1868, feared that issue would keep from the Democracy those moderates who opposed the excesses of Radical reconstruction, yet hesitated about committing themselves " to associations that may be perverted to affect the national credit."

On April 3, in a speech at Bridgeport, Connecticut, Seymour attacked the financial policy of the government, pointing out that merchants could borrow money at 6% but that the government—when the fact that interest was in gold was

[75] Cook and Knox, *op. cit.,* pp. 309-322.

[76] March 14, 1868. This speech, with that of S. J. Tilden at the same time, published by the *World* as " World Tract No. 1 ".

[77] New York Historical Society Library, Seymour Mss. Box 4.

taken into account—had to pay 10%. Although the war had ceased some years before, the government was spending $150,000,000 a year to maintain an army to keep the South in subjection; " a people that ought rather to be helping us bear the cost of governing the nation." [78] The New York *Tribune* quoted the report of the Secretary of War and the World *Almanac* to show that he had grossly overestimated the expenses connected with the South.[79]

On June 25, at the Cooper Institute in New York City, Seymour opposed either contraction or expansion of the paper currency. He said that the paper dollar of the government was " a government falsehood ". A uniform currency for all classes was necessary—should it be uniformly good or uniformly bad? Contraction, he said, would carry ruin and bankruptcy into every part of the country. Expansion on the other hand would still further debase the currency. The reason for the paper currency not being at par with gold was " because the national credit is dishonored." He called on the people to demand honesty and efficiency in government and an end to military expenses in the South in order to bring the greenbacks to par.[80] If the greenback agitation had died down, and if the expenses of reconstruction had been contracted, it is quite probable that resumption would have taken place before 1879. The Springfield *Republican* on June 29 applauded Seymour's sentiments as " what every voter ought to hear and every Republican ought to applaud and echo."

The greenback issue, as suggested above, tended to divide the country between East and West rather than on party lines. The Eastern Democrats, as a whole, were hardly less opposed to Pendleton's " Ohio Idea " than the Eastern

[78] Cook and Knox, *op. cit.*, pp. 374, 384.

[79] April 9, 1868.

[80] Cook and Knox, *op. cit.*, pp. 322-334.

Republicans, while most Westerners, Republicans as well as Democrats' supported it. Benjamin F. Butler declared that nine-tenths of the bondholders resided east of a meridian drawn down through Lake Ontario. It was the rich East against the poor West.[81] The Western Democratic merchants were not bondholders like those of the East, and they agreed with Pendleton on the greenback issue, as their capital was in their businesses and in real estate, rather than in government securities.[82] On January 16, 1868, the *Nation* reported an alarming growth of greenback sentiment among the Western Republicans. Senator Sherman of Ohio said in the Senate that the Greenback issue would decide every election in the Northwestern States in the fall of 1868. " I might show you by resolutions of political parties, both Republican and Democratic, that we can not avoid or evade this issue . . . no man can be elected to Congress unless he commits himself for or against the proposition." [83] John Sherman of Ohio supported a bill to compel the holders of the 5/20 6% bonds to accept a 4½% bond specifically payable in gold as a preventive of worse measures. Both Sherman and Morton of Indiana compromised on the issue by declaring that the government had the right to redeem the 5/20's in paper, but did not have the right to issue new paper for that purpose.[84]

The Funding Bill, as Sherman's proposal was called, provided for an issue, bond for bond, to cancel the 5/20's. This new issue was to be redeemable in gold after thirty years with interest at 4½%, or in forty years with interest at 4% for the last ten years. The bonds and interest were

[81] Oberholtzer, *op. cit.*, vol. ii, p. 161.

[82] New York *Herald*, June 17, 1868.

[83] *Ohio Archaeological and Historical Quarterly*, vol. xxxvii (1928), pp. 253-254, article by Moore.

[84] Dewey, *op. cit.*, p. 348.

to be exempt from Federal taxes, except the income tax. A gold fund from the customs receipts was to be used to meet the interest and retire the principal when due. The bill was introduced in July, 1868.[85] An earlier bill, introduced by Sherman in February, 1868, provided for a 5% forty-year bond instead of a 4½% issue. The New York *Tribune* commented that the bill really meant that if the holders of the 5/20's refused to convert their bonds into the new issue they would be paid in greenbacks—or else it meant nothing whatever.[86]

Among those Republicans who embraced the greenback cause was Thaddeus Stevens of Pennsylvania. He hailed Sherman's funding plan as an admission that the existing bonds were not payable in gold, else why replace them by an issue specifically payable in gold?[87] Stevens in 1862, as Chairman of the Ways and Means Committee, had said that the 5/20 loan was " at 6%, reedemable in gold in twenty years, the best and most valuable permanent investment that could be desired; "[88] yet in 1868 he was reported to have declared that he would vote for " no such swindle upon the taxpayers," but if he knew the Republican party proposed to do this he would vote " for the other side, Frank Blair and all."[89] Stevens in the House denied that he had declared himself for the Democratic ticket under any conditions. " I have only declared against fools and swindlers who have fabricated the most atrocious falsehoods as to my position on the currency question."[90] However, it was

[85] McPherson, *op. cit.*, p. 382.

[86] In New York *World* February 15, 1868.

[87] Letter in Washington *Express*, August 1, 1868.

[88] Oberholtzer, *op. cit.*, vol. ii, p. 161, cites *Congressional Globe*, February 6, 1862, p. 686.

[89] *Ibid.*, cites *Nation*, July 23, 1868.

[90] New York *Herald*, July 29, 1868 from Lancaster, Pa. *Express*, July 25, 1868.

true that Stevens was in favor of paying off the 5/20's in paper. Another prominent Eastern Radical who embraced the greenback doctrine was Benjamin F. Butler of Massachusetts. Rhodes gives as a reason for Stevens' and Butler's attitude on the question their alarm at the growing disaffection of the Republicans towards negro suffrage. They believed that Pendleton had hit upon a popular issue which they did not intend he should make a Democratic monopoly.[91] Butler was opposed to paying the bondholders in gold and the pensioned veterans and widows in paper. " But there were more bondholders in Congress than a majority of each House, and they naturally had their way." [92]

About July 1, 1868, Butler attempted to commit the House of Representatives to a 10% tax on the interest on government bonds. " Although this was in the direction of repudiation, it was more easily defensible than the plan of discharging the principal in paper money." [93] *The Nation* denounced it as an attempt " to cheat the public creditor out of the tenth part of his interest," and pointed out that the public credit was suffering not from the Southerners nor the Democrats, but from a knot of " arch-radicals " headed by Butler.[94]

One straw which showed the way the wind was blowing in Ohio was a special election to fill a seat in Congress held in the Dayton district in January 27, 1868. The victorious Republican candidate, General John Beatty, won on an out-aud-out greenback platform with a majority four times as great as that obtained in the district by Hayes in the race for Governor in 1867.[95]

[91] *United States*, vol. vi, p. 193.

[92] *Butler's Book* (Boston, 1892), p. 920. For an elaborate statement of his views see pp. 931-354.

[93] Rhodes, *op. cit.*, cites *Nation*, July 2, 1868.

[94] July 9, 1868.

[95] *Nation*, February 6, 1868.

The conflict within the Republican party on the currency issue was reflected in the national platform adopted at Chicago on May 21. The plank [96] was outspoken in its denunciation of all forms of repudiation, but failed to specify in what repudiation consisted. It asserted that the national debt should be paid according to the spirit as well as the letter of the law, but the spirit was not defined. The party called for equalization of taxation, but no reference was made to taxing the bonds. It declared that the national debt should be paid over a fair period and that interest rates should be lowered " where honestly possible ". These provisions were eloquent in their vagueness. Designed primarily in opposition to the Ohio Idea, the platform made no mention of greenbacks or the 5/20's. The greenbackers denied their scheme was repudiation, and insisted it was in accord with both the spirit and the letter of the Legal Tender Act.[97] This position of the Republican Party recalls the ambiguous position taken on " Free Silver " in the 1896 platform.

Where the Republican platform straddled the financial issue, the Democratic platform went after the bondholders hammer and tongs with out-and-out greenback planks.[98] And this in spite of the fact that both Belmont, the national chairman, and Seymour, the president of the Convention, in their introductory speeches were outspoken in defending the national credit. The Democrats endorsed rapid payment of the National bonds and declared that, where they " do not expressly state upon their face, or the law under which they were issued does not provide, that they shall be paid in coin, they ought in right and justice to be paid in the lawful money of the United States " (i.e. legal tenders). The party de-

[96] *Official Proceedings*, pp. 84-85.

[97] New York *World*, May 26, 1868.

[98] *Official Proceedings*, pp. 58-60.

manded taxation of government bonds and called for one currency for the government and all the people, including the laborer and the bondholders.

4. THE TARIFF

The tariff is not often thought of as an active issue in the few years following the Civil War, and the Republican platform of 1868 did not mention it.   The Democratic platform included a statement strikingly similar to the tariff plank of the 1928 platform.   The party demanded " a tariff for revenue upon foreign imports, such as will afford incidental protection to domestic manufactures, and as will without impairing revenue impose the least burden upon, and best promote and encourage the great industrial interests of the country." [99]

There is reason to think that some Republican leaders had the tariff more in mind than was evident from their public statements.   Indeed, the desire to continue protection was one reason why the Republican party was so anxious to maintain its political power in the South.   Many radicals " realized that a return of the South to Congress meant a union of South and West which would deprive the growing business interests of the country of the favors that radical rule would insure them." [100]

Following the end of the war, the internal taxes were gradually lowered or eliminated, but the war-time tariff rates were retained, and with the fall of prices which followed the war the manufacturers received a degree of protection which they had never asked for.   Taussig, writing of the war tariffs, says they were intended to be temporary and it was only reasonable to expect that they would be reduced.   Most

[99] *Official Proceedings*, p. 59.

[100] H. K. Beale, "The Tariff and Reconstruction," in *American Historical Review*, January, 1930, pp. 276-294.

of the public men of the time, had the question been put to them direct, would have agreed that the war rates needed lowering. Even Morrill, as late as 1870, said in Congress that it was a mistake for the friends of " a sound tariff to insist on keeping the war rates, if lower rates would raise the needed revenue." The reason why the rates were not reduced lies in the now familiar story of the power of the lobby, the pre-occupation of Congress with other matters, and the gradual adaptation of industry to the existing rates. Thus the " feeling that no reform was needed obtained a strong hold." [101]

In 1867 a bill sponsored by Special Commissioner of the Revenue David A. Wells, which provided for lower duties on raw materials, but left the rates on manufactured articles little changed, failed of enactment although it passed the Senate by a vote of twenty-seven to ten.

This failure to reduce the tariff encouraged the protectionists in fighting for the retention of the war duties wherever they could not secure an increase, a contest in which they were, with few exceptions, successful.[102] Up to 1868, indeed, the only change in the tariff which was at all significant was the Wool and Woolens Act of 1867 with higher rates on those commodities. In 1872 a general 10% reduction was made, but the higher rates were restored soon afterwards.

The New York *Tribune* during the Impeachment Trial stated that among the defenders of the President were free traders who feared that, if Benjamin F. Wade, president pro. tem. of the Senate, became President, he would aid the cause of protection. " The Free Traders say. . . . Mr. Johnson is only false to the Constitution and laws of the United States; Mr. Wade is false to the interests of the manufacturers of Great Britain." They were charged with

[101] Taussig, *History of the Present Tariff* (New York, 1885), pp. 19-20.
[102] *Ibid.*, p. 24.

attempting to influence the vote of the Free Trade Republican Senators, especially Grimes and Fessenden.[103]

Godkin, of the *Nation,* reported to the London *Daily News* on April 30 that the protectionists had made a successful effort to commit Wade to the protective tariff position.[104] In March Wade was quoted as saying: "We should strive to take the burdens off industry and to secure our laboring classes relief from foreign competition. . . . That means . . . a high tariff." He was in favor of reducing the internal taxes and collecting from foreign competitors the amount thus lost.[105] On May 10 Godkin reported that Wade's high tariff views were hurting him in the West; on May 14 that Wade had declared that, if he could accomplish nothing else during his anticipated term as President, he was determined to bring about an increase in tariff duties. This statement had aroused the free-traders and even the moderate Western protectionists against him.[106]

With Senator Wade out of the picture as a possible President even for nine or ten months, the tariff position of General Grant, the Republican nominee, became of more interest. The New York *Evening Post,* after Grant's nomination, thought he would favor a tariff for revenue only sufficient to bring in with other sources of revenue the funds necessary for an economical administration of the government.[107] There was no ground for assigning tariff opinions to the hero of Appommattox, for he knew little of economics and less of tariffs.

One bit of evidence that the sentiment against tariff reform, which was making headway among the Republicans

[103] New York *Tribune,* May 14, 1868.
[104] London *Daily News,* May 12, 1868.
[105] Philadelphia *Evening Star,* March 16, 1868.
[106] London *Daily News,* May 22, May 27, 1868.
[107] In New York *Times,* May 27, 1868.

at this time, aroused some apprehensions is found in a Washington dispatch to the Cincinnati *Commercial* for April 24. It was reported that those most concerned for the success of the Republican party felt that it would be disastrous for the party to give countenance to "the obstinate extortionate factionists" who wish to commit the party to the maintenance of a prohibitory tariff which would give monopolists the power to regulate the prices of necessities.[108]

During the campaign the tariff played a very small part. As an issue, the tariff had to wait for four years until the tariff reformers among the Liberal Republicans united with the Democrats; and even then it received little attention.

Big business in the sense in which the words were used in later years had not yet become a dominating political force. It is true, however, that the banking interests were a unit in opposition to the greenback plank of the Democratic platform, and occasional groups of manufacturers met in convention to pass political resolutions.

During the spring of 1868, the National Manufacturers Association held its first annual meeting at Cleveland, with about thirty in attendance. The Association was organized on December 18, 1867, with the object of obtaining an adjustment of taxes satisfactory to the manufacturers. A committee to lobby in Washington was appointed at that time and gave its report at the annual meeting. The report advocated economy in government, the abolition of useless offices, and the reduction of taxes. "Your only hope is in and through Congress. The executive branch of the government is hostile to every reform that can lessen taxation or purify the government." The meeting adopted resolutions which gave credit to the Association for the tax reduction Act of March 31, 1868. The Civil Service Reform bill of Representative Thomas H. Jenckes of Rhode Island

---

[108] Cincinnati *Commercial*, April 27, 1868.

was endorsed, and a purification of the public service demanded. The protective tariff principle was endorsed, and an extension of its benefits demanded. The national banking system was endorsed. On the bond issue, the Association recommended that the debt should be refunded at par into long term, 3.65% gold principal bonds which would be used to extend the system of National banks.[109]   This was similar to Senator Sherman's forty-year 4½% refunding proposal, placed before Congress in July, 1868. In 1868 also occurred the first meeting of the Woolen Manufacturers Association of the Northwest, convened in Chicago on February 19. The proceedings, as reported, contained no references to the tariff although the Chicago *Republican* (February 20) commented that, " According to the British Free Trade organs in this city, these men are the enemies of the farmers of the Northwest ". The *Republican* considered the Chicago *Tribune* one of these organs.[110]

[109] New York *Times*, May 29, 1868 (Cleveland, May 27).
[110] June 22, 1868.

CHAPTER II

The Democratic Party

I. THE DEMOCRATIC PARTY AFTER THE WAR

It is hard to explain why the Democratic party in the four years following the Civil War, having the support of some 45% of the voters of the Northern States and with a President in office who sympathized with their program, was able to exert such a limited influence in shaping the policies of the nation. The figures [1] show that 44% of the voters in those States which had not been in the Confederacy were Democrats at the time when the Republican party had its greatest strength—the State elections of 1865. The percentage rose to 45.4% in the Congressional elections of 1866 and 49.5% in the State elections of 1867, and sank to 46.7% in the Presidential election of 1868. If to these figures were added the uncast votes of the intimidated and largely disfranchised Southern Democrats, we should find that during the period from 1865 to 1868 (and on to 1876 for that matter) a majority of the white men of this country were Democrats. Another way of putting it is to say that, had the Southern whites been in control of their States as they have been since 1877, the Democratic party would have polled a majority of all votes cast. Of course, this does not mean that the Democrats would have carried either Congress or the electoral college.

We have then, the spectacle of a political party receiving

[1] Computed from figures in *American Annual Cyclopedia*, 1866-1868; *Tribune Almanac*; *Democratic Almanac*; McPherson, *History of Reconstruction*.

the support of nearly one-half of the voters of the country, and yet finding itself in a position of political impotence greater than at any time in its history before or since.

The reason for this situation lay first in our system of voting by States and Congressional Districts, which leaves minorities, however large, unrepresented, and second in the divisions within the party—largely an inheritance of the war.

In 1866 the Democrats had hoped that the break within the Republican party would result in their acquiring the support of the Moderate Republicans, and particularly of those who supported the President in his quarrel with Congress. The Conservative Convention at Philadelphia, in August, 1866, marked the high point of this movement, and by November there was little left of it; so little, indeed, that the 40th Congress, elected at that time contained only twelve Democratic Senators and fifty Democratic representatives. The failure of the movement for a Democratic-Conservative coalition was due to the fact that it was considered to be an attempt to advance the President's interests, and declined as Radical Republican misrepresentation lowered the President in public estimation, and also to the fact that the Johnson Conservatives and the Democrats deeply distrusted one another.[2]

The collapse of this movement showed the Democrats that they must stand squarely on their own feet if they wished to retrieve their political fortunes—that a union of all anti-Radical elements into a new " Conservative " organization was impractical as well as undesirable from a party point of view. This does not mean that the Democrats gave up the idea of securing support from disgruntled Republicans— the situation seemed to call for as much effort in this direction as ever—but it did mean that the party organization must remain intact, no matter how candidates might be

[2] Beale, *The Critical Year* (New York, 1930), *passim.*

chosen or platforms constructed, to draw Conservative voters.

Although the Democratic party did not frame national legislation during this period, and was unable to block the program of its opponents, it served a very useful purpose, by keeping alive the spirit of opposition to Radicalism, with two results. The Southern whites did not lose heart altogether and were ready to reclaim their power when Radicalism had spent its force: the Radical party was prevented from going to the very worst extremes. Within eight years after 1868, the Republican party abandoned the Radical principles of 1865-1868 as the bases of their party program. It is not too much to say that the existence of a determined Democratic party in the North prevented the complete Africanization of the South,[3] and kept alive the principle of " State Rights " as opposed to the centralizing tendencies of the party in power.

The position of the Republican party following the death of Lincoln was not without its difficulties. With Lincoln out of the way there developed a contest for party leadership in which the malcontent Radicals strove to make their views the views of the party. President Johnson at first seemed to side with this faction, thus giving them an inside track in the race for party control. By the time Johnson came to an open break with them, in the winter of 1865-1866, the Radicals had consolidated their position. Due to the war hysteria and war animosities which were given renewed vigor by the popular resentment at Lincoln's assassination, the Radicals had acquired a backing among the people of the North which made it possible for them to oppose successfully the President and the Conservative element in the party. The Radicals were able to appeal to a wide range

[3] Minor, *The Story of the Democratic Party* (New York, 1928), p. 296, quotes Senator John Sharp Williams.

of sentiments.   This is shown by the diversity of character
which marked their leaders, from the vindictive Stevens to
the idealist Sumner.

The Radical game was unwittingly played by the former
Confederates who were in virtual control of most of the
Southern States in 1865 and 1866.   Their assumption that
their States would be allowed to deal with the problems
arising out of emancipation resulted in the enactment of
various " Black Codes " regulating the position of the freedmen.   These codes were a marked recession from the extreme restrictions which the slave codes had imposed upon
the negro, but they fell short of granting him full economic
and political equality with the whites.   Thus the Radicals
were able to point with alarm at an assumed intention of the
" rebels " to reenslave the negro, and they were able to claim
that if their policy of repression for the whites and outside
support for the negroes was not followed the gains of the
war would be lost.   The rejection of the fourteenth amendment by the Southern States strengthened the hands of the
Radicals and contributed to the belief among the Republicans that the South remained disloyal at heart and that
the negro needed Northern protection if his emancipation
was to be more than a futile gesture.

By the winter of 1866 the attempted Conservative-Democratic fusion had failed, the President had been outlawed by
the party which elected him, and the Democrats, repudiated
by the Congressional elections of that year, found themselves
unable to stem the tide of the increasingly vindictive Radical
programme.

2. THE ELECTIONS OF 1867

The results of the Congressional election of 1866 were
very discouraging to the Democrats, but they did not have
to wait long for better omens.   State elections were held in

1867 in nineteen States:[4] all of New England; all of the Middle States except Delaware and Maryland; West Virginia, Kentucky, Tennessee, Ohio, Michigan, Wisconsin, Minnesota, Iowa, and California. In 1866 the Republicans had carried all of these States except Maryland and Kentucky. In 1867 the Democrats carried not only those two but also Connecticut, New York, Pennsylvania, New Jersey, and California. Still more significant was the fact that in each of the nineteen States the Democratic majorities increased or the Republican majorities decreased. Even in local elections, not state-wide, as in Indiana and Illinois, the Democrats made large gains. In New England the Republican majority for Massachusetts shrank from 65,000 to 28,000, the vote for the Democratic candidate for governor increasing from 36,000 to 70,000. Boston elected a Democratic mayor. The result in Connecticut represented a smaller shift of votes but was more heartening to the Democrats especially as it came early in the year (April 17). In 1866, James R. Hawley had defeated James E. English for Governor by 541 votes. In 1867 English won over Hawley by 987 votes.

In New York the principal office to be filled was Secretary of State. In 1866 Reuben E. Fenton had defeated John T. Hoffman for governor by nearly 14,000. In 1867 H. A. Nelson, Democratic candidate for Secretary of State, defeated J. B. McKean by nearly 48,000 votes. In New Jersey the election of 1867 was for members of the legislature. This body was changed from a Republican joint

[4] March—New Hampshire; April—Connecticut, Rhode Island, Michigan; August—Kentucky, Tennessee; September—Maine, Vermont, California; October—Pennsylvania, Ohio, Iowa, West Virginia; November—Massachusetts, New York, Maryland, Minnesota, Wisconsin. Election data in this section from *American Annual Cyclopedia*, 1866-1867; *Tribune Almanac*, 1867-1868; *Democratic Almanac*, 1867-1868; McPherson, *op. cit.* See Appendix A.

ballot majority of 11 to a Democratic joint ballot majority of 33. In Pennsylvania (more evenly balanced then than now) a Republican majority of 17,000 in 1866 was changed to a Democratic lead of 922 on a light vote for a justice of the State Supreme Court. In Maryland Odin Bowie became Governor by a majority of 41,000, polling 74% of the votes cast. The Democratic candidate for State Comptroller in 1866 had received only 59% of the vote cast. California had no Congressional election in 1866, but in September, 1867, not only was a Democratic Governor chosen but also three Democratic Congressmen; [4a] and in October a Supreme Court election was won by the Democratic candidate.

The most widely discussed election this year was the contest in Ohio where R. B. Hayes, Republican, opposed Allen G. Thurman for governor. In a spirited canvass in which negro suffrage was widely discussed, Hayes won by less than 3,000. In 1866 the Republicans had carried the State by over 42,000. At the same time (October, 1867) the Ohio voters rejected a negro suffrage amendment to their Constitution by 38,000 votes, and elected a Democratic legislature; winning both houses and changing a Republican majority of 46 on joint ballot to a Democratic majority of 8. The campaign was a very vigorous one. The Republicans used such slogans as " Honest Black Men are preferable to White Traitors "—" Democrats Murdered our President." " If any man pull down the American flag, give him a Post Office—A. Johnson." [5] But the Republicans committed two tactical errors. They identified their candidates too closely

[4a] The three California members of the fortieth Congress, elected on September 4, 1867, did not qualify for their seats until November 21, 1867. McPherson, *op. cit.*, pp. 183, 348; *Biographical Directory of the American Congress*, p. 294. There was no general election in California during the year 1866. *American Annual Cyclopedia*, 1866, p. 84.

[5] *Ohio Archeological and Historical Quarterly*, vol. xxxvii, nos. 2 and 3, 1928—article by Moore, p. 243.

with negro suffrage, and their majority in the legislature proposed a constitutional amendment disqualifying all Army
deserters from voting.   This was to debar " Peace " Democrats, but it was discovered that about one-fourth of the
Ohio deserters had left the Army after Lee's surrender to
avoid Indian and Mexican service.   In July, 1867, through
th efforts of Representative Ashley of Toledo, Congress
lifted the stigma of desertion from all those who left the
Army after April 15, 1865.   But the Ohio legislature had
already placed itself on record.[6]   The Republicans attempted
to make the war records of the Democrats the issue, and
Senator Wade delivered such bitter attacks on the Democrats
as to arouse a hostile reaction, especially in Southern Ohio.
Outside oratorical talent was drawn upon for both sides, the
speakers including Voorhees of Indiana for the Democrats
and John A. Logan of Illinois and Senator Zachariah
Chandler of Michigan for the Republicans.[7]

A recent commentator remarks that Hayes descanted on
negro suffrage to such an extent that he overdid it and gave
Thurman an opening he failed to seize.   " Had Thurman
ceased talking about States rights for which nobody cared,
and discussed equal suffrage and the 14th amendment to the
Constitution to which many people were still opposed ", he
might have defeated Hayes.[8]

The legislative triumph of the Democrats in Ohio led to
complications within the party.   During the campaign, it
was generally understood that if the Democrats won the
legislature Clement L. Vallandigham was to have the Senate
seat then to be filled.   The tentative slate presented Thurman
for Governor, Vallandigham for Senator, and George H.

[6] Moore, *op. cit.*, pp. 242-243.

[7] Porter, *Ohio Politics During the Civil War Period* (New York, 1911),
pp. 244-248.

[8] Eckenrode, *Rutherford B. Nayes (etc.)* (New York, 1930), p. 85.

Pendleton as the choice of the Ohio Democrats for President.

The Senate seat in question was that of Benjamin F. Wade, whose term was to expire with the 40th Congress (March 3, 1869). One radical Democratic weekly stated in January, 1868, that Vallandigham was the choice of the majority of the Ohio Democrats, although Thurman would get the seat. Vallandigham was advised to try for the House of Representatives in November as a better theatre for his talents. Thurman should contest Hayes' election, and secure the governorship after the illegal negro votes for Hayes had been thrown out. As for " Ben Wade's nasty seat," it would " be a credit to this State " if it were left vacant for a couple of sessions and fumigated.[9]

When the Democratic members of this newly elected legislature met in caucus, they gave Thurman 51 votes and Vallandigham 24 for the Senate seat. Vallandigham was deprived of the coveted seat because of the jealousy of the other leaders, because it was felt that Thurman had earned a reward for his vigorous campaign against Hayes, and because there was a feeling that the Senate would not seat any man of his war record. Vallandigham was much disappointed by his failure. Upon his return home he " appeared for days as if a dark shadow had fallen upon his soul." [10] He felt that one reason for his defeat was the support given Thurman by Pendleton. This feeling towards Pendleton helps to explain why Vallandigham was not more active in supporting " Gentleman George " for the Democratic nomination for President.[11]

Newspaper comment on the results of the elections of

[9] Cincinnati West and South, January 11, 1868.

[10] Porter, *op. cit.*, p. 253; J. L. Vallandigham, *Clement L. Vallandigham* (Baltimore, 1872), pp. 422-423.

[11] *Infra*, pp. ——.

1867 was varied. The Springfield *Republican* said the Democratic gains meant a popular reaction against the policy of disfranchising the Southern whites for the benefit of the negroes.[12] The New York *World* on January 10, 1868, reminded its readers that ten months previously the Democratic party was proclaimed by its opponents to be dead—if so, " its corpse has been performing some singular feats." General Grant, according to the *World,* had been courted by the Democrats, but " since the Great Reaction " the party " feels no need of this crutch and is quite willing its rival shall us it to support its tottering steps ". The Republican party confessed that its salvation " is staked upon General Grant's epaulettes," and the Democratic gains made his nomination by the Republicans virtually certain, and eliminated Chief Justice Chase as a Republican candidate. Carl Schurz of Missouri, in a letter to his wife on October 12, 1867, wrote that the Presidential campaign would require a real effort by the Republicans even with Grant, whose nomination appeared to have been rendered practically certain. " The Republican party now needs to have its best men at the wheel." [13]

The Round Table, a New York weekly of the better class, anti-Radical in sympathy, attributed the Republican losses to the negro suffrage issue and to a growing feeling of kindliness and generosity on the part of the North towards the South. The editor thought it possible that the Republicans might even be displaced in the national government by the Democrats.[14] Later *The Round Table* expressed doubt that any condidate whatever could be elected President upon

[12] In Merriam, *The Life and Times of Samuel Bowler,* vol. ii, p. 34.

[13] *Schurz, Intimate Letters of* (in Wisconsin Historical Society Publications), p. 408—written after the Ohio, Iowa, Pennsylvania and West Virginia elections.

[14] October 19, 1867.

a negro equality and negro suffrage platform, and said that the elections of 1867 had given the Democrats a chance for success they little dreamed of before.[15]

The Democratic reaction did not change materially the party lineup in Congress, as few seats were contested at this time. With their majorities safe for another year, the frightened Radicals determined to take advantage of the respite, and to put through at once the programme they had evolved. The reconstruction and consequent readmission of the Southern States on a negro suffrage basis was hastened, as it became evident that Southern Republican votes might be needed in 1868.

The elections of 1867 also had the effect of turning many wavering Republican Conservatives towards the Radicals, as a decisive Democratic victory in 1868 would mean the scrapping of the entire system of reconstruction that had been evolved in the two preceding years.[16] While willing to see the South treated with more leniency than had been shown by the Radicals, many Conservatives were not willing to leave the problem of Southern reconstruction in exclusively Southern hands.

3. THE DEMOCRATIC PARTY ON THE EVE OF THE CAMPAIGN

In January, 1868, largely due to the gains made in the preceding year, the Democratic party found itself in possession of five governors and eight legislatures, as follows: Governors H. H. Haight of California, James E. English of Connecticut, Saulsbury of Delaware, John W. Stevenson of Kentucky, and Odin Bowie of Maryland; the legislatures of California, Delaware, Kentucky, Maryland, New Jersey, New York, Ohio, and Oregon.[17]

[15] November 16, 1867.

[16] Alexander, *op. cit.*, vol. iii, p. 189.

[17] McPhetres, *Political Manual for 1868*.

One result of the Democratic gains was a tendency for former Democrats, who had acted with the Republicans during and after the war, to drift back to their old allegiance. Commenting on this, Horatio Seymour wrote to Samuel J. Tilden on December 13, 1867, that the ex-Democrats were seeking to return to the party " not as penitents but as leaders." He pointed out the danger of their dividing the party men who had stood together in the years of trial. " Do not suffer those who come in sunshine and leave us in storms to walk into our councils and shape our policy with a view to their own gain." The Democratic organization and leaders should remain unchanged. He suggested a conference of party leaders to be held in Albany in January. " The rival candidates for the Presidency will all try to get men drawn into their interests. Let us keep our power by holding ourselves free." [18] William A. Wallace, Pennsylvania State Chairman, agreed that a meeting of party leaders of all the Northern and border States should be held. He suggested to Tilden February first at Washington as the date and the place.[19]

An Albany meeting, as suggested by Seymour, was held on January 2nd, and was attended by leaders from both New York city and " upstate." [20]

A more elaborate gathering of the national leaders of the Democracy took place on January 8 (Jackson Day) at Washington under the auspices of the Democratic Residential Executive Committee. Among those who spoke were President Johnson, Senators Reverdy Johnson of Maryland and James Doolittle of Wisconsin, Attorney General Henry Stanbery, Judge Jeremiah Black of Pennsylvania, and Gen-

[18] *Tilden Letters*, vol. i, pp. 214-215.
[19] *Ibid.*, p. 215, December 30, 1867.
[20] Washington *Express*, January 4, (Albany, January 3).

eral Thomas Ewing, Jr., of Kansas. Others present were Montgomery Blair of Maryland, Senator Patterson of Tennessee, Secretary of the Interior Browning, and Robert J. Walker, former Secretary of War.[21] As seen by this list, the Conservative or "War" Democratic side of the party predominated in this meeting. The speeches at this meeting stressed the essential unity of principles of President Johnson and the Democratic party. This emphasis on the desirability and possibility of cooperation between the "War" Democrats and the Administration on the one hand, and the regular Democratic organization on the other was very widely advocated, both in the party and out of it.

On February 11 a meeting of Democrats in New York city issued an address urging the "necessity for new measures and new men." [22] On March 2, August Belmont, Chairman of the Democratic National Committee, following the selection of New York as the place and July 4 as the time for the meeting of the Democratic National Convention, issued a letter to the various State Chairmen urging them to appeal to the Conservatives who had not before acted with the Democrats.[23] Charles A. Dana, who became editor of the New York *Sun* in January, said that the Democracy "should remove the debris of its broken down platforms out of its path; adopt measures consonant with its liberal principles; bow its old fogy leaders to the rear." [24] The New York *Journal of Commerce* (Republican) foretold Democratic defeat if they "take up an old party hack or any man of obnoxious or extreme party views." The New Haven *Register* (Democratic) called for party peace

[21] *Ibid.*, January 9, 1868.

[22] *Leaflet*, New York, 1868, "The Path to Conservative Triumph," in New York Public Library.

[23] *National Intelligencer*, April 14, 1868, and elsewhere.

[24] Wilson, *Dana*, pp. 384-385.

and united action by Conservatives and Democrats.[25] The New York *Times* (Republican) advised the Democrats to look for new men to meet the new issues and warned them not to nominate anyone who took a prominent part in the party struggles of the war.[26]

Among the elements which the Democrats could bring together by a Conservative policy, according to the New York *Herald* (Independent) were: merchants hurt by the protective tariff; workingmen out of work; the Irish and the Germans; the Catholics; women opposed to negro suffrage; all the opponents of military government; those shocked by the Radical assaults on the Supreme Court; and conservative classes generally. The *Herald* recommended that the Democrats refrain from selecting their Presidential nominee until the last minute, and attempt to reconcile the greenbackers of the West and the financial interests.[27]

The position of the Southern States in the party raised some delicate questions. With a large portion of the Northern voters still looking upon the ex-Confederates as "rebels" and with something of the war-time sentiment remaining for the former slaves, an active participation by the Southern Democrats in the councils of the party would be likely to have a bad effect on Northern public opinion. The situation called for the Southerners to " lie low " and say little, trusting to their friends in the North to obtain relief for them. There remained enough of the " unterrified " and " unreconstructed " attitude in the South to worry the Northern Democrats. The Washington *Express,* on March 30, warned the Southern press that a victory of the Northern Democracy would not result in a forcible end of existing

[25] In *National Intelligencer*, April 14, 1868.

[26] May 1, 1868.

[27] January 23, 1868.

troubles in the South. " The Northern people have no idea
of substituting bullets for ballots."   On May 23 the New
York *Times* said editorially that the star of the " war "
Democrats was in the ascendant with a general recognition
on the part of Democrats, South as well as North, that it
would be hopeless to carry on a contest with the " loyal "
sentiment of the nation.   Yet in June the *Times* felt that
Southern ideas more faithfully represented the prevailing
temper of the Democracy, and would not be abandoned without a struggle.[28]   The Springfield *Republican* on July 1 did
not think that the Conservative elements of the party had
made much headway.   It referred to " the mere, stupid,
causeless, aimless hatred of the negro " which pervaded the
Democracy.   The *Republican* thought it a pity that the
Democrats did not seize upon the real issues of the day.

The movement to nominate the Republican Chief Justice
as the Democratic standard bearer was an indication of the
strength of the idea that the Democracy should take new
leaders on a new platform in order to appeal to the Conservatives.   Colonel John D. van Buren,[29] a personal friend
of Chase, on May 1 wrote to Seymour that he did not believe
the Democratic party was likely to win the Presidency unless a breach in the other party could be made.   Under
existing conditions, van Buren expected the Republicans to
carry Ohio, Pennsylvania, and Illinois, besides all the
Southern States to be admitted under the Reconstruction
Acts.   Chase was the Moses to lead the party out of the
wilderness.[30]   James G. Bennett's New York *Herald,* which
by May was active in support of Chase, gave the Democrats

[28] June 1, 2, 1868.

[29] Not " Prince John " VanBuren who died in 1866, obituary notice in
American Annual Cyclopedia, 1866.

[30] May 1, 20, New York Historical Society Library, Seymour Mss.
Box 4.

the same advice: repel the Conservatives and lose—or attract them with Chase as a candidate and win. The Cincinnati *Commercial* (Republican) edited by the able Murat Halstead took the same position.

In February, 1868, Bennett told the Democrats that they should nominate their candidate for President at as late a date as possible. " Train all your men and keep all their friends in hope until it is too late to back out, and then try and nominate with a sole view to victory," was his advice.[31]

In spite of the widespread sentiment that the Conservative Republicans should be invited to places at the head of the table, Seymour's advice to Tilden was on the whole consistently followed. Although overtures were made to those who had been acting with the Republicans, no last minute convert such as Chase was given a place on the national ticket and the party chairmanships, state as well as national, went to regular Democrats. The nearest approach to recognition of the Conservatives was the nomination of General Frank Blair, of Missouri, for Vice-President, but Blair like his brother Montgomery, though an office holder under Lincoln, had been in open opposition to the Radical Republicans for some years. The platform adopted by the party contained little that would entice Conservative support, though an appeal to them was included in it.

It seems accurate to say that the party victories of 1867, added to the failure of the Democratic-Conservative movement of 1866, convinced the Democratic leaders that an excellent chance for success existed under a policy which would not in any way endanger the integrity of their party organization. Three years were to pass before the party was ready for the " New Departure " of 1871 which led to the Democratic-Liberal Republican union of 1872. To some

[31] Charles O'Conor to Tilden, February 10, 1868, *Tilden Letters*, vol. i, p. 218; O'Conor saw Bennett at Tilden's suggestion.

the fact that the fusion ticket of 1872 failed even more decisively than the party ticket of 1868 will indicate that Seymour's position was a sound one. To others, however, it will seem that the Democratic party in 1868 would have come nearer to national success had more attention, with some real concessions, been paid to the Conservative element. The nomination of a Conservative Democrat such as General Hancock on a platform more moderate in tone than the one adopted might have given a different result.

The divisions within the Democratic party were too numerous and deep seated to permit such a solution. The divergence of Eastern and Western opinion on financial issues and the friction between the " war " and " peace " elements in the party resulted in a Western victory in the adoption of the platform, and in the defeat of those candidates before the National Convention who had a pronounced " War Democrat " record. There was a decided effort especially on the part of the Eastern Democrats to narrow the issues down to one—opposition to the violation of Constitutional principles by the Radical Congress. As the New York *World* put it : "The Constitution was the issue." [32] It was urged that the Democrats should forego discussion of questions upon which they were divided, such as the greenback question, and concentrate their efforts on rescuing the Constitution from the hands of the Radicals.[33]

The division of sentiment within the party was not shown as clearly as might have been expected by the action of twenty-two Democratic State Conventions, held in 1868 before the National Convention.[34] Nine States: Ohio,

[32] May 26, 1868.

[33] Franklin Pierce to J. D. Hoover, April 22, 1868, *Franklin Pierce Papers*, Library of Congress, vol. vii.

[34] Data on Conventions from *American Annual Cyclopedia*, 1868, *passim*, the following Democratic State Conventions are mentioned: January—

Indiana, Minnesota, Illinois and Michigan from the Middle West; Pennsylvania and Maine from the East; and Tennessee and Oregon, endorsed the greenback idea; but only four of them (Ohio, Indiana, Oregon, and Illinois) instructed their delegates to the National Convention to vote for Pendleton. Only two State Conventions at this time (Connecticut and New Jersey) went on record as opposing the " Ohio Idea," while the other State Conventions were silent or non-committal on this issue.

The sentiment of the party on the subject of negro suffrage was much nearer a unit. Of the twenty-two State Democratic Conventions, held between January and July, eleven from all sections went on record as opposing negro suffrage, North or South. Only one gathering, that of South Carolina in April, approved negro suffrage in any form. The other ten Conventions either were silent on the subject, or announced their belief in State control of suffrage. This was the position taken by the party in the national platform.

A summary of the action taken by the various Democratic Conventions shows that the greenback plan was more widely accepted than was the candidacy of Pendleton, its chief apostle. Some opposition to this plan existed in the East; in fact the Eastern opposition was stronger than the actions of the State Conventions would show. However, it was logical enough for the platform of the National Convention to take a greenback position while refusing to nominate Pendleton. Negro suffrage was generally denounced except in New England, and the principle that suffrage was a State matter, not subject to Federal control, was so widely

Ohio, Indiana, New Hampshire, Connecticut; February—North Carolina, Tennessee, Minnesota; March—Pennsylvania, New York, Oregon; April —South Carolina, Illinois; May—Missouri, Michigan; June—Delaware, Tennessee, Maryland, Alabama, South Carolina, New Jersey, Maine.

accepted that its inclusion in the National platform was to be expected. In denouncing the Radical plan of reconstruction, military government in the South, and attacks by Congress on the Supreme Court and the Executive, the party was a unit.

The Republican party was also faced with internal division, but the dominant radical group had been successful in putting over its reconstruction programme in Congress. Outright opposition to this, from within the party, had become almost inarticulate. The reconstruction acts of 1867 were in full force in the South, and were being supported by Federal military power. The collapse of the conservative Republican—Johnson—Democratic movement of 1866 left those Republicans who resented the radical programme without leadership. They were divided into three groups. Moderate Republicans such as Fessenden and Trumbull were working and voting, temporarily at least, with the radicals. The old Lincoln supporters in Johnson's cabinet—Seward, McCulloch and Welles—were firm in their support of the President, and many former Republicans such as the Blairs, Senator Doolittle and Chief Justice Chase, were either out and out Democrats, or were rapidly drifting into that position. This situation gave the Democrats an excellent opportunity to undermine the radical position. The story of the campaign is largely that of their failure to do this. In the spring of 1868 the Democrats were very much stronger than they were in the fall. Instead of adding to and consolidating their gains, the Democracy by giving the " unreconstructed " and greenback elements a free rein drove the moderate Republicans to the support of the Republican platform and ticket.

4. THE SPRING ELECTION IN 1868

The results in the State and local elections in the spring of 1868 [35] encouraged the Democrats in their belief that a widespread reaction against Radicalism was under way.

The first election of any significance held in 1868 was curiously enough a Republican victory: on January 27 the Republican candidate for Congress, Beatty, won in the Dayton, Ohio, district.[36] Clement L. Vallandigham, disgruntled by his failure to receive the Senate seat he wanted, published in his Dayton *Ledger* a pessimistic prophecy of Democratic defeat in November, and the failure of the movement to nominate Pendleton for President. He attributed Beatty's victory to " the Democratic policy of trimming to catch Republican votes by ignoring old fashioned, straight out Democratic principles and Democrats." The New York *Herald* commented that Vallandigham, badly used by his party, meant to " smash the machine." [37] According to the New York *World,* Vallandigham had " gone over to the enemy " and was a " sinister and treacherous rival " of Pendleton.[38] Some Ohio papers regretted the attack by the *World* but that paper refused to recant. It likened him to Benedict Arnold and said that: " If his revenge had not incited him to treachery, he would have found ample protection from criticism in our contempt." [39]

More favorable results from the Democratic point of view were found in local town elections in New Hampshire, Maine and New York held in the latter part of February and early

[35] Election figures in this section from *American Annual Cyclopedia,* 1868; *Tribune Almanac,* 1869; *Democratic Almanac,* 1869; McPherson, *Reconstruction,* see Appendix A.

[36] *Supra.*

[37] February 2, 1868.

[38] February 5, 1868.

[39] February 5, 1868.

in March.   In each case, Democratic gains as compared with the vote of the preceding fall were recorded.   The *World* printed a list of sixteen New York towns and cities, showing that in 1866 only two had been Democratic; in 1867 seven; and now fourteen of the sixteen gave Democratic majorities.[40]

The first State-wide election in 1868 was that of New Hampshire.   In a total vote for Governor some ten thousand greater than a year before, the Republican majority with the same candidates was reduced from thirty-one hundred to eighteen hundred.   E. L. Godkin wrote to the London *Daily News* that the Republican victory was in reality a victory for the reconstruction policy of Congress, and was a repudiation of the President.[41]   The New York *Tribune* on March 11 was exultant—" New Hampshire is True " ! The election was supposed to strike the keynote for the Presidential contest, and it did.   *Harper's Weekly* was especially glad that the Democrats lost since they used such outside oratorical talent as Henry Clay Dean, C. C. Burr, and Daniel W. Voorhees.   The Democrats were emboldened to throw away the mask by flaunting such men, most of them " Peace " Democrats, before the people.[42]

The next State election, in Rhode Island on April 1, gave the Republicans a majority of 4,300 as compared with 4,200 in 1867; but the percentage of the Democratic vote rose from 30.2 in 1867 to 35.8 in 1868.

On April 6 two more elections gave comfort to the Democrats.   In Michigan a new State Constitution providing for negro suffrage, was defeated by a vote of 110,000 to 71,000.   In local elections in Michigan, the Democrats showed increased strength in the southern and central

[40] March 4, 5, 1868.

[41] New York, March 11, in London *Daily News* of March 23, 1868.

[42] March 28, 1868.

counties where the situation was considered so serious that Schuyler Colfax and Ben Wade were brought in to speak for the Republicans.[43]

The Connecticut election, however, attracted the most attention. The previous year, Governor English (Democrat) had been elected by a majority of nearly one thousand. The Springfield *Republican* on March 27 was confident of Republican victory. The Democrats, not only in Connecticut, but all over the country were " depressed and spiritless." Carl Schurz of Missouri, in a letter to his wife on March 29, reported that the Connecticut Democrats were hardly stirring at all,[44] while A. E. Burr of the Hartford *Times,* a Democrat, writing to his friend Gideon Welles on March 29, said: " The Republicans are using money like water in Connecticut," but he reported popular sympathy with the Democrats and an expected victory for English, though the legislature would go Republican.[45] English was re-elected by a majority of over 1,700, or nearly twice that of the year before. The districting system for the legislature enabled the Republicans to retain control of that body with the result that Senator Dixon who was up for reelection lost his seat.

The reelection of English brought forth paeans of joy from the Democrats. The Utica *Observer* (Seymour's home-town paper) said the result meant " Radicalism, impeachment, Grant, and all their host routed, scattered, almost annihilated. On a vote as large if not larger than ever before polled, the Democratic majority of the State has been doubled! " It was a repudiation of the Radicals and a rebuke to fanatics. And so on in other Democratic papers.[46]

The Springfield *Republican* attributed the result to fraud

---

[43] Dilla, *Politics of Michigan* (New York, 1912), p. 97.

[44] Schurz, *Intimate Letters,* p. 431.

[45] Welles Mss., New York Public Library, Manuscript Division.

[46] E. g., New York *World,* April 7, 8, 1868.

and to disgust with the idea of negro suffrage. The Democrats did not repeat the mistake they made when they sent
" virulent Copperheads " into New Hampshire. Their party
had no " cumbersome sentiments. It is never troubled with
gratitude. It knows no remorse. . . It learns by its mistakes and never repeats its errors." [47]   The Cincinnati *Commercial* thought that the result would encourage the Democrats to nominate a " thorough partisan " such as Pendleton
for President, and thus insure their defeat in November,
although English himself was a " war " Democrat.[48]

On April 17, the Albany *Argus* summed up the electoral
progress of the Democracy to date, and found great comfort therein. The New York cities of Albany, Utica,
Rochester, and Troy had given Democratic majorities.
Forty towns in Michigan which were radical in 1867 had
voted Democratic. In Western cities, too, the Democrats
made large gains—St. Louis, Milwaukee, Cincinnati and
others. On April 21 Chicago was carried by the Democrats
in a judicial election.[49]

The Oregon Congressional election remained before the
summer. In 1866 the Republican candidate won by over
1,500 votes. In 1868, the Democrat, Joseph S. Smith, won
by a majority of 209. This change of over 1,700 votes in
a total canvass of some 22,000 bore out the trend shown by
elections in other States. The Oregon legislature also
changed from Republican to Democratic control. Gideon
Welles recorded in his diary that the Oregon vote was " the
first reaction to the Chicago (Republican) nominations." [50]
Grant and Colfax had been nominated by the Republican
National Convention on May 21. The result in Oregon

[47] April 7, 15, 17, 1868.
[48] April 7, 8, 1868.
[49] Chicago *Republican*, April 27, 1868.
[50] June 2, 1868, vol. iii, p. 375.

was telegraphed to President Johnson who, in reply, referred to Oregon as one of the States which " in the approaching elections, will redeem the nation from misrule and corruption." [51]

The next State elections took place after the Democratic nominations, and with few exceptions were Democratic defeats. Why were the high hopes aroused by the victories of the spring dashed to the ground in the summer and fall? Why did the seemingly steady tide towards the Democrats recede so definitely in a few months? The answer is to be found in the platform and ticket of the Democratic National Convention which was in session early in July.

[51] *Johnson Papers*, Library of Congress, telegrams received and telegrams sent, p. 113.

CHAPTER III

CHIEF JUSTICE CHASE AND THE REPUBLICAN PARTY

1. CHASE'S POLITICAL POSITION

AMONG the most interesting features of the campaign of 1868 was the position taken by Chief Justice Chase. His political career up to this time had been varied. His party affiliations may be listed as follows: 1832 National Republican; 1836-1840 Whig; 1844 Liberty; 1848 Free Soil; 1851 Democratic; 1852 Liberty; and 1856 Republican.[1] He had been Governor of Ohio, Senator, and Secretary of the Treasury under Lincoln. In this position he had drifted towards the more radical element in the Republican party, and was talked of as a successor to Lincoln in 1864. The movement failed, and he left the Cabinet. In December, 1864, Lincoln appointed him Chief Justice to fill the vacancy caused by the death of Taney.[2]

Chase was prominent as an abolitionist for many years before the war. After the conflict, he continued to be a Republican and was considered a leader of the Radical element. He retained his interest in the negro, and advocated legislation that would insure equal rights in the South. In May 1865, he made a trip to the South to investigate the position of the freedmen. In Charleston he spoke to the negroes, advising them to use their new-found liberty in a way to merit the respect of their friends. If the government would not make all negroes voters, they should go to work and show that the government was mistaken in

[1] *Ohio Archaeological and Historical Quarterly*, vol. xv, p. 316 (July, 1906), article by Senator Foraker.

[2] New York *Herald*, June 19, 1868.

68

the delay. "If you show that, the mistake will be corrected."[3] He wrote President Johnson from Charleston on May 12, hoping for the success of the Administration, and adding " it will be an exceedingly great pleasure to me if I can in any way promote its complete success."[4] It is possible to construe Chase's Southern trip as an effort to look over the political situation in the South with a view to his own chances, but this would be ungenerous. The trip was made when the South was being overrun by various Northern leaders, and Chase's lifelong interest in the negro was reason enough for the journey.

Chase's championship of the Radical cause at the close of the war was due to his sympathy with the freedmen. But two influences gradually brought him into opposition—his resentment as a jurist of the military encroachments upon the judiciary in the South, and his belief in States' Rights. Although he had worked with the Republicans since 1855, he never entirely abandoned the fundamental Jeffersonian doctrine of the rights of the States. In 1865 the way was cleared for a new examination of the problem of State and Federal relationships. After the war, Chase told Don Piatt, " While we freed the negro, we enslaved ourselves." He believed that State sovereignty was the only system upon which conflicting sectional interests could be reconciled, and the freedom of a people spread over a continent be preserved. Centralization of power at Washington must be checked, or the war would prove the forerunner of many woes. Piatt commented that Chase was a more consistent States' Rights man than any Southern statesmen except Henry A. Wise and John Tyler.[5]

[3] Speech in *Harper's Weekly*, July 4, 1868.

[4] Schuckers, *Life (etc.) of S. P. Chase* (New York, 1874), p. 523.

[5] Piatt, *Memories of Men who Saved the Nation* (New York, 1887), pp. 125-127.

Chase's attitude towards military government in time of peace is well known through his participation in the Reconstruction decisions, such as Cummings v. Missouri. His refusal to hold circuit court at Richmond for the trial of Jefferson Davis until all military authority was removed from Virginia is famous. As he stated in a letter written in September, 1868: "I do not believe in military government for American States; nor in military commissions for the trial of American citizens; nor in the subversion of the executive and judicial departments of the general government to Congress, no matter how patriotic the motive may be." [6]

Another element in the situation was his political ambition, which Lincoln referred to as a "mild insanity." [7] Chase was thrice a candidate for the Republican nomination for President, in 1856, 1860, and 1864. As Chief Justice, his old desire persisted and even seemed to have grown with the years and opportunity. [8] Hayes, of Ohio, then in Congress, wrote in December 1865, that Chase "does not show any uneasy ambition—or rather he seems to have made up his mind that his political career is ended; that it is of no use to worry about it; and yet it is not by any means his choice." [9] But a month later, Chase himself wrote: "I think I have a good deal of executive faculty and often wish I were in some more active employment than hearing causes which take up my whole time." [10] In a letter to Jay Cooke, in August, 1866, he admitted the impropriety of a Chief Justice engaging in an active campaign. He wished to visit

[6] *To Col. A. J. H. Duganne*, Schuckers (*op. cit.*), p. 592.

[7] Rhodes, *op. cit.*, vol. vi, p. 168.

[8] *Ibid.*

[9] Hayes, *Diary and Letters* (Columbus, O., 1924), vol. iii, p. 9 to Mrs. Hayes, December 7, 1865.

[10] Oberholtzer, *Jay Cooke*, vol. ii, p. 61, to Jay Cooke, Jan. 9, 1866.

the Convention of Southern Loyalists to be held in Philadelphia in September, but recognized that " the howl which knaves and fools would raise over the fact of my attendance would do more harm than good." [11]   This desire to attend what was essentially an Anti-Johnson rally illustrates the confusion which existed in his mind.   In 1866 he expressed a desire to attend a demonstration against the President; in 1867 he attempted to win the Radical Republican nomination for President; and in 1868 he sympathized with the President in his trial before the Senate, and lent a willing ear to suggestions that he be the Democratic nominee for President!   Chase's instability is shown in a letter early in 1868, in which he refers to the irksomeness of his judicial position, and says he would be better satisfied if called to administrative duties.[12]   Carl Schurz wrote his wife that he pitied Chase, who was like a " wounded lion " as Chief Justice and that a position envied by others made him feel himself a martyr.   " The Presidential fever is a deadly malady," observed Schurz.[13]

By April 1868, with the impeachment trial under way, it had become evident that Grant was to be the Republican nominee.   Chase, while already mentioned for the Democratic nomination, had not yet committed himself to accept it if offered.   Recognizing the futility of his aspirations, he wrote in May that if he knew his own heart, he desired more to merit than to receive the approval of his fellow citizens. However, he would not guarantee that he would look towards the White House again for " I make no boast of an *iron will*." [14]   About the same time he wrote that he had

[11] Oberholtzer, *op. cit.*, p. 61, August 24, 1866.

[12] To H. B. Walbridge, January 2, 1868. *Chase Papers*, Historical Society of Pennsylvania Library, box no. 15.

[13] Schurz, *Intimate Letters*, p. 433, April 4, 1868.

[14] To John H. Gilmore, May 17, 1868, Warden, *An Account of . . . S. P. Chase* (Cincinnati, 1874), p. 695.

long since dismissed the subject of the Presidency from his thoughts, and was now, more than ever, satisfied with the dismissal.[15]

In his attitude towards the Presidency, Chase probably deceived himself more than others and was sincere when he considered the Presidency primarily as an opportunity for service and a chance to show his powers to the best advantage.[16] In his pursuit of political ambition in 1868 he lost something of the respect of his contemporaries and consciously lowered the dignity of the office.[17] He was insatiably ambitious; and he allowed himself to be played upon by bad counsellors. In his efforts to attain the Presidency he corresponded familiarly and often indiscreetly with men of the widest possible differences of political opinion. In 1868 we find him writing with equal familiarity to Horace Greeley and Theodore Tilton, Radical Republican editors, and Alexander Long of Cincinnati and Clement L. Vallandigham of Dayton, Peace Democrats with very unsavory war records. Both Blaine and Piatt commented on this curious range and nature of his political friendships.[18] When Charnwood in his life of Lincoln labeled Chase " unhappily a sneak," [19] he did him an injustice. Chase was an honorable man of great ability with an overweening ambition that led him into curious relationships. He realized the impropriety of his ambition for the Presidency and struggled against the Presidential disease—but in vain.

[15] To J. R. G. Pitkin, May 13, 1868, *ibid.*, p. 693.

[16] Hart, *Chase* (Boston, 1899), p. 362.

[17] *Ohio Archaeological and Historical Quarterly*, vol. xv (July, 1906), article by Foraker.

[18] Blaine, *Twenty Years of Congress* (Norwich, Conn., 1886), vol. ii, p. 395; Piatt, *op. cit.*, pp. 98, 117.

[19] Page 329.

2. CHASE AND THE REPUBLICAN NOMINATION

Before considering the relation of Chase to the scramble for the Democratic nomination, we shall examine his efforts to head off Grant and secure the Republican nomination.

Chase's opposition to the selection of Grant was natural, for he desired the honor himself and he also felt the danger in electing a military hero. As one of the founders of the Republican party, he felt that he was the legitimate candidate, and no other civilian of equal prestige was suggested.[20] Among his supporters were the old abolitionists and the national banks,[21] and as early as 1866 an organization in his behalf was suggested. In the summer of 1867, Chase sent an agent to sound out the Western Republicans and, although he received some favorable reports from Illinois, Wisconsin, Iowa and Missouri, he found that his name aroused little popular enthusiasm, and that he had no strong friends among the political leaders of the West.[22] His disappointment is described in a verse current at the time:

> " Says Salmon P. Chase, says he
> I'll fish, by Jupiter Ammon!
> He went to Ohio
>   And threw in his fly—oh!
> But never a sign of a salmon." [23]

The summer of 1867 marked the high point of Chase's Republican chances. Grant had not yet broken with Johnson, and the Radicals doubted the General's soundness on reconstruction and the negro. Some began to favor Chase, but the shrewd leaders and the rank and file wanted Grant

---

[20] Hart, *op. cit.*, pp. 362-363.

[21] Poore, *Perley's Reminiscences of Sixty Years in the National Metropolis* (Philadelphia, 1886), vol. ii, p. 237.

[22] Hart, *op. cit.*, p. 363.

[23] Poore, *op. cit.*, p. 238.

and were eager to get him on their side.[24]   As Blaine writes
" At an earlier stage, there had been an effort to direct
public thought towards some candidate who was more dis-
tinctly a party chief, and who held more pronounced political
views; but public sentiment pointed so unmistakably to
General Grant that this . . . was speedily abandoned." [25]
Rhodes characterizes Chase's efforts to receive the nomination as clumsy and eager.[26]   Certainly a degree of eagerness
is disclosed in a letter from Chase to James A. Garfield
(August 7, 1867) in which he indicated his Republican regu-
larity by endorsing Congressional reconstruction, to which
the President must yield or face impeachment.[27]   After his
chances for a nomination had become very slight, and the
Chief Justice was called upon to preside over the impeachment trial, he was opposed to the attack on the President.
One is inclined to consider the letter to Garfield a statement
for political effect.

The elections of 1867 which showed a marked Democratic
advance and an increase in popular support for the greenback heresy, were interpreted by some as a blow to Chase.
The New York *Herald* referred to the rejection of negro
suffrage, and took the view that like a dazzling castle in the
clouds, the gorgeous, imposing Presidential structure of
Chase had melted away and vanished.   Grant remained the
only available candidate.[28]   Grant himself recognized that
the Democratic revival would probably make his nomination
necessary to the Republicans.   In the fall of 1867 he was
telling General Sherman, with a show of reluctance, that

[24] Rhodes, *op. cit.*, vol. vi, p. 158.

[25] Blaine, *op. cit.*, vol. ii, p. 386.

[26] Vol. vi, p. 162.

[27] Hart, *op. cit.*, p. 356.

[28] October 16, 1867.

events might force him to take the nomination.[29] As late as October 15, the New York *Tribune* still thought Chase the best qualified man for the place.[30] But the *World* more wisely took the view that the October elections had transferred Chase to the back seats among the used-up politicians, " near the shadow of old Nick Biddle." [31]

Chase himself now recognized that Grant was very likely to receive the prize. He admitted in a letter in December, 1867, that " some feel that the political currents are now running in military channels," and added " If not now nominated, my name will never again be mentioned in connection with any political office with my consent." [32] But that he had not yet given up is proved by his sending to a correspondent, in January, 1868, some political pamphlets to show what his sentiments were in 1843 and 1863. " You know," he wrote, " I am not a man much given to change." [33]

Evidences of the growing sentiment for Grant may be seen in a Grant rally held at Cooper Union, New York City, on December 4. The meeting selected a committee to issue a call for Grant which W. B. Astor, Hamilton Fish, Peter Cooper, W. E. Dodge, Cornelius Vanderbilt, and Henry Hilton signed.[34] Evidently the doughty general was not to suffer for lack of funds. The *Nation* in December endorsed him editorially.

Yet in January, Chase was considered still in the running not only by the *Herald* but by a number of prominent journals. The New York *Tribune* on January 3 stated

[29] Howe, *Home Letters of General Sherman* (New York, 1909), p. 362.

[30] Quoted in Todd, Presidential Election of 1868. In *American Magazine of History*, vol. ii, p. 153 (1907).

[31] Quoted in Oberholtzer, *Jay Cooke*, vol. ii, p. 27 n.

[32] Warden, *op. cit.*, p. 676, to John Paul, December 20, 1867.

[33] *Ibid.*, January 2, 1868.

[34] Copy of call in *Johnson papers*, Library of Congress, vol. 128.

that " We want a statesman, we desire Mr. Chief Justice
Chase. The party contains no purer, no worthier, no more
gifted man." [35]   *The Round Table* said that if Grant withheld his opinions on negro suffrage the Radicals would meet
the situation by nominating Chase and thus in all probability
elect the Democratic candidate.[36] The radical *Nation* on
the contrary thought on January 9 that, if Chase were
nominated, he would get the electoral votes of the reconstructed States in the South and win.

It is interesting to find some inkling of Grant's opinion
of the situation. He told General Sherman in January
that he would avoid the nomination if possible, but considered it doubtful whether Chase could win. Grant didn't
want to see Pendleton elected, for he had been an open
enemy of the war.[37]

The Chase strength in the South seemed rather remarkable to the Springfield *Republican,* especially as the freedmen
had no reason for preferring him to General Grant. The
Republican referred to a " preposterous " report from
Alabama of a plan to run Chase as a third candidate on an
extreme Radical platform, hoping to throw the election into
the House. If Grant should be nominated, he would win.[38]
Another report of an intrigue involving Chase was reported
to the New York *Herald* from Washington on January 21.
Chase and his friends were said to be offended by lack of
recognition from the Grant supporters, and were secretly
working against the Republicans. It was predicted they
would make a trade with the Democrats.[39] In view of

[35] In Oberholtzer, *United States,* vol. ii, p. 153.

[36] January 9, 1868.

[37] *Home Letters of General Sherman,* p. 370.

[38] January 2, 1868.

[39] January 23, 1868.

Chase's later advances towards the Democracy, this report may be of some significance.

New Hampshire and Connecticut were reported by the *Herald* to have endorsed Grant, with the friends of Chase aloof especially in New Hampshire. Should the Democrats carry these states in the spring elections, Chase's chances would be greatly improved, but according to the *Herald* if the Republicans should carry them on a Grant platform, Chase would be eliminated. Ohio was later reported to Chase as having withstood the tide for Grant. He was told that during the winter two-thirds of the members of both houses of the Ohio legislature were really in favor of Chase as the Republican candidate.[40]

In spite of the optimistic reports, Chase saw the handwriting on the wall and on February 19 admitted that Grant could have the nomination if he wanted it. His own nomination was improbable.[41] About the same time, the New York *Herald* recognized that Chase's chances for the nomination were poor, and thought that he would doubtless cease to push his claims. Grant had completely taken the Radical wind out of Chase's sails, although the developments during the impeachment trial might result in Chase jostling him aside in the Convention. The Western Republicans still feared Chase, and were anxious for Grant to be nominated.[42]

On March 2, Chase professed that he had never had any sanguine expectations that he would be President, although there had been now and then some indications that he might, " but none strong enough to raise in me any troublesome

[40] T. T. Brand, Columbus, June 17, 1868, *Chase Papers*, Library of Congress, vol. 100.

[41] Warden, *op. cit.*, p. 677, to Judge Underwood, Richmond, February 19; to A. N. Cone, February 12, *Chase Papers*, Library of Congress, Letter Book No. 8.

[42] February 12, 13, 27, 29, March 2, 1868.

thoughts." At the present (a very brief present!) he had no wish whatever to have his name connected with that office.[43] A week later a Washington dispatch to the Philadelphia *Evening Star* stated that Chase was reported to have withdrawn from the contest for the nomination, although he himself had not said so.

In speaking of the withdrawal of Radical support from Chase, Rhodes says until the impeachment trial he had been their favorite candidate for the Presidency, not excepting Grant.[44] That this gives too rosy a hue to his prospects during the winter of 1867-68, the preceding pages show.

Although Chase realized the dangers inherent in a military candidacy, his secretary, J. W. Schuckers, records that the nomination of Grant did not antagonize him, for he felt that Grant " was as likely to make a safe and successful President as any other purely military man." He knew that the nomination of a military man by the Republicans had become necessary and inevitable.[45]

In an editorial of March 26, the New York *Herald* gave a résumé of Chase's candidacy during the preceding six months. In Ohio, in October, 1867, the defeat of negro suffrage had been generally considered a blow to his Presidential aspirations. In New York, in the November election, the Republicans stressed as an issue Chase's availability as a candidate and they lost. The Grant-Johnson correspondence (admitted the *Herald*) and the election in New Hampshire, won by the Grant Republicans in that State, settled the last doubts, even in the mind of Chase.

[43] To W. S. Hatch, Warden, *op. cit.*, p. 678.

[44] *United States*, vol. vi, p. 140.

[45] Schuckers, *op. cit.*, p. 560.

3. CHASE AND THE IMPEACHMENT TRIAL

On March 5, the President was impeached before the Senate, and on March 30 the trial began.   Chase entered the impeachment trial without thought of making political capital out of it.   On March 10, he had written Col. William Brown of Kentucky that, whatever may have been his former desires in connection with the Presidency, he wished now to have his name completely disconnected with it.   He was satisfied he was not a suitable candidate for either party.[46]   Similar statements appear in several of his letters in March and April to Gerrit Smith, veteran abolitionist and personal friend, to whom he wrote: " The subject of the Presidency has become distasteful to me.   Some will say ' sour grapes ' ; and there may be some ground for the application of the proverb." [47]

One reason why Chase was inclined to favor President Johnson in the impeachment trial was that the chief beneficiary of the President's conviction would be Benjamin F. Wade of Ohio.   Wade and Chase had been rivals in Ohio for many years, and Chase could not have looked with pleasure upon Wade's elevation to the Presidency.[48]   When the trial was nearing completion, Chase's daughter Kate, wife of Senator Sprague of Rhode Island, was quoted in the Philadelphia *Evening Star* (May 15) as declaring that she would leave her husband if he voted for conviction. " The idea," she said, " of that horrid Ben Wade being put over my father ! "   If the fiery Kate actually said this, her husband called her bluff, for he did vote for conviction.

Quite apart from personal considerations the Chief Justice as a jurist agreed that the President was within his con-

[46] Warden, *op. cit.*, p. 680.

[47] *Ibid.*, pp. 680-683 ; Schuckers, *op. cit.*, p. 576.

[48] Hart, *Chase*, p. 358 ; also New York *Herald*, March 2, 1868.

stitutional rights in removing Stanton.   Chase had said in
the summer of 1867 that Johnson possessed the unquestioned
right, under the Civil Tenure bill, to remove Mr. Stanton.[49]
In the following April, Chase wrote that the removal of
Stanton was the proper mode of protecting and defending
the Constitution and that to him the whole impeachment
business seemed wrong, and " if I had any option I would
not take part in it." [50]   To another correspondent, he voiced
his determination to see that Johnson got a fair trial, as
far as it lay within his power.[51]

Chase was virtually read out of the Republican party
shortly after the trial started, since the Radicals believed his
conduct in the trial would be determined by his hopes for
the Democratic nomination.[52]   Godkin on March 14 reported to the London *Daily News* that Chase had at last
come to grief with his former friends, for the radicals had
denounced him as a traitor and as an ally of the President.[53]
This the Springfield *Republican* found it difficult to believe.
It nevertheless published a report that his son-in-law, Senator
Sprague of Rhode Island, had sent money to New Hampshire to help the Democrats in the recent spring election
there, and that Kate Chase Sprague was lobbying for the
President.[54]   On the other hand, the Washington correspondent of the Philadelphia *Evening Star* reported that the
feeling against Chase among the Republicans was dying out,
as it was recognized that so far he had done only his duty.[55]

[49] J. C. Kennedy to President Johnson, February 22, 1868, *Johnson
Papers*, Library of Congress, vol. 132.

[50] Warden, *op. cit.*, p. 685, to Gerrit Smith, April 19, 1868.

[51] *Ibid.*, p. 682, to J. E. Snodgrass.

[52] New York *Herald*, March 14, 1868.

[53] London *Daily News*, March 27, 1868.

[54] March 17, 1868.

[55] March 17, 1868.

Harper's Weekly defended Chase and declared when all was over that the nation honored him more than ever.[56]

In order to discredit Chase as President of the Court of Impeachment, the Radicals were free in their accusations that he was coquetting with the Democrats. The New York *Tribune* reported that the Democrats and Johnson were suggesting Chase for President in order to influence his actions during the trial, and in order to stir up trouble among the Radicals.[57] Godkin reported to the London *Daily News* on March 25 that the Radical feeling against Chase was growing in bitterness, and that he was accused of seeking the Democratic nomination for President.[58] Perhaps the most widely noticed criticism of the Chief Justice came from the New York *Independent* on April 16, in an editorial entitled "The Folded Banner." In this article the *Independent* announced that it had long supported Chase for the Presidency but it now ceased the advocacy, and expressed the belief that he would not accept a Republican nomination if offered, but would take one from the Democrats. This editorial followed an interview with Chase by the editor, Theodore Tilton. Chase resented this article.

But the insinuations that he was seeking a nomination by the Democrats were denounced by Chase's friends as a roorback of the impeachers to discredit him in public estimation.[59] His own attitude is shown by a letter on March 29 in which he stated he once would have been gratified by a Republican nomination, but he discovered he could not be an impartial judge in the impeachment trial without dissatisfying a large number of Republicans. Since then he had not been a candidate for a nomination, and hoped only to do the

[56] March 21, 1868.

[57] New York *Herald*, March 20, 1868.

[58] London *Daily News*, April 7, 1868.

[59] *National Intelligencer*, March 30, 1868.

duty before him.[60]   On April 5 Chase wrote to his friend
Colonel John D. van Buren that his position was well understood, and that few desired or expected anything of him
except the discharge of his duties as presiding officer.   " In
this expectation I trust no one will be disappointed." [61]

That his impartial position as a judge in the trial was
recognized in some quarters is shown by the statement in
the New York *Herald* on May 7 that his conduct of the trial
commended him to the respect of all, which was of more
value to him than party successes, cliques, and caucuses.[62]
Van Buren wrote him on May 9 that he alone had gained
any substantial reputation out of the impeachment trial.[63]

Among the most widely advertised charges against Chase
was that on May 11 he had gathered Grimes, Trumbull, and
Henderson together and influenced them to vote for acquittal.   It was alleged that there was a " Chase conspiracy " to
acquit the President with the formation of a new Conservative party in view.   The New York *Tribune* on May 18
hysterically stated that Chase " decided the vote of Mr. Van
Winkle.   He did his utmost—happily in vain—to carry off
Messrs. Anthony and Sprague.   We doubt that Mr. Henderson would have voted as he did but for the Chief Justice's
exertions."   Chase denied both charges' and wrote to
Greeley that he had not exerted himself to influence anybody, one way or the other.[64]   The *Independent* a few days

[60] *John C. Underwood papers*, Library of Congress, to John C. Underwood.

[61] Copy in Chase Mss., Historical Society of Pennsylvania Library,
box no. 15.

[62] This was the day the *Herald* commenced advocating his nomination
by the Democrats.

[63] *Chase Papers*, Library of Congress, vol. 99.

[64] Schuckers, *op. cit.*, p. 581; *Chase Papers*, Library of Congress, ser. 2,
vol. iii.

later summarized these and other accusations against the Chief Justice. He had been Johnson's chief defender and did his utmost to prevent a verdict against the President. He was influential in securing votes for acquittal. The explanations for his conduct were to be found in his disappointed ambitions, his dislike for Senator Wade, and his desire for a nomination by the Democrats. On May 27 the *Independent* said that it a thousand times preferred Grant to Chase.

Rhodes recognizes that Chase " presided at the impeachment trial with dignity, impartiality and correctness." [65] Hart says he permitted his friends to continue to urge him for the Presidency,[66] and that his private letters written at this time " were most unsuitable and were ludicrous; " [67] but it can be said for Chase that he freely stated that he was not a candidate for any nomination and, while he left a few loopholes in some of his letters, his correspondence during the trial can hardly be considered as a part of a campaign for a nomination from either party. His correspondents included such diverse characters as Theodore Tilton of the *Independent* (extreme Radical), Murat Halstead of the Cincinnati *Commercial* (Conservative Republican) and Alexander Long (Copperhead Democrat).

One point is clear. It is not true as stated by Winston that the impeachment trial cost him the Presidency.[68] By March 30, when the trial opened, Grant had received the approval of the Radical group in control of Congress and popular sentiment was behind them. Such feeling for Chase as had survived to this time could hardly have overcome the lead possessed by Grant.

[65] *United States*, vol. vi, p. 163.

[66] Hart, *op. cit.*, p. 361.

[67] Rhodes, *op. cit.*

[68] Winston, *Johnson* (New York, 1928), p. 453.

CHAPTER IV

THE REPUBLICAN NOMINATIONS

I. GRANT'S POPULARITY

THE tremendous popularity of the hero of Appomattox was such that he was quite a " catch " for any political party. Grant had never taken an active part in party politics, although his pre-war political sympathies were with the Democrats. His one pre-war Presidential ballot was cast for Buchanan in 1856, and his vote would have been recorded for Douglas in 1860 had he been able to satisfy the Illinois residence requirement.[1] Since the war, he had been considered a supporter of the President. He had accompanied Johnson on a portion of the swing around the circle, and had been selected by the President to replace Stanton and thus bring the tenure of office dispute before the courts. In January, 1868, his quarrel with Johnson over this affair brought the General into opposition to the President, and he wished to see Johnson convicted by the Court of Impeachment.[2]

Considering Grant's earlier political sympathies and his support of the President until January, 1868, it was only natural that at first he should have been thought of for the Democratic nomination. That there was such a movement among a number of New York Democratic leaders was recorded by Thurlow Weed, still the close ally of Secretary Seward. " I learned that Peter Cagger, Dean Richmond

[1] Rhodes, *op. cit.*, vol. vi, p. 188.

[2] McCulloch, *Men and Measures* (New York, 1888), p. 403.

84

and others, successors of the old Albany regency, were quietly preparing the way for General Grant's nomination and, remembering that in 1828 Tammany Hall took the wind out of the sails of the Clintonian party by making General Jackson, an active Clintonian, its candidate, I determined that the adversary should not steal our thunder a second time." [3] As Richmond died on August 27, 1866,[4] this statement by Weed indicates that the Democrats of New York did not lose much time in attempting to capture the General for their 1868 ticket.

The New York *Round Table* in July, 1867, reported that up to that time Grant was urged for the Presidency only by the group that got up the Conservative Convention of 1866. But the fall elections of 1867 showing a strong Democratic swing led the Radicals to cast their doubts aside and to accept Grant as the man to avert their threatened defeat. The sentiment for Grant among the Democrats declined as his availability for the Republicans became more and more obvious. On January 4, 1868, General Charles G. Halpine (Miles O'Reilly), a New York War Democrat, and admirer of Grant, author of the Appomattox apple-tree poem, wrote to the President that he wished the Democrats would nominate Grant on a platform endorsing Johnson but he admitted this result was unlikely.[5] Just before Johnson's break with Grant, the New York *World* recognized that Grant's record was consistent enough with a Democratic nomination; and it is not strange that before the reaction in the fall elections his military popularity caused some discouraged Democrats to look towards him. On January 28 came the open rupture between the General and the Presi-

[3] Barnes, *Memoir of Thurlow Weed* (Boston, 1884), p. 458.

[4] Obituary notice in *American Annual Cyclopedia*, 1866.

[5] *Johnson Papers*, Library of Congress.

dent which precluded any possibility of the Democrats nominating Grant.[6]

As early as September 8, 1867, Samuel Bowles of the Springfield *Republican* predicted that " Grant will take the game at a swoop." John Sherman agreed with this. Following the State and local elections in October and November, 1867, the popular demand for Grant increased among the Republicans,[7] and received added support by party leaders who had previously hesitated to recognize his availability. The New York *Tribune,* however, still preferred Chase.[8] The New York *Herald* thought that, if Grant should be nominated on a platform calling for the Africanization of the South, he would be defeated despite his popularity.[9] On December 4 a Grant meeting was held at Cooper Union in New York City,[10] and on December 19 the *Nation* came out for Grant. On January 3 the New York *Tribune* hauled down its colors, though somewhat ruefully. " Perhaps we must take him; but we do not feel like cheering over it; certainly not so long as great statesmen remain in our ranks." After his nomination, the *Tribune* became one of the most outspoken supporters of Grant. On January 11 *Harpers Weekly* said that the people expected and required General Grant to be the President for his "wise and temperate touch" would heal the nation's wounds.

By the beginning of Grant's quarrel with Johnson (January 28), the movement for his nomination by the

[6] Johnson-Grant correspondence — January 28, February 11, 1868; *American Annual Cyclopedia,* 1868, New York *World,* February 12, 14, 1868.

[7] For situation in Illinois, see Cole, *The Era of the Civil War* (Springfield, 1919), p. 408.

[8] November 7, 1867, in Alexander, *op. cit.,* vol. iii, p. 190.

[9] November 16, 1867.

[10] Copy of call in *Johnson Papers,* Library of Congress, vol. 128.

Republicans had achieved such proportions that it is doubtful if it could have been stopped even if the quarrel had not occurred. He was not eager for the nomination. As late as January 30, General Sherman wrote that he would avoid it if he could.[11] The state of Republican sentiment in Congress for Grant was shown by a bill which was introduced in the House of Representatives in January to give him, as General of the Army, power to assume control over the government of the ten " unreconstructed " Southern States. This bill passed the House but was not taken up in the Senate. Representative James Brooks, a New York Democrat, said that it appeared to him to be a bill to organize the Southern States so as to elect a particular person to the Presidency.[12]

The New York *World,* on January 22, summarized Grant's position in relation to the Republican nomination, saying that as the movement for his nomination by the Republicans gained force he was " at first shy; he then wavered; then enveloped himself in a thick mystery; and at last, he has changed his politics." The *World* thought that Grant's ambition had got the better of his discretion, and that by making it impossible for the Democrats to nominate him he had restored full freedom of choice to the Republicans. The first issue of the New York *Sun,* under the editorship of Charles A. Dana (January 25, 1868) stated " The *Sun* will support General Grant as its candidate for President." [13] On February 5, the New York State Republican Convention, at Syracuse, endorsed his candidacy by acclamation. This was the first formal expression of a State Convention and " set the party aflame." [14] From February to May there

---

[11] *Sherman Home Letter,* p. 370.

[12] *American Annual Cyclopedia,* 1868, pp. 161, 168.

[13] Frank M. O'Brien, *The Story of the Sun,* p. 145.

[14] Alexander, *op. cit.,* vol. iii, p. 191.

remained little doubt that Grant would be chosen and his unanimous nomination by the Republican convention of May 20 was a matter of course.

The difference between the two parties in unity and organization is shown by the fact that, while the Democrats voted on twenty candidates in their Convention and a total of forty-seven were mentioned for the nomination, only three were mentioned for the Republican nominations — Grant, Chase, and Colfax [15]—and only one of these names survived until the Convention met.   The Democrats, it is true, had no such popular hero as Grant and were badly divided as to sections and policies.   Yet the Republicans were also divided on the greenback issue, and Radicals and Conservatives were fighting within the party.   The Republican party discipline was such, however, that the greenback issue was shelved and the Conservatives ignored.   This last procedure was justified by the fact that most of them, including such men as John A. Dix and Secretary Seward, finally climbed on the Grant band wagon before the election.

2. THE REPUBLICAN NATIONAL CONVENTION

The Republican, or Republican National Union Convention, met at Chicago in Crosby's Opera House on May 20 and 21.[16]   As was to be the case in the Democratic Convention, a meeting of Soldiers and Sailors took place on May 19, in Chicago, at the German Turners' Hall.   The soldiers were presided over by Governor Fairchild of Wisconsin, late a general.   Resolutions were adopted in favor of the nomination of Grant and attacking the seven recalcitrant Republican Senators who had voted to acquit the President.

[15] Merriam, *Life of Samuel Bowles* (New York, 1885), vol. ii, p. 55.

[16] For general description of Convention see Oberholtzer, *United States,* vol. ii, pp. 154-157; A. S. Hill in *North American Review*, vol. 107, pp. 167-186 (July, 1868) ; *Official Proceedings.*

On the floor of the National Convention all the States—North and South—were present except Texas. Some opposition to the admission of the Southern delegates existed, but the temporary organization completed under the leadership of the New York delegation forced their admittance. The reason why delegates from States not represented in Congress were admitted was that their votes were desired for trading purposes in the maneuvers incident to the Vice-Presidential nomination.[17] A dozen or more negroes were among the Southern delegates, but equally novel was the presence of the Confederate Governor of Georgia, Joseph E. Brown, who had been " reconstructed." His address to the Convention in which he explained how he had received political light was warmly received.[18] Present on the platform was Jesse Grant, father of Ulysses. The temporary chairman, Carl Schurz of Missouri, delivered the " keynote address " and then turned the meeting over to the permanent president, Joseph R. Hawley of Connecticut.[19] Following the permanent organization of the Convention, a petition for Grant's selection from the Soldiers and Sailors Convention of the preceding day was presented.[20] The platform in twelve planks was reported and unanimously adopted on the second day, May 21.

The party's reconstruction policy in the South, as embodied in the Congressional legislation, was endorsed and the success of those measures was acclaimed. Support was pledged to the constitutions adopted in the Southern States in accordance with that policy. More specifically, equality

[17] Stebbins, *Political History of New York* (New York, 1913), p. 311, cites New York *Times*, May 21, New York *Herald*, May 21.

[18] *Official Proceedings* (Chicago, 1868), pp. 32-36 (hereafter referred to as *O. P.*).

[19] *O. P.*, pp. 8-10.

[20] *O. P.*, p. 30.

of suffrage for all " loyal " men in the South was approved although—with unblushing inconsistency—the control of suffrage in the North was admitted to lie with the States.

Pendleton's " Ohio Idea " was denounced in the resolution which declared all forms of repudiation to be a national crime.   To avoid any suspicion of bad faith, the national debt should be paid according to the spirit as well as the letter of the law, over a fair period, and should be refunded at lower interest rates wherever honestly possible.   These lower interest rates would be possible, the party professed to believe, when Democratic " repudiation " was no longer threatened or suspected.   The demand for tax reform (including taxation of government bonds) was ostensibly met by the statement that taxation should be " equalized " as far as the nation's faith would permit, and the rates of taxation should be rapidly reduced.   To bring about this reduction, it was necessary to end the corruption nursed and fostered by President Johnson, and to substitute economy for his profligacy.

The party paid tribute to the memory of President Lincoln, and deplored his untimely end.   President Johnson's accession had proved to be a national calamity.   He had acted treacherously, usurped the functions of Congress and of the Federal Courts, and had refused to execute the laws.   He had vilified Congress, had denounced it as unconstitutional, and had attempted to block the reconstruction of the Southern States.   He had perverted the patronage of his office.   The House of Representatives had justly impeached him, and he had been properly pronounced guilty by thirty-five Senators.

The above pronouncements on reconstruction, the national finances, and President Johnson occupied eight planks.   The remaining four resolutions were devoted to the veterans and the Irish.   Those who had served in the armed forces of the Union were the saviors of their country, and the bounties and pensions which were their due were sacred obligations which would never be forgotten. The widows and orphans of those who gave their lives were the wards of the people.

The European doctrine of inalienable citizenship was denounced, and it was declared that naturalized citizens as well as native-born should not be liable for punishment by any foreign power for any act done or word spoken in the United States. This right should be upheld by the Federal government. Foreign immigration should be encouraged, and sympathy was expressed for all oppressed peoples struggling for their rights.[21]

In addition to the twelve planks summarized above, Carl Schurz proposed two more which were added to those already adopted. These additions commended former rebels who had become loyal and were cooperating with the Republicans. Such men should be permitted to resume their political privileges. The Declaration of Independence was proclaimed the true foundation of democratic government.[22]

Some of the outstanding features of the platform may be examined briefly. The suffrage provision made "loyalty" the test in the Southern States. That the loyalty intended was loyalty to the Republican party is shown by Schurz' addition. The financial planks were outspoken in denunciation of " repudiation," but failed to specify in what repudiation consisted.

The attacks on President Johnson were quite similar to his strictures on the Republican-controlled Congress, especially on the issues of corruption and usurpation of constitutional functions. The Irish vote was enticed by the planks condemning the doctrine of inalienable citizenship and the

[21] Twelve plans in *O. P.*, pp. 84-85.

[22] *Ibid.*, pp. 89-90.

pronouncement in vindication of the rights of naturalized citizens while abroad.   Those resolutions had reference to the difficulties in which Irish-Americans had found themselves because of their participation in the Fenian agitation, then active in Ireland.

The platform was notable for two omissions.   No gesture of friendship towards the South was included, and the tariff was not mentioned, although the predominant opinion in the party favored a retention of the war duties.   Viewed as a whole, it may be labeled a fighting platform.   No inducements were held out to Democrats to forsake their old allegiance.   The party entered the campaign determined upon a direct assault upon the enemy.

Following the unanimous adoption of the platform, General John A. Logan of Illinois placed Ulysses S. Grant in nomination.[23]   No other name was suggested, and he received the unanimous vote of the 650 delegates present.[24] The expected saturnalia of noise and enthusiasm took place, after which the contest for the Vice-Presidency began. Eleven names were presented:[25] Henry Wilson of Massachusetts (by a Virginia delegate); Schuyler Colfax of Indiana; Benjamin F. Wade of Ohio; Reuben E. Fenton of New York; James Speed of Kentucky; Andrew G. Curtin of Pennsylvania; James Harlan of Iowa; S. C. Pomeroy of Kansas; and J. A. J. Cresswell of Maryland.   Each of the above except Wilson was presented by a delegate from his own State.   The following were also presented: Wm. D. Kelley of Pennsylvania, by an Alabama delegate, and Hannibal Hamlin of Maine by a Wisconsin delegate.   Cresswell of Maryland announced he was for Wade.   Six ballots

[23] *O. P.*, p. 90.

[24] *O. P.*, p. 95.

[25] *O. P.*, pp. 98-116.

were necessary for a choice.[26]   On the first ballot all those placed before the Convention received votes, but the four leaders were Wade (147), Fenton (126), Wilson (119) and Colfax (115).   There was a total of 648 votes and 324 were necessary for a choice.   The ballots for the four leaders were as follows

Ballots	1	2	3	4	5	6
Wade	147	170	178	206	207	38
Colfax	115	145	165	186	226	541
Fenton	126	144	139	144	139	69
Wilson	119	114	101	87	56	—

As is shown, the concentration on Colfax came after the fifth ballot.[27]   Wilson's name was withdrawn at this time, and the Massachusetts vote went for Colfax on the sixth and last.   The choice was made unanimous after the result of the sixth ballot was announced.[28]

According to the usual practice of National Conventions, the party's national committee was chosen for the next four years.   The national chairman was William Claflin of Massachusetts, and the secretary was William E. Chandler of New Hampshire.   Four regional executive committees (Central, Western, Southern, and Pacific Coast), composed of national committeemen from those sections, were designated.   Horace Greeley was the member for New York.[29]

As shown by the balloting, there was something of a contest over the tail end of the ticket.   Fenton was desig-

[26] Balloting in *O. P.*, pp. 118-132.

[27] Oberholtzer, *United States*, vol. ii, p. 157; and Rhodes, *op. cit.*, vol. vi, p. 159 state that Colfax was chosen on the fifth ballot.   Stanwood, *History of the Presidency* (Boston, 1898), vol. i, p. 321, gives the figures for ballot 6 as being ballot 5.

[28] *O. P.*, p. 132.

[29] *O. P.*, p. 137.

nated by the Republican State Convention of New York held at Syracuse on February 5 as its choice, to be voted for by the State delegation as a unit. Roscoe Conkling and Thurlow Weed, however, opposed him. Weed preferred Colfax, Wilson, Blaine, Edwards (of Vermont), or Grow (of Pennsylvania).[30] Fenton's vote in the Convention, outside of New York, came largely from the South, in the proportion of nearly two to one.[31] Bowers, citing Eddy's life of Colfax, attributes Colfax's selection to the influence of a Methodist Conference then in session in Chicago.[32] Wade, the heir-apparent who lost out in the impeachment trial despite his own vote, wished the Vice-Presidential nomination as a consolation prize.

In Washington, following the receipt of the news of the Convention's choices, a crowd called on Grant and Colfax. Grant spoke briefly, disclaiming the power of a public speaker and declaring his intention to discharge any duties thrust upon him with fidelity and honesty of purpose. Colfax praised Grant and placed him next to Washington.[33]

The reception of the nominations by the metropolitan press was on the whole very favorable. The *Times, Tribune, Sun, Herald,* and *Commercial Advertiser* united in declaring Grant a wise choice.[34] The *Sun* thought him stronger than his party.

The harmony of praise for Grant found little echo in the mind of George W. Julian of Indiana, foreshadowing later difficulties. Julian thought the idea of Grant's nomination distasteful, but swallowed the dose and supported the

---

[30] Alexander, *op. cit.,* vol. iii, p. 192; Barnes, *Memoir of Thurlow Weed,* p. 459.

[31] Alexander, *op. cit.,* vol. iii, p. 193.

[32] Bowers, *op. cit.,* p. 224.

[33] Oberholtzer, *op. cit.,* vol. ii, pp. 157-158.

[34] Stebbins, *op. cit.,* pp. 315-320.

party's choice.[35] Gideon Welles recorded in his diary that the choice of the Convention created no enthusiasm for Grant who, he declared, was untruthful, weak and superficial.[36] To his son John Welles he wrote on June 28 in a similar vein, and announced his intention of abstaining from an active part in the campaign.[37]

It is of interest to see how Grant himself regarded his nomination. On June 21 he wrote to his friend General Sherman that his nomination would force the Democrats " to adopt a good platform and put upon it a reliable man who if elected will disappoint the copperhead element of their party. This will be a great point gained if nothing more is accomplished." [38]

Colfax's selection as Grant's running mate was also generally praised in the New York press. The *Times* thought his selection eminently judicious, while the *Tribune* agreed that he was the best man for the position. The *Sun* thought him a wise choice, and Weed's *Commercial Advertiser* expressed pleasure at his selection rather than Fenton. The Buffalo *Express* also thought Colfax added strength to the ticket, if it were needed.[39] The New York *World* naturally criticized the selection on the grounds that both Grant and Colfax came from the Middle West, and the friends of Fenton, Wilson and the other defeated aspirants were not satisfied with Colfax.[40]

The campaign following the nomination contained the

[35] Julian, *Political Recollections* (Chicago, 1884), pp. 319-320.

[36] *Diary*, vol. iii, p. 370, May 27, 1868.

[37] *Welles Papers*, Library of Congress, vol. 65.

[38] *W. T. Sherman Papers*, Library of Congress, vol. xxiii, copy attested by A. Badeau.

[39] Stebbins, *op. cit.*, pp. 315-320.

[40] *Ibid.*, p. 317, May 22, 1868.

usual amount of personal attacks on the nominees. The
Democrats paid their respects to Grant as an inept soldier,
a thief and a drunkard, who lacked confidence in his own
success. In May the New York *World* cited figures of the
relative strength of Grant's and Lee's armies in the campaign of May and June 1864, to show that Grant was Lee's
inferior as a fighter, and that as a commander he was care-
less of the lives of his men.[41] This was not permitted to
go unanswered by the Republican press. The New York
Sun, claiming to use official figures, gave a computation
which was very much more creditable to Grant.[42]

Another attack on Grant's military career was the publication of his " General Order No. 11 " of December, 1862,
in which he expelled all Jewish traders from his military
department. The order stated that " The Jews, as a class "
had violated every regulation of trade established by law.
Grant's father Jesse R. Grant was accused of being involved in unlawful cotton speculations with the connivance
of his son.[43]

Of more substance, was the charge that Grant drank ex-
cessively. The New York *World* was prominent among the
journals making this allegation.[44] In April President Johnson had paid his respects to Grant by stating, in an interview, that when Grant abandoned the Presidential party, on
the " Swing Around the Circle" in 1866, he did so because
of his drunken condition.[45]

That there was considerable truth in the stories about
Grant's drinking is shown by an entry in Welles diary for
October 10. Welles described Grant's drinking habits as

[41] May 25, 1868.

[42] August 10, 1868.

[43] Cincinnati *Commercial*, August 10, 1868.

[44] July 7, 8, 12, etc.

[45] Cincinnati *Commercial*, April 3; New York *World*, April 10, 1868.

follows: "Grant loves drink for the sake of drink. He is not like Blair, convivial, social and given to a spree, but a soaker behind the door and in the dark. He is not a convivialist, but, solitary and alone when the spell is on him, pours down whiskey. There are intervals of days and weeks when he does not drink at all, and he seldom partakes a glass in company." [46]

Grant's honesty was also impugned. It was alleged that when Grant was entertained, with his staff, by a lady in Mississippi during the war, he went off with a large part of the lady's family silver, and that a Shetland pony used by his son was stolen.[47] A New York City Democratic Club hung up a sign which read "Grant's ingratitude to McClellan makes countless thousands scorn." [48]

An unusual form taken by the Democratic attacks on Grant was the circulation of a rumour that Grant, despairing of success, proposed to withdraw as a candidate. In August the Washington correspondent of the New York *World* reported "extraordinary rumours" concerning the return of General Grant from a Western tour. Letters had been received from members of his party "showing an anxiety on the part of the General to throw up his candidacy" because of the lack of spirit in the Republican campaign, and the popular tide running in favor of the Democrats. It was rumoured that the nomination would be tendered to General Sherman. These rumours were indignantly denied by Republican leaders.[49] The Washington correspondent of the New York *Herald* commented: "Grant will not withdraw. He finds he can not do it. He may wish to fly the

[46] *Manuscript Diary*, Library of Congress. Omitted in published *Diary*, vol. iii, p. 450.

[47] Referred to by *Nation*, August 20, September 3, 1868.

[48] *Ibid.*, August 4, 1868.

[49] Washington *Express*, August 13; Albany *Argus*, August 13, 1868.

course but he can not." It was stated that this was decided
at a conference between Grant and the party managers, and
that it was agreed that if Grant should be elected Colfax
would be the actual President. The *Herald* wanted to know
if Grant was contemplating an early retirement, if elected.[50]
Grant was said to be " on the stool of repentance for having
been so blind as to entangle himself with the fortunes of a
sinking party." [51] More than a month after this rumour
made its rounds, the Utica *Observer* printed a story intended
to show that Grant had little hope of his own success. He
was asked if office holding under Johnson would injure a
man's standing with the next administration. Grant was
alleged to have replied " I think not, sir. I can not see
any possible objection Mr. Seymour could have to such
gentlemen." [52]

The attacks on Grant did not receive the approval of all
Democrats. In June Vallandigham was stated to have
sharply rebuked those Democrats who assailed Grant's military services.[53] Godkin reported to the London *Daily News*
on September 5 that Pendleton had publicly repudiated all
personal attacks on Grant, and so had the Democratic Convention of Massachusetts.[54] General N. B. Forrest also
came to Grant's defense. He denounced as a lie the story
that Grant had stolen property from a lady who entertained
him. Forrest told a representative of the Cincinnati *Commercial* that he had a high opinion of Grant, though opposed
to him in everything.[55]

[50] August 18, 1868.

[51] Albany *Argus*, August 19, 1868.

[52] September 22, 1868.

[53] Washington *Express*, June 2, 1868.

[54] London *Daily News*, September 19, 1868.

[55] Cited by Godkin, September 5, *ibid*.

On September 24 the *Nation* admitted that Grant was not an ideal candidate.   He was not a mixer or a handshaker. " As a show candidate Grant is probably the worst that ever took the field."   Frèmont as a candidate in 1856 had more popular appeal.

Schuyler Colfax, Grant's running mate, was also the target for a variety of attacks.   It was said, truly enough that he was no statesman, and that he was unfriendly to Grant.   But the most widely-circulated attack related to Colfax's alleged membership in the Know Nothing Party before the war.   He was pictured as an enemy to all foreign-born citizens and all Catholics.   A letter reputed to have been written by him was printed in which he stated that he once made an oath never to vote for foreign-born candidates for public office, and to remove all foreigners and Catholics from office whenever he might have the power.[56]   The New York *Tribune* branded this letter as a forgery.   A " stupid and malignant falsehood." [57]   In 1855, while a Know Nothing, Colfax was alleged to have referred in a speech to immigrants as " ignorant, degraded paupers " who should be barred from voting and office hold-ing.   " God knows that, were I a candidate for any office, [I] would tell these paupers and vagabonds, these vile, dirty, filthy degraded, idiotic foreigners [that] I did not want their votes; if I ever am a candidate, I hope to God I never will get them."   This tirade was also branded a forgery by the New York *Tribune*.[58]

Colfax also came in for his share of petty abuse.   For example, it was charged that he refused to see a soldier who

[56] Washington Constitutional Union, June 17, in New York *Tribune*, June 20, 1868.

[57] June 20, 1868.

[58] Utica *Observer*, October 30 from Vincennes, Indiana *Sun*. New York *Tribune*, November 2, 1868.

called upon him because the soldier lacked a card to place on the silver waiter held by a " pampered menial." [59]

The comment on the platform by the New York papers was varied. The *Times* [60] thought it as good as was to be expected, although a Republican Convention in 1868 ought to have been able to present something other than promises in regard to tax reduction and government economy. The *Tribune* [61] pronounced the platform fair, temperate and firm, while the *Evening Post* [62] thought it less broad than might be desired on equal suffrage. The *Herald* [63] labeled it conveniently evasive and withal as elastic as Indian rubber. Weed's *Commercial Advertiser* [64] called it a platform to which the party would not give entire and cordial support. The *World* [65] naturally disapproved it, and condemned the suffrage plank especially as a " jumble of nonsense." The *Round Table,* [66] New York weekly, thought the platform at first blush " obnoxious to nothing except the rules of good taste and English grammar."

On May 29 Grant wrote his letter of acceptance. It was a brief document as such epistles go, and was not distinguished for literary form. He endorsed the platform, and stated the impossibility of laying down a policy to be adhered to right or wrong for four years. Economy in administration together with the restoration of nation-wide

[59] *Nation,* September 3, 1868.

[60] May 22, 1868.

[61] May 23, 1868.

[62] May 25, 1868.

[63] May 23, 1868.

[64] May 21, 1868.

[65] May 28, 1868.

[66] May 30, 1868. Also see Stebbins, *op. cit.,* pp. 315-318 for other comment.

tranquility and prosperity he announced to be his aims. No mention was made of the governments in the Southern States cursed under the Congressional plan, no mention was made of negro suffrage, and no reference was made to the greenbacks.[67] Although the letter avoided all reference to the issues foremost in the public mind, his concluding words, " Let us have peace" struck a popular chord, and did much to advance his chances for election. The Republicans were able to quote it with telling effect as a contrast to the more radical suggestions contained in Blair's (the Democratic nominee for Vice-President) " Brodhead Letter," which suggested that the President compel the army to undo the Radical programme in the South.[68]

The next day, May 30, Colfax wrote his letter of acceptance. It was much longer than Grant's, and was for the most part an eulogy of the platform, Grant and the Republican party.[69] Grant's " Let us have peace " is engraved on his tomb in New York city. Who can quote from memory a single word or phrase of the letter of Colfax?

[67] *O. P.*, p. 139.
[68] *Infra*, pp. ——.
[69] *O. P.*, pp. 140-141.

CHAPTER V

CHASE AND THE DEMOCRATIC NOMINATION

I. ORIGINS OF THE CHASE MOVEMENT

THE most striking name suggested for the Democratic nomination for President in 1868 was that of Chief Justice Chase. As has been indicated, by the beginning of March when the impeachment trial started Grant was virtually assured of the Republican nomination. As the trial progressed, Chase's attitude estranged what little support he still had for the Republican nomination. It is at this time, March 1868, that the first suggestions are made that the Chief Justice might be considered as a Democratic Presidential possibility.

Blaine speaks of a favorite scheme in the inner councils of the New York Regency to strike beyond the Democratic lines and nominate Chief Justice Chase. This proposition, he writes, was little discussed in public but was deeply pondered in private by influential members of the Democratic party, and Chase presented no obstacle and no objection. Blaine did not believe that Chase's nomination would have been wholly inconsistent for the following reasons: (1) He was a Democrat in his early career; (2) he was later sent to the Senate with Democratic aid; (3) he had been a consistent advocate of original Democratic principles; (4) he had come into opposition with the Radical Republicans and their measures; (5) he had criticised the military governments in the South; (6) he had been influenced by his Democratic associates on the Supreme Court; (7) his participation in the majority opinions in the Cummings versus Missouri and *ex parte* Garland decisions had made friends for him in the South; (8) these influences towards the Democratic party had been strengthened by the impeachment trial.[1]

Albert Bushnell Hart writes that in 1868 " some of the shrewdest [Democratic] leaders—among them Samuel J. Tilden—favored a new departure in which the party should accept the results of the war, including the new conditions of the South as accomplished facts, and should make a stand against the threatened concentration of government in Washington . . . it was upon this basis that overtures were made to Chase to consider the Democratic nomination." [2] Dunning, also speaks of the desire of the more conservative Democratic leaders to heal the party breach of 1860 " by a solemn consecration of the reunited Democracy to its traditional doctrines, strict construction, tariff for revenue, hard money and, in general, the interests of the masses against the classes." [3]   But in contradistinction to the theory that the Chase movement originated with the Democratic leaders was the theory of Chase himself that it arose in response to a growing popular demand.[4]   And the *Annual Cyclopedia* for 1868 states that the movement did not originate with Chase or with his personal friends; it developed in the Democratic ranks shortly after the impeachment trial.

In March the first suggestions linking the name of the Chief Justice with the Democratic nomination were made in the party press. The Albany *Argus,* edited by William Cassidy, prominent " up-state " Democratic leader, printed

---

[1] *Twenty Years*, vol. ii, p. 393.

[2] Hart, *op. cit.*, p. 365.

[3] Dunning, *Reconstruction* (New York, 1907), pp. 129-130.

[4] Warden, *op. cit.*, pp. 700-701; Schuckers, *op. cit.*, p. 583; Oberholtzer, *United States*, vol. ii, p. 169.

an editorial on "Chief Justice Chase and the Court of Impeachment." The *Argus* stated that the Democratic National Convention would have as its task the selection for the Presidency of the man who best represented the opposition to the Congressional conspirators and their military chief, and who in defense of the Constitution most effectually asserted the supremacy of civil over military rule. On March 14 a Democratic journal in New York City, the *Atlas*, announced that Chase might be the Democratic nominee. The mention of his name in this connection, it remarked, was itself proof of the freedom from personal prejudices with which the Democracy enter upon the campaign; and if nominated, Chase would be as warmly supported as Horatio Seymour.[5] The first metropolitan paper of national reputation to give an impetus to the suggestion was the Republican *Sun*, the new editor of which—Charles A. Dana—was an admirer of both Grant and Chase. Dana thought it would be good policy for the Democrats to nominate Chase. Thus the two foremost men of the country would lead the opposing parties. "It would be a spectacle worthy of the best days of the republic." [6]

The *Sun* continued to discuss the subject for a number of issues, and printed the opinions of other papers on the subject. The Hartford *Times* and Washington *Constitutional Union* were among the Democratic papers favoring Chase. Among those opposed to him was the Augusta (Ga.) *Constitutionalist*, which labeled him a Democratic deserter. The *Sun* considered this opposition to be a point in his favor as it indicated his ability to poll negro votes.[7] All this advocacy of Chase for the Democratic nomination by the *Sun* and other papers resulted in a report from Chase's friends in

[5] In New York *Sun*, March 16, 1868.

[6] Wilson, *Dana*, p. 395.

[7] New York *Sun*, March 17, 18, 19, 20, 1868.

Washington, denying that he had consented to the use of his name by the Democrats.[8]

The New York *Herald,* which later was among the most ardent supporters of Chase's nomination by the Democrats, did not yet take the movement seriously. It was twaddle and moonshine, according to the *Herald,* and the Democratic politicians were using Chase's name to scare the Radicals. They spoiled their plans by working too fast.[9] The last week in March, the Cincinnati *Gazette* considered friendly to Chase and in a position to present his views, published an article which was considered to be inspired by him. It stated that if Chase was the Democratic candidate he would have to run on a platform consistent with his past life. Chase's views, according to the *Gazette,* included opposition to military government, approval of impartial (not universal) suffrage, and sound money with no more greenback issues.[10] The New York *Herald* thought that striking out the military features of reconstruction would scrap the whole scheme, and that if Chase took this attitude he was within speaking distance of the Democracy.[11]

Of all the New York newspapers supporting the Democratic party, none was more influential than the *World,* edited by Manton Marble. On March 26 the *World* charged that the *Sun* was advocating Chase's nomination in order to win back lost subscribers, and added that because the Chief Justice had done his duty the Radicals were willing to injure him by insinuating that he was courting a Democratic nomination. The *World* did not believe Chase capable of seeking or even accepting a Democratic nomination. On April 2 it thought it equally absurd to suppose that either Chase

[8] March 20, 1868.
[9] March 22, 1868.
[10] In New York *Sun,* March 23, 1868.
[11] March 26, 1868.

or the Democratic party were " looking for a chance to arise out of the present trial for their coming together in a party alliance."

2. CHASE'S OWN ATTITUDE

That the position of the *World* was in accord with the views of the Chief Justice at that time, and may have been inspired by his friend van Buren is indicated by a letter from Chase to van Buren on April 5, in which he thanks van Buren and Manton Marble for the article (of April 2) in the *World* making his position clear. No one in Washington, he stated, except over-zealous partisans expected him to do anything but impartially discharge his duties as presiding officer at the trial. Not content with letting his letter end on that safe note, Chase then expressed his political sentiments. He longed for the restoration of the Union. If the North were willing to concede and the South to accept, a policy of universal suffrage and universal amnesty, peace would follow.[12]

The position of the *World* that Radical opposition to the Chief Justice was responsible for the suggestion of his name as a Democratic candidate was accepted by Godkin, who wrote to the London *Daily News* on April 4 that the rumours that Chase was to be the Democratic candidate were spread by the Radicals without foundation.[13] The Washington correspondent of the New York *Commercial Advertiser* (Thurlow Weed's paper) reported that the Chief Justice's friends took the same view—it was a roorback of the impeachers to discredit him in public estimation.[14]

Chase was meanwhile reported in the Cleveland *Leader* to

[12] Warden, *op. cit.*, pp. 683-684, and *Chase Papers*, Library of Congress, Letter Book 8, pp. 346-8.

[13] London *Daily News*, April 17, 1868.

[14] In *National Intelligencer*, March 30, 1868.

have said that he did not seek the Presidency. He held that as a Justice of the Supreme Court he was necessarily out of party politics, and regretted that his recent actions had been attributed to a party or perverse feeling. The Washington *Express* was gratified to find that the Chief Justice was not seeking the Presidency.[15] But in two letters to Alexander Long, Chase was less emphatic in his determination to eschew all politics. On April 8 he wrote to Long that " nothing would gratify me more than to see the Democracy turn away from past issues and take for its mottoes: suffrage for all, amnesty for all; good money for all; security for all citizens at home and abroad against governmental invasion." Here the President of the impeachment trial, then under way only slightly over a month, is laying down a Chase platform for the Democratic party. But he hastens to add: " But I am neither aspirant nor candidate myself I want no more political distinction or position." [16]

But he did not long remain in this negative position. On April 19 he wrote to Long that, if the Democratic party did accept his doctrines as stated in his previous letter, " I should not be at liberty to refuse the use of my name." However, he disclaimed any desire for a nomination.[17] It is of interest to know that J. W. Schuckers, Chase's private secretary, was in Cincinnati in April and in touch with Long.[18] This frankness ("not be at liberty to refuse the use of my name") exhibited in a letter to a prominent " Peace Democrat " while he was giving the impression to all others that he was out of the running is very puzzling. Did Chase at this time, while the impeachment trial over

[15] Washington, D. C. *Express*, April 10, Utica *Observer*, April 11, 1868.

[16] Warden, *op. cit.*, p. 684.

[17] Schuckers, *op. cit.*, p. 579.

[18] Long to Schuckers, April 29, 1868, in *Chase Papers*, Historical Society of Pennsylvania Library, box No. 23.

which he presided was in session, desire the Democratic nomination? We must answer yes and no. Yes to the extent that his craving for the Presidency was still present, and no to the extent that as an honorable judge he wished to keep clear of all political entanglements.

It has been mentioned that the New York *Independent* on April 16, in its editorial " The Folded Banner," read Chase out of the Republican party. This resulted in a reproachful letter from Chase to Theodore Tilton, written the same day as the " not be at liberty to refuse the use of my name " letter to Long! Chase wrote that he had said he would not accept a Republican nomination " because I felt like saying it, and thought you knew me well enough to believe me. I certainly never dreamed of a proclamation by you in the *Independent*, based upon it." As for the statement in the *Independent* that Chase would accept a Democratic nomination, Tilton evidently knew Chase's mind better than he did himself, for on this point Chase commented, " I refused to say to you that I would not accept it, but I did not say that I would; nor did I say anything to that effect. I have never sought or expected it." [19]

The day after this *Independent* article appeared, on April 17, Chase had another visitor, this time Col. William Brown of Kentucky. He told Brown that Tilton had done him a great injustice, and that the statements in the *Independent* were not authorized. He said further according to Brown, " I am a thorough Radical but I am no extremist," and that if he had the power he would resume specie payments at once which would hardly ingratiate him with the Western Democracy.[20] If Brown was correct, Chase must have said

[19] Schuckers, *op. cit.*, pp. 579-580; Warden, *op. cit.*, pp. 687-689; *Chase Papers*, Library of Congress Letter Book 8; Historical Society of Pennsylvania Library, box 15.

[20] Cincinnati *Commercial*, May 3, 1868.

what he did in a moment of exasperation against the frankness of Tilton, for within three weeks he was proclaiming himself a Democrat.[21]

The comments by the Republican papers of New York City were quite generally sympathetic to Chase. It might be wondered what their attitude would have been if the editors had seen Chase's letters of April 19 to Tilton and Long. The New York *Times* congratulated him on a victory over aims and purposes which were utterly at variance with judicial usefulness. The *Evening Post* thought that something was wrong in the Republican party if a man of Chase's abilities stood ready to abandon it.[22] The *Tribune's* Washington correspondent thought the *Independent* article " a simple defiance of good taste," and protested against damning him with faint praise. There was no warrant in saying that he would accept a Democratic nomination.[23] The *Nation* (April 30) thought this report in the *Tribune* was inspired by Chase himself. *Harper's Weekly* hoped that he was not deserting the party, and looking towards the Democrats, and preferred to believe that the *Independent* was in error. The *Independent* stated that it had advocated Chase in the past because he was a representative Radical, and would have ceased its advocacy if Chase had merely become a representative of the Conservative Republicans, but he did not now represent the Republican party at all.

Chase continued to protest his lack of ambition for the Presidency, and at the same time to point out the road upon which he could walk with the Democracy. On April 29, he wrote to Colonel William Brown that he had ceased to have any hopes for the Presidency: " You doubtless notice the talk there is about uniting all the opponents of military

[21] Schuckers, *op. cit.*, p. 580.

[22] In Cincinnati *Commercial*, April 17, 1868.

[23] April 25, 1868.

ascendancy and military commissions in one candidate, and making me that candidate. But I have no idea . . . that there will any such unite upon me, and I am very sure that I shall not seek the nomination from any party." [24] A few days later he informed Richard Gaines that he was a Democrat, but insisted he was not a candidate for the nomination. That the fears of his former fellow Republicans that he had gone over to the enemy were at least partly right is indicated by his assertion " I was a Democrat then [during the Free Soil struggle], too Democratic for the Democratic party of those days, for I admitted no exception on account of race or color or condition to the impartial application of Democratic principles to all measures and to all men. Such a Democrat I am today." [25] A similar sentiment was shown in a letter to Horace Greeley on May 19. " I believe myself to be as you say a ' thorough Democrat, according to the true definition of that much-abused term,' and nothing would rejoice my heart more than to see the Democratic party reforming its policy to Democratic ideas and principles. I do not expect it to do so this year . . . whether it does or not, I ask nothing from it or any party." [26]

The Utica *Observer,* Seymour's home paper, on April 29, considered Chase's break with the Radicals an example of unselfish patriotism " which will not be lost upon the American people." This approval of Chase's position is of some significance, coming from a paper that was very close to Seymour, and which ardently championed his nomination if Seymour would consent to run. It might be said to foreshadow the support of Chase's candidacy later given by Seymour.

[24] Warden, *op. cit.,* p. 690.

[25] Schuckers, *op. cit.,* p. 580.

[26] *Ibid.,* p. 582; Warden, *op. cit.,* pp. 696-697.

On May 7 the " Chase movement " received a powerful addition to its supporters in the New York *Herald,* which started a campaign for his nomination by the Democracy which it continued to the meeting of the Convention in July. The *Herald,* up to this time, had treated the suggestion as absurd,[27] and Chase himself had wondered why it turned its guns on him so often.[28]   But it now thought that Chase was nearer the Presidency than ever.   Around him a new party was forming which would be supported by all opponents of Radical reconstruction and military rule.   Chase for President and a soldier, like Thomas, Sheridan, Schofield, or Meade for Vice-President, could sweep the country.   On the next day the *Herald* thought that Chase would serve equally well as the candidate for the combined anti-Radicals, whether Johnson should be acquitted or convicted.   His candidacy would make the campaign one of issues rather than personalities, and would neutralize Grant's war record. On May 13 the *Herald* referred to a significant Chase movement having been started in Washington on May 11 at a reported meeting of Chase with the Republican senators opposed to impeachment.   At this meeting, according to the *Herald,* the formation of a new party was discussed with Chase as its candidate for President.   *Leslie's Weekly* for May 30 gave a detailed account of the alleged meeting, including the Cabinet assignments to be made under Chase. On May 15 the *Herald,* in substantiation of its earlier story reported that at the meeting, Grimes, Fessenden, Trumbull and Henderson had proclaimed their intention to vote for acquittal.   On May 18 the Washington *Chronicle* stated that at this alleged meeting Chase had conspired with the anti-impeachment senators to defeat Grant and get the Democratic platform so framed as to proclaim his principles.

[27] March 24, 26, April 13, 1868.

[28] Letter March 26, in *Chase Papers,* Library of Congress, letter book 8.

On the same day Chase replied, denying that any meeting had been held. The whole story was utterly false, although it was true that if the Democratic platform should take an advanced position on the issues of the day, it would attract back to the party those who left it to join the Republicans.[29]   Corroborating Chase came a denial from Senator Trumbull.[30]

3. THE THIRD PARTY PROPOSAL

Chase had an interview on May 13 with H. S. Bundy, a former member of Congress from Ohio, in which he was said to have told Bundy that he intended to be a candidate for President on the Democratic ticket, and—failing in this —a candidate for a third party. He did not doubt his success in either contingency. Impeachment would fail, and would divide the Republican party. Senators Trumbull, Fessenden, Henderson, Grimes and Fowler would be leaders of one division of the Republican party, and they had pledged him their support ten days before.[31]   After this article appeared Bundy wrote to Chase on May 22 and stated that, contrary to the article, Chase did not express any intention of becoming a candidate for President on the Democratic ticket. The conversation had turned on impeachment and the Congressional plan of reconstruction, both of which Chase disapproved.[32]   This letter by Bundy was given to the press by its author, probably to correct the errors of the first report of the interview. On May 31 Chase answered Bundy. He was sure that he had never said he was opposed to Congressional reconstruction—on the contrary he upheld the main features of the plan, although there were some

[29] *Chase Papers*, Library of Congress, ser. 2, vol. iii.
[30] Chicago *Tribune*, May 21, 1868, in New York *Times*, May 23, 1868.
[31] Chicago *Republican*, May 16, 1868.
[32] *Chase Papers*, Library of Congress, vol. 100.

objections to its military features. Chase objected to being represented as having abandoned any of his old principles —especially his approval of reconstruction on a basis of equal rights.[33]

It should be said that Chase, while not an active third party organizer, would have been willing to act with a Conservative party opposed to Radicalism if it had been organized, and would probably have expected to head its ticket. The idea of a third party centered around Republicans opposed to Grant was not new. As early as January 1868, the Washington correspondent of the New York *Herald,* reported the possibility of Chase, supported by the banks, running against Grant if the General received the nomination, with the idea of throwing the election to the House of Representatives.[34] The idea of a third party had also been suggested to President Johnson at this time. The calling of a " Peoples Convention " was suggested to make nominations apart from the two regular parties, with the ticket pledged to a new Congress with all States represented.[35]

The rumours of a third party persisted. On May 16 the New York *Times* reported from Washington that both Chase and Johnson were involved; Chase was to be the candidate for President and Johnson was to carry out the reconstruction acts, and form a new Cabinet of Republicans. The patronage of the administration was to be used in Chase's favor, and it was hoped that the new party would throw the election to the House, if not win outright. Strong Democratic support was expected, although Chase would not accept a Democratic nomination. The New York *Herald*

[33] *Ibid.,* letter book 8.

[34] January 4, 1868.

[35] W. D. Jewett to J. R. Doolittle, January 5, 1868, copy in *Johnson Papers,* Library of Congress, vol. 129.

thought that Chase should launch his independent candidacy
before the meeting of the Democratic National Convention.
With Chase already in the field, the best chance for the
Democrats would be to support him.   The dissenting Republican senators, according to the *Herald,* would be found
in support of Chase.[36]   In addition to these, it was reported
to the Cincinnati *Commercial* that the following were in
favor of the third party proposal: The President, Secretaries Seward, McCulloch, Browning, Randall and Stanbery;
Thomas Ewing, Sr.; Robert J. Walker, Reverdy Johnson,
Jay Cooke, Thurlow Weed and William Cullen Bryant.[37]
But the *Times* stated that the organization of a third party
by the dissenting senators was what the Radical Republicans
wished as it would justify the charge of desertion, and would
leave the extremists in control of the party.   The story, said
the *Times,* was a Radical invention to injure these senators
and to break the force of Johnson's acquittal.[38] The *Herald's*
Washington correspondent agreed that the offer of a nomination to Chase or any of the dissenting senators would give
rise to charges of collusion in acquitting the President,[39]
while the Cincinnati *Commercial* considered that the inclusion of the President would result in the failure of the
movement.[40]

An active step towards the organization of a third, or
Conservative party was taken on May 14 when a committee
of Conservatives from Philadelphia visited Washington,
hoping to organize a Conservative party under Chase.[41]
The leaders were John W. Frazer and John Welch.   They

[36] May 16, 18, 1868.

[37] May 20, 1868.

[38] May 30, 1868.

[39] May 30, 1868.

[40] May 24, 1868.

[41] Cincinnati *Times* in Cincinnati *Commercial,* May 17, 1868.

saw Chase, who was reported to have told them that, while he was not a candidate, he would accept a nomination if offered. The committee then called on various Conservative senators to obtain support for Chase. On May 17, the Philadelphia *Despatch* announced the organization in Philadelphia of a Citizens Conservative Association of Pennsylvania in favor of Chase for President as the Conservative candidate.[42] Further reports concerning the progress of the third or Conservative party movement were given in the Philadelphia *Evening Star* of May 19 and 20. A third party convention was to be called in Baltimore, and a paper supporting the movement to be started in Washington. Chase was reported to have said that if the Democrats selected an extremist such as Pendleton or Seymour he would run as an independent.

Actually however, Chase continued to deny any connection with a third party. On May 22 he wrote Murat Halstead of the Cincinnati *Commercial* that he had no concern with third parties or first or second parties, and did not want any nomination although he did wish the Democratic party would consent to be democratic.[43] On June 1, however, he admitted to Halstead that he would " not feel at liberty to decline " a nomination really representing " the wishes of the masses " of whatever party opposed to those in power.[44] He expressed his surprise at the strength of the movement for his nomination by the Democrats.

While the third party movement did not bring a new ticket into the field, it was followed with interest by the Democratic leaders. Colonel John D. van Buren, friend of both Chase and Seymour, on May 20 wrote to Seymour

[42] Philadelphia *Despatch* in New York *Herald*, May 17, 1868; New York *Times*, May 18, 1868.

[43] Warden, *op. cit.*, p. 698.

[44] Warden, *op. cit.*, p. 700.

suggesting how the dissent among the Republicans could be used to block reconstruction and bring about a Conservative-Democratic union under Chase.   This letter was written four days after the acquittal of the President on the eleventh article.   He suggested that the seven Republican senators who voted for acquittal, together with Chase's son-in-law Sprague and his colleague Anthony and the Democratic senators, would make a sure one-third and more of the Senate to sustain a veto.   This combination could keep out the carpet-bag senators from the South and could form the basis of a party with Chase at the head.   The new party would advocate universal suffrage of whites and blacks in voting for new constitutions in the South and for *universal amnesty*.   Van Buren proposed that the constitutions only were to be voted for by this universal suffrage; leaving to each constitution to prescribe suffrage restrictions in each State.[45]   This letter shows an attempt to get around Chase's insistence on universal suffrage by making one concession, and then nullifying it by tying it up to the principle of States Rights.

4. CHASE AND NEGRO SUFFRAGE

Nothing came of this third or fusion party idea.   Chase's candidacy soon settled down to a straight question of the Democratic nomination or nothing.   The revolt in the Republican ranks was not yet strong enough to break down party lines, and most of the seven dissenting senators supported Grant in the campaign.

The discussion of his candidacy was to a considerable extent centered around the possibility of an adjustment of views on negro suffrage which would be acceptable to the Democratic party and to Chase.   The leaders of the party would not have considered any compromise upon this point

[45] New York Historical Society Library, *Seymour Papers*, box 4.

if the chances of victory without it had been brighter. Chase himself realized the seriousness of the obstacle, and at times made concessions, suggesting equal instead of universal suffrage, and that suffrage was a matter to be decided by each State for itself. But he repeatedly reverted to his original advocacy of universal suffrage. It might be said that he was a Republican where the negro was concerned and a Democrat on other issues. The New York *World* stated that one reason why it had suggested that the negro suffrage issue be kept out of the party platform was to determine, by the party reaction to this suggestion, the possibility of Chase as a candidate. Its rejection by a considerable portion of the party press ended Chase's chances, the *World* believed.[46]

From the point of view of this suffrage issue, the letter from John D. van Buren to Seymour on May 20 has additional interest. In a sense van Buren's proposal foreshadowed the suggestion soon after made by Chase that the " application " of the principles of equal suffrage could be left to the several States, suffrage being a power of the States. Van Buren's intimacy with Chase should be emphasized. He was virtually Chase's eastern campaign manager just before and during the National Convention. A letter from Hawley to Tilden contained a suggestion as to an adjustment on the suffrage issue that also foreshadowed Chase's later position. Postmaster General Randall told Hawley that Chase's sentiments concerning the negro could be accommodated by adopting a plank conceding to each State the management of the question of suffrage.[47]

On May 25 Chase wrote to " a personal friend " that he still adhered to his old creed of equal rights even though the Republicans had read him out of the party. He stated

[46] June 17, 1868.
[47] *Tilden Letters*, vol. i, pp. 227-228.

that while he did not desire nor expect to be a candidate for office again, it would gratify him if the Democratic party would endorse the principle of universal suffrage.[48]   The press comment on this letter was varied.   The Springfield *Republican* thought it would win sympathy among candid Republicans but would hardly do him any good among partisan Democrats; [49] while the Syracuse *Journal* deemed it a direct bid for the Democratic nomination, but believed that the Democrats would take him at his word and refuse it.[50] The letter confirmed the confidence of the New Bedford *Mercury* in his integrity.[51]   These papers were all Republican.   A Democratic paper, the Hartford *Times*, thought that there was no probability of the Democratic National Convention taking the position indicated by Chase in his letter.[52]   Godkin, writing the London *Daily News* on May 29, considered the Chase movement among the Democrats stronger than ever, with Hancock the only other candidate talked of.   The Democrats, he reported, were ready to swallow negro suffrage as an " accomplished fact." [53]

On May 29 Chase wrote to Hiram Barney that he believed he could " refuse the throne of the world if it were offered to me at the price of abandoning the cause of equal rights and exact justice to all men."   He mentions an unexpected visit from a very prominent Maryland Democrat [54] who expressed a strong wish that Chase be presented to the people.   Chase spoke during the conversation of their probable disagreement on negro suffrage.   " Yet with all his

[48] In New York *Herald*, June 9, 1868, widely reprinted.

[49] June 10, 1868.

[50] In New York *Herald*, June 12, 1868.

[51] In New York *Herald*, June 12, 1868.

[52] In New York *Herald*, June 12, 1868.

[53] London *Daily News*, June 12, 1868.

[54] Governor Odin Bowie?

repugnance to universal suffrage, he persisted in saying that he believed my nomination at this time was the very best thing that could be done for the country. Such indications . . . afford ground for hope that a change is going on . . . which warrants good hopes for the future." [55] On the day he wrote this letter (May 29) an even more prominent Democrat, Chairman August Belmont of the Democratic National Committee wrote to him. Belmont had been mentioned as a probable supporter of Chase because he was a banker, but this was the first effort he made to " sound him out." Belmont told him that leading Democrats were favorable to his nomination and reminded him that with the settlement of the slavery question the issue which had separated him from the Democratic party was eliminated.[56] Chase replied on May 30, his letter being shown to several influential Democrats; and it is probable that its outspoken expressions on some points lessened his chances.

In his reply Chase affirmed his Democratic principles. He had been separated from the party by the slavery question which was now settled, but which had been replaced by the reconstruction question. He favored that part of the Congressional programme that insured universal suffrage. The exclusion of the Southern whites from the ballot by Congress was wrong, as were military government and proscriptive oaths. If the Democratic party would endorse universal suffrage, the party would carry the South in November, he had been told by many Southern Democrats, and as he believed. He was apprehensive of the dangers to American institutions from the aggressions of Congress upon the executive. The Chief Justice still insisted " that

---

[55] *Chase Papers*, Historical Society of Pennsylvania Library, box 15.

[56] Blaine, *Twenty Years*, vol. ii, p. 394; Schuckers, *op. cit.*, p. 563; Oberholtzer, *United States*, vol. ii, p. 170; *American Annual Cyclopedia*, 1868, p. 750.

I do not desire the office of President nor a nomination for it.   Nor do I know that, with my views and convictions, I am a suitable candidate for any party.   Of that my country-men must judge.   If they think fit to require such services as I can render, they are without doubt entitled to them. If they have no requisition to make upon me, I shall be entirely content." [57]

In spite of his eagerness for the nomination, this letter was creditable to the writer.   He stood firmly on his principle of universal suffrage, and did not even suggest the possibility of a modification of his views.   Such a modification came shortly after.

On June 2 the Washington correspondent of the New York *Herald* reported an interview with Chase, and gave what were alleged to be his views.   Chase insisted he was not a candidate for the nomination, and did not want it. His position as Chief Justice would not admit of his accepting a nomination unless the nation were in great peril, and under no circumstances would he take it at the sacrifice of his convictions.   As for suffrage, the Chief Justice believed in the removal of all political disabilities.   Freedom and manhood suffrage should be an unquestioned right, but he was opposed to conferring it by any authority other than the States themselves.   Here we see Chase trimming his sails.   On other issues, the interview reported Chase as in favor of an early return to specie payments, and as condemning the trial of citizens by military commissions in time of peace.[58]   Was this report authentic?   Schuckers without out questioning its accuracy referred to it when writing to Chase on June 3.[59]

[57] Schuckers, *op. cit.*, p. 584; Belmont, *Letters, etc.* (privately printed, 1890), pp. 114-117.

[58] New York *Herald*, June 3, 1868.

[59] *Chase Papers*, Library of Congress, vol. 100.

About the middle of June Chase prepared a statement of his views which, according to Schuckers, " was not only in harmony with his own antecedents but was such as a Democratic Convention might adopt in perfect consistency with Democratic principles." [60]   The statement was sent to John J. Cisco.   It was printed in New York on June 18 as " an authoritative statement " of Chase's platform, said to have been drawn up by Chase himself.   We are particularly interested in the attitude taken towards suffrage in this statement. " Universal suffrage is a democratic principle, the application of which is to be left under the Constitution of the United States to the States themselves; and universal amnesty and complete removal of all disabilities on account of participation in the late rebellion are not only wise and just measures of public policy, but essentially necessary to the beneficial administration of the government in the States recently involved in civil war with the United States, and to the full and satisfactory reestablishment of the practical relations of those states with other States of the American Union."   The remainder of the statement consisted of a denunciation of military government and the trial of citizens by military commissions.   Taxes should be reduced and collected impartially, and so apportioned as to bear on wealth rather than labor.   All national obligations should be honestly and exactly fulfilled, but no special privileges should be allowed to any class or corporation. [61]

This statement shows Chase plainly shifting his position on universal suffrage to a point where it harmonized with a strict States Rights doctrine, and therefore was more

[60] Schuckers, *op. cit.*, p. 567, also " Mr. Chase's Views " in *Chase Papers*, Historical Society of Pennsylvania Library.

[61] Schuckers, *op. cit.*, p. 567; New York *Herald*, June 19 with slight verbal changes; in New York *Evening Telegram*, June 18, 1868; in Cincinnati *Commercial*, June 19, 1868, and elsewhere; printed in the New York *Herald* on July 3, 1868 as extracts of a letter from Chase.

acceptable to the Democracy. The Cincinnati *Commercial* on June 20 recognized the significance of this change, and thought that if the report were true his chances for the Democratic nomination were better than those of any other mentioned. But the *Commercial* did not believe he would desert his principles even for the presidency. Gideon Welles thought that the statement of Chase's views indicated quite a change. " I am glad to see these improved opinions; hope they are true, and that he will vigorously maintain them." [62]

This position of the Chief Justice on suffrage, which left the door ajar to accommodate those Democrats who were opposed to negro suffrage but were willing to accept it in principle if the individual States could apply that principle, seems perilously near to endangering the substance, while retaining the form, of the principle of equal rights for which Chase insisted he was an unyielding advocate. The degree of change which Chase's views on the subject of negro suffrage had undergone is shown by comparing the proposal in this platform with the proposal made by Chase two years before as to the wording of the fourteenth amendment. He then suggested virtually the same provision as that finally placed in the amendment—that States denying the suffrage to any of their adult male inhabitants except ex-rebels should suffer a proportionate loss in their Congressional representation.[63]

Oberholtzer says of Chase, " there was that in his character which would effectively prevent him from truckling to man or party, from yielding his opinions or his principles." [64] Does this adjustment of his views bear out such a statement?

[62] *Diary*, vol. iii, p. 385, June 19, 1868.

[63] Schuckers, *op. cit.*, p. 527. Letter to Justice S. J. Field, April 30, 1866.

[64] *United States*, vol. ii, p. 169.

But Chase would not admit that his approval of State control of suffrage constituted modification of his position. On June 17 he wrote van Buren, that he had been told that a considerable number of Democrats would be satisfied with a platform recognizing universal suffrage as a Democratic principle, the application of which was to be left to the States themselves under the Federal Constitution.[65]   On the same day (June 17) Chase wrote his old abolitionist friend, Gerrit Smith, seemingly seeking moral support for his position. " The New York Convention gives me no uneasiness.   It is said that the Convention will be willing to declare universal suffrage a principle of the Democratic faith to be applied in the States by the States respectively, under the Constitution of the United States.   If the nomination is offered to me on that or any equivalent basis, will it not be my duty to accept it?   If not offered I certainly shall be entirely content.   That it will be seems to me unlikely." [66] He informed James Lyons of Richmond that, while he was personally in favor of undiluted universal suffrage, " I welcome gladly every advance towards the general object by free concessions of impartial if not universal suffrage." " Suffrage " he concludes, " will give assurance of safety and protection to labor; amnesty will provide men fit for public trusts.   Can there be anything better?   Will not patriots bury the past, recognize the present, and provide for the future? " [67]   And in a letter to J. F. Hawley on the 17th, Chase feared that the published statement of his views " will be taken as evidence that I seek the Democratic nomination and also to dictate the platform to be adopted by the party, neither of which impressions will be at all correct." [68]

[65] *Chase Papers*, Library of Congress, letter book no. 8.

[66] *Ibid.*, ser. 2, vol. iii.

[67] Schuckers, *op. cit.*, pp. 587-588.

[68] *Chase Papers*, Library of Congress, letter book 8.

On June 19 in reply to Bryant's letter of June 13 Chase suggested a platform with a plank for universal suffrage and universal amnesty or recognition of the fact that universal suffrage is a democratic principle, the application of which is to be left to the States under the Constitution.   In either case, he added, " I might I suppose honorably accept a nomination." [69]   Bryant in reply spoke of his letter " as admirable in every respect."   Chase had deprecated his chances of receiving the nomination, as usual, and Bryant seems to have taken him at his word, for in spite of the fact that, when Bryant first wrote, it seemed impossible for the Democratic Convention to avoid nominating him, he recognized that Chase has " surveyed the ground from a higher point of view and with a more comprehensive vision." [70]

It is difficult to believe Chase really thought that State control of suffrage would result in negro suffrage in the Southern States.   To the extent that State control meant restrictions on negro voting, even under the terms of the then pending fourteenth amendment, the principle violated Chase's thesis of equal rights.

Thomas Ewing, Sr., wrote his son on June 22 that he was unable to perceive that Chase's acceptance of State control of suffrage was a departure from his avowed principles. " Chase is in favor of two things—the Constitution of the United States including the rights of the States under it— and suffrage without distinction of race, and I think he never said he would violate the first in order to secure the last—and it is not an inconsistency or a departure from principle to refuse the attainment of an end however desirable by an assumption of unjust powers.   If you talk with

[69] Warden, *op. cit.*, pp. 701-702.

[70] *Chase Papers*, Library of Congress, vol. 100; American Historical Association *Annual Report*, 1902, vol. ii, p. 519.

Chase on the subject, suggest this view to him." [71]   The letter was sent to Chase, who on returning it wrote that the author was entirely right as to his views on suffrage and States Rights.

About the first of July a declaration of principles in conventional platform style, consisting of 15 planks, was drawn up either by Chase or by van Buren, or both, and submitted to various Democratic leaders in New York and Washington as a statement of views acceptable to Chase, and upon which he could accept a nomination.   The suffrage plank read: " Public and private interests rest more securely on the broadest basis of suffrage " but under our Federal system " wisdom and duty require that the application of this principle be left in the several States, under the Constitution of the United States to the people of each State, without interference by the National government." [72]   Evidently Chase was determined to retain this method of approach with those who differed from him on the equal rights question.   In a letter to van Buren on July 2 he admitted that the platform (" your platform ") is " not exactly what I should like *best* " but he feels he may stand upon it in harmony with all Democrats.[73]   A careful reading of this platform fails to bring to light any point inconsistent with Chase's views other than the suffrage declaration.   As Chase probably wrote the fifteen points himself, what he meant by " not exactly as I should *best* like " was that he would have preferred an out and out universal suffrage declaration, but he realized it would not be acceptable to the Democracy.

The question remains—in putting forward his approval

[71] *Thomas Ewing Papers*, Library of Congress, vol. xix; New York *Herald*, July 6, New York *World*, July 6, 1868; dated June 25 in the *Herald*.

[72] Schuckers, *op. cit.*, p. 568; *American Annual Cyclopedia*, 1868, p. 750.

[73] *Chase Papers*, Historical Society of Pennsylvania Library, box no. 15.

of State control of suffrage, linked with an insistence on a recognition of equal suffrage as a democratic principle, did Chase deliberately trim his sails and place one of his life-long principles in jeopardy in order to obtain the Democratic nomination? In view of the fact that the evidence, as will be shown, clearly indicates that after the impeachment trial Chase deliberately angled for the nomination in spite of his protestations to the contrary, the answer to the above question must be yes. Possibly he thought that if he were once in the White House with the backing of the Democratic party, he could use the executive power to foster a broadening of the suffrage by those white men who would be in control in the South in the event of Democratic victory.

5. CHASE AND THE DEMOCRATIC LEADERS

All of the press agitation for Chase and the organization of his friends could do little to insure his nomination unless it were seconded by the leaders in the Democratic party. The movement for a third, or Conservative party had been followed with interest by the Democratic leaders, especially in New York, and when it subsided the agitation for Chase's nomination by the Democrats took on fresh vigor, a fact indicated by Belmont's letter to Chase. Various other Democrats by this time (May 29) had either committed themselves to Chase, or had been reported as favoring him. Among them were S. S. Cox,[74] Daniel W. Voorhees, " The Tall Sycamore of the Wabash," [75] and Horatio Seymour. Seymour had written to a friend that Chase had " more qualifications for the Presidency than any other man in the country." [76]

[74] Cox to Schuckers, May 11, 1868—*Chase Papers*, Historical Society of Pennsylvania Library, box 23.

[75] New York *Herald*, May 21, 1868.

[76] *Chase Papers*, Historical Society Pennsylvania Library—William Brown to Chase, May 27, 1868.

On May 29 Seymour committed himself in favor of Chase at a meeting of the New York Democratic leaders held at Albany. Among those present were Peter Cagger and William Cassidy. Seymour was reported to have said that Pendleton could make himself the leader of the future by cooperation in the Chase movement now; and that Chase differed from the Democracy only on the negro question. He added that Chase was right on the tariff, taxation, amnesty and restoration of the South, and that the Democratic party was in a transition state and must be progressive in fact as well as name. Seymour's remarks were well received.[77] The news that he had committed himself for Chase was received by the Chicago *Republican* as evidence that he realized the nomination was an empty honor. " If he thought there was a reasonable chance for success, no one would be less inclined to let it slip through his fingers." The Springfield *Republican* attributed Seymour's action to his own ill health, which barred him from the nomination.[78] The real reason why Seymour advocated Case's nomination rather than that of an out-and-out Democrat was that he felt that no such candidate could defeat Grant.[79] Seymour's support of Chase was reported to the Chief Justice on June 1 by his New York friend John J. Cisco, who stated the Chase movement was gaining rapidly, with the masses pushing the leaders in New York city.[80] The New York *World* on June 1 reported that Chase's name was taking well with those Democrats who were not closely bound by party ties.

[77] Brooklyn *Eagle*, in New York *Herald*, May 31, 1868; New York *Herald*, June 19, 1868.

[78] Chicago *Republican*, June 10, 1868; Springfield *Republican*, June 1, 1868.

[79] Howard Carroll, *Life of Seymour*, p. 66, typescript in New York Historical Society Library, *Seymour Papers*, box 3.

[80] *Chase Papers*, Library of Congress, vol. 100.

The leaders, except a few, were non-committal. These argued that Chase would be a valuable candidate because he could carry the Senate and House with him. The Chase movement in New York was mentioned by Welles in his diary for June 6. He thought it was not sincere. " It is New York party management and means Seymour . . . whatever the popular sentiment the New York leaders wont have Chase." On June 15 he wrote, " Doolittle [Senator James R. Doolittle of Wisconsin] has been to New York and says the talk for Chase is strong, yet he can not suppose the leading men can be earnest. Blair [Montgomery Blair] says Belmont and the bankers are the instigators—that it is a money scheme." [81]

A certain substantiation of Welles' suspicions is given by a letter marked " private " from Sanford E. Church, prominent New York Democrat, to Tilden on June 10. " Chase is out of the question. He would be the weakest man we could have. We will use him well, but must not think of nominating him." [82] Church favored Hendricks. Just what was the purpose for which Chase was to be used is not clear, although the result of the Convention would seem to confirm Welles' opinion that it was the nomination of Seymour. Welles was probably wrong, as the evidence indicates that the nomination of Seymour, while not displeasing to the New York leaders, was not looked for by them.

Further evidence on the possibility that the Democratic leaders were " using " Chase may be read into a letter from van Buren,[83] who was virtually Chase's New York manager, to Horatio Seymour on June 19: " I dont know what to

[81] *Diary*, vol. iii, pp. 379, 382.

[82] *Tilden Letters*, vol. i, p. 229.

[83] " Van Buren is his (Seymour's) most trusted friend "; S. Ward to Chase, June 26, 1868, *Chase Papers*, Library of Congress, vol. 100.

make of the Chase matter. It seems pretty clear we shall have no difficulty in carrying our troops over to him, the rank and file are over anxious to run that way, so much so that they will suffer a disappointment. The officers, as you see by the *World,* kick. I have seen a Washington private letter saying that Wade Hampton and other prominent Southern men favor Mr. Chase. I should not wonder for he would be able to take Southern men into full confidence at once." [84] What does van Buren mean by the rank and file, who are anxious to support Chase, suffering a disappointment? When the trap is sprung and Chase slides out of the Convention? Chase had the greatest confidence in van Buren. During the Convention he wrote to him " My confidence in your friendship and judgment combined is very great, and I wish that everything could be either through you or under your supervision." [85]

On June 24 Welles recorded in his diary that Robert H. Pruyn of Albany told him that Seymour or Chase would be nominated at New York. Pruyn, Welles commented, " is one of the leading Democrats of New York and he speaks, I have no doubt, the purpose and interest of the leaders of that party in the State, which does not mean Chase." [86] On June 25 Seymour, making a public address to the New York city Democrats urged that victory could be had only under Chase. His nomination would disintegrate the Republican party, carry the House of Representatives for the Democrats, and by uniting Conservatives and Democrats, secure a majority in the Senate. [87]

The New York *Herald* on June 5 reported McClellan as favorable to Chase. However, in a letter on June 14 to

[84] Seymour Papers, box 4, New York Historical Society Library.
[85] July 8, 1868, Schuckers, *op. cit.,* p. 590; Warden, *op. cit.,* p. 707.
[86] Vol. iii, pp. 390-391.
[87] Alexander, *Political History of New York,* vol. iii, p. 198.

Barlow, McClellan said: ". . . The main thing is to wrest
the government from the hands of the Radicals.   Party
success is a small matter in comparison . . . If the party
do take up Chase, I trust that they will be well informed as
to his *present* opinions and feelings." [88] After the nomination
of Seymour, McClellan expressed himself more openly about
Chase's Democratic candidacy.   He wrote he had feared
Chase would be the nominee.   " I confess that I have not
yet reached that point of disinterestedness which would have
allowed me cheerfully to see my bitterest personal enemy,
next to Stanton, elected by my friends, and he too not long
since a most rabid Radical." [89]   His views were shared by
Montgomery Blair, who was ardently in favor of the nomination of his brother Frank, and who derided the Chase
movement.   For example, Blair wrote to Tilden that Chase
was without influence with the " Lincoln Republicans " and
was the " only human being that I believe Lincoln actually
hated." [90]   On June 18 William Cassidy wrote to Seymour
" Montgomery Blair is bitter against Chase." [91]

Pendleton could hardly have been expected to fall in
line with Seymour's suggestion that he support Chase.   The
reasons are plain enough—Chase had been a member of the
war administration which Pendleton opposed.   Chase was
and remained an opponent of the greenback movement as
well as being the father of the national bank system; and
both Chase and Pendleton were from Ohio and the ambitions
of one would be certain, if confined to the same party, to
circumscribe those of the other.   On June 8 Pendleton said
the Western Democrats could not discover how the Eastern

[88] *McClellan Papers*, Library of Congress, vol. 93.

[89] To " Prince ", Ste. Maurice, August 4, 1868, *McClellan Papers,*
Library of Congress, vol. 93.

[90] *Tilden Letters*, vol. i, pp. 232-233, June 5, 1868.

[91] *Seymour Papers*, Albany.

Democratic leaders hoped to bring the party to endorse the ex-secretary of the Treasury who, with Jay Cooke, was the author of the assumption that the 1,700 millions of 5/20 bonds were payable, principal and interest, in gold. Pendleton doubted Chase's willingness to accept a nomination from a party with which he had been at war during the whole of his political career.[92] But among Pendleton's supporters was one who was not completely against Chase. C. L. Vallandigham announced himself as a Pendleton man, but was not unfriendly to the Chief Justice. Vallandigham's paper, the Dayton *Ledger,* on June 6 said that if the party were so hard pressed for material as to be forced to go outside its ranks, Chase would be the man.[93] Vallandigham in an interview answered the two objections to Chase—negro suffrage and the redemption of the bonds. State control of suffrage was the means of adjustment of the first; Chase's relation to the original issue of greenbacks with their legal tender feature might prove the key to the second. Vallandigham preferred Chase to Johnson, Doolittle, Dix, Blair, or Hancock.[94]

A résumé of the situation as it existed among the assembling delegates to the Democratic Convention was given to Chase by Frederick A. Aiken, writing from New York on June 25. Aiken was one of the editors of the *Constitutional Union* at Washington, and took an active part in furthering Chase's cause while the Convention was in session.[95] He quoted one Wallace of the New York *Herald* to the effect that great unanimity existed among the people of New York in Chase's favor, and that this pressure, already heavy, would

[92] New York *Herald,* June 11, 1868.

[93] In Cincinnati *Commercial,* June 8, 1868.

[94] Dayton, June 11, 1868, New York *Herald,* June 13, 1868.

[95] Chase to H. Barney, June 26, 1868, *Chase Papers,* Historical Society of Pennsylvania Library, box 15.

increase.   " Still he has not been able to fix upon any great
number of delegates who have declared in the same way."
Wallace told Aiken that on the previous day he had seen
a petition for Chase's nomination, signed by ten thousand
Republican Germans.   Belmont had said that he was for
Chase " with all my heart."   F. O. Prince, Massachusetts
delegate and Secretary of the National Democratic Committee, told Aiken that of all the candidates yet presented
" he is most in your favor and says that the Massachusetts
delegation on the first opportunity will vote as a unit for
you." Josiah G. Abbot, chairman of the Massachusetts delegation was a " strong Chase man," as was Josiah Bardwell,
delegate at large, a wealthy Boston merchant, who was ready
to spend money like water if Chase was nominated.   Aiken
reported that Pendleton's strength " is all let out in advance."   The New York argument against Pendleton was
that he had a future before him, and " defeat the second
time will forever destroy it."   At the rooms of the New
York State Central Committee Aiken was told that Chase
had been the principal subject of conversation during the
past four weeks.   He was anxious to open up a Chase headquarters in New York, and asked the Chief Justice for three
hundred dollars for that purpose.[96]   Various other leaders
were reported in favor of Chase.   Charles G. Halpine, City
Registrar of New York and editor of the *New York Citizen*,
Mayor John T. Hoffman and M. O. Roberts of New York,
Jeremiah Black of Pennsylvania and General James Long-
street of New Orleans, were among them.[97]   The New
York *Herald* on June 8 placed William M. (Boss) Tweed
among the supporters of Chase.

On June 27 there appeared in the London *Spectator* a

[96] *Chase Papers*, Library of Congress, vol. 100.

[97] New York *Tribune*, June 12, 1868; Philadelphia *Evening Star*, June
15, 1868.

penetrating exposition of the significance of Chase's candidacy to the Democratic party. After asking what the Democrats would gain by the election of Chase as a Democrat the *Spectator* explained that Chase, if accepted and elected, would of course select moderate men, but he would be compelled by party etiquette to choose a Cabinet nominally at least Democratic and to use his patronage as far as he could on the Democratic side. " If he won the Republicans would at once pass the Jenckes Civil Service Reform bill." The party would seem to win, and in America as elsewhere, there are masses of waverers who float towards the strong. The root of bitterness for the Democrats, their discord with the government as to enfranchisement would be removed, and they would have time to apply their ideas to new issues.[98]

Before leaving the investigation of the candidacy of the Chief Justice, we must examine the development of his own views in the period between the end of the impeachment trial and the meeting of the Democratic National Convention. The shift in his position on negro suffrage has already been discussed.

He was reported (May 22) to have advised the negroes to leave the Republican party which had betrayed the negroes of the North on the suffrage question, and to have told them that the Democrats were willing to adopt a platform of universal suffrage and universal amnesty.[99]

Chase was also reported to have said that " the time has come for all who love their country to band together against the Jacobins."[100] It is quite likely that Chase did advise the negroes to abandon the Republicans and that he likened that party to the French Jacobins. In all his statements at

[98] In New York *World*, June 9, 1868.

[99] Philadelphia *Press* in New York *Herald*, May 24, 1868.

[100] J. E. Butler to Chase, June 12, 1868, *Chase Papers*, Library of Congress, vol. 100.

the time concerning the Southern situation, he was outspoken in denunciation of the Republican programme. For example, on May 27 he wrote to Hamilton Smith criticising the Republican disposition to subvert the constitutional authority of the executive and judicial departments, decrying their programme of reconstruction through military government. After stating his views and saying that he would take a nomination only if offered on his own terms, he concludes " If with this explanation your views of public duty should induce you to make use of your old facility of writing and scatter your words like leaves of Vallambrosa through the West, I certainly shall find no fault." [101]

Chase's eager interest in the movement for his nomination is revealed by his letters to his private secretary Schuckers. On June 2 from Richmond he wrote asking that newspaper clippings be sent him, although on June 6 he wrote " my private judgment is that the talk about me will come to nothing. The Democracy is not Democratic enough." On June 9 he wrote that " the military plan is the best ' talk horse '. Be sure you adopt it on all political matters which concern me or seem to concern me." [102]   It may be significant that copies of these three letters from Chase to his secretary are not in the letter book containing his letters of this period.

When the Democratic National Convention was in session Chase was not discreet in answering requests for blanket endorsements of the Convention platform and possible candidates. This being so, unusual interest attaches to a report in the Washington *Express* of June 19 that Chase had " written a letter to be read in the National Democratic Convention placing himself squarely on any platform the Convention may determine, but urges on the members of the

[101] *Chase Papers*, Library of Congress, letter book 8.   Handwriting of Schuckers.

[102] *Ibid.*, ser. 2, vol. iii.

Convention that negro suffrage be recognized and universal amnesty demanded." The Cincinnati *Commercial* commented (June 20) that this report was very improbable, yet Chase said some very foolish things in his correspondence and he may have written as reported, possibly to Alexander Long.

Chase's views are summarized in a " Democratic declaration " written in platform style, found in his papers at Philadelphia. This declaration is in his handwriting, and was probably written about the latter part of June. It read as follows:

The American Democracy reposing entire confidence under God in the wisdom, virtue and patriotism of the people and recognizing the duty of faithfully applying the eternal principles of the Democratic faith announced by Jefferson in legislation and administration, as required by the progress of events, do now in view of the approaching election of President and Vice-President, declare:

1. That the Democracy cherishes and will maintain the perpetual union of the United States under the National Constitution.

2. That the Coordinate Departments of the Government, Legislative, Executive and Judicial, must be maintained in their integrity without encroachments by either upon the other.

3. The plain principles of the Constitution and the spirit of all free government require that the military be always subordinate to the civil authority.

4. That no State of the Union can withdraw or be withheld from the Union except by revolution effected either by force or by equal consent; and when any State, by violence or otherwise, is deprived of a Republican form of government in the Union, it becomes the right of the people of each State, aided by the National government in pursuance of the guaranty conferred in the Constitution, to reestablish their State government in conformity with the principles and provisions of the Constitution of the United States.

This last paragraph, if coupled with his belief that the Federal troops should be withdrawn from the South, is similar to Frank Blair's position in his famous " Brodhead Letter " of June 30, for which he was so vigorously attacked during the campaign.   It meant revolution, bloodless as far as the National government was concerned, but rough on the carpetbaggers.

On June 25 Chase wrote to van Buren a letter which he did not send.   He thanked him for support during the civil war and later.   Chase feared that the publication of his private letters by various correspondents had resulted in his being misrepresented.   He reaffirmed his belief in negro suffrage in the Southern States and gave his objections to the Republican tendency to centralize power at Washington, and especially in the House of Representatives.   He agreed with van Buren that there was a pressing need for an administration which would restore the doctrines and practices of Jeffersonian Democracy.   He hoped the Democratic party would forget the things that were behind it, and pass forward in an effort to reestablish the government on " the solid basis of equal rights with justice and constitutional liberty."[103]

On June 29 there were published " a few stray planks of Mr. Chase's platform " which were as follows: The public lands should be disposed of for the benefit of the people. The government should develop the resources of the public domain.   He was opposed to secret sessions of the Senate. He was opposed to the appointment of executive committees of Congress to sit during the Congressional recess.   He was a friend of the immigrant.[104]

It was about this time that Chase was working in col-

[103] *Chase Papers*, Historical Society Pennsylvania Library, box 15.

[104] Philadelphia *Evening Star*, June 29, 1868; New York *Herald*, June 29, 1868.

laboration with van Buren on the fifteen-paragraph statement of his position which has been referred to in the discussion of negro suffrage.

The origin of the " fifteen point platform " is in some doubt. It seems probable that van Buren actually wrote it, possibly in Washington with the assistance of Chase.[105] Van Buren had evidently been in Washington in conference with Chase during or soon after the preparation of the document for Chase wrote: " I have taken the liberty of sending the copy left with me as a platform acceptable to some New York Democrats, to several gentlemen of various opinions and as yet have met with no one not ready to accept it." The platform was made public on July 1, and passed around in Washington as a statement of principles " acceptable to some New York Democrats." Chase felt that if the platform should be accepted by the Democratic Convention " A new era of Democratic ascendancy, analogous to that inaugurated by Jefferson, will begin for our country." [106] Chase had arrived at the point where he was thinking of himself as another Jefferson, or Moses, to lead the party out of the wilderness.

The document under discussion was written in regular Convention style, and may be summarized as follows:

1. The party accepts the doctrine of equal rights to all men.

2. The war is over—thanks offered to the soldiers of the Union —ex-Confederates are welcomed back into the fold.

3. Slavery is accepted as ended, and the necessity for constitutional amendment to define and protect the new status of the negro is recognized.

4. Universal suffrage is accepted in principle. Its application is to be left to the States.

[105] *Chase Papers*, Historical Society of Pennsylvania Library, van Buren to Chase, June 25, 1868; Chase to van Buren, July 2, 1868.

[106] *Chase Papers*, Historical Society Pennsylvania Library, box 15, July 2, 1868.

5. Southern whites should be reenfranchised and universal amnesty extended.

6. Usurpations by Congress of the powers of the coordinate branches of the Federal government should be checked.

7. Military government and military commissions condemned.

8. Armed forces should be reduced in numbers and those in the South withdrawn except those " absolutely necessary for the support of the civil authority."

9. Accession to the Union of neighboring States on their own volition is welcomed (Canada?)

10. Rights of American citizens should be upheld in foreign countries. (American Fenians on trial in Canada or Ireland?)

11. Indian affairs are marked by corruption. The Indians should be protected.

12. Laws favorable to labor should be passed to make possible every " opportunity of individual improvement ".

13. The public debt should be honestly paid but creditors are not entitled to special favors in the interpretation of the laws. The courts should decide cases of conflicting interest.

14. Reduction of taxes and rigid economy in government is needed. Taxes bearing specially upon labor should be removed.

15. The cooperation of Conservative Republicans is invited.[107]

This platform merits a careful examination. The chief issues that divided the country at this time were negro suffrage, military government in the South, and whether the Civil War bond issues should be repaid in greenbacks or gold. As to the first point, in his fourth plank the Chief Justice sanctions the compromise subterfuge of permitting the individual State to " apply " the principle of equal suffrage. The issue of military government in the South is met in the seventh and eighth planks. In the latter the outspoken denunciation of the system is tempered with an admission that troops "necessary for the support of civil

[107] Text in Schuckers, *op. cit.*, pp. 568-700; *American Annual Cyclopedia*, 1868, pp. 750-751.

authority " should be retained in the South. It is difficult to see why such an exception should have been made by Chase. Even the Conservative Republicans, upon whom he counted for support, were becoming more and more opposed to the system. He wobbled violently on the greenback issue. It was Chase's " hard money " record that attracted conservative eastern Democrats to him and made his candidacy possible. Yet in the thirteenth plank it is declared that the debt should be " honestly " paid, a statement with which even Pendleton would agree. Furthermore, the platform takes a direct slap at the bondholders by gratuitously denying them any special favors; and it declares that controversial questions concerning the debt should be settled by the courts. It is hard to think of this plank as other than a " straddle ".

The platform was acceptable to many delegates and other prominent men of the party.[108] The New York *Sun,* commenting while the Convention was in session, thought the doctrine and the man " considerably in advance of the old fogy Democracy of the present day." [109] On July 1 the day the platform was published, Chase wrote to Alexander Long stating his belief that military governments should be withdrawn from the South without delay.[110] Evidently Chase wanted the Democrats to know that his published platform meant what they wanted it to mean, and that they should not take the exception in the eighth plank seriously.

Tilden and Seymour were reported satisfied with the platform. Chase expressed his pleasure, and added: " It would give me still greater satisfaction if either of these gentlemen would adopt it as his own." [111] Seymour was reported to

---

[108] *American Annual Cyclopedia,* 1868, p. 750.

[109] Cited by Oberholtzer, *United States,* vol. ii, p. 173.

[110] Warden, *op. cit.,* p. 704.

[111] Chase to van Buren, July 2; *Chase Papers,* Historical Society of Pennsylvania Library.

have accepted the platform with the understanding that it provided for negro suffrage.[112]

When the Democratic National Convention opened on July 4, the progress of the Chase movement had resulted in a general knowledge of his position, a friendly feeling towards his candidacy by various party leaders and something of an organization to work for him among the delegates. No State delegation was pledged to him, however. The interplay of the various factors in the Convention will be taken up in a later section.

[112] New York *Times*, September 4, 1868, cited by Alexander, *op. cit.,* vol. iii.

CHAPTER VI

WESTERN ASPIRANTS FOR THE DEMOCRATIC NOMINATION

I. PENDLETON OF OHIO

THE most marked division within the Democratic party in 1868 was that between East and West. The principal issue lying beneath this division was the greenback theory, which was most widely advocated in the West and most generally opposed in the East, although there were exceptions on both sides. Of those most prominently mentioned for the nomination, three—George H. Pendleton, Thomas A. Hendricks, and Frank Blair—were from Western States. Pendleton was the chief exponent of the greenback theory, which was also approved by the other two. Hendricks was not so intimately identified with the theory, and for that reason was more acceptable to the East. Blair did not base his candidacy upon this issue, but rather stood primarily for the overthrow of the reconstruction program of the Radical Congress.

George H. Pendleton of Ohio had been the party's candidate for Vice President in 1864, and had represented the Cincinnati district in Congress for four terms (1857-1865). Young (forty-three in 1868) handsome, well educated (including a year in a German university) and of ample means and assured social position, " Gentleman George " was the idol of the Ohio democracy.

While Pendleton was not the originator of the " Ohio Idea," he was among its first sponsors and his name had become linked with it to such an extent that the Western Democrats from West Virginia to Nebraska looked upon him as their champion in the effort to free them from the shackles of the " bondholders."

Pendleton and Chase were considered to differ widely on financial questions, yet the New York *World* on June 9 called attention to an alleged similarity between their views. Chase and Pendleton both wished to have one currency for the laboring masses and for the bondholders. Pendleton said give them both greenbacks, Chase said give them both gold. They both wished to lighten the debt burden of the government—Pendleton by paying the 5/20's in greenbacks and Chase by paying them in gold, and with improved credit refunding the obligations at 4%. Pendleton and Chase differed most decidedly on the National Banking system established by Chase, which Pendleton wished to see eliminated.

Pendleton's war record was calculated to arouse enthusiasm among the dyed-in-the-wool Democrats, although it was hardly an asset to him in appealing to the " war " Democrats who supported Lincoln. His father was a native of Georgia, and the son always looked southward with a friendly eye. He was not an obstructionist, pure and simple, while in Congress during the war. Rhodes speaks of him as one of the Democratic leaders with whom the Republicans found it easy to work.[1] His war record might be summarized by saying that he guarded, to the best of his ability, the Democratic minority and the principles of his party but was never seditious or treasonable. He was a Democrat of the old school on the States Rights issue. The *Nation* thought that his nomination on his own platform would excite more enthusiasm among the regular Democrats than that of any other man, except possibly Horatio Seymour.[2]

[1] *United States*, vol. vi, p. 160.
[2] June 4, 1868.

The opposition to him was strongest in the East, and was chiefly due to dislike of his financial theories. Another objection was that his greatest strength lay for the most part in States which the Democracy could not hope to carry with any candidate, and his candidacy would weaken the party in those States where success was possible.

We have seen how he made himself the leader of the greenback movement in 1867 and how in January 1868, when the first States held their Democratic conventions, he was in high favor and received instructed delegations both in Ohio and Indiana. The vote in Ohio was unanimous. During the winter and spring other Western State Conventions either committed their delegates to his support (like Oregon[3] on March 19 and Illinois on April 15) or adopted a strong " greenback " plank in the State platform which had virtually the same result (like Iowa on February 26). West Virginia, Nebraska and Kentucky were among the States which could be depended upon to give him, and did, unanimous support in the National Convention in July.[4] The Chicago *Times* reported the Democracy of Illinois as ardent for Pendleton as that of Ohio. The sentiment " has been in no sense manufactured . . . the attempts to defeat it or turn it have signally failed, and now it is irresistible.[5] The *Times* gave as an argument for his nomination the lack of refinement in the White House since Buchanan. " Gentleman George " was just the man to restore culture to the Chief Magistracy.[6] The Cincinnati *Commercial* boldly prophesied his nomination.

Ohio, as was to be expected, showed the most ardor for Pendleton. Washington McLean's Cincinnati *Inquirer*

[3] *Oregon Historical Quarterly*, vol. iii, p. 42, article by Fenton.

[4] Bloss, *Pendleton* (Cincinnati, 1868), pp. 104-106.

[5] April 21, 1868.

[6] May 1, 1868.

which was virtually Pendleton's organ, contended that the
national debt and taxation would be the paramount issues,
and that on these Pendleton was strongest. The Northwestern States would decide the election and " the available
candidate in all the great doubtful States is George H.
Pendleton." [7]   Prominent among the Democrats of Ohio
was Vallandigham.   In spite of the fact that he felt he had
not received proper consideration in the choice of United
States Senator by the Democratic legislature elected in 1867,
Vallandigham and his paper — the Dayton *Ledger* — supported Pendleton for the Presidential nomination.[8]   Pendleton was a party to the arrangement which sent the defeated
candidate, for Governor, A. G. Thurman, to the Senate instead of Vallandigham.   There was some doubt, however,
as to the sincerity and constancy of Vallandigham's support
in the National Convention itself.

On June 11 the New York *Herald* reported an interview
with Pendleton in which it said he was in favor of a prompt
payment of the National debt, opposed to the whole National
Bank system and equally to sudden contraction or expansion
of the greenbacks.   He demanded also that greenbacks be
used to pay the holders of bonds wherever permitted by law,
such payment being legal he contended in all cases except
the " 10-40's" and those issued before the legal tender act.
Pendleton also stated his opposition to negro suffrage.   Two
days later the New York *Times* reprinted from the Cincinnati *Enquirer* a " Pendleton Platform " embodying his
known views on public finance.   The *Times* commented that
the Republicans would be very glad to see this " plank " inserted in the Democratic platform, as it would simplify the
labors of the canvass very decidedly in the East.

Eastern support for Pendleton was not lacking, although

[7] In New York *Herald*, May 21, 1868.

[8] Interview in New York *Herald*, June 13, 1868.

it was overshadowed by the opposition. His chances for
the nomination were acknowledged to be good. There was
considerable Pendleton strength in Western Pennsylvania,
and one-fifth or one-sixth of the Western delegates to the
State Convention favored him.[9] The Pittsburgh *Post* supported him on the greenback issue.[10] Jeremiah Black of
Pennsylvania was told by a Cincinnati correspondent that
a Democratic victory could be had only by going with the
Northwest for Pendleton. "Pennsylvania can second his
nomination. With your cooperation the vote of Pennsylvania is certain for him." [11] An estimate of Pendleton's
candidacy was given by former Governor William Bigler of
Pennsylvania to Tilden on February 3. Bigler feared that
Pendleton had formulated an issue on which the party could
not unite—"at all events it can not be made the leading
issue." [12] He thought the greenback issue would not live
till July 4. There were also some Pendleton supporters in
New York City. But they were not the men who control
the votes in the Convention, commented the *World*.[13] Tilden,
hopeful that Seymour could be induced to accept the nomination, was opposed to Pendleton.

Evidence that Washington McLean attempted to win
Horatio Seymour over to Pendleton's support is offered by
a note from McLean to Seymour on March 30, saying that
he would visit the East in April and wished to see him.[14]
The effort was not successful. At a meeting of Democratic
leaders in Albany on May 29 where Seymour endorsed

[9] Bigler to Tilden, March 16, 1868, *Tilden Letters*, vol. i, p. 223.

[10] In Washington *Express*, June 1, 1868.

[11] J. L. Dawson, June 14, 1868, *J. S. Black Papers*, Library of Congress, vol. xlviii.

[12] *Tilden Letters*, vol. i, pp. 216-217, 223-224.

[13] New York *World*, June 1, 1868.

[14] New York Historical Society Library, Misc. Mss. McLean.

Chase, Seymour suggested that Pendleton's chance would come in the future if he now supported Chase.[15]   In the National Convention Seymour spoke of himself as one who had been in a position of " marked opposition " to Pendleton's nomination.[16]   Seymour's attitude was primarily due to his dislike of the " Ohio Idea."   There was reason in his suggestion that Pendleton give way to Chase, for Pendleton had been a candidate for the Vice-Presidency in 1864, and a second defeat would end his career.   He was young enough to wait for a chance to run under more favorable conditions.

August Belmont, the National Chairman, was among Pendleton's opponents.   His position as a financial leader made this stand inevitable.   The choice of New York for the Democratic National Convention was ascribed to his influence and it was thought to be a blow at Pendleton.   The date, July 4, was considered to be late enough to permit the Pendleton boom to subside, and to allow the Eastern Democrats to concentrate their strength on someone who could defeat him.   When the Congressional Democratic Committee in Washington requested that the Convention meet in June, Chairman Belmont refused to act.   This also was ascribed to his desire to see Pendleton defeated.[17]   The New York *Times* predicted that Belmont's opposition would be decisive for " pockets are often more potent than friendships and to the former Mr. Belmont holds the key." [18]

Those opposed to Pendleton had difficulty in agreeing upon a candidate.   Seymour would have been the man if he had not refused the use of his name.   As it was, Hancock [19]

---

[15] New York *Herald*, May 31, June 19, 1868.

[16] *Official Proceedings*, p. 153.

[17] New York *Times*, May 6, 1868.

[18] *Ibid.*

[19] New York *Herald*, May 20, 1868.

and Hendricks [20] were widely considered, and a considerable portion of Chase's appeal to Eastern Democrats lay in his known hostility to Pendleton's views on currency and banking. On May 20 the New York *Herald* predicted that the real contest would come between Hancock and Pendleton. Five weeks later the *Herald* substituted Hendricks as the man who would oppose Pendleton.[21]

The difficulty which Seymour's coyness caused the New York party workers in their efforts to find a man to stop Pendleton is seen in a letter which one of Tilden's friends sent him, on May 25: " I fear that we are to be embarrassed by the want of a candidate to oppose Mr. Pendleton. Governor Seymour should have consented to the open using of his name, or else we should have agreed upon some other man. Is it possible at this late date to unite (upon) a man with whom we can head off Pendleton? I fear we can not go into the fight with great confidence and enthusiasm with him as our standard bearer." [22] The efforts to unite upon one man failed, and as late as July 4 the *World* reported no concentration of the forces opposed to Pendleton. But the *Sun* professed to believe that Seymour's speech at the Cooper Union on June 25 had " knocked Pendleton's financial theories completely out of mind." [23]

As soon as Pendleton's candidacy for the nomination reached serious proportions, the attack on his war record began. On January 26 the New York *Herald* labeled him a " crippling copperhead candidate " who would be easily defeated. Grant viewed his record with apprehension.[24] E. L. Godkin reported to the London *Daily News* that

[20] *Ibid.*, June 30, 1868.

[21] *Ibid.*, June 27, 1868.

[22] W. F. Allen, Albany, *Tilden Letters*, vol. i, p. 231.

[23] In *National Intelligencer*, June 30, 1868.

[24] General Sherman to his wife, January 30, 1868, *Home Letters*, p. 370.

Pendleton and Seymour because of their war records were obnoxious to the large body of moderates whose support the Democrats must have in order to win.[25]   The New York *Times* made the same point, while the *Tribune* considered Pendleton a representative of the ideas which would triumph in the event of the failure of the Democrats to nominate Chase.   His nomination would result in a square open fight which the *Tribune* welcomed.[26]   That Pendleton's reputation as a copperhead might defeat the party was the opinion of such war Democrats as Charles G. Halpine,[27] John D. Caton[28] (former Chief Justice of the Illinois Supreme Court), Gideon Welles [29] and Thomas Ewing, Sr.[30]

The South, to be sure, gave Pendleton considerable support.   But the Southern Democrats were on the whole reticent about pressing their preferences for the nomination,[31] realizing that their support of anyone would handicap him. And even in some Southern quarters there was a recognition of the argument that Pendleton lacked drawing power among war Democrats and Conservatives.   The Mobile *Register,* the Richmond *Enquirer,*[32] the Memphis *Avalanche,*[33] and the Charleston *Mercury,*[34] admitted Pendleton's Southern popularity but supported Hancock because, with a military candidate, success was more likely.

[25] London *Daily News*, April 7, 1868.

[26] *Times*, May 1, *Herald*, June 10, *Tribune*, July 3, 1868.

[27] In Memphis *Avalanche*, February 19, 1868.

[28] Chicago *Republican*, February 20, 1868.

[29] To E. T. W., June 9, 1868, *Welles Papers*, Library of Congress, vol. 65.

[30] *Thomas Ewing Papers*, Library of Congress, vol. 19.

[31] E. g. Richmond *Enquirer*, in *National Intelligencer*, May 8, 1868.

[32] In *National Intelligencer*, May 8, 1868, Cincinnati *Commercial*, May 7, 1868.

[33] May 16, 1868.

[34] In New York *Herald*, May 21, Cincinnati *Commercial*, May 19, 1868.

When the date for the Democratic National Convention approached, the hopes of the Pendleton men were high, and they made a gallant fight for their man, but without success. The story of this struggle in the Convention, and its relation to the final outcome is reserved for a later section.

2. HENDRICKS OF INDIANA

When we turn to Thomas A. Hendricks we encounter an entirely different type of candidacy. The strongest factor in the movement to nominate Hendricks was the possibility that the East would unite upon him to head off Pendleton, and the weakest factor was that Pendleton's supporters would block his nomination by means of the two-thirds rule as they considered it treason to the West. As it turned out, when Hendricks appeared to be reaching a commanding position in the balloting, the Ohio delegation stampeded the convention for Seymour.

The first important mention of Hendricks' name was in a letter from Seymour to Tilden on March 4, 1868, in which Seymour wrote that he thought Hendricks would be as good a candidate as the party could get.[35] Seymour did not continue his support of Hendricks and made no public endorsement of him. He later turned to Chase. Had he continued to feel as he expressed himself to Tilden and had he actively worked for Hendricks, it is quite possible that Hendricks would have received the nomination. Other Democratic leaders in New York were also favorably inclined towards Hendricks. The Manhattan Club, which included most of the party leaders in New York City in its membership was reported about the first of May to have gone for Hendricks.[36] Among those who thought that Hendricks would make a good candidate was Sanford E. Church, who wrote Tilden

[35] *Tilden Letters*, vol. i, p. 221.

[36] New York Correspondence, Philadelphia *Ledger* in Cincinnati *Commercial*, May 3, 1868.

to that effect on June 10.[37]   On June 1 the New York *World*
reported that the Tammany group, while publicly advocating
the nomination of Seymour, were in reality looking towards
Hendricks.   Some of the New Jersey Democrats, notably
those from Trenton, were in favor of Hendricks in the
New Jersey Democratic Convention of June 10.[38]

Curiously enough, among his fellow Democrats in Congress Senator Hendricks' nomination was not widely urged
in spite of his personal popularity, according to a report to
the Springfield *Republican* on May 24.[39]

Gideon Welles was one of the Cabinet who thought that
Hendricks would make a suitable candidate.   " He would
unite as many as any one, perhaps, and is a politician as good
perhaps as any suggested by the anti-war Democrats."
Welles thought Hendricks and Hancock would both strike
the Democratic Convention favorably.   His friend, A. E.
Burr, a Democratic leader in Connecticut, reported to him
on June 19 that the delegates from Connecticut were most
inclined to favor Hendricks, although they were ready to go
for Hancock or Senator Doolittle as well.[40]

During the two months preceding the Democratic Convention, various journals gave lists of names suggested for
the nomination.   Hendricks was included in most of them.[41]
The *World* on June 1, vigorously presented his case.   His
war record would draw many moderate Republicans to the
ticket; he would be acceptable to the Northwest and, if the
East would find him more acceptable than Pendleton, " there
is no doubt that the West, including Pendleton's friends, will

[37] *Tilden Letters*, vol. i, pp. 228-229.

[38] New York *World*, June 11, 1868.

[39] May 25, 1868.

[40] *Welles Papers*, New York Public Library, Mss. Div.

[41] *National Intelligencer*, May 27, 1868; New York *World*, June 1,
22, 1868; New York *Herald*, July 3, 1868.

readily acquiesce." A week later the *World* reported gains
for Hendricks in the East where, to all appearances, the
question rested between Hendricks and Chase.[42] The New
York *Sun* on June 19 professed to regard it as settled that
neither Chase, Pendleton or Seymour would be the nominee;
but that the prize would go to Hendricks, although he had
not sought the nomination. " There is probably no man of
his eminence in either party who has excited so few animosities among his political associates." [43]

As the time for the assembling of the Convention
approached, the report was circulated that the New York
leaders had decided to concentrate their forces on Hendricks.[44] A brother-in-law, Dr. Pierce, was reported to
have visited Washington, Philadelphia, and New York, and
to have made arrangements which would insure Hendricks
over one hundred votes as soon as his name was presented.[45]
Actually, as we shall see, he did not reach the hundred mark
until the nineteenth ballot.[46] On June 29 the New York
World reported a general impression that Hendricks would
be the nominee. On the 30th the Cincinnati *Commercial*
said all the signs pointed to Seymour, Hendricks or Hancock.

A report on July 1 said that Hendricks had written a
letter declining to be a candidate, and declaring Pendleton
the choice of the Northwest. After this message was received, the Indiana delegation then assembled in New York
was said to have met and decided to support Pendleton as
long as Ohio.[47] The rumour that Hendricks had withdrawn
according to the New York *World* for July 2, arose from

[42] June 8, 1868.

[43] In Cincinnati *Commercial*, June 23, 1868.

[44] Cincinnati *Commercial*, June 21, 1868; New York *Times*, July 3, 1868.

[45] Cincinnati *Commercial*, June 25, 1868.

[46] *Official Proceedings*.

[47] New York, July 1, 1868, in Cincinnati *Commercial*, July 2, 1868.

this same decision of the Indiana delegation. The *World* continued that while there had been some feeling against Hendricks on the part of the Pendleton supporters it had died out, " and there is now the best of feeling between the friends of Pendleton and Hendricks." The Hendricks candidacy arose from circumstances neither he nor Pendleton could control. The New York *Times* on July 3 repeated the story of the letter of withdrawal, and stated it was in the hands of an Indiana delegate, Lafe Devlin, to be read in the convention if Hendricks' name was mentioned. The *Evening Post* for the same day reported that the letter in question " seems to mean that he will not stand in the way of Mr. Pendleton."

On July 3 the Cincinnati *Commercial* printed, from Washington, a denial by Senator Hendricks that he had written a letter withdrawing as a candidate. A similar denial was printed in the Washington *National Intelligencer* for July 3 as coming from the Indiana delegation in New York who intended however, to support Pendleton during the early ballots.[48] The Louisville *Courier* (July 3) stated that Hendricks "maintains the same attitude he has always, advising his friends to act in good faith for Mr. Pendleton."

3. BLAIR OF MISSOURI

Among the other western aspirants a particularly dramatic place was occupied by General Frank Blair of St. Louis, the son and namesake of old " Blair of the *Globe* " and the brother of Montgomery Blair of Lincoln's Cabinet. He possessed a good war record; none of the political generals of the Civil War had a better. Before the war he had been the admitted leader of the Missouri abolitionists. He was as radical as any man among them. During the war he left the Missouri Radicals when a decided majority of them

[48] New York, July 2, 1868.

turned against him in his quarrel with General Frèmont. It was charged at the time that President Lincoln revoked Frèmont's emancipation order at Blair's instigation. "Blair's strong forte was invective. Apparently he was never so happy as when making others miserable." He was a born fighter, and physically " he was the bravest man I ever knew," records one who knew him in Missouri. In physical appearance he was slender and wiry, a bundle of bones and nerves without a particle of surplus flesh, with auburn hair and a sandy complexion.[49] Blair returned to St. Louis from the army in June 1865, and continued his opposition to the Radical Republicans then in control in Missouri. He opposed the radical constitution of 1865 on the ground that the prevalence of war hatreds made it an improper time to adopt a new constitution.[50] Blair supported Johnson in his quarrel with Congress, as did his father and brother.

By 1868 General Blair was fairly on the Democratic side of the fence and was being talked of for the Presidential nomination. An early mention of his name was in the Chicago *Republican* for March 9, 1868, in a tabulation of Democratic possibilities.

Montgomery Blair's interest was awakened, and he busied himself in writing to the Democratic leaders. He wrote to Barlow of New York who passed his letters on to Tilden, who in turn sent them to Seymour with a covering letter in which he stated that " the case with Frank Blair seems to be about this: He is a gallant young man and of very popular manners. He could be relied on for friendly disposition towards you and our people in this State as well as anybody out of it, and would administer the government on Jeffersonian principles. His friends think he will have

[49] Hume, *The Abolitionists* (New York, 1905), pp. 188-189.

[50] Barclay, *The Liberal Republican Movement in Missouri* (Columbia, Mo., 1926), pp. 53-54.

Missouri and some other votes [in the National Convention]; and be more extensively a second choice. On the other hand, he would have the antagonisms created by other members of his family—not by himself—to encounter. And I think generally that the first impression of our people is not of attraction towards him as a candidate. I think it advisable for his friends to get votes for him in the West if they can; and have said so to some of them—but without forecasting at all our action." [51]

This statement by Tilden perhaps meant that Blair's candidacy might be used by the Eastern Democrats as an offset to Pendleton. A Washington dispatch in May to the Cincinnati *Commercial* spoke of a " quiet movement " for Blair which had made some headway. Some distinguished and influential Democratic leaders of Pennsylvania and New York supported him, it was said, and he had strength in New England, while his active hostility to negro suffrage would make him very acceptable to the South. [52]

Montgomery Blair continued his correspondence with the New York Democratic leaders by a letter to Tilden on June 5, in which he stated that Frank's hopes were revived by the Chase momevent, which would help him by loosening up partly feeling and checking Pendleton. If any Democrats could go for Chase they could go for Blair, " the true heir of Lincoln." He added that the Lincoln Republicans who were the only Republicans disposed to support the Democrats against Grant were opposed to Chase. [53] Montgomery's advocacy of his brother's nomination also took the form of opposition to Hancock. The Cincinnati *Commercial* commented that the idea of nominating Blair was insanity. He

[51] *Seymour Papers*, New York Historical Society Library, box 2, May 11, 1868.

[52] May 21, 1868.

[53] *Tilden Letters*, vol. i, pp. 232-233.

might do for the tail end of the ticket but " if it be necessary to go outside the party for a candidate, Chase is undoubtedly the man." [54]

Welles confided to his diary on July 1, " Frank Blair has some qualities for the emergency which is approaching—is spoken of by friends,—but, but—poor Frank has destroyed himself by his—[drinking?] " [55] This reference to Blair's drinking habits forecast the bitter attacks made upon him on that score by the Republicans after his nomination for the Vice-Presidency.

In addition to the St. Louis *Republican,* the St. Louis *Dispatch* (Democratic) also favored Blair, and was opposed to the candidacy of Chase. The *Dispatch* insisted that a War Democrat must be chosen.[56] On July 2 the *Tribune* published a summary of Blair's views, issued " apparently with his approval," in which he placed before the convention an outspoken platform of opposition to the Radical Reconstruction program. He was opposed to negro suffrage, which he regarded as " a cardinal issue of the canvass." The reconstruction acts he held unconstitutional, and he called for a platform declaration to that effect. He demanded withdrawal of the military support of the reconstruction governments in the South, which would result in the collapse of these " bastard and spurious " organizations. Laws disfranchising ex-Confederates embraced in amnesty proclamations, and test oaths for voters, he branded as unconstitutional and arbitrary. The *Tribune* dubbed this set of doctrines " Revolution, plain and simple—an appeal from the decision of the ballot box to force and violence."

On June 30 Blair wrote a friendly delegate to the National Convention, Colonel James O. Brodhead, a letter which was

[54] June 8, 1868.

[55] In *Manuscript Diary*, Library of Congress.

[56] In New York *Times,* June 3, 1868.

even more explicit as to the remedy for existing evils.　In this epistle, printed in the New York *World* to determine whether his name should be presented to the Convention or not, he stated that his conception of " the real and only issue in this contest " was the overthrow of Radical Reconstruction in the South.　This reconstruction would have been accomplished by November, insuring a Radical majority in the Senate, and making it impossible to undo the Radical plan by Congressional action.　" Must we submit to it." How can it be overthrown? " he asked, and answered—by the authority of the President.　If a Democratic President enforced or permitted to be enforced the Reconstruction Acts, the Radicals, including twenty spurious Senators and fifty spurious Congressmen, would control Congress " and his administration will be as powerless as the present one of Mr. Johnson."　The President, continued Blair, should declare the reconstruction acts null and void, " compel the army to undo its usurpations at the South, disperse the carpet bag State governments, allow the white people to reorganize their own governments, and elect Senators and Representatives.　The House of Representatives will contain a majority of Democrats from the North and they will admit the representatives elected by the white people of the South, and with the cooperation of the President it will not be difficut to compel the Senate to submit once more to the obligations of the Constitution."　By putting this issue plainly to the country all future strife would be avoided.　The constitution had to be restored before men could restore the finances.　" It is idle to talk of bonds, greenbacks, gold, the public faith and the public credit.　What can a Democratic President do in regard to any of these with a Congress in both branches controlled by carpet baggers and their allies? " " We must have a President who will execute the will of the people by trampling into dust the usurpations of Congress, known as the reconstruction acts. I wish to stand before the Convention on this issue," Blair concluded.[57]

This plain-speaking placed Blair before the Convention on a platform that contained no hint of temporizing. In some quarters it was hailed with delight and gave him renewed strength with the Southerners and others. The Republican reaction to the letter is indicated by the New York *Times,* which labeled it as a revelation of the views of that unregenerate Democracy " whose aim is to counteract the results of the War and to revive the rule of race and color by bloodshed and anarchy." If the Democratic party in framing its platform and selecting its candidate acts upon Blair's view, concluded the *Times,* " it will go to the country as the promoter of another civil war." [58]

Stebbins inclines to the view that the Brodhead letter was too radical to permit the Democrats to hope for victory under its author; " hence the dropping of Blair's name from consideration." [59] The ideas expressed by Blair, were, according to Oberholtzer, " the fair inheritance of the party." [60] Like President Johnson, Blair had shifted from the position of a Republican of the most outspoken type during the war to a complete and unreserved Democrat. On July 5, after the Convention had opened, Blair wrote a letter to answer the objection that his Brodhead letters would frighten away the moderates:

I do not think that people would be alarmed at the prospect of undoing the infamous acts of Congress, and I do not believe in lying and double dealing even for the office of President of the United States. . . . Alarm the people? Why, they are alarmed now. The country is in revolution. . . . It will not serve the

[57] New York *World,* July 3, 1868.

[58] July 4, 1868.

[59] Stebbins, *op. cit.,* p. 332.

[60] *United States,* vol. ii, p. 166.

cause of the people by putting in a President with the same set
of opinions as the present occupant of the White House. . . . [61]

Here Blair showed himself to possess a ramrod for a
backbone. Not one inch did he retire under fire. And
while his views were much too outspoken to be politically
expedient for the Democratic party, it should be pointed out
that the heart of his proposal—the undoing of the Radical
reconstruction in the South through executive action—was
the policy eventually followed by Hayes.

[61] New York *Herald*, July 6, 1868.

CHAPTER VII

Johnson and the Eastern Aspirants for the Democratic Nomination

I. ANDREW JOHNSON

AMONG these who desired the Democratic nomination for President was Andrew Johnson himself. Having broken with the Radical Republicans and suffered their attacks for three years, even to standing trial for removal from office, it was natural for the President to seek vindication through reelection. An ardent Democrat before the war, he had opposed the secession of his native State and had remained in his seat in the Senate when Tennessee seceded. When he became president he at first showed signs of following a policy in harmony with the wishes of the Radicals, but by the winter of 1865-1866 had taken the opposite course. Johnson had gone over completely and unreservedly to the Democrats,[1] and was a leading champion of moderation and conciliation in dealing with the South, opposed to negro suffrage and military government, yet he had not been accepted by the Democratic party as a member in full standing and, as far as the Presidency was concerned, he was as impossible a candidate for either party as John Tyler had been in 1844.[2] Logically the President would have been the leader for those making war on the work of Congress, but there was little disposition to select him as the Democratic nominee for 1868.[3]

[1] Oberholtzer, *United States*, vol. ii, p. 166.

[2] Wilson, *Division and Reunion, 1829-1889* (New York, 1894), p. 271.

[3] Dunning, *Reconstruction*, pp. 339-340.

The strength of the Democratic opposition to his nomination was not fully realized by Johnson, and up to the meeting of the Convention he hoped that he might receive the prize. Schouler states that while no doubt Johnson had visions of another term, this fact did not influence his acts as President.[4] He desired above everything else to strike another blow at his former allies—the Republicans. " I was born a State-Rights Democrat and I shall die one," he said.[5] What he failed to see, at least two members of his Cabinet saw clearly enough. Secretary McCulloch declares in his reminiscences that in spite of the fact that the President and the Democrats agreed on the paramount subject of reconstruction, " it was quite certain long before the Convention was held that he would not be their candidate." [6] Secretary Welles did not think that the President cared so much about the office as about receiving a vindication.[8]

Johnson's break with the Republican party in 1865 was hailed by the Democrats with enthusiasm, and the New York *News* and New York *World* as early as that year suggested that he might be available as a Democratic candidate in 1868.[9] But the President's position as a possible Democratic leader was weakened by the developments of 1866, notably his famous " Swing around the circle." The National Union Convention held in Philadelphia in August 1866, had as one of its purposes the formation of a Conservative party uniting Democrats and Conservatives under the President's leadership. The movement came to nothing and the President became more and more isolated

---

[4] Schouler, *United States* (New York, 1913), vol. vii, p. 10.

[5] Winston, *Andrew Johnson*, pp. 339-340.

[6] *Men and Measures*, p. 345.

[8] *Diary*, vol. iii, p. 383, June 15, 1868.

[9] Cited by M. H. Albjerg in *South Atlantic Quarterly*, October, 1927, p. 409.

politically. His growing unpopularity and tactless acts resulted in the loss of such support as he retained in the New York press. The New York *Herald* counseled him to consider the Republican victories in the Congressional election of 1866 as the verdict of the people as a jury. On September 12, 1867 the *World* warned the Democratic party against identifying itself with the President, for that would make the party responsible for his " blunders and mismanagement perpetrated against its judgment and in contempt of its wishes." [10] Having alienated every important New York daily by 1867, and most of them a year earlier, Andrew Johnson not only had lost his right arm, figuratively speaking, but he might have read his political doom in the change of front of this powerful metropolitan press.[11]

Gideon Welles recorded in his diary the reasons as he saw them for Johnson's lack of support by the New York Democrats. He wrote that the Tammany leaders, fearing that the adoption of the President by the party might injure their organization, were careful not to endorse Johnson himself although they encouraged and supported his policy. " They feared that the President . . . a man whom they did not elect, might become popular; they were distant, cold, reserved towards him." [12]

Although Johnson's acquittal in the impeachment trial removed the possibility of Constitutional ineligibility, the movement for his nomination did not make much headway after May 16. The progress of other candidacies while the trial was under way, notably those of Chase, Hancock, and Pendleton, had so committed the party leaders that the President had little chance. The President was so informed by some of his correspondents the last week of June. One

---

[10] Albjerg, *op. cit.*, pp. 413-414.

[11] *Ibid.*, p. 414.

[12] *Diary*, vol. iii, p. 399, July 9, 1868.

told him that following a meeting of Democratic leaders at the Manhattan Club on June 25, it was probable that the nominee would be selected " from policy," although the President would be warmly endorsed.[13]   Another correspondent, although finding Johnson's name frequently mentioned by delegates to the Convention, thought it evident his name and claims would be ignored.[14]

An important additional bar to the President's nomination by the Democrats lay in his refusal to turn the patronage of his office over to the party leaders.   Secretary McCulloch has stated Johnson's position on the subject of patronage. " In appointments money was not potent.   Offices were not merchandise.   The President never permitted himself to be under personal obligations to any one."   McCulloch says of his own Department that the President desired it to be honestly administered, independent of all political considerations except for the brief period in 1866 when the short-lived Johnson-Conservative party was being formed.   The Administration had been conducted in the interests of neither the Republican nor the Democratic parties, and officeholders opposed to the President poltically were not disturbed.[15]

Democratic leaders after the failure of the Johnson-Conservative party movement of 1866 evidently expected him to turn toward the regular Democratic organization, and his correspondence for 1867 contains letters from many Democrats suggesting names for Presidential appointments. Among those writing were Tilden, James Brooks, and Fernando Wood of New York city, Edgar Cowan and Charles R. Buckalew of Pennsylvania, Frank Blair, Jr., of

[13] Lillian Foster, June 26, 1868, *Johnson Papers*, Library of Congress, vol. 142.

[14] W. W. Warden, June 28, 1868, *Johnson Papers*, Library of Congress, vol. 141.

[15] *Men and Measures*, pp. 344, 377.

Missouri, D. W. Voorhees of Indiana, and General George W. Morgan of Ohio.[16] The *World* on February 19, 1868, commented on the failure of the President to give patronage to the Democrats by saying that the President had kept the obligation to the party which elected him, and he had bestowed no offices on men who voted the Democratic ticket in 1864. The Washington *National Intelligencer,* edited by Johnson's friend John F. Coyle, on March 17 lamented that Radical influences seemed to control the distribution of office " even in the Navy Department, of which this is less true than any."

Connected with the question of patronage was the demand by many Democrats that the President reconstruct his Cabinet along Democratic lines. Their chief target was Secretary McCulloch, and his retention in the Cabinet was held by some writers to be the chief bar to Johnson's nomination. Secretary Welles records that Seward's retention also helped alienate the New York Democrats. " For a year he has bestowed some favors on Democrats, but Seward was still with him. It is impossible that he should be nominated at New York." [17] But the attacks on McCulloch were particularly bitter and sustained. The *National Intelligencer* wanted to know what the friends of the President could say when his persistent retention of McCulloch was thrown in their faces.[18] McCulloch, according to the same paper, had even promised to support Grant in return for being retained in office.[19]

The suggestion, or even demand, that Johnson reconstruct his Cabinet, eliminating McCulloch and Seward, continued to the days when the Convention was in session. In a letter

[16] *Johnson Papers,* Library of Congress, vols. 111-114 inc.

[17] June 15, 1868, *Diary,* vol. iii, pp. 383-384, 400.

[18] June 27, 1868.

[19] July 1, 1868.

of July 8 to his friend Edmund Cooper, a leader among the Johnson forces in the Convention, the President defended the retention of his Cabinet. He considered his Cabinet members ties binding the Conservatives to the measures the Democrats professed to support. Together with the seven Republican Senators who voted to acquit him, they were a strength of the first importance. He concluded: " And now when the final issue is made it is no time to change front and, while the enemy is in the field, to select some new leader to fight the last battle. To change front now would be an acknowledgment of weakness which would inspire the adversary with hope and confidence." [20] McCulloch was an able executive, loyal to the President and to the country, and Johnson is entitled to the highest praise for not yielding to the pressure for his removal.

The movement in favor of the President for the Democratic nomination received much of its support from the South. This in itself was something of a handicap due to the general sentiment that the selection of the candidates should be left to the Northern wing of the party. That Johnson was restored in the affections of the Democrats of Tennessee (from whom he differed so sharply in 1861) is shown by the action of the Democratic Convention of that State in instructing its delegates to the National Convention to vote for him (February 15). North Carolina's Convention (February 7), also came out strongly for the President.[21] These States, together with Alabama, Florida, Georgia, South Carolina, Virginia and Texas, gave him their undivided vote on the first ballot in the Convention. Alabama and Tennessee continued to do so for six ballots.[22]

In New York City in January, a meeting of the Andrew

[20] *Johnson Papers*, Library of Congress, vol. 142.
[21] *American Annual Cyclopedia*, 1868, pp. 554, 721.
[22] *Official Proceedings*, pp. 77-108.

Johnson " Veterans Volunteer Club " endorsed the President for reelection.[23]   And on January 30, at Cooper Union in New York city, a mass-meeting to sustain the President was addressed by Senator J. R. Doolittle of Wisconsin, who endorsed him and protested against the nomination of a Peace Democrat.[24]   On June 24 ten New York Democrats wrote to the President, asking him if he would allow his name to be presented to the Convention.   Johnson replied on July 2, just before the meeting of the Convention that he was not ambitious for further service, unless called by a popular demand so general as to be an endorsement of his record as President.   Such an endorsement, however, he did not expect.   This letter was not published until the morning of July 7, the day the balloting started.[25]

Another move by the President calculated to advance his cause with the Convention was his Amnesty Proclamation of July 4.   His intention to make such a move was known in some quarters as early as May.   Philo Durfee wrote to Seymour on May 26 that the President would issue a proclamation of amnesty.[26]   The Baltimore *Gazette* reported in June that the friends of the President anticipated some " official demonstration which will secure him the nomination." [27]

On July 1 Welles recorded in his diary that an amnesty proclamation, prepared by Secretary Seward, was read to the Cabinet by the President.   It included an exception for those still under indictment.   The President was not pleased

[23] H. F. Lieberman to President Johnson, January 24, 1868, *Johnson Papers*, Library of Congress, vol. 132.

[24] New York *Herald*, January 30, 31, 1868.

[25] New York *World*, New York *Express*, July 7, 1868; rough draft in *Johnson Papers*, Library of Congress, vol. 141.

[26] *Seymour Papers*, Albany.

[27] In New York *Times*, June 24, 1868.

with the exception and asked why this unhappy controversy should be prolonged.   The next day Johnson laid before Browning and Welles a draft which contained no exception. Browning thought the omission a mistake.[28]   When the Proclamation appeared, the exception was included.   It was not until December 25 of the same year that the President issued a proclamation granting amnesty to all involved in the rebellion.[29]   The New York correspondent of the Cincinnati *Commercial* on July 2 told of the coming proclamation, and thought that the President might get thirty or forty Southern votes in the Convention.[30]

The proclamation was published on July 4.   It pardoned all persons involved in the rebellion except those under indictment in any Federal Court.   In the fourth paragraph the President virtually gave his political platform.   He stated that " it is desirable to reduce the standing army, and to bring to a speedy termination military occupation, martial law, military tribunals, abridgment of freedom of the speech and of the press, and suspension of the writ of habeas corpus, and the right of trial by jury—such encroachments upon our free constitutions in times of peace being dangerous to public liberty, incompatible with the individual rights of citizens, contrary to the genius and spirit of our Republican form of government, and exhaustive of the national resources." [31] The New York *Times* thought it " an overture to the Convention " but did not think it would be successful.[32]

2. WINFIELD S. HANCOCK

Meanwhile, the movement to nominate an entirely differ-

[28] *Welles Diary*, vol. iii, pp. 394-395.
[29] *American Annual Cyclopedia*, 1868, p. 754.
[30] Cincinnati *Commercial*, July 3, 1868.
[31] *American Annual Cyclopedia*, 1868, p. 753.
[32] July 4, 1868.

ent type of candidate had been steadily gaining ground. As it became obvious that the Republicans would select General Grant as their candidate, more and more Democrats had listened to those who advocated the nomination of General W. S. Hancock, the most popular Democratic soldier except perhaps McClellan. In 1867 Hancock the " Superb " had been appointed commander of the Military District which included Louisiana and Texas, succeeding General Phil Sheridan. His career as commander, which lasted from November 1867, until March 1868, when he resigned, endeared him to the Democrats, North no less than South.

Upon taking command at New Orleans on November 29, he issued a general order in which he stated the principles upon which he proposed to act. Both Louisiana and Texas had been centers of a great deal of violence between the Democrats and the Radicals, and previous commanders had aided the radicals in overriding constitutional guarantees. General Hancock announced that " the great principles of American liberty are still the lawful inheritance of this people, and ever should be. The right of trial by jury, the habeas corpus, the liberty of the press, and the rights of property must be preserved." [33] Referring to this order, Hancock told his wife that " I am expected to exercise extreme military authority over these people. I shall disappoint them. I have not been educated to overthrow the civil authorities in time of peace. I intend to recognize the fact that the civil war is at an end, and shall issue my order or proclamation accordingly." [34]

The publication of this order brought congratulations from many quarters. Jeremiah Black of Pennsylvania wrote from Washington that it had " the very ring of the revolutionary mettle. Washington never said a thing in

[33] *Civil Record of ... Hancock* (1880), p. 5.
[34] Hancock, *Reminiscences of Hancock* (New York, 1887), p. 120.

better taste or at a better time." [35]   President Johnson made it the subject of a message to Congress (December, 1867). He compared Hancock's action with that of Washington in refusing to elevate himself above the law. Although not implying that Hancock was the only army officer who was influenced by the example of Washington, Johnson said that the distinguished honor belonged to him of " being the first officer in high command south of the Potomac, since the close of the Civil War, who has given utterances to these noble sentiments in the form of a military order."   The President suggested that Hancock's patriotic conduct be given public recognition by Congress.[36]   Obviously this was not in any hope that Congress would act on the recommendation, but simply to place the President on record as supporting the General's position.

On December 5 Hancock proceeded to give practical effect to his principles by withdrawing an order issued by his predecessor which interfered with the selection of jurors. Hancock accompanied this action by the statement [37] that he would "maintain the just power of the judiciary" and was "unwilling to permit the civil authorities and laws to be embarrassed by military interference." [38]   He followed this on January 1 with General Order No. 1, in which he again came to the defence of the civil courts and stated that " the administration of justice appertains to the regular courts.   The rights of litigants do not depend on the views of the General—they are to be adjudged and settled according to law. . . . Arbitrary power, such as he has been urged to assume, has no existence here." [39]

[35] *Reminiscences of Hancock*, pp. 225-226.

[36] *American Annual Cyclopedia*, 1868, p. 126.

[37] Special Orders 203, New Orleans, December 5, 1867.

[38] *Civil Record*, p. 15.

[39] *Civil Record*, p. 22; *American Annual Cyclopedia*, 1868, p. 430.

Hancock's position continued to please those opposed to Radical reconstruction. Christian Rawlins of Louisiana declared that " General Hancock is gaining in golden opinions of all sorts of men, only a few of the dirty politicians howl and curse. I am satisfied that our political horizon begins to brighten up and that constitutional liberty will revive." [40] The Chicago *Republican* (March 9) spoke of Hancock as hard at work in Louisiana making political capital. This was unfair. Mrs. Hancock in her Reminiscences states that " before yielding up his command in the Fifth Military District, General Hancock was approached by friends and urged to be a candidate for the Presidency. He would not listen to these appeals, nor allow his name to be used in any manner to further his own advancement; everything that was done was through enthusiastic friends and supporters." [41]

When the Radical Governor of Texas, E. M. Pease, wrote him protesting against his course Hancock replied (March 9) that for the future of their common country he could " devoutly wish that no great number of our people have yet fallen in with the views you appear to entertain. Woe be to us whenever it shall come to pass that the power of the magistrate—civil or military—is permitted to deal with the mere opinions or feelings of the people." This was just before his resignation. His attempts to remove corrupt officials in New Orleans were overruled by General Grant in command of the army, and he asked to be relieved on March 16—his request being granted on the 18th.[42] The entire period of his command was marked by a consistent discountenancing of trials by military commission instead of the courts.[43]

[40] *Johnson Papers*, Library of Congress, vol. 128, January 6, 1868.

[41] P. 135.

[42] *American Annual Cyclopedia*, 1868, p. 430.

[43] Walker, *General Hancock* (New York, 1895), p. 302.

General Hancock's attitude was a refreshing change from that usually held by military commanders at the time. He was too popular a man for the Senate to reject when the President nominated him for the post, and perhaps there was a hope on the part of the Radical Senators that the possession of great power over the civilian population, together with the disorder endemic in the far South at that time, would combine to lead Hancock to excesses that would alienate him from the Democracy. That Hancock rose superior to his environment and maintained the principles of civil liberty when even civil officers, under radical inspiration, were flouting them, is a tribute to his character as well as to his principles.

Unfortunately however, another chapter in Hancock's military career was the occasion for much criticism. At the time of the assassination of Lincoln Hancock had been in command of the Military Department in which Washington was located, and therefore had general supervision over the apprehension, trial and execution of those implicated in the assassination. By 1868 a very strong feeling had grown up that justice had not been done in all of these trials and executions, especially in the case of Mrs. Surratt. This feeling was strengthened by the fact that when John Surratt, who escaped capture in 1865, surrendered himself and was brought to court, the charges against him were dismissed in 1868.

Those opposed to Hancock's nomination were free in their strictures upon the General for the part they alleged he played in the execution of an innocent woman. The Washington correspondent of the Cincinnati *Commercial* (April 24) summed up the criticism: Mrs. Surratt " was a Catholic, and her execution created a great deal of feeling in the Catholic Church. It is very true that Hancock only obeyed orders, but still in obeying orders he hung a woman who is now believed to have been innocent. . . . You can't go before the people and say that Hancock only obeyed orders. They'll tell you that he ought to have resigned his commission before obeying any such an order."

Mrs. Hancock in her Reminiscences defends her husband from the charge of responsibility for Mrs. Surratt's execution. The accusation, she wrote, was as unfair as any man had ever been called upon to meet. While the troops were under his command, including those that guarded the prisoners, all orders came to him from the Secretary of War. From him they went to General Hartranft, who was Governor of the Military Prison, and who had immediate charge of the prisoners and gave the verbal order for the executions. " President Johnson was wholly responsible for it. Not once, but many times, did my husband urge upon the President unanswerable reasons for granting a pardon." [44] Hancock had stationed couriers at intervals along the route from the White House to the arsenal so that if the President granted a reprieve the order would reach him at once. He had personally attended the execution for the same reason.

In opposition to Hancock's candidacy, Montgomery Blair used a proclamation issued over Hancock's name at the time calling upon negroes to arm and assist in hunting down the President's assasin. Mrs. Hancock insists that this proclamation was really written by Attorney General Holt and Secretary Stanton, and only published formally over the Commanding Officer's signature. Blair's use of this proclamation is termed " malicious " by Mrs. Hancock. [45] The two Democratic papers in Washington, the *Express* and the *National Intelligencer,* both came to Hancock's defense on this charge. [46]

[44] Pp. 108-109.

[45] P. 108.

[46] *Express*, June 26, 1868; *Intelligencer*, June 27, 1868.

Because of his admirable military record and his soundness on financial issues, the Republicans genuinely feared Hancock. Carl Schurz expressed this apprehension in a letter to his wife on May 24. Referring to the Republican chances for victory in November, Schurz wrote that something depended on the Democratic candidate. An extreme Copperhead would be easy to beat, " but if a man like General Hancock shall be nominated, we shall have to work very hard. Nevertheless I think that even in that case the old forces can be lead to victory once more." [47]

As early as December 1867, while at New Orleans, Hancock had found occasion to place himself on record as regards the financial issues. To R. S. Walker, Hancock wrote on December 12 that he considered the payment of the public debt a matter of necessity. With the nation's honor safeguarded, the actual interests of the people must be protected. " The laws in reference to the loans, the advertisements in connection therewith and the terms of the bonds will determine the point of honor. As a matter of policy alone, the debt should be paid." [48] This rather noncommittal statement indicates that Hancock realized that the financial question, about which he knew very little, was highly controversial. But on the whole the statement placed him in opposition to Pendleton, especially since he included a reference to the advertisements in connection with the bond issues during the war. As the movement for Hancock's nomination continued, his name was most often mentioned as one who would appeal to the two classes of voters least likely to be attracted to Pendleton—the war Democrats and those opposed to the repayment of the national bonds in other than gold.

In February the New York *Herald* commented that

[47] Schurz, *Intimate Letters*, pp. 437-438.
[48] New York Historical Society Library, Misc. Mss. Hancock.

Hancock having failed to catch on adequately with the Democrats, President Johnson had put General Sherman forward as a candidate. " An occasional echo from the mountains of Pennsylvania " was reported in favor of Hancock, " but Hancock, they say out west, was the hangman of Mrs. Surratt and so they wont have Hancock." [49] In Pennsylvania, Hancock's home State, the consideration of his name had reached a stage where former Governor William Bigler was able to write to Tilden on March 4 that, although Pendleton and Jeremiah S. Black had some supporters, Hancock was the only man seriously considered in that State.[50] However, in a letter to Black on April 9 Bigler, referring to the Pennsylvania Democratic Convention then recently in session, said that the Convention was divided between Pendleton, Hancock and Packer supporters and that "there were difficulties in the way of handsomely naming anyone." [51]

We find van Buren writing from Washington to Seymour on April 21 and reporting strong support for Hancock, including Senator Doolittle, who said he was the man with the best chance of carrying Pennsylvania. " They all want to know how *you* feel to his nomination. I told him you were for saving the country and for any Democrat who could be surest to win. . . ." Van Buren offered to take a message from Seymour to Hancock. On May 1, van Buren again wrote to Seymour that the Hancock movement was loud and noisy. " Hancock himself is willing." [52] On April 26 a meeting of influential Democrats was held in New York, where it was finally agreed to support the nomination of Hancock for President and Groesbeck of Ohio for Vice-

---

[49] New York *Herald*, February 17, 20, 1868.

[50] *Tilden Letters*, vol. i, pp. 220-221.

[51] *J. S. Black Papers*, Library of Congress, vol. 48.

[52] *Seymour Papers*, New York Historical Society Library, box 4.

President.[53]   A little later Washington dispatches reported
that Senators Bayard, Dixon and Buckalew all favored
Hancock.

But the strongest support for Hancock came from the
soldiers. A meeting of the executive committee of the
Cleveland Soldiers and Sailors Convention of 1866 was
called for New York city on April 28, not only to arrange
for a Soldiers and Sailors Convention to be held in connec-
tion with the Democratic National Convention but also to
advance Hancock's name for the nomination.   General
Gordon Granger presided over the meeting which included
Generals Steedman, Slocum, McCook and others.   They
were all unanimously for Hancock for President, the "Game-
Cock of the Army," with Hendricks for Vice-President.
The meeting appointed a committee to consult with Governor
Seymour on the subject of Hancock's nomination.[54]   The
New York *Citizen,* claiming to be the mouthpiece of the
War Democrats, came out for Hancock with the prediction
that should Pendleton be nominated the War Democrats
would support Grant.[55]   On the other hand, it seems clear
that, though acceptable to the moderates as well as the War
Democrats, Hancock would not be acceptable to the Peace
Democrats.   The Western Democrats, especially those supporting Pendleton, were opposed to any soldier as a
candidate.[56]

Hancock received considerable support from the South.
The Memphis *Avalanche* supported him, and thought that
Hancock and Hendricks would receive the support of every
Democrat and of every Conservative in the country.[57]   A

[53] Utica *Observer,* April 29, 1868.

[54] Utica *Observer,* May 7, 1868.

[55] In Cincinnati *Commercial,* April 29, 1868.

[56] New York, March 25, in London *Daily News,* April 7, 1868.

[57] Memphis *Avalanche,* May 23, 1868; Cincinnati *Commercial,* May 19,
June 24, 1868; *Corcoran Papers, Library of Congress,* vol. xv.

military leader should be chosen, and Hancock had more availability than any other. Among other journals which preferred Hancock were the Charleston *Mercury,* the Macon *Telegraph* and the Mobile *Register* while he enjoyed the support of such leading Southerners as Howell Cobb, and General N. B. Forrest.

3. GEORGE B. MCCLELLAN

The New York *Herald* on March 29 suggested that the old ticket of 1864—McClellan and Pendleton—might be necessary as a compromise between the East and the West. "Little Mac," according to the *Herald,* was stronger than his party in 1864 and his absence from the United States since then had not hurt him. Pendleton's war record was not worse than Seymour's and the ticket would not have the platform of 1864 as a handicap. The possibility of McClellan's selection continued to be recognized as when the *National Intelligencer* on May 1 included him among those whom that paper would cordially support. But his availability did not continue to impress the *Herald* for on May 18 we find it dismissing McClellan as eclipsed by Grant, and as being tired and already defeated.

The talk of McClellan as a possibility died down to such an extent that the *Nation* on May 7 was able to say that nobody was then talking of him as a Democratic candidate. Yet the New York *World* on June 1 still listed McClellan as one of those proposed for the nomination. The *World* stated that there was a strong desire for him both among the Democrats of the Northwest and of New York City. The Washington correspondent of the Cincinnati *Commercial* on June 5 spoke of financial support. "There is a feeble voice raised from Belmont's banking house in favor of McClellan, as if to insure Republican success by running the man who didn't take Richmond against the man who did."

But McClellan's attitude towards these suggestions remained the same—he did not want the nomination. The New York *Times* on June 3 reported that a letter had been received from him in reply to one asking permission to use his name. " The General earnestly begs that this shall not be done, urges the nomination of a new man—a statesman who will command the respect, admiration and enthusiastic support of the combined anti-Radical elements of the whole country, and pledges himself as soon as the nomination is made to come home and canvass wherever needed in behalf of the New York nominees." The New York *Herald* interpreted this letter to mean that the General was in favor of Chase; a conclusion not borne out by a letter from McClellan to S. L. M. Barlow on June 14 in which he expressed surprise that Chase should be a leader of the anti-Radical crusade.[58]

Lacking any support by the principal, the McClellan movement made little headway as the time for the Convention approached, although the *World* on June 22 again listed him among the possibilities, as did the *Herald* on July 3. On July 5 the *Herald* spoke of two cliques among the managers of the New York delegation—a Seymour clique and a McClellan clique. Certain New York Democratic financiers, who had made some financial sacrifices in behalf of McClellan in 1864, would like to obtain a return. These men constituted the New York McClellan Central Committee. " Their chance is very slim," added the *Herald*.

The actual feebleness of the McClellan movement when the Convention met is shown by two facts. The Democratic (or Conservative) Soldiers and Sailors Convention held in New York on July 4, though expected in view of McClellan's popularity to endorse him, selected Hancock instead; and in the Convention itself McClellan received only

[58] *McClellan Papers*, Library of Congress, vol. 93.

one vote—on the twelfth ballot—and a half vote on the twenty-first ballot.   He returned to the United States in October and did not take as active a part in the campaign as the Democratic leaders wished.

4. HORATIO SEYMOUR

The man who received the Democratic nomination for President was the one man, except McClellan who refused to be a candidate.   He took the nomination under protest, and thereby missed a chance for immortality as the only man ever to refuse a formal Presidential nomination by one of the major parties.

Horatio Seymour is described by Chauncey M. Depew as " an elegant and accomplished gentleman, with a high-bred manner which never unbent, and he was always faultlessly dressed.   He looked the ideal of an aristocrat, and yet he was and continued to be until his death the idol of the Democracy." [59]   A description by a more recent writer pictures him as " six feet tall and of handsome features with perfect figure." [60]

There were several reasons why Seymour was widely considered for the Democratic nomination.   His irreproachable private life, his financial integrity, and his high social position contributed to public confidence in him.   If nominated and elected, he would be able to act with authority and independence, for he was popular among the Democrats of all sections, and had fewer party enemies than any other leader of national prominence.[61]   As governor of New York he had show administrative talents of a high order.   It is

[59] Depew, *Speeches, 1896-1902*, p. 105.   In Alexander, *Political History of New York*, vol. iii, p. 111, note.

[60] A. J. Wall, *Sketch of the Life of Horatio Seymour* (New York, 1929), p. 62.

[61] Alexander, *op. cit.*, vol. iii, p. 208.

not too much to say that Seymour merited the name of statesman to a greater degree than any other Democrat of his time since the death of Douglas.

On the other hand, as a party candidate in New York he had consistently run behind his ticket, and had been defeated three out of the five times he was a candidate for governor. He had never held national office, and though his whole political career had been identified with New York, his name was not associated with any outstanding measures of state policy.[62]   He was unjustly connected with the New York draft riots of 1863.   For that reason, and because his record as a Democrat was entirely regular, he did not attract Conservative Republicans.   This Seymour probably realized.

At an early date Seymour let it be known that he was not a candidate.   On November 11, 1867, he wrote to the editor of the Oneida *Democratic Union* that for personal reasons he was not and could not be a candidate.[63]   What the reasons were is uncertain.   His health was not robust, and the strain incident to a campaign may have given him pause. Rumours arose that the ill health involved was a hereditary tendency to insanity.   This report apparently first appeared in print in the Cincinnati *West and South* for March 14, 1868.   After Seymour's nomination in July the statement that there was insanity in his family was widely circulated by the Republican press.

Another equally fantastic reason was assigned for his refusal to become the nominee.   It was reported that in 1864, while Governor, he had been in treasonable communication with Confederates in Canada, and that he realized this fact in the hands of the Republicans would defeat him.   This report first appeared in the Ohio *State Journal* some time in

[62] Alexander, *op. cit.*, vol. iii, p. 208.

[63] *Public Record of Seymour*, pp. 338-339.

March.[64] Seymour considered it serious enough to demand an answer. On March 28 he wrote from Utica denying the story as absurd. " I never had any confidential correspondence with Messrs. Clay and Holcombe [Confederate Commissioners in Canada]. I do not know them. If I ever, at any time, wrote to either of them, it must have been some merely formal matter of which I have not the slightest recollection." [65]

A more reasonable explanation for Seymour's hesitancy is that he felt that an unswerving Democrat would not have as good a chance of election as a Conservative. This is indicated by his support of Chase.[66] The Chicago *Republican* said that he advocated Chase's nomination as he thought there was no chance for himself.[67]

But in spite of his letter of November 11, his friends continued to urge him, and on January 2 a meeting of Democratic leaders in Albany made an effort to induce him to run.[68] George L. Miller, a relative of Seymour and editor of the Omaha *Herald,* wrote William Cassidy of the Albany *Argus* that Seymour was powerful all through the West, except in Ohio and Kentucky, and was a strong second to Pendleton in even those States. Miller wanted to know if Seymour would accept if nominated.[69] Cassidy sent this letter to Seymour on January 15, with a copy of his reply that " New York would send a delegation that would be unanimous for Seymour whenever the other States de-

[64] Date unknown. New York *Herald*, April 1, Utica *Observer*, March 30, 1868 from New York *Sun.*

[65] Utica *Observer*, March 28, 1868. Addressee not given.

[66] New York *Times*, August 18, 1879. Typescript copy in New York Historical Society Library, *Seymour Papers*, box 1.

[67] June 10, 1868.

[68] Washington *Express*, January 4, from New York *Express*, January 3, 1868.

[69] *Seymour Papers*, Albany.

manded him." [70]   Such letters exasperated Seymour, and on January 22 he wrote again, to a "citizen of Onandago County": "I assure you that I am not a candidate for the office of President. In my letter [of November 11] I said what I meant; and I am annoyed to find it looked upon by some as a strategic movement. I am very much gratified that my friends are willing to support me for the office of President—as much pleased as if I wished that office." [71] The Albany *Argus* refused to take this as closing the matter, stating its belief that every Democrat in New York was ready to protest against Seymour's decision.

Tilden's correspondence at the time also shows a disposition among many Democrats to reject Seymour's disclaimers. Bigler wrote him that at the bottom of all the sentiment for Hancock "as far as civilians are concerned, is the feeling and purpose [for Seymour] I expressed to you." [72]   On March 7 Francis Kernan, later United States Senator, wrote to Tilden that Seymour's health was all right. As Kernan believed Seymour was the best man for the canvass, he hoped the New York delegation would be composed of men friendly to his nomination. [73]   Another correspondent, writing from the Comptroller's office at Albany on May 25, thought Seymour should have permitted his name to be used or else some other man should have been agreed upon, in order to head off Pendleton. [74]

Most important of all, on June 25, Pendleton wrote to Washington McLean of Cincinnati endorsing Seymour. "I would rather trust him than myself with the delicate

[70] *Ibid.*

[71] Albany *Argus*, February 3, 1868. Also *Public Record of Horatio Seymour*, p. 339.

[72] *Tilden Letters*, vol. i, pp. 220-221.

[73] *Ibid.*, pp. 222-223.

[74] *Ibid.*, pp. 231. W. F. Allen.

duties of the next four years," he stated. " You know I am sincere . . . I am ready—anxious—to give up the nomination to anybody who can get one single vote more than myself." [75] This letter was written for use among the delegates to the National Convention, and indicates that the Pendleton forces planned to effect the nomination of Seymour, to keep our Hendricks or Chase, in the event that Pendleton himself was unable to secure a nomination. But the fact that Seymour was acceptable to Pendleton under any condition calls attention to the almost complete lack of animosities existing around his name in Democratic circles. Such opposition as existed came chiefly from the West, because he was considered a " hard money " man, and too much in sympathy with the Eastern financial interests. The Cincinnati *West and South* stated as early as February 29 that Seymour's nomination was a foregone conclusion, for was not August Belmont " our master, as well as master of the situation? "

Seymour boldly stated his opposition to the " Ohio Idea " in a speech before the Democratic Convention at Albany on March 11.[76] His entire record placed him in opposition to any such scheme. His western friends felt that if he would be willing to modify his position on the financial issue he would make the triumph of the party in the West much easier. One such friend asked him to bridge over the greenback question so that it would remain an issue in the West, " leaving you of the East free to tide over it as best you can." [77] While Seymour ran for President on a platform with a greenback plank, he did not pretend to be a convert to the " Ohio Idea " during the campaign. Seymour's popularity in the Middle West, in spite of his opposition to

[75] New York *World*, July 10, 1868.

[76] *Public Record*, pp. 309-322.

[77] *Seymour Papers*, Albany, George L. Miller, Omaha, May 17, 1868.

the Greenback craze, is indicated by the fact that in November he polled 45% of the total vote in the five States of Ohio, Indiana, Illinois, Michigan and Wisconsin.[78] His western strength was relatively greater than the Eastern strength of any Western Democrat.

The belief was widely held that the New York leaders retained the intention of nominating Seymour, and that Seymour was a party to the scheme. Gideon Welles states in his diary that the demonstration for Chase in New York was not sincere. " It is New York party management and means Seymour." Welles looked upon Seymour as " subtle, artful and not always sincere." He had " a ring of special admirers, or cronies, who think much of management, a merry taint." He thought Seymour meant to be nominated.[79]

The New York *Herald,* on May 25, reported a rumor that New York party leaders planned to nominate Seymour in order to carry New York in November, regardless of the result in Ohio and the West. The New York *World* reported on June 29 that Seymour's address at the Cooper Union on June 25 had created some doubt in the minds of the politicians, some claiming that he was a candidate, and others insisting that he was not, and did not desire the nomination. The New York *Tribune* thought the Cooper Union speech was a bid for the nomination for by rallying the Democrats on the Reconstruction Acts as the issue, it killed off Chase, and by opposing repudiation, it sought to dispose of Pendleton.[80]

But Seymour remained adamant in his refusal to allow his name to be used, notwithstanding the various reports of intrigue, plots and secret purposes. On July 2, two days

[78] *American Annual Cyclopedia,* 1868, *passim.*

[79] Vol. iii, p. 379, June 6, 1868; p. 381, June 10, 1868.

[80] June 26, 1868.

before the Convention opened, the New York delegation held a meeting to decide on a common basis of action. No candidate was settled upon, but it was decided not to present Seymour's name " for the simple reason that he positively declines to be a candidate." Seymour stated that what he had said before, from a sense of duty, he must now repeat from a sense of honor. His name must not be pressed by his friends.[81]

5. MINOR CANDIDATES

Among the more interesting minor candidacies were those of Admiral David G. Farragut, Gen. William T. Sherman and Charles Francis Adams. These gentlemen realized the absurdity of mentioning them for the Democratic nomination, and gave no countenance to the talk in their behalf. The fact that they were seriously mentioned by active party workers and by important newspapers is an illustration of the chaotic condition into which Democratic leadership had fallen.

Farragut's name was suggested to Chairman Belmont of the Democratic National Committee on March 12.[82] Two days later the New York *Herald* published an editorial entitled, " The Next Presidency and the Democracy—Admiral Farragut their only chance." The *Herald* continued its advocacy for a month or more, and called for his nomination either by summary proclamation of the National Committee or by the National Convention, to be promptly assembled for the purpose.[83] Evidence that the Farragut suggestion was seriously considered by a few men is indicated by Gideon Welles' correspondence [84] and by a letter to Seymour, from

[81] New York *World*, July 3, 1868.

[82] *Letter*, March 15, in *Herald*, March 18, 1868.

[83] New York *Herald*, March 20, April 4, 13, 1868.

[84] *Letter*, John R. Donehov, April 6, 1868, *Welles Papers*, Library of Congress, vol. 64.

van Buren on May 1, stating that "the preferences for
Farragut here are more numerous and among more thoughtful men than I had at first supposed."[85]   On May 25 Tilden
was asked by William F. Allen of Ohio, "Has Farragut
been heard from and what of him? I am for a fight to
win."[86]   But the movement for Farragut's nomination made
little real headway, for he sternly refused to be considered.
When he was approached he peremptorily refused the use of
his name, and said, in substance "that he had already
reached a far higher position than he had ever dared to
hope for, and higher he thought than his merits deserved."
The Admiral's name was not mentioned in the Democratic
National Convention, nor did he take any part in the
campaign.

The short-lived movement for Farragut's nomination was
obviously inspired by a desire to select a candidate whose
popularity would offset the popular sentiment for Grant. The
same feeling accounted for the overtures which were made
to General Sherman by certain Democrats.   In February,
1868, during the Stanton controversy, President Johnson
attempted unsuccessfully to get Sherman to come to Washington,[87] possibly with the object of getting his support in
place of that of Grant.   About the same time the New
York *Herald* reported that the President had put forward
General Sherman as a Democratic candidate.[88]

On May first Senator Sherman was informed that a
number of prominent Democrats, including Tilden, desired
his brother's nomination, and that he could receive it by

[85] *Seymour Papers*, New York Historical Society Library, box 4.

[86] *Tilden Letters*, vol. i, p. 231.

[87] Telegram, Johnson to Sherman, February 19, 1868. *Johnson Papers*,
Library of Congress, vol. 132.

[88] February 17, 1868.

acclamation, if he would say that he would not decline.[89]
The General received a number of letters voicing the same
sentiment, in June,[90] to which his reply was a positive declination to consider the nomination.[91] This ended the matter,
and his name was not mentioned in the National Convention.
Sherman was eager for Grant's election, although he did not
expect to campaign actively for him.[92]

Even more fantastic than the proposals to nominate Farragut and Sherman was the suggestion of Charles Francis
Adams. At this time Adams was completing his service as
Minister to England, and he remained abroad until after
the Democratic Convention. Although it was known that
he was out of sympathy with the Radical Republicans he
gave no evidence that he would accept a Democratic
nomination.

On May first the New York *Times* paired Adams with
Hancock as the two towards whom Democratic sentiment
was drifting, and the Chicago *Republican* on May 6 stated
that he might well be " the coming man " for the Democrats,
although the *Republican* later reported that the idea of his
nomination seemed to have been abandoned. The Democratic Boston *Post* advocated Adams and Hancock or
Hancock and Adams as the Democratic ticket. The New
York *World* on July 3 reported Adams supporters among
the national convention delegates from Massachusetts, New
Hampshire and Vermont. However, he received no votes
in the Convention.

Many other names were mentioned for the Democratic

[89] James H. van Alen to John Sherman, May 1, 1868, *John Sherman
Papers*, Library of Congress, vol. 126.

[90] *W. T. Sherman Papers*, Library of Congress, vol. 23.

[91] *Ibid.*, to S. S. Hayes, Chicago, June 25, 1868.

[92] To Mrs. Sherman, June 7, 1868. *Home Letters*, p. 376; to Grant,
June 24, 1868, *W. T. Sherman Papers*, Library of Congress, vol. 23.

nomination.   Among the more prominent was Connecticut's
" favorite son," Governor James E. English.   The English
movement was given some importance by his reelection as
Governor in April 1868.   However, on April 20 he discouraged the suggestion by writing Judge George M. Curtis
that he could not consent to the use of his name for either
position on the ticket.   He wished only to work for what
he thought the best interest of the whole country.[93]   In
spite of this his State delegation placed him before the Convention, and he received nineteen votes on the twenty-first
roll call.[94]   Another man supported by his State for the
nomination was Senator James R. Doolittle, of Wisconsin,
a former Republican but at this time a member of the Democratic Congressional Committee.[95]

[93] New York *Herald*, June 15, 1868.

[94] *Official Proceedings.*

[95] *National Intelligencer*, May 27, 1868.

CHAPTER VIII

THE DEMOCRATIC NATIONAL CONVENTION

I. PRELIMINARIES

THE National Democratic Convention met in New York at noon, July 4, in the newly-completed Tammany Hall on 14th Street, near Union Square. The weather was exceptionally hot, " as hot as weather can well be. Too hot for the warm work on hand here," as Chief Justice Chase was informed by his daughter Kate.[1] Elaborate preparations had been made for the gathering. Triumphal arches of evergreen, flags and bunting were thrown across 14th Street, bearing portraits of Jefferson and Jackson. Inside the hall, an elaborate chandelier, 24 feet high and 18 feet in circumference, with 320 gas jets, was the outstanding feature.

Delegates began to arrive in the city a week before the opening, and various hotels were assigned as officials' headquarters. Besides the State delegations, a number of clubs were present in strength. From the capital came the Young Men's Democratic Associations of Washington, and the Soldiers and Sailors Convention held at the same time was responsible for the presence of the Soldiers and Sailors Democratic Association. A delegation of German Americans was present, and the Keystone Club of Philadelphia was well represented. Chase's Committee of One Hundred, from

[1] July 5, 1868, *Chase Papers*, Historical Society of Pennsylvania Library.

Philadelphia, determined upon by the meeting on June 10, was on hand to work for their favorite.[2]   Among the groups attracting most attention was the "Pendleton Escort," some 350 men who were present to shout for Gentleman George. About 3 o'clock on the afternoon of July 2 the Escort, preceded by a squad of police and a band, paraded two by two, clad in linen dusters and linen hats, wearing badges fashioned in the likeness of a greenback, and bearing a banner with the inscription: "The People demand of the United States payment of the bonds in greenbacks and equal taxation. One currency for all. Pendleton the People's nominee. Convention ratify their choice."[3]   The *Nation* called the " Escort " a disappointment, as Pendleton's journals " had led us to expect a multitudinous and fierce host, capable of overawing even the Democracy of this metropolis."[4]

The few days preceding the opening were used by the various delegations for organization meetings. Friends of various candidates scurried about trying to gain promises of support for their candidate. Some of the delegations were already committed. Thus Ohio, Illinois, Kansas, Minnesota, Kentucky, Delaware, Iowa, West Virginia, Nebraska, Oregon, and Indiana were pledged to Pendleton, Wisconsin and Rhode Island to Doolittle, Tennessee and Alabama to Andrew Johnson, Louisiana and Mississippi to Hancock, New Jersey to Joel Parker, Pennsylvania to Asa Packer, and Connecticut to English. The chief hope of those seeking votes from these States was to obtain support for their candidate as second choice.

Among the most important of the delegation meetings held before the Convention were those of New York. On

[2] New York *World*, July 1, 1868, for description of preparations.

[3] New York *Times*, July 3, 1868, Rhodes, *United States*, vol. vi, p. 164, speaks of their arriving on July 3.

[4] July 9, 1868.

July 1 a preliminary meeting, under the chairmanship of Tilden, took no action in regard to candidates,[5] but a meeting on July 2 decided to accede to Seymour's wishes and not present him to the Convention. The presentation of Sanford E. Church was desired by a large portion of the delegation,[6] and he was later nominated by Tilden. This sentiment for Church was based on no expectation that he would be chosen but on a desire to withhold the vote of the State until the strength of the leading candidates had been developed.

Tammany Hall had been completed just in time for the Convention. One hour before it met the Tammany Society, with its Grand Sachem, Mayor John T. Hoffman, took possession and dedicated the Hall to Democracy. Judge Albert Cardozo read the Declaration of Independence.[7] A military pageant and parade, participated in by the members of the Soldiers and Sailors Convention then meeting in the city, was held in the forenoon of the 4th, and fireworks were displayed that night.[8]

The delegates represented all phases of the Democracy of the day, from such courtly Eastern aristocrats as Belmont and Seymour to the " great unwashed " of the backwoods. Samuel Bowles, of the Springfield *Republican,* reported that the Convention represented a contest within the party, " between the exponents of a new era and the exponents of the copperheadism of the war . . . between in a certain sense the men of honor and culture and growth, and men of brutality and ignorant instinct and course passion." [9] Union Generals were present, together with their late foes. But the great names of ten years before were not on the rolls.

[5] New York *World,* July 2, 1868.

[6] *Ibid.,* July 3, 1868.

[7] Breen, *Thirty Years of New York Politics* (New York, 1899), p. 167.

[8] *Ibid.,* p. 168.

[9] Merriam, *Bowles,* vol. ii, p. 40.

For the most part these leaders of a vanished age had died or gone into retirement.   Nevertheless, Bayard of Delaware, Preston of Kentucky, Blair of Maryland, and Chestnut of South Carolina recalled the bygone days of party glory.

The delegates [10] had 317 votes, each State having the same as in the Electoral College, but there were at least two delegates for each vote so that 781 were accredited, including those from the District of Columbia and Colorado, without votes.   The delegation of each State was twice its vote, except that Florida had 23 present to cast its three votes, Virginia 22 present to cast ten votes, and South Carolina 23 present to cast six votes.   Arkansas sent A. H. Garland, of " ex-parte Garland " fame.   Delaware sent James A. Bayard; John B. Gordon of Georgia was present; Indiana had Daniel W. Voorhees.   Iowa sent General A. C. Dodge; Kentucky, Generals William Preston and S. B. Buckner; Missouri, Col. James O. Brodhead.

The New York delegation was rich in names associated with the party's history.   Among them were Seymour, Tilden, Church, S. S. Cox, August Belmont, "Boss" Tweed, A. Oakey Hall, later Mayor; and Peter B. Sweeney, of Tweed's organization.

North Carolina sent Zebulon B. Vane.   The Ohio delegation contained General George W. McCook, Vallandingham, and Senator Thurman.   Pennsylvania's representatives included former Governor William Bigler, and Heister Clymer.   Rhode Island's list included Amasa Sprague, brother of Senator Sprague.   Tennessee sent General N. B. Forrest, Edmund Cooper, friend of President Johnson, and T. A. R. Nelson of Johnson's defense counsel.   The temporary President of the Convention, Henry L. Palmer, was among the Wisconsin delegates.

The position of the Southern delegates generally was

[10] List of delegates in *Official Proceedings*, pp. 31-40.

peculiar. They realized they were tainted with rebellion in many Northern minds, and that it would not be politically expedient for them to take too active a part, or to have too much to say, in the work of the Convention. The Chicago *Times* wished that General Lee had been included among those who received the heartfelt welcome of the Northern Democracy. " The people would rise up to do Lee reverence." [11] The presence of the ex-Confederates, as well as such copperheads as Vallandigham of Ohio, offered the Republicans an opportunity to " wave the bloody shirt " which they did not miss. The Union Republican Congressional Committee published a seven-page leaflet listing, with comments, the former " rebels and copperheads." [12]

2. THE SOLDIERS' CONVENTION

The military atmosphere in the Convention was by no means an unrelieved gray, however. The Soldiers' and Sailors' Convention, in session in New York at the same time, provided an array of Union Generals to give their blessing to the Democracy.

This meeting of military men opposed to Grant was an offshoot of a similar convention held in Cleveland in September 1866, to support the President. A committee chosen by this earlier body, and headed by Gen. Gordon Granger, had decided in April to hold the service men's gathering at the same time as the National Convention.[13] A call for the election of delegates was issued on June 15, signed by Gen. H. W. Slocum of New York.[14] A possible connection between this call and the New York managers of the national gathering is seen in a letter from S. E. Church to Tilden,

[11] In Chicago *Republican*, July 9, 1868.

[12] Washington, 1868.

[13] Utica *Observer*, April 29, 1868, New York *Herald*, April 30, 1868.

[14] New York *World*, June 15, 1868.

on June 10.   Church asked about the proposal that military
men be represented on July 4.   If it was to be provided for,
he suggested that a call from some New York military men
be issued at once.   He also wondered in whose interest the
military gathering was called.[15]

The meeting was held at Cooper Union, at 11 A. M., on
July 4.   Thirty-one states and territories were represented.
Among the officers present were Major Generals James B.
Steedman of Ohio, Henry W. Slocum of New York,
William Morgan of Ohio, John A. McClernand of Illinois,
William B. Franklin of Connecticut, and Thomas Ewing,
Jr., of Kansas.   The prevailing choice was Hancock, with
General Frank Blair a good second.[16]   McClernand was
selected as temporary chairman and Franklin as permanent
chairman.   The political nature of the gathering was emphasized in speeches.   General McQuade frankly acknowledged
that they came to New York to cooperate with the Democratic party in putting down Radicalism.[17]   Moreover, a
resolution to commit the gathering to a blanket endorsement
of the platform and candidates of the Democratic Convention was adopted by a vote of 287 to 7.[18]

Following the adoption of the platform by the National
Convention of July 7, the Soldiers Convention responded
with a resolution of approval which was read in the National
Convention on the afternoon of the same day.[19]   The
Soldiers Convention held a series of meetings until July 8,
when it adjourned.[20]   Its National Executive Committee sat

[15] *Tilden Letters*, vol. i, pp. 228-229.

[16] New York *World*, July 2, 1869, July 3, 1868.

[17] *Ibid.*, July 5, 1868.

[18] New York *Evening Express*, July 7, 1868. In *Seymour Papers*,
New York Historical Society Library, box 1.

[19] *Official Proceedings*, p. 102.

[20] New York *Evening Express*, July 8, 1868; New York *World*, July
9, 1868.

on July 8 to plan their campaign for Hancock.[21]   A letter
was sent to the Chairman of the Kansas delegation in the
National Convention, which announced their preference for
Hancock.   If an Eastern civilian should be nominated, then
the soldiers' first choice for the second place on the ticket
was General Ewing of Kansas, and if a Western civilian
should be named for President, then they wanted General
Franklin of Connecticut.   A similar letter was sent to the
chairman of the New England delegations.   Both were read
in the National Convention on July 9, when nominations
were being made for Vice-President.[22]

Judged by results, the Soldiers and Sailors Convention was
a failure, although it came near to success when on July 8
General Hancock almost received the nomination.   If he
had been chosen, the movement represented by this gathering would have added greatly to his strength, and might
possibly have given the election a different result.

3. THE CONVENTION IN SESSION

When the Democratic Convention was called together at
noon on July 4, Chairman August Belmont made a short
speech.   He paid a graceful compliment to Tammany, the
Convention's hosts, and welcomed the delegates to New
York city, " the bulwark of Democracy," and to the Empire
State which claimed the right to lead the Democracy to
victory in November.   He eulogised the Democratic party
of the past, and attacked the Radicals for their reconstruction policy with its accompanying taxes, debt, and " vicious
irredeemable, and depreciated currency."   The country he
said, looked to the Democratic party to " stay this tide of
disorganization, violence, and despotism."   The motto of
the Democracy, in its march to victory should be " The

[21] New York *World*, July 9, 1868.
[22] *Official Proceedings*, pp. 164-166.

Union, the Constitution and the Laws." [23]   These remarks, which were enthusiastically greeted, including the mention of greenbacks let the Convention know where their national chairman stood on the currency question.   The *Nation* thought this speech " artful." [24]   Forceful it certainly was, but " artful " is hardly the word to describe a speech which referred directly to the chief bone of contention, the financial issue.   The New York *Herald* said that judging by Belmont's speech the Democrats " have not heard of any great changes . . . but twaddle on in their arrogant self-sufficiency and artful blindness as if the nation had not four years ago repudiated them absolutely for these very vices." [25] Did the *Herald* expect the National Chairman to approve McClellan's defeat and welcome all that followed in the years of peace after Appomattox?

Belmont presented Henry L. Palmer, of Wisconsin, a temporary chairman, who spoke briefly, congratulating the Convention because once more every State was represented. The quadrennial burr under the Democratic blanket made itself known almost immediately.   It was necessary for the Convention to adopt temporary rules, to serve until a committee on permanent organization had been selected and had reported.   After some dispute, the rules of the last Democratic Convention were adopted.   The New York *World* thought this a blow to Pendleton's supporters, who wanted the two-thirds rule dropped, as it made it more likely that the permanent rules to be adopted later would include the same feature.[26]

The call of the National Committee for the Convention,

---

[23] *Official Proceedings*, pp. 3-5.   References to *Proceedings* omitted hereafter.

[24] July 9, 1868.

[25] July 6, 1868.

[26] July 4, 1868.

dated February 22, was then read. It set the representation of each State at double the number of Senators and Representatives at the last (1860) apportionment. It is interesting to note that the vote of each State was one-half this total, or the same as that in the Electoral College. Thus each delegate had one-half a vote, in some cases (Florida, Virginia and South Carolina) less than one-half. The right of the territorial delegates to vote was denied by a vote of 184 to 106. Following this, provision was made for the appointment, by each State delegation, of one member each for the Committees on Permanent Organization, Credentials and Resolutions.

A motion to adjourn until 7 P. M., was lost, and a motion to adjourn until Monday at 10 A.M., was carried. The New York *World* stated that the adjournment until Monday, eliminating the evening session, was looked upon as a blow to Pendleton, as the anti-Pendleton men wanted time to unite.[27] Henry C. Murphy of New York, was the Chairman of the important Committee on Resolutions, which included C. C. Langdon of Alabama, James A. Bayard of Delaware, William Preston of Kentucky, Edmund Cooper of Tennessee and Wade Hampton of South Carolina. The Southern leaders were thus well represented in this body.

After the opening prayer on the second day of the Convention (Monday, July 6), the privilege of seats on the floor of the Convention was extended to the members of the National Workingmen's Association, which had been in session on July 3. They had adopted resolutions endorsing the greenback idea and the replacement of national bank notes by greenbacks.[28] The report of the Committee on Organization was then submitted. Horatio Seymour was named as President, and a Vice-President and Secretary

[27] July 4, 1868.
[28] *American Annual Cyclopedia*, 1868, p. 549.

were chosen from each State. Among the Vice-Presidents was General Thomas L. Price, of Missouri, who later took the Chair on occasions when Seymour was absent and William M. Tweed of New York. The Committee recommended the adoption of the rules of the last Democratic National Convention. The question was raised whether the two-thirds rule, which applied to nominations for President and Vice-President, meant two-thirds of those voting or two-thirds of the total membership. The chair held that question not in order, and the report of the Committee on Organization was accepted. Seymour then took the chair, advancing up the main aisle amid cheers, arm-in-arm with Governor Bigler of Pennsylvania and Governor Hammond of South Carolina.

The choice of Seymour, who had presided over the Convention of 1864, did not come as a surprise. The Springfield *Republican* gave as a reason for his election the desire of Ohio to get him out of the way, and of New York to keep him out of harm's way.[29]

Upon taking the chair, Seymour delivered an address which was enthusiastically received. He attacked the Republican platform and nominee, paying particular attention to the financial issue. " In one resolution they 'denounce all forms of repudiation as a national crime.' Then why did they put upon the statute books of the nation laws which invite the citizens who borrow coin to force their creditors to take debased paper. . . . If Repudiation is a national crime, is it no crime to invite all the citizens of this country thus to repudiate their individual promises? " He condemned the Republicans for maintaining the supremacy of the military over the civil powers in the Southern States. He likened 1868 with 1789, and called on the party to lead the country out of the difficulties caused by a war, as in 1789 Washing-

[29] July 7, 1868.

ton led the way. It will be noted that his speech offered no comfort to the Western greenbackers, and that there was not a sentence in it not in harmony with the expressed views of Chief Justice Chase.

Following the reading of resolutions from a Special Council of the National Labor Union, which advocated the payment of bonds in greenbacks, the substitution of legal tenders for national banknotes, and equal taxation of all forms of property, the Convention demonstrated the courtesy of the time by enjoying " a very hearty laugh at the folly of a deluded champion of the Womans' Rights movement, who, having failed of any encouragement from the Republicans brought her cause to Tammany Hall." [30] The "folly" mentioned was a memorial from the Womans' Suffrage Association. When announced, the delegates called " Read it! Read it!" with loud cheers and laughter. The Memorial was then read and referred to the Committee on Credentials. It was issued by the Central Committee of the Womans' Suffrage Association, and was signed by Susan B. Anthony. The memorial asked the Democratic party to endorse the principle of woman suffrage. The party had maintained its power, in the years before the war, by broadening the suffrage to include all white men. By granting it to women a renewed lease of power would be achieved. " The party that takes this onward step will reap its just reward."

Resolutions praising President Johnson, congratulating him on his aquittal, and approving his amnesty proclamation were read amid cheers and referred to the resolutions committee. Shortly afterward a resolution requesting the President to issue a proclamation of amnesty without exceptions was adopted. A resolution pledging the delegates in advance to support the nominees of the Convention was unanimously adopted. It was then decided, by a vote of 189½

[30] Woods, in *North American Review*, vol. 107, p. 448.

to 90½, to act on the platform prior to the nomination of candidates.   Governor Bigler of Pennsylvania was the only delegate to speak against this proposal.   The result may be counted as a Western, or Pendleton victory.   The controversial issue before the Convention was the financial one. Some States not to be counted upon for Pendleton, due to the local situations, were in favor of a greenback plank in the platform.   The chance of placing their views in the platform would be much stronger if done before the nomination of a candidate, should a hard money man be selected. For the same reason, the inclusion of a greenback plank might be considered a deterrent to the nomination of a hard money candidate.

Following the reading and reference of resolutions on bond payment and Congressional reconstruction, the Convention adjourned until 4 P. M., the same day.   The afternoon session was devoted to the Soldiers and Sailors Convention.   A Committee from that convention was received, headed by Generals Franklin and Slocum, and an address of the Soldiers and Sailors was read attacking the Radicals for their Southern policy and offering the cooperation of the veterans with the Democracy.   Following this General Thomas Ewing, Jr., spoke, announcing the determination of the veterans to unite with the Democrats, in defense of the principles of the Constitution.

When the Convention met for its third day of deliberation President Seymour was "slightly indisposed," though present, and the chair was taken by Gen. Thomas L. Price of Missouri.

Resolutions prepared by Alexander H. Stephens, Vice-President of the Confederacy, were read amid applause, and referred to the Committee on Resolutions.   Stephens upheld the principles of State Rights, including State control of suffrage, and advanced the thesis that the subjugation of the Southern States, after the war, involved the destruction of the Union. As soon as his resolutions were read, W. A. Richardson, Chairman of the Illinois delegation, moved that hereafter all resolutions be submitted to the Committee on Resolutions without reading in the Convention. If this were not done, Richardson feared that the Convention might " commit some mistake, or endorse some doctrine that we can not defend upon the stump, and ought not to defend." No action was taken on this subject. Resolutions from a California Labor Convention were read. They denounced negro rule and pronounced the eight-hour day a Democratic measure.

The Committee on Resolutions at this point presented the platform of the party. Following its unanimous adoption there was a scene of the wildest enthusiasm, delegates and spectators rose en masse; cheer upon cheer resounded through the building, and the demonstration continued for several minutes.

4. THE PLATFORM

During May and June various rumours of the form the platform was to take had been in the air. For example, some New York leaders were reported on May 15 as having decided to submit to the Convention an out-and-out Chase platform, hard money, qualified negro suffrage and all.[31] The position of the National Democratic Committee was reported to be confined to three planks—opposition to Congress, opposition to negro supremacy, and in favor of the reconstruction of the national unity.[32] Reports were abroad that the Democrats proposed to ignore the suffrage and financial issues. On June 18 the New York *World* declared that neither negro suffrage nor the financial issue were major

[31] Philadelphia *Evening Star*, May 15, 1868.
[32] *States and Union* in *West and South*, June 6, 1868.

issues. The important questions were: (1) The defence
of the powers of the President against Congress, (2) the
defence of the authority of the Supreme Court against Congress, and (3) the rights of the States. The New York
Herald (June 22) agreed that negro suffrage was not a
" living question," but included the financial issue with the
restoration of civil authority over the military and the vindication of the Constitution, as the vital questions. The
Memphis *Avalanche* on June 16 gave a platform " the
Northern Democracy intend to inscribe on their banners, in
letters of fire " which stressed State rights; opposition to
banking and tariff monopolies, and restoration of economy
in government, but did not include the reconstruction acts,
the suffrage issue or the greenback issue. The New York
Tribune on the day the Convention opened reported that a
number of Eastern party leaders would attempt to put
through a non-committal platform ignoring the war, slavery,
President Johnson, States Rights, universal suffrage, and
reconstruction and repudiation—" in short keep very shady
and lie very low generally." The *Evening Post* on July 6
also reported that a platform had been circulated among the
delegates, and was likely to be adopted, which expressed no
preferences on the financial and suffrage issues. " The
design is very plain. The Democratic party cannot be
united on any declaration of principles."

The platform as adopted by the Convention was in three
parts.[33] An introductory paragraph recognizing slavery and
secession as closed questions was followed by eight planks in
which the party demanded: 1. Immediate restoration of all
the States to their rights in the Union, and of civil government to the American people. 2. Amnesty for all past
political offenses and the regulation of suffrage in the States
by their citizens. 3. Rapid payment of the public debt—

[33] *Official Proceedings*, pp. 58-60.

" where the obligations of the government do not expressly state upon their face, or the law under which they were issued does not provide, that they shall be paid in coin, they ought, in right and justice, to be paid in the lawful money of the United States." [34]   4. Equal taxation of all property including government bonds.   5. One currency for the government and all the people, including the laborer and the bondholder.   6. Economy in administration.   Reduction of the Army and Navy.   Abolition of the Freedman's Bureau and all agencies for negro supremacy.   Equalization and lessening of the burden of taxation, increase in the credit of the government and restoration of the greenbacks to a gold basis.   Repeal of all laws for enrolling State militia in the national forces in time of peace.   " A tariff for revenue upon foreign imports, such as will afford incidental protections to domestic manufacturers, and as well, without impairing revenue, impose the least burden upon, and best promote and encourage the great industrial interests of the country." [35]   7. An end to corruption and useless offices in the government.   Restoration to the executive and judicial departments of their rightful authority and independence, and the subordination of the military to the civil power, in order to end the usurpations of Congress.   8. Equal rights and protection for naturalized and native-born American citizens at home and abroad.   The maintenance of the rights of naturalized citizens against the doctrine of immutable allegiance. [36]

Then followed eight supplementary paragraphs in which the Radical party was arraigned for its oppression, tyranny and disregard of rights.   The pledge to carry on the war

[34] This in answer to the denunciation of all forms of repudiation in the Republican platform.

[35] The Republican platform did not mention the tariff.

[36] The Republican platform continued a similar provision.

exclusively for the preservation of the Union had been repeatedly violated. Instead of restoring the Union, it had dissolved it, subjecting ten States, in time of peace to military despotism and negro supremacy. Rights guaranteed in the first ten amendments had been nullified. It had curtailed the rights of the Supreme Court and subjected the Chief Justice to atrocious calumnies for refusing to prostitute his office to support the false and partisan charges against the President. The corruption of the Radical party had been unprecedented. The President had been deprived of the power to appoint his own cabinet officers. Any attempt by Congress to interfere with State regulation of suffrage was denounced as an unconstitutional usurpation, tending to centralism and despotism.[37] "We regard the reconstruction acts, so-called, of Congress, as such an usurpation, and unconstitutional, revolutionary and void."

The party maintained that the soldiers and sailors of the Union, who vanquished a gallant and determined foe, must be ever gratefully remembered and all guarantees given to them must be carried out. It advocated the granting, or selling at a minimum price, of the public lands only to actual occupants. The lands should not be granted in aid of public improvements, but when necessary, the proceeds of their sale.[38] The party stated that the President, for his resistance to Congressional aggressions, was entitled to the gratitude of the American people;[39] and it appealed to Conservative Republicans to unite with it in the struggle for the liberties of the people.

[37] The Republican platform advocated negro suffrage in the South. State control of suffrage in the North.

[38] *American Annual Cyclopedia*, 1868, p. 549. This resolution agreed with one passed by a Convention of the "National Labor Union" held in New York City on July 3.

[39] The Republican platform condemned President Johnson's course and approved his impeachment.

A careful reading of this document brings out a number of evasions. The platform did not mention negro suffrage, or universal suffrage, but was content to dispose of the subjest by asserting it a matter for State control. The opportunity to attack the inconsistent position of the Republican platform on this issue was passed up, possible out of deference to those Conservatives who wished to see the negroes of the South granted the ballot.

An account of the drafting of the suffrage plank was given by Wade Hampton in a speech at Charleston on July 24. He said that when the proposal was made to declare that the right of suffrage belonged to the States, he "asked that they would declare that these questions [of suffrage] belonged to the States under their Constitutions up to the year 1865." The Northern members pointed out to Hampton that such a statement might cause offense at the North. As they pledged themselves to do everything in their power to restore the Constitution and relieve the Southern States, Hampton withdrew his suggestion and accepted the suffrage plank as it appeared in the platform. This was offered by Bayard of Delaware. Hampton then suggested that the reconstruction acts be denounced as unconstitutional, which was done.[40]

The platform approved the greenback theory in all its glory, but no reference was made to the national banks and their notes, objects of attack by Pendleton and his supporters. A revenue tariff was proposed, but not one burdensome to American industry. The lion's tail was given a flip for the benefit of the Fenians who had gotten into trouble in Canada and Great Britain. The President was praised, as was fitting, probably as much to keep him in support of the party in the campaign as for any other reason. The ex-Confederates were complimented as " gallant and deter-

[40] *McPherson Scrap Book*, Library of Congress, vol. vi, pp. 1, 12.

mined," while the Union veterans were tempted with a pledge to keep the Treasury doors open for them.

The denunciation of the reconstruction acts was in a manner to please the Southern Democrats and was the point most vigorously attacked during the campaign. The heart of the platform was in this statement, together with the espousal of the greenback theory. The platform, as a whole represented the victory of the Western and out-and-out Democratic forces in the party as opposed to the Northern and conservative forces. Although an appeal was made to Conservatives to support the platform, and the ticket named upon it, the document was one likely to drive them back to the Republican fold.

When the greenback plank, which was " unexpectedly positive and emphatic," was read the acclaim of the delegates " drowned any hope of reversing the judgment of the Committee which might have been entertained by Mr. Belmont and the handful with him in the Convention who as financial experts believed in national honesty as the best and cheapest policy." [41]   The reconstruction plank, later so vehemently attacked by the Republicans, was given additional force by the nomination of Blair for Vice-President, whose known views, in the " Brodhead letter " were so pronounced. The Republican press charged that Wade Hampton of South Carolina had written this plank.[42]

Comment on the platform by historians has been uniform in criticism of it as weak. Burgess wrote that there is no question that with its paper money doctrine, and its hostility to reconstruction and universal suffrage, it " was a shaky foundation for any party to attempt to stand upon at that

[41] Woods, in *North American Review*, vol. 107, p. 449.

[42] Chicago *Republican*, August 1, 1868, *Independent*, August 6, 1868, New York *Tribune*, October 17, 19, 22, 1868, New York *Times*, September 21, 1868.

juncture." [43]　Minor, in his history of the Democratic party, calls the financial plank a departure from the old Jeffersonian and Jacksonian hard-money principles.　It was a surrender to expediency.[44]　Alexander Johnston in Lalor's Cyclopedia speaks of both the financial plank and the opposition to universal suffrage as being departures from party doctrine.[45] Perry Belmont, son of Chairman August Belmont, has termed the financial plank one "leading to inevitable defeat." [46]

Contemporary comment was on the whole, equally adverse, even from such journals as the New York *Herald*.　The *Herald* labeled the platform, like that of the Republicans, platitude and buncombe, and thought that either platform would do for either party.　The New York *Times* called it a strange mixture of fact and fancy, of courage and duplicity, of propositions both muddy and lucid.　The Chicago *Republican* considered it "a mass of catch phrases," distinguished by "the flexibility of its meaning," some parts of which were stolen from the Republican platform, and botched in the stealing.　The *Nation* thought it "nearly as good as Republicans could have desired."　There is "not a vestige even of the old Democratic party in the platform." [47]　On July 16 the *Nation* thought there might have been expected a platform including planks calling for free trade, compensation for slaves, and hard money, but none of these things are in the platform adopted.　John A. Logan of Illinois in Congress called it a "whited sepulchre, full of

[43] *Reconstruction and the Constitution* (New York, 1902), p. 209.

[44] P. 301.

[45] Vol. i, p. 784.

[46] *National Isolation an Illusion* (New York, 1925), p. 253.

[47] New York *Herald*, New York *Times*, Chicago *Republican*, *Nation*, July 9, 1868.

dead men's bones." [48]   Gideon Welles was disappointed.[49] The Democratic Almanac for 1869 written after the election, referred to the platform as a milk and water, noncommittal affair, not calculated to call out the enthusiasm of the Democracy.[50]

The Greenback plank was generally considered the most outspoken part of the platform.   The effect of the adoption of this provision on the securities exchange was recorded by the New York *Herald* " as favorable to an advance in rail- way stocks and a decline in government securities." [51]   The *Journal of Commerce* reported the market " a little sensi- tive " on the subject of the platform, and the financial portions of it " have had, on the whole, an unfavorable effect upon the street.   The proposition to tax the government bonds is not new." [52]   The financial writer in the New York *World* (July 8) wrote that the platform, " when read and understood today, has given strength and firmness to all government bonds " as the Democratic policy, if carried into effect would advance the price of bonds to par in gold before maturity.[53]

The platform denunciation of the Reconstruction Acts as unconstitutional called forth angry comments, and led Re- publican commentators to charge that the Southern and copperhead elements in the party were dominant.   The New York *Times* said the Democrats required " another great defeat to bring it to its senses.   The copperhead element is rampant, insolent and defiant." [54]   This element showed

[48] *Pamphlet,* " Principles of the Democratic Party " (1868).

[49] *Diary,* vol. iii, p. 397, July 8, 1868.

[50] P. 40.

[51] In New York *Evening Express,* July 8, 1868.

[52] *Ibid.,* July 9, 1868.

[53] New York *Evening Express,* July 9, 1868.

[54] July 9, 1868.

itself "unabashed and even triumphant," according to Godkin.[55] The Springfield *Republican* stated that Vallandigham, the "Jonah of the party from 1861 to 1866," was still its prophet, still its ruler, still its grave-digger. He has been its leading spirit . . . and he leads it again to defeat." [56]

After the adoption of the platform, Seymour resumed the chair and had the two-thirds rule, as adopted by the Conventions of 1860 and 1864, read in order that action could be taken by the Convention on any desired interpretation of the rule. The rule was "that two-thirds of all the votes cast shall be required to nominate a candidate for President and Vice-President of the United States." Chairman Clymer of the Committee on Organization announced that it had interpreted the two-thirds rule to mean two-thirds of the total vote, or electoral college, not merely two-thirds of those voting on a particular roll call. The Chair stated this was the construction placed on it by previous conventions, and that the entire vote was 317, two-thirds of which, or 212, was necessary for a nomination. Thus simply, and with little debate, the two-thirds rule was retained.

Before the roll of the States was called for nominations, it was ruled by the Chair that nominations might be made at any time after the nominating roll call had been completed, and while the balloting was under way.

5. THE BALLOTING

The first name presented to the Convention was that of James E. English of Connecticut.

Illinois, Indiana, Iowa, Nebraska, Oregon and West Virginia when called made no nomination, but stated their purpose to vote for Pendleton. Hancock was presented by

[55] July 8, 1868, London *Daily News*, July 21, 1868.
[56] July 8, 1868.

the majority of the Maine delegation, and Pendleton by the minority.   Joel Parker of New Jersey was next placed before the Convention by Henry S. Little of that State. Sanford E. Church of New York was presented by Tilden. Pendleton, already referred to by several delegations, was presented again, in one sentence, by General George W. McCook of Ohio.   The longest nominating speech was made for Asa Packer of Pennsylvania by George W. Woodward of that State.   President Johnson was named by Thomas A. R. Nelson of Tennessee.   The majority of the Wisconsin delegation nominated Senator James R. Doolittle.

The first ballot gave Pendleton the highest number, 105 votes, and President Johnson second with 65, all but four from Southern States.   This was the highest he received. Three individuals received votes in this first ballot who had not been formally presented to the Convention, Reverdy Johnson 8½, Hendricks, 2½, Blair ½.   Applause punctuated the roll call whenever popular names were mentioned. On the second ballot the changes of Texas from Johnson to Hancock, and Virginia from Johnson to Blair were the most significant.   Johnson's vote declined to 52.   On succeeding ballots he continued to decline.   After the second vote, a motion to recess until 4 P. M. was lost.   Pennsylvania retired for consultation.   Upon their return at the close of the third ballot, their vote was cast for Asa Packer, as before. Pendleton went from 104 to 119½ and Hancock gained 5 to 45½ on this vote.

On the fourth roll call North Carolina cast its nine votes for Seymour.   This was greeted with delight by the galleries, " but the delegates took the matter very coolly." Seymour was not then in the chair, but came forward and declared he was not a candidate, and could not with honor accept a nomination if offered, " which I do not expect." [57]

[57] Woods, in *North American Review*, vol. 107, pp. 455-456.

Vermont had given its five votes for Hendricks on the third and fourth ballots. Efforts to adjourn and to take a recess were defeated before the fifth ballot, but a recess was taken after that. During this recess an effort was made to permit the territories to appoint a member each to the national committee. Tilden objected, saying that it was enough that New York, with 4,000,000 population, should be neutralized by the small States of the Union. The question was disposed of by providing that members should be appointed by the local organization of any Territory becoming a State during the next four years. Little change was recorded in the sixth ballot, taken after the recess, and it became apparent the Convention was approaching a deadlock. A resolution from the Soldiers and Sailors Convention, approving the platform adopted, was then read, following which an effort to take a recess until 6 P. M. was lost, 218 to 99, and an adjournment until 10 o'clock the next morning was carried by the same vote.

Before the balloting was resumed on the fourth day, an Indiana delegate, speaking for a majority of his State delegation, formally presented the name of Thomas A. Hendricks. A representative of the minority announced their purpose to continue to vote for Pendleton while there remained a reasonable hope for his nomination. On the next ballot (the seventh) Indiana voted 9½ for Hendricks, 3½ for Pendleton. This brought Hendricks from 30 to 39½ votes. Pendleton also increased his vote, from 122½ to 137½, most of his gain coming from the South. It was pointed out by an observer that the Southern delegates, having obtained the platform they wanted, followed the Northern lead as regards candidates, and after the first few ballots gave their votes wherever the Northern vote was heaviest.[58]

Following the seventh ballot, New York retired for con-

[58] Woods, *op. cit.*, p. 455.

sultation, and on the eighth her vote was changed from
Church, where it had been from the beginning, to Hendricks. Evidently the defection in the Indiana delegation
gave New York her cue—now was the time to get behind
Hendricks and eliminate Pendleton. On the eighth ballot
Hendricks went to 75 and Pendleton reaches his highest vote,
156½, his increase still coming largely from the South at
the expense of Hancock. But on the 9th roll call Hendricks
went to 80½, Pendleton dropped to 144 and Hancock re-
covered to 34½. From the ninth to the twelfth ballots
Pendleton continued around 145, while Hendricks climbed to
89, with Hancock remaining about 30.

When California was called on the twelfth ballot one-half
vote was cast for S. P. Chase. It was greeted by applause.[59]
McClellan also received one vote from Tennessee. On the
thirteenth ballot California's half vote for Chase was not
added to. Franklin Pierce received the compliment of one
vote from Tennessee. On the next two ballots Pendleton
declined to 129½ and Hendricks to 82½, while Hancock
climbed to 79½ when Pennsylvania transferred to him her
26 votes. This started a swing to Hancock, his vote rising
to 144½ on the eighteenth ballot, which was the highest he
received. Hendricks held his own, receiving 87 on the
eighteenth. Pendleton declined to 56½ on that ballot, and
was evidently out of the running.

Illinois, which had voted as a unit for Pendleton for the
first sixteen ballots, on the seventeenth divided her vote between Pendleton, 8½, and Hendricks, 7. On the eighteenth
it was cast again as a unit, this time for Hendricks. A delegate named Maloney objected, insisting that his vote be given
for Pendleton. He moved that each delegate be permitted
to vote as he saw fit, but the Chair ruled that the manner in
which the votes of each delegation was to be cast was a

59 Woods, op. cit., p. 457.

matter to be decided by the delegation. Maloney objected to this ruling and the controversy showed signs of becoming general when an adjournment, moved by a Massachusetts delegate, was declared carried.

George L. Miller, a Nebraska delegate, twenty-five years later, published a description of Seymour's course at this point as presiding officer. The proceedings were very stormy and " Seymour saw that it was time for enraged men to cool off, and for passions to be allayed, and he determined to have them take a day for it." When he put the question on adjournment, the affirmative was very light, and the negative thunderous. Nevertheless, he brought the gavel down with a thump, declared the adjournment carried, and left the Chair to avoid argument.[60]

The Washington *National Republican* during the campaign attributed the adjournment to the deliberate purpose of the Tammany Democracy to slaughter Hancock, and Seymour " did the deed himself by declaring the Convention adjourned against the fact." [61]

At the time of the adjournment Hancock had nearly one-half of the votes, and a landslide in his direction seems to have been underway. His nomination was taken for granted—a cannon in front of the Convention Hall was fired in his honor, and some papers announced his selection.[62] His nomination probably would have taken place on the nineteenth or twentieth ballot if adjournment had not occurred. But his strength declined during the night and within four more ballots Hendricks had reached and passed him.[63]

[60] March 4, 1893, *Seymour Papers*, New York Historical Society Library, box 3.

[61] September 4, 1868.

[62] Woods, *op. cit.*, p. 459.

[63] Mrs. Hancock, in her *Reminiscences* (p. 136) states that Hancock

At the beginning of the fifth day Col. James C. Brodhead of Missouri presented the name of F. P. Blair, who received 13½ votes on the next ballot. This did not start a rally for him, however, for on the twentieth ballot he received 13, and on the twenty-first none. Delegate A. H. Rose of California then proposed the name of Justice Stephen J. Field of the United States Supreme Court, a Californian. He received but 15 votes (with only 3 of California's 5) on the nineteenth ballot, 9 in the twentieth and 8 in the twenty-first. Of greater significance was the withdrawal of Pendleton's name by Vallandigham of Ohio. Vallindigham read the letter written by Pendleton to Washington McLean on July 2 in which he stated that, if at any time a name should be suggested which in the opinion of McLean would be stronger before the country than his, he asks that his name be withdrawn.[64] The reading of this letter was accompanied by great cheering. Vallandigham explained that McLean thought it should have been read early in the afternoon of the preceding day, but that it was not done because the Ohio delegation insisted on continuing their support of Pendleton.

The nineteenth and twentieth ballots proceeded with little change, except that Hancock gained slightly from 134½ to 142½, and Hendricks made a substantial gain from 107½ to 121, accounted for by the addition of Arkansas and New Jersey.

Hendricks continued to gain on the twenty-first reaching 132, most of his increase coming from the South. It began to look as if a Hendricks landslide was in the making. The twenty-second roll call then started. It was a see-saw between Hendricks and Hancock with New York still voting

received offers of support during the night of July 8, if he would make certain commitments. He declined.

[64] New York *World*, July 10, 1868.

for Hendricks—until Ohio was reached. At this point occurred the resubmission of Seymour's name which resulted in his selection, against his will, when the New York leaders joined in the demand for his candidacy.[65]

The roll of the States was then called for the purpose of placing names before the Convention for Vice-President. But when it had reached California, a motion to take a recess was made. The delegates immediately voted to leave their seats for one hour for the purpose of consultation before proceeding with the nomination of a vice-presidential candidate.

The first name presented upon reassembling was that of General John A. McClernand of Illinois by an Illinois delegate. General McClernand, who was present, withdrew his name. " This compliment is far above any merit which I possess." The next name was that of General Asa C. Dodge of Iowa by an Iowa delegate. He was followed by General Charles W. Blair of Kansas who named Thomas Ewing, Jr., of Kansas. He submitted the letter from the Soldiers and Sailors Convention advocating the nomination of General Ewing if an Eastern civilian were chosen for the Presidency. General Frank P. Blair was then named by Preston of Kentucky. The nomination was seconded by another former Confederate, General James B. Steadman of Louisiana. Maryland, Minnesota, Missouri, Nebraska, North Carolina, Oregon, Pennsylvania and Nevada each endorsed the name of Frank P. Blair. When South Carolina was called, Wade Hampton arose and stated that the soldiers of the South accept the right hand of friendship extended to them by the soldiers of the North. He also then seconded Blair. Tennessee, Virginia and finally New York fell into line, and the names of General Ewing and A. C. Dodge were withdrawn by the delegates who presented them.

[65] The details of this last ballot are given in the chapter on Convention Strategy. See *infra*, pp. 240-242.

The roll call followed, and Blair was unanimously chosen. An interesting fact was that the chairman of the Tennessee and Texas delegations introduced ex-Confederates to cast the votes of their States. Gen. N. B. Forrest of Tennessee thanked the Convention for the kind and courteous treatment accorded to the Southern delegates. General Smith of Texas promised that the Southern soldiers would give General Blair as warm a reception "when we come to vote" as they did on the field of battle.

Only routine work remained to be done after this. The usual resolutions thanking New York city, the officers of the Convention, etc., were adopted, including one offered by Vallandigham sympathizing with the working men of the United States. A Committee of one from each State was then named to inform the nominees of their selection.

Finally, just before adjournment, Francis Kernan of New York offered a resolution tendering the thanks of the Convention to Chief Justice Chase for " the justice, dignity, and impartiality with which he presided over the Court of Impeachment." With this last gesture of conciliation towards the politically ignored Chief Justice, the Convention adjourned sine die " amid enthusiastic cheers for Seymour and Blair."

CHAPTER IX

CONVENTION STRATEGY — CHASE, PENDLETON AND SEYMOUR

I. THE FAILURE OF THE CHIEF JUSTICE

THE preceding account leaves out of the picture the devious paths followed by the friends of the most prominent candidates in their efforts to secure the prize. Not least active were the supporters of the nomination of Salmon P. Chase. When the Democratic delegates began to gather in New York about the first of July, they found the supporters of Chase numerous and active. His daughter, Kate Chase Sprague, was tireless in her efforts for her father's nomination. Her residence at 94 Fifth Avenue was a center of Chase agitation. Hardly less prominent was John D. van Buren, friend of Chase and Seymour, at whose home at 11 West Ninth Street, Seymour stayed during the Convention.[1] In a sense van Buren was Chase's New York chief of staff. The Committee of One Hundred named by the Chase meeting in Philadelphia on June 10 gathered in full strength on July 3, with headquarters at the Chandler House on 14th Street across from Tammany Hall. Its Chairman was Frederick P. Stanton of Maryland, with Frederick A. Aiken of Washington as Secretary. Kate wrote her father on July 7 warning him against Aiken's intemperance and indiscretions; but Ben: Perley Poore refers to Aiken as Mrs. Sprague's master of ceremonies, who introduced the delegates from the rural districts to her.[2]

[1] Seymour to G. L. Miller, June 20, 1868. *Seymour Papers*, New York Historical Society Library.

[2] Poore, *Perley's Reminiscences*, vol. ii, p. 238.

Other friends were present and active, including two war-time New York office holders under Chase, Hiram Barney, ex-collector of the Port, and John C. Cisco, former Assistant Treasurer. Chase's resignation as Secretary of the Treasury grew out of the appointment of Cisco's successor.[3] Another friend, James C. Kennedy, was in the inner circle and wrote letters to Chase on Kate's stationery. Hamilton Smith, whose friendship with Chase dated back to 1833, was on hand.[4] The active workers among the delegates were not numerous but at least two must be named: Peter B. Sweeney of New York City whose support was obtained by van Buren, and Amasa Sprague of Rhode Island, brother-in-law of Kate. Chase's secretary, J. W. Schuckers, was also present and worked in close cooperation with Kate. Horatio Seymour was accounted a supporter of the Chief Justice and he worked for him with his own delegation, but his position as President of the Convention prevented him from conducting a more active canvass for votes. One observer wrote " of the few Democratic leaders who from the first worked openly for Chase, Seymour was the chief." [5]

No sooner had Chase's friends began to gather in New York than he wrote another indiscreet letter to Alexander Long and immediately repented of it. Long had written to him asking him to pledge himself to support the nominee of the Convention, if the choice fell on another. Chase replied on July 1 that he would vote with satisfaction for any " of the distinguished citizens whose names have been prominently mentioned in connection with the office " unless, contrary to his expectations, a platform should be adopted to which he could not agree. He insisted that he was not

[3] June 29, 1864, Schuckers, op. cit., p. 243.

[4] Warden, op. cit., p. 219.

[5] Woods, in North American Review, vol. 107, p. 454.

solicitous for the Presidency, though he would not decline to accept a nomination if offered.[6]

Realizing his indiscretion, Chase wrote confidentially to van Buren on the same day that, in reply to Long's request, he had written a letter that "goes a little too far." He asked van Buren to protect him from any mistakes. He had told Long not to use his letter, nor some notes of a conversation to the same effect, except after full consulation with van Buren and with his advice and consent. He asks van Buren to see Long and allow no mistake to be made. "Suppress both . . . if either seems to make any pledge which you . . . think I ought not to make." [7]

That Chase was wise in regretting his letter to Long is indicated by reports in the press of July 3 that a pledge from Chase to support the candidates of the Convention had been received by his friends.[8] Long had probably permitted a leak. Not content with this, Long on July 3 sent Chase a letter enclosing a statement pledging support to the nominees of the Convention, and asking Chase to approve it. This pledge was to be given to the one who would present Chase's name to the Convention. Long stated that a frequent question among the Pendleton men was "Will Mr. Chase abide by the result of the Convention and vote for the nominees?" He suggested that Chase could give the statement any date he preferred and "should it become necessary to make it public the letter to which it is intended to be a reply we can prepare." [9] It was not a very comfortable position for the Chief Justice to be in—writing a pre-dated reply to a fictitious letter, and the matter handled by a petty politician with an unsavory war reputation.

[6] Warden, *op. cit.*, p. 704; Historical Society Pennsylvania Library, *Chase Papers*, Box 15.

[7] *Ibid.* Also cited by Oberholtzer, *United States*, vol. ii, p. 177n.

[8] New York *World*, New York *Evening Post*.

[9] *Chase Papers*, Historical Society Pennsylvania Library.

Chase replied on July 4, sending Long a letter to be used if really necessary, but not without van Buren's advice and consent. He warns Long that "my self respect is worth more to me than fifty Presidencies." [10] On July 5 Chase wrote van Buren telling of his correspondence with Long and adding, " I have never in my life bound myself to the support of unknown candidates upon an unknown platform." [11] There is something pathetic about this last statement, after his indiscretion of July 1 had led Long to the suggestion of his letter of July 3.

Chase's blanket endorsement of the nominee, before the nomination was made, continued to find its way into the press. The New York correspondent of the Cincinnati *Gazette* stated that Chase had said in a private letter, " an extract of which is being used in the Convention " that if he voted at all in November, it was probable that " I shall vote the Democratic ticket, no matter what the result as to the nomination." [12] The Washington correspondent of the New York *World* reported that on July 8 Chase told him that the Convention had so many excellent men to choose from, that it could hardly fail to select a good nominee.[13]

In this situation Chase's desire to get in the good graces of the Convention led him to write and possibly say things that he could hardly have believed. It is one of the least pleasant incidents of Chase's efforts to receive the nomination. As shown by his letters to van Buren, the Chief Justice realized that he had gone too far, and endeavored to retrace his steps, but his original statment got out, and he was placed in an awkward position. Most of this took place

[10] Warden, *op. cit.*, pp. 704-705. Also notation by Chase on letter from Long.

[11] Schuckers, *op. cit.*, p. 589.

[12] In Washington *Express*, July 11, 1868.

[13] New York *World*, July 10, 1868.

before the nominating ballots were commenced. Evidence that Chase really contemplated voting for the yet unselected nominee is contained in a letter to Kate on July 7. " If I vote at all this fall, I shall in all probability vote for the Democratic nominee." [14] But this is not a blanket endorsement of any possible nominee.

Chase's lack of self-control seemed to be chronic; for we find him taking peculiar ground on the platform which, as we have seen, was hardly a Chase document.

Chase's " fifteen point " platform published on July 1, although satisfactory to Seymour and others, did not meet general approval, and suggestions were made that he modify it. After the Convention had adjourned, the Springfield *Republican* remarked that Chase's platform " was accepted formally by the leaders; but subsequently he was called upon to modify his views somewhat which he refused to do, and he was therefore dropped and a new platform made." [15]

On July 3 Chase wrote van Buren with some care, telling of changes in the fifteen-point platform which had been suggested to him and stating his own position. He asked van Buren and Craig to consult together and act as his interpreters. The fourth, or suffrage plank in the Chase platform pledged the party to accept universal suffrage in principle, although leaving its application to the States. It had been suggested that instead of accepting universal suffrage in principle, the phrase " a broad basis of suffrage is a democratic principle " be substituted. Chase told van Buren that the change would be indifferent to him personally, but it would probably cost thousands of votes by the openings it would give to attack. His name could only be of service " by forming a link of connection between the body of the Democratic Party as now constituted, and a multitude of

[14] *Chase Papers*, Historical Society Pennsylvania Library, Box 15.
[15] July 14, 1868.

Republicans ready to accept democratic ideas on all other questions."

In the Chase platform no direct mention is made of the governments established in the South under the Reconstruction Acts, although the necessity for the War amendments is recognized. (Paragraph three.) It was suggested to Chase that he hold the Reconstruction Acts unconstitutional "as the Supreme Court would probably decide." In commenting on this Chase forecasted accurately the result to be expected if a declaration of their unconstitutionality be adopted by the Democratic party. It would be a mistake. As Chief Justice, he certainly would not oppose what the Court might decide, but no such decision had yet been made. As Chief Justice, he might have added, he should not be asked to state an opinion prior to it becoming the basis of a cause before the Court.[16]

It would have been well for the Democrats had they heeded his advice, even though not nominating its author. It is hard to understand why Chase did not repudiate the Democratic platform when submitted by its committee.

The activity of Kate Chase Sprague was such that Chase felt it necessary to warn her. " I am afraid, my darling, that you are acting too much the politician. Have a care. Don't do or say anything which may not be proclaimed from the house tops." [17]   One may wonder if Chase would have been willing for his correspondence with Long to be proclaimed from the house tops. The New York correspondent of the Cincinnati *Enquirer* (July 4) reported that Kate's activities had been especially active among the New York leaders, and that she had had long interviews with Belmont and Tilden, who had promised to help the Chase movement.[18]

[16] Historical Society of Pennsylvania Library, *Chase Papers.*

[17] July 7, 1868. Historical Society of Pennsylvania Library, Box 15.

[18] In New York *Herald*, July 7, 1868.

Kate wrote to her father on July 2, " I am glad that you are not going to be greatly disappointed if the nomination is not for you. I should like to see this bright jewel added to your crown of earthly distinction. I believe it will be. But we can live and be very happy and just as proud of you without it. Will the country do as well?" [19] On July 5 she reported, " There is a noble work being done here by your friends, and whether success or failure crown their efforts, they will be always proud to have had a hand in it." [20] On the 7th, before the balloting had started, she exclaimed in a letter to her father: " There are snares and pitfalls everywhere. Oh, if the Convention would only have the courage to do right." [21] The failure of Chase was probably as great a disappointment to her as to him. As Chase was a widower, she, his eldest daughter, would have been his hostess and " the first lady of the land." Chase was credited by the Washington correspondent of the Louisville *Courier Journal,* with desiring the nomination as much for her sake as for his own. He constantly spoke of her in connection with his ambition; when he thought his nomination certain, he rejoiced most of all for Kate; and when his failure was made known to him, his first words were, " Does Mrs. Sprague know? And how does she bear it?" [22]

The Chase Executive Committee of one hundred chose a subcommittee of nine to draft an address to the Convention,[23] which was duly published on the morning of July 4. Meanwhile a number of Treasury employees, like John Wilson of Illinois, Third Auditor of the Treasury, and former Treasury employees like Cisco and Barney of New

[19] Historical Society of Pennsylvania Library, Box 15.

[20] *Ibid.*

[21] *Ibid.*

[22] Warden, *op. cit.,* p. 705, from *National Intelligencer.*

[23] New York *Herald,* July 4, 1868.

York, were laboring valiantly for Chase. The Chase Committee continued to work for their man after July 4. The New York *Evening Express* for July 7 said they were still holding sessions in the Chandler House headquarters and that they were still hopeful of success.

In spite of the size of this organization, the most promising work for Chase was done by the small " inner circle " of friends which included van Buren, Kate, Cisco, Smith and Kennedy. Assistance was lent them by a little group of some twenty negroes who advanced the argument that Chase would carry more Southern negro votes than any other candidate.[24] Truly this was astonishing. Negroes, within four years of the Civil War, attempting to influence the action of a Democrat National Convention! At the same time, Henry Ward Beecher, pastor of the Brooklyn Plymouth Church and former Abolitionist, placed one foot gingerly in the Chase bandwagon only to withdraw it hastily. On Sunday, July 5, the day after the opening of the Convention, he preached two political sermons. In the morning he spoke against military candidates, and in the evening against the greenback idea.[25] In the first sermon he said: " It remains to be seen if the Americans will . . . rise to rewarding men of moral principle, of Christian character, of civil capacity. . . ."[26] This sounded very much like an endorsement of Chase, and indeed, the two sermons were generally construed to this effect. Beecher found he had disturbed a hornet's nest. With his usual facility in changing sides, he then issued a denial.[27] Still another abolitionist,

[24] F. Powell to President Johnson, July 3, 1868. *Johnson Papers,* Library of Congress, vol. 141.

[25] Springfield *Republican,* July 7, 1868.

[26] Washington *Express,* July 8, 1868.

[27] Speech, July 10, 1868, New York *World,* July 13, 1868. Also Cincinnati *Commercial,* July 14, 1868.

this time an old friend of Chase, Gerrit Smith, was reported to have declared for his nomination, with Charles O'Conor of New York for Vice-President. A letter to this effect was said, on July 2, to be in the hands of the Chase men.[28] It is probable that this report was accurate, as Smith urged Chase to take the nomination if offered.[29]

But the Chase forces pinned their greatest hopes to the encouragement given them by Horatio Seymour. That Seymour was sincere in his advocacy of Chase's nomination seems well established. He had spoken in favor of the Chief Justice for some weeks before the meeting of the Convention. When he said in the Convention on July 7 that honor forbade him to be a candidate, he was probably thinking of his advocacy of Chase.

A caucus of the New York delegation, held on June 30 to make certain changes in the delegation, took no formal action as to candidates. But it was the general feeling among the majority that the delegation should cast their first vote for Seymour, who was to rise in his place, forbid the use of his name, and speak for Chase.[30] Two circumstances prevented the execution of any such plan—the subsequent decision of the delegation to vote for Sanford E. Church on the early ballots, and the selection of Seymour as presiding officer of the Convention. Van Buren wrote Chase on July 2 that " Everything looks well now for New York making you her candidate. I have had a talk with Peter B. Sweeney, who is the real man in New York, and worth more than Belmont, Tilden, Barlow, Marble and twenty more such. He is earnest in the matter and will do

---

[28] New York *Sun*, July 2, in Cincinnati *Commercial*, July 4.

[29] Chase to Smith, July 24, *Chase Papers*, Library of Congress, ser. 2, vol. iii; Chase to C. D. Cleveland, Oct. 14, Historical Society of Pennsylvania, Box 15.

[30] New York *Herald*, July 2, 1868.

all he can and that is a great deal. The city delegation except one man is all sure, and that one is Morrissey—so
Sweeney says." Tilden, van Buren reported, "is setting
back against you." [31] Kate wrote her father the same day:
"The point now is to select the man to be spokesman in the
convention. Governor Seymour, Mr. van Buren, insists
. . . is perfectly sincere in his intention under no circumstances to be a candidate." [32]

James C. Kennedy, also writing on Kate's stationery on
the afternoon of July 3, assured Chase that he had spent the
day with the New York delegates, and had talked with
Belmont, who was favorable. "I am satisfied you will be
nominated. . . . The trouble seems to be as to what the
New York delegation shall do, at first." Kennedy thought
the delegation would vote as a unit for Seymour on the
first ballot, and that Seymour would decline in Chase's favor.
"I cannot see how it's possible at this time to prevent your
nomination." [33]

But on July 4 the New York delegation decided to vote
for Church on the first ballot, or more. The poll of the
delegates was Church 38, Chase 10, Hendricks 8, Reverdy
Johnson 4, Pendleton 3, Judge Nelson (of the Supreme
Court) 2, and Seymour (who had declined) 1. [34]

Why did New York decide to support Church? He was
obviously not of Presidential calibre, and to run him against
Grant would have been absurd. One explanation is that the
delegates, desiring the nomination of Chase, realized that
the Pendleton supporters, who controlled over one-third of
the Convention, would block it at the outset, and even if not

[31] Historical Society of Pennsylvania Library, *Chase Papers*.

[32] *Ibid.*

[33] *Chase Papers*, Historical Society Pennsylvania Library.

[34] New York *World*, July 5, 1868. Also Philadelphia *Evening Star*,
July 8, 1868.

successful in blocking it, would be disgruntled if Chase or any other Easterner should be nominated before Pendleton had a chance to poll his maximum vote in the Convention. Therefore New York voted for a " favorite son " until Pendleton's strength had become dangerous. Then, in order to split the Pendleton forces, the New York delegates swung to Hendricks, a Western man, with the idea that after Pendleton and Hendricks had both been eliminated, they could head a drive for the nomination of her real choice,— Chase. A Republican observer wrote that the demonstration of New York in favor of Church " was without any sincere hope or purpose of bringing the Convention to his support, and was arranged to keep up with ulterior designs." [35]

After New York had decided to vote for Church in the early ballots, a note of uncertainty is found in Kate's report to her father. On July 5 she wrote: " Everything, as far as developed looked well—only New York—friends inside that close corporation say their action is cautious and those outside call it timid." [36]

On July 7 the *Herald* gave a different version of the New York situation. The New York leaders proposed to use Chase to circumvent Pendleton, and Seymour was the man to be chosen. " It would now appear that Seymour, satisfied that he has circumvented himself in this game, has generously withdrawn in favor of Church. . . . We suspect the cat is still hid in the meal." The next morning, however, the *Herald* professed to believe that New York would start the Chase movement in the Convention that day, and that it was to be supported by Pennsylvania, the South and the entire Eastern States. Welles in his diary for July 8 admitted he thought it likely that New York really meant to go

[35] Woods, *op. cit.*, p. 452.
[36] *Chase Papers*, Historical Society Pennsylvania Library.

for Chase, although "I can hardly believe it." [37] He had previously been convinced that New York intended all along to nominate Seymour.

On July 8 New York was voting for Hendricks. A meeting of the delegation was held on the morning of the 9th, and Seymour urged that it turn to Chase when the balloting was resumed that forenoon. He was opposed by Murphy of Brooklyn. The delegation voted 37 for Chase, 24 for Hendricks, and one for Pendleton. It was then agreed to present Chase's name as soon as the vote for Hendricks began to decline.[38] Samuel Ward wrote to Chase on July 10 that all Ohio votes had been secured for Chase, in support of New York.[39] Wisconsin, according to report, was to second New York in presenting Chase.[40] Long wrote Seymour, on July 14, that a Wisconsin delegate showed him a paper favoring Chase, and signed by more than twenty German editors then in New York, which was to have been read in the Convention after Wisconsin seconded New York's presentation of Chase. Massachusetts, Michigan, Tennessee, and Rhode Island were reported to be ready to follow New York and Wisconsin.[41] Other States said to be similarly inclined were Georgia, Maine and New Jersey.[42] A. E. Burr of Hartford wrote his friend Welles, on July 14 that when New York, on the morning of the 9th, voted to present Chase's name, the delegates already knew

[37] Vol. iii, p. 397.

[38] New York *Herald*, July 10, 1868 in *Stebbins*, op. cit., p. 343. New York *World*, July 10, 1868. *Herald* gives vote as 36 to 27. Also *American Annual Cyclopedia*, 1868, p. 749.

[39] *Chase Papers*, Library of Congress, vol. 100.

[40] New York *Evening Post*, August 26, 1868.

[41] Copy in *Chase Papers*, Historical Society Pennsylvania Library, Box 3.

[42] S. Ward to Chase, July 10, 1868. *Chase Papers*, Library of Congress, vol. 100.

about the proposal of Ohio to present Seymour, and knew
that the time to vote for Chase would never come.[43] That
this decision to turn to Chase was inspired by Seymour is
shown by an incident later related by van Buren. " The
night before the grand denouncement (or the night of July
8) Tilden sought me out at twelve at night and in a tone
of great irritation said ' What the devil does the Governor
man? '—' What about? ' said I. ' Why, he has been around
all the evening buttonholing the New York delegation one
by one, electioneering with them to go for Chase in the
morning.' I told him I did not know his meaning—he had
better ask Seymour himself." [44]

On the morning of the 9th, when Hendricks strength was
increasing, Vallandigham is said to have tried to induce
Tilden to let New York at once execute its stroke for
Chase; [45] but the fact that Hendricks did not weaken, combined with the fact that Tilden essentially disliked Chase,
caused the New York leader to refuse. Even so, the men
behind Chase cherished high hopes of an immediate swing to
him by both Ohio and New York.

But could Ohio really be counted upon to join New York
in nominating Chase? Here Chase's friends miscalculated.
The correspondent of the Cincinnati *Commercial* had some
inkling the day before (July 8) of what would actually
happen. He wrote his newspaper that when Pendleton was
forced out, Ohio would swing to Seymour. That is, the
majority of the Pendleton men would hasten to beat the
Chase game by presenting the eminent ex-governor of New
York. He reported, and it seems correctly, that in the even-

[43] *Welles Papers*, Library of Congress, vol. 65. Alexander, *op. cit.,*
vol. iii, p. 203 for statement this was true of Tilden.

[44] *Chase Papers*, Library of Congress, vol. 101, July 24, 1868.

[45] Alexander, *op. cit.*, vol. iii, p. 203; Rhodes, *op. cit.*, vol. vi, pp.
166-167.

ing of July 8 a stormy discussion in the Ohio delegation
resulted in the passage of a resolution that the delegates
would not, under any circumstances, support Chase, although
at least one stated that he preferred Chase to Hendricks.[46]
Vallandigham, who was supposed to be a Chase man, was
not present to vote on this resolution.   At a later date, Donn
Piatt declared that a single speech had swayed this meeting
of the delegation.   " A drunken harangue made by an eminent Democrat the night before the nomination lost him
[Chase] Ohio and just enough votes to insure defeat." [47]
The Democrat who thus denounced Chase to the Ohio delegation was apparently Henry Clay Dean of Iowa.[48]

The result was that in the crisis of the Convention, as we
shall see, the Ohio delegation did not swing with New York
to support Chase—who would probably have been nominated on the twenty-second ballot if it had done so.   It
swung instead to Seymour, and made a dramatic presentation
of his name.   If Ohio had but said the word, the correspondent of the Cincinnati *Commercial* lugubriously stated
in his review of the critical day, " Chase would have been
nominated in a whirlwind of enthusiasm." [49]   This is no
doubt true, though one competent observer did not think
so.   On September 9 van Buren wrote Chase that even if
Seymour had stood adamant in his refusal to listen to a
nomination, Chase's success was not certain; that many
delegates had told him that if Chase had been nominated " it would have produced an open and serious bolt
in the convention, and that it would *not* have been made
unanimous." [50]

[46] Cincinnati *Commercial*, July 9, 1868.

[47] *Memories*, p. 119.

[48] Cincinnati *West and South*, July 11, 1868.

[49] Cincinnati *Commercial*, July 10, 1868.

[50] *Chase Papers*, Historical Society Pennsylvania Library.

On September 23, van Buren wrote to Chase that he just had learned that if Seymour had persisted in his refusal to run, the Ohio men " had it all arranged to propose John T. Hoffman; what they wanted was to draw New York away from you. Hoffman would not have refused, and the city delegation, your strongest friends, would have been demoralized. I have this from a sure source, and I saw some things at the time which confirm it." [51]

The failure to bring Chase's name formally before the Convention was a part of the strategy of his supporters. As stated by van Buren early in June " Of course it will not do to put your name in the Convention to be fought over as competing with Pendleton or any other regular Democrat. It must be done by a degree of general assent." [52] On July 7 Chase wrote his daughter: " I think it will be much better not to have my name before the Convention at all unless it goes upon such a demand as will insure its acceptance by the necessary votes." [53] The *World* on July 8 remarked that Chase's friends " are credited with a good deal of discretion in not bringing his name prematurely before the Convention." He is more likely to succeed on July 9, than " if his claims had been urged today." If the plan for Seymour to present his name on the morning of the 9th had been carried out, it is possible that the stampede would have been for Chase instead of for Seymour. Vallandigham wrote on July 18: "As a matter of opinion, I believe that had New York withheld her vote for Mr. Hendricks, Judge Chase would have been nominated within an hour." [54] Chase himself believed that he would have been selected on the twenty-second or twenty-third ballot " if a

[51] *Ibid.*

[52] June 9, 1868. Historical Society Pennsylvania Library, *Chase Papers*.

[53] *Ibid.*, Box 15.

[54] In *National Intelligencer*, July 28, 1868.

portion of the Ohio and a portion of the New York delegations had not concerted the nomination of Seymour." He
understood that Georgia, Wisconsin, Rhode Island, Massachusetts, Maine and New Jersey were ready to fall in with
New York as soon as his nomination was presented. A
knowledge of this caused the Ohio delegation to act for
Seymour.[55]

As has been indicated, the sentiment in the Convention
itself, as shown by applause, was somewhat divided. He
was roundly cheered and also determinedly hissed on more
than one occasion. When the resolution offering him the
thanks of the convention was offered on Monday (July 6),
it became " the signal for a burst of enthusiasm almost without a paralled in Convention annals." The *World* predicted
that Chase would receive nine votes on the first ballot (three
each from Massachusetts, Rhode Island and North Carolina),[56] but his name did not appear in the balloting until the
twelfth roll call on July 8, when he received one-half a vote
from California, which was repeated on the 13th, 17th, 18th,
the 19th votes. This one-half vote, reported the *World,*
gave rise to excitement " greater than had before been produced at any stage of the proceedings." [57] An observer
records that it was greeted by applause as hearty as that
greeting the financial resolutions of the platform. " But
the Chase managers were not yet ready to press his name." [58]
Schuckers attributes the failure to take advantage of the enthusiasm caused by the one-half vote to " absence of an
organized movement among the delegates favorable to Mr.
Chase," with the result that " the golden opportunity " was

[55] To Gerrit Smith, July 24, 1868. *Chase Papers,* Library of Congress,
ser. 2, vol. iii. To Jay Cooke, July 11, 1868, *ibid.,* Letter Book 8.

[56] July 7, 1868.

[57] July 9, 1868.

[58] Woods, *op. cit.,* p. 457.

not improved.[59]   On the next to the last ballot, the twenty-
first, Chase received four votes from Massachusetts.   This
was greeted with both applause and hisses.   The Columbus
Crisis, whose editor was present at the Convention, considered these four votes for Chase a signal that the trap was
to be sprung for Chase.   Ohio prevented the jaws from
closing by her action on the next roll call.[60]   Considering
what happened on the twenty-second ballot, and the fact
that New York came *before* Ohio on the roll call, the twenty-
second was the place where Seymour, relinquishing the chair,
should have spoken for Chase on the floor, but Hendricks'
strength was increasing, and New York wished it to decline
before presenting Chase.

Thus ended what chance Chase ever had of being the
nominee.   It had at one time been a large chance.   The
opposition of one delegation only, Ohio, defeated him, and
even in that delegation he had a few friends.   Yet he received very little sympathy.   The Boston *Advertiser* quoted
Elijha Wright as saying, " It was a sad thing, that going
down to Jericho and falling among thieves; but poor Chief
Justice Chase, going down to the Dead Sea of Democracy,
has fallen among fools as well as thieves, and needs something strengthening for his head, as well as oil for the
wounds he is likely to get." [61]   The Chicago *Republican,*
July 10, in an editorial " Exit Chase," said " few have
descended more rapidly in public estimation than Chief
Justice Chase. . . . Dishonored, self-debauched, friendless,
he goes to his long home, an example of the calamitous, disgraceful consequences of political prostitution."   The *Independent* on July 16 said Chase " was on every man's tongue,
but in no man's heart. . . . He flew into and flew out of

[59] Schuckers, *op. cit.,* p. 565.

[60] In Cincinnati *Commercial,* July 27, 1868.

[61] *Ibid.,* July 11, 1868.

Tammany Hall like that cuckoo which Wordsworth declared to be not a substantial bird, but only a ' wandering voice.' "

Hart states that Chase's failure to receive the nomination was because he " was willing to swallow the Democracy, but not be swallowed by them "—he held out for universal suffrage.[62] But this is an inaccurate view of Chase's relations to the Democracy at this time. His statements about other candidates and the platform show that he came perilously near to being swallowed by the Democracy. As for universal suffrage, he was willing to yield even on that vital subject.

On July 10, with the Convention adjourned, Chase wrote van Buren in words strongly tinged by suspicion of Seymour's course. " Well, all is over. I shall sleep soundly, regretting the result only for the sake of friends and country. I was told that Seymour was for himself before the Convention met,—but would not believe it. I thought *you could not be* deceived and I knew you would not deceive." Chase asks for the return of his letters in which he referred to the platform, " I want them in Memoriam." [63] But he did not long maintain this suspicion of Seymour's sincerity. Later he wrote that " I do not hold Governor Seymour at all responsible for what occurred. I believe he was sincere throughout. He yielded where almost any man would have yielded. I had no claim either on him or the Convention." [64] " He simply yielded when almost any man would have yielded, but when his honor and duty required him not to yield." [65] Seymour himself, in a letter five years later, some months after Chase's death, declared that the failure

[62] Hart, *Chase*, p. 368.

[63] *Chase Papers*, Library of Congress, Letter Book 8.

[64] To Dr. John Paul, October 1, 1868, *Chase Papers*, Library of Congress, Letter Book 8.

[65] To W. B. Thomas, July 17, 1868, *ibid.*

of Chase to receive the nomination was due in part to the desire of the Convention to wind up its work, and New York had decided upon presenting Chase's name " unless it could secure the nomination of Mr. Hendricks. There would have been strong opposition to Mr. Chase at the outset, but I think in the end he would have been nominated. But time was needed to bring this about, and the delegates were impatient to return to their homes." [66]

It now remains to explain just how the favorite of the West, Pendleton, was defeated, and just what happened when Ohio turned from him to Seymour of New York.

2. PENDLETON'S FAILURE

Pendleton had come before the Convention with a better organization than any other candidate. His supporters had been actively at work for at least six months. Pendleton himself remained in Cincinnati, but a large group of friends were on hand to shout, argue and intrigue for him. They were outwardly very confident, and 168 votes were claimed for him—not counting any from the South; even some of his opponents conceded him 160. Actually the highest vote he received in the Convention was 156½ on the eighth ballot.

The two-thirds rule of the Democratic Convention was the greatest obstacle confronting Pendleton. The New York *Sun* for June 30 reported an attempted intrigue by which it was hoped this obstacle would be removed. On June 29 a group of New York City and Brooklyn leaders was told by Douglas Taylor, a supporter of Church from " up-state," that an offer, straight from Pendleton headquarters, had been made to give Church the support of the Pendleton men for the Vice-Presidential nomination, if he and his friends would bind themselves to aid in the repeal of the two-thirds rule. The *Sun* reported that in order to block this game

[66] Schuckers, *op. cit.*, p. 572.

the Church men decided to attempt again to get Seymour's permission to use his name.[67]

It appears that Pendleton's Ohio supporters were not satisfied with their delegation, and on July 5 six changes were made in order to obtain " men combining parliamentary experience, ability as public speakers and a hearty zeal for Pendleton." These changes placed Thurman, Vallandigham, George E. Pugh and two others on the delegation, and removed Washington McLean. Vallandigham, suspected, and to an extent rightly so, of being for Chase, was placed on the delegation in order to get him committed to Pendleton, and to appease him for his loss of the Senate seat to Thurman. His admission to the delegation caused some indignation. It was reported that certain Eastern delegates feared his presence in the Convention would hurt the party.[68]

On the first six ballots Pendleton increased from 105 to 122½. In the second day's balloting, his vote rose from 137½ to 156½ on the eighth roll call, and then declined to 107½ in the sixteenth and 56½ in the eighteenth. Thirty-three votes were cast for him from beginning to end without change—Ohio 21, Iowa 8, Oregon 3 and Massachusetts 1. The defection of Indiana on the seventh when Hendricks received 9½ of the State's 13 votes came at the time when Pendleton's strength was gaining rapidly. With the 9½ votes thus lost, Pendleton would have had 166 votes on the eighth ballot, or 7 more than a majority. While the two-thirds rule is not to be disregarded, it is possible that if Pendleton had received an actual majority, the enthusiasm would have started a stampede. Certainly the majority mark was held to be significant by the enemies of Hancock and Hendricks, for when those names were approaching a majority they were cut off, Hancock by an adjournment and Hendricks by the Seymour landslide.

[67] In Cincinnati *Commercial*, July 2, 1868.
[68] New York *Herald*, July 6, 1868; Cincinnati *Commercial*, July 6, 1868.

After the second day, July 8, the friends of Pendleton acknowledged that it was useless to press his name further, and were making arrangements to throw his remaining vote elsewhere. They were aided in this decision by the receipt of a telegram from Pendleton, requesting the withdrawal of his name.[69] On the next morning, before the balloting started, Vallandigham read the letter from Pendleton to McLean, dated before the Convention, authorising the withdrawal of his name, and stated that McLean thought it should have been read the day before. The charge was made by the New York *Herald* for July 16 that the Ohio delegation voted on the night of July 8 to continue to support Pendleton, and that after this decision was reached Vallandigham went into consultation with two New York delegates, with the result that on the morning of the 9th Pendleton's name was withdrawn and Seymour carried through with a rush. The *Herald* charged that those responsible, on the Ohio side, were Vallandigham, McCook, Pugh and Thurman. On July 18 Vallandigham replied to this story. He denied that the Ohio delegation, on the night of July 8, had decided to continue to support Pendleton. McLean announced that Pendleton's letter of withdrawal would be read in the morning, but the delegation did not decide whom they would support instead. In the morning the delegation met again, before the Convention, and although Hancock received a majority of the votes of the delegation, it was decided to cast one vote for Packer, which was done. Vallandigham denied his alleged meeting with two New York delegates. D. S. Alexander gives a story of a meeting of Ohio and New York representatives similar to that of the *Herald,* except that Vallandigham is not mentioned. He states that Tilden was the New Yorker who arranged the

[69] New York *World,* July 9, 1868.

plot, which was decided upon at a meeting at Delmonico's on the evening of July 8.[70]

Commenting on the result of the Convention, the *Independent* considered Pendleton the chief conqueror, for he dictated the platform, defeated his rivals and created the successful nominee, while at the same time he " put the Eastern Democracy under bonds to do him a good turn in the future," with the result that his chances for 1872 were very bright.[71]

3. SEYMOUR'S NOMINATION

It now remains to explain just how Seymour obtained the nomination. We have seen that in spite of his repeated statements that he was not a candidate, reports had continued to circulate that New York intended his nomination. The New York *Sun* had early stated that Seymour's zealous friends " are arranging a programme by which they hope to secure his nomination." Hendricks, it said, was to be offered the second place on the ticket as a bid for Western support.[72] Although the New York delegation, on July 2 had agreed to accept Seymour's declination,[73] the rumours continued. It was reported by the New York *Tribune* on July 4 that a group of Eastern leaders proposed to nominate Seymour on a non-committal platform, which would omit all reference to such controversial issues as greenbacks and universal suffrage. A. E. Burr, editor of the Hartford *Times,* wrote Gideon Welles from New York on July 4 that Seymour " declines every day for the purpose of securing the nomination, and the New York delegation mean to secure it for him if possible. I think they will fail." [74]

[70] Vol. iii, p. 203.
[71] July 16, 1868.
[72] In *National Intelligencer,* June 30, 1868.
[73] New York *World,* July 3, 1868.
[74] *Welles Papers,* Library of Congress, vol. 65.

The " Albany Regency " was the force behind the move to nominate Seymour, according to the New York *Herald* for July 5, and his refusal " is but a stroke of strategy " in the Regency's " nice little game." It is the same trick plotted to secure his nomination as Governor in 1862—to " keep him back until his rivals are worn out and killed off and then to charge with him . . . and take possession of the field." The Albany Regency argued that with Seymour as the candidate they were sure at least of New York State and, holding New York, they held the whip hand for 1872.

New York cast its 33 votes for Church according to agreement during all six of the ballots on July 7, and on the first ballot of the next day. Gideon Welles recorded in his Diary that this " was a blind and meant Seymour." He believed that both the New Yorkers and Seymour himself intended that he should be nominated, and that New York " had been playing an insincere game." [75]

On the second roll call of the second day (the eighth ballot) New York dropped Church and switched to Hendricks. There is some evidence that this support of Hendricks by New York was bonafide and met with Seymour's approval.[76] A friend of Hendricks told Chase afterwards that what Seymour had said and done left him with the assurance that the first choice of the New York delegation was really Hendricks.[77] The explanation that it was intended as a screen for Chase is more probable, although it was freely charged that Seymour was the intended beneficiary.[78]

[75] Vol. iii, pp. 396-397, July 7, 1868.

[76] G. L. Miller to H. S. Miller, March 4, 1893, *Seymour Papers*, New York Historical Society Library, Box 3.

[77] Chase to W. B. Thomas, July 17, 1868. *Chase Papers*, Library of Congress, Letter Book 8.

[78] New York *Evening Post*, July 9, 1868.

It is probable that the switch of New York from Church to Hendricks on the eighth ballot was due primarily to the desire to stop Pendleton, by casting a vote in the direction most likely to injure him.   The move was sincere, in that New York was willing to see Hendricks nominated rather than Pendleton.   This is shown by the fact that the New York delegates continued to vote for Hendricks to the next to the last roll call.   At the same time, Hendricks was not the first choice of most of the New Yorkers but they were not united on any preference.   The vote for Hendricks, then, was a makeshift to keep Pendleton out, and to give more time for further deliberation.   At this time the New York delegation was not planning to put Seymour forward, because of his refusal to allow his name to be used.   Ohio, which finally led the move for Seymour, was still voting for Pendleton.

When the enthusiasm for Hancock was at its height, near the end of the second day's balloting, the New York delegation went out to consult, and according to A. E. Burr, they " held to their previous plan of defeating every one till Seymour should be brought forward.   Seymour kept on declining and every time making a little stump speech for himself." [79]   New York's refusal to join the Hancock land-slide indicates that the delegates had not yet decided what they really wished to do, and remained by Hendricks in order to prolong the proceedings.

We have seen that a meeting of the Ohio delegation was held on the evening of July 8, that it held a stormy discussion and that it adopted a resolution refusing to support Chase the next day.   According to Vallandigham, it adjourned without agreeing upon a candidate.[80]   There may

[79] To Welles, September 4, 1868. *Welles Papers*, Library of Congress, vol. 65.

[80] *National Intelligencer*, July 28, 1868.

be found in newspapers of the day various reports of another meeting held later on that night at Delmonico's between various New York and Ohio leaders — McLean, Thurman, Pugh, Tilden, Ben Wood and Barlow are among those mentioned—at which was concocted the plan used next day to bring Seymour forward with an overwhelming rush.[81]   This group is said to have met again in the morning of the 9th at the Fifth Avenue Hotel and decided upon the details of the scheme.   The arrangement, according to those newspaper reports, was kept secret from the rank and file of both delegations.   Indeed the delegations were so far from suspecting what was on foot that the next morning they formally decided upon quite different courses of action. The Ohio delegates, as the Convention was about to open, informally agreed to cast a complimentary vote for Packer and then, if an opportune moment presented itself, throw their ballots to Seymour.   The New York delegates at the same time, after hearing Seymour reiterate his refusal to be a candidate, adopted his resolution to move for Chase as soon as Hendricks' vote fell off.[82]

When the Convention reconvened on the morning of the 9th, Ohio ran up the white flag for its favorite son : that is, Pendleton's name was formally withdrawn by Vallandigham. On the first three ballots then taken, Hendricks' vote increased from $107\frac{1}{2}$ to 132.   Under the circumstances, New York could not drop him and turn to Chase.   The rise in the vote cast for the Indianian alarmed all his opponents.   It frightened Tilden; it frightened Thurman, McLean and the other Ohio leaders.   There was danger that a sudden new combination would place Hendricks within striking distance of victory.   Indeed, E. L. Godkin learned later that at this

[81] Cincinnati *West and South*, August, 29; New York *Herald*, September 6, etc.

[82] New York *World*, July 10.

crucial point a bargain was being made between the Hendricks men and the Hancock men to unite, nominating the former for President and the latter for Vice-President.   As the figures for the twenty-first roll-call were being read, Ohio realized that she must act, and act promptly.

What then occurred can be briefly told.   Vallandigham— always a Chase man—,rushed to Tilden and beseeched him to have New York cast her vote for Chase with Ohio to follow.[83]   Tilden replied that New York could not do this as long as Hendricks' strength remained so formidable. Vallandigham then decided that the one alternative method of beating Hendricks was to swing the Ohio delegation to Seymour.   Taking Seymour to an anteroom, he asked him to withdraw from the Convention, leaving it to act on his name.   This Seymour refused to do.   Vallandigham then told him that the Ohio delegation was determined to nominate him.   Seymour, still adamant, stated that he would rise in the Convention and refuse a nomination.   Thereupon Vallandigham once more went to Tilden and asked him to present Chase but Tilden declined.   It was obvious that Ohio must take the bit in her teeth.   There were a few seconds of hurried consultation.   Then McCook of Ohio gained the floor and presented the name of Horatio Seymour to the Convention.

A scene of confusion followed.   Seymour came forward, declared that his name must not be used, and notified the secretary not to receive the vote.   He then withdrew from the platform.   Vallandigham promptly rose and insisted that Seymour's name must stand.   Kernan of New York followed him with an emphatic assertion of the same opinion.[84]   Meanwhile Seymour, who had returned to the

[83] Warden, *op. cit.*, pp. 707-708.

[84] Warden, *op. cit.*, pp. 707-708; Alexander, *op. cit.*, vol. iii, p. 203; Rhodes, *op. cit.*, vol. vi, pp. 166, 167.

platform, tried to decline once more and to propose the name of Chase. But friends stopped him. One of them, Joseph Warren of Buffalo, seized him by the arm and virtually forced him off the rostrum. He was surrounded, protesting but hesitant, bustled out a rear door and driven rapidly in a carriage to the Manhattan Club.[85] Various observers later stated that, as he was thus carried off, his cheeks were wet with tears, and it is reported that, meeting Peter Harvey of Boston on the stairs, he exclaimed, " Pity me, Harvey, pity me." Tilden, undoubtedly, had a great deal to do with the hasty moves by which Seymour was thus rushed from the Convention and held incommunicado in the principal Democratic Club of the city.[86]

When Ohio took this bold action, the Convention was in a mood to be stampeded. The conclusion of the twenty-second ballot gave Hendricks 145½, Hancock 103½ and Seymour but 22. But when the last State on the list was reached, Wisconsin, a delegate rose and announced that she would abandon Doolittle and vote for Seymour.

This started the procession. In quick succession Kentucky, Massachusetts and North Carolina followed, changing their votes to Seymour. A scene of wild enthusiasm ensued, the chairman of a dozen other delegations springing to their chairs to obtain recognition from the presiding officer and switched their States' votes to Seymour. While the excitement was at its height, a cannon outside the building began firing in honor of the now certain nomination. It was answered by cheers within the hall. After every State had changed its vote, Tilden gained the floor. The previous night, he said, he had believed that Seymour's nomination was impossible unless Ohio should demand it, and " to that I thought New York ought to yield. We were without any

[85] New York *World*, July 10, 1868; *Official Proceedings*, pp. 153-155.
[86] Cincinnati *Commercial*, August 31, 1868.

connection or combination that bound our faith or our honor." In conclusion Tilden declared that the New York delegation — last or nearly last of all — now voted for Seymour.

With the landslide thus complete, but before the final result of the ballot was announced, a delegate from Wisconsin moved the ratification of the nomination by the spectators in the galleries. A half-hour demonstration followed.

The Cincinnati *Commercial* thought that Seymour was a party to the plot for his nomination. " When the telegraph informs us that in the confusion of the glorious moment Horatio Seymour quietly escaped from the Hall, the truth of history should have added that he was almost smothered with internal laughter at the success of the New York game." [87] Godkin wrote to his London paper that the nomination had hardly been made, when " the Convention perceived it had made a mistake, but there was no help for it." [88] The result had been brought about in part by the firing of a cannon and the playing of a band, which started the galleries to shouting " in what was really wild enthusiasm," long before the actual nomination was made, and while there was still time for the friends of Hendricks to save their man. The enthusiasm of the galleries " too obviously " affected the votes of the delegates.[89] Myers, in his History of Tammany Hall, speaks of the galleries being filled with " seasoned wigwam shouters, cheering vociferously for Seymour." [90]

Chase thought the nomination of Seymour had been concerted by a portion of both the Ohio and New York dele-

[87] July 11, 1868.

[88] London *Daily News*, July 11, 1868.

[89] *Nation*, July 16, 1868.

[90] Page 216.

gations.[91]   Chase's friend Hiram Barney wrote to him that he believed Seymour's selection had been agreed upon long before the Convention met—"But his friends could not have calculated upon the humiliation of his running upon Pendleton's platform." [92]

The *Herald* on July 10 professed to believe Pendleton to be the " chief wire puller " who at the proper moment sprung the trap.   The New York *Times* on July 11 said that the entire affair on the part of the New York Democrats was one of " dissimulation, treachery and fraud." They divided the Convention into shreds by their " sustained and shameless cunning " and the Convention was " an easy prey to the trick by which Seymour was sprung upon the Convention."   Gideon Welles recorded in his diary that to speak of Seymour's nomination as spontaneous was nonsense.   " All worked as New York intended." [93]   The Springfield *Republican's* New York correspondent reported that the New York game was to nominate either Chase or Seymour.   " The process was the same with either candidate.   It was Ohio's power to choose between them, and she took Seymour." [94]

Stanwood does not believe that it can be proved that the nomination of Seymour had been planned before hand.   If so, " not a line of evidence was ever adduced to prove it, a few persons only could have been in the secret, and the enthusiasm of the delegates was genuine and sincere.   Indeed, the Convention had selected one of the strongest men in the party." [95]   Stanwood's statement needs only minor

[91] To Gerrit Smith, July 24, 1868.   *Chase Papers*, Library of Congress, ser. 2, vol. iii.

[92] July 10, 1868.   *Chase Papers*, Historical Society Pennsylvania Library.

[93] July 9, 1868, *vol.* iii, p. 398.

[94] July 10, 1868.

[95] *Presidency*, vol. i, p. 326.

revision. The nomination was planned before hand, the evening before, in fact, but it was abandoned when vetoed by Seymour. The next morning the plan was revived, and put through in spite of Seymour's protests.

If the above is true, it follows that Seymour was not a party to his nomination. Vallandigham, in a speech at Dayton on July 28, said that Seymour was chosen "to my personal knowledge, against his will and without a pledge or promise to anyone, on any subject. He is under no obligation of any sort, other than that which binds the patriot and gentleman." [96] Vallandigham wrote on another occasion that "Positively Governor Seymour had no knowledge or intimation of the movement till twenty minutes previous to his nomination." [97] The New York *Sun* also believed that Seymour was sincere in declining, and was coerced by circumstances. "He is not in the slightest degree amenable to the charge of low trickery, false dealing, and slippery hypocrisy in gaining an honor which might have been his at any time." [98] The *Nation* had no doubt of Seymour's sincerity in declining, as "he is sagacious enough to know that he cannot be elected. . . . It is no kindness to Horatio Seymour to make him a Presidential candidate, and he knows this as well as we do." [99]

While there was some talk in the Convention about the possibility of some one less prominent than Seymour, Chase, Hendricks, Hancock or Pendleton receiving the nomination, as an answer to the deadlock between the leaders, it came to nothing. Doolittle, Reverdy Johnson, and Frank Blair were suggested, but the Convention was so near a nomination on various occasions that the supporters of the leaders were not

[96] Cincinnati *Commercial*, July 29, 1868.
[97] July 18, in *National Intelligencer*, July 28, 1868.
[98] In Utica *Observer*, July 14, 1868.
[99] July 23, 1868.

likely to listen to dark-horse suggestions. At four different times before the final selection a nomination was near, and was averted only by unscheduled actions. If Indiana had not given Hendricks 9½ of her 13 votes on the seventh ballot, Pendleton would have had a majority on the eighth, and a landslide might well have occurred. If a snap adjournment had not taken place after the 18th, Hancock probably would have been nominated, and if Ohio had not gone for Seymour on the 22nd, Hendricks' nomination on the 23rd was to have been expected. Finally, if Seymour when attempting to decline the use of his name when suggested during the 22nd roll call, had asked his friends to vote for Chase, he would have precipitated an exciting half-hour or more. When the smoke of battle had drifted away, Chase might well have been the nominee. But these things did not happen and Seymour did not decline.

CHAPTER X

THE DEMOCRATIC NOMINEES BEFORE THE COUNTRY

I. RECEPTION BY THE DEMOCRATS

THE reception of the nomination of Seymour and Blair by the Democrats was on the whole favorable, but it was far from being unanimously enthusiastic.

The papers which gave Seymour an unqualified endorsement included the *World,* the *National Intelligencer,* and the Cincinnati *Enquirer.* The *World* said that Seymour had more political courage than Chase. His selection was " the best possible result that could be obtained." [1] The *National Intelligencer* on July 10 praised Seymour highly for his national reputation, oratorical ability, the purity of his character and his patriotism. His talents were equaled by but few Presidents. The Cincinnati *Enquirer,* referring to the differences between Seymour and Pendleton on the greenback issue, stated that they were removed by Seymour's acceptance of the nomination on a greenback platform. Seymour " has no equal in any party, and no rival." [2] Among other journals approving the nomination were the Portland *Argus,* New Haven *Palladium,* Pittsburgh *Daily Post,* Troy *Daily Press,* Rochester *Union,* Providence *Herald,* Hartford *Times,* Philadelphia *Age,* Baltimore *Gazette,* the New York *Leader,* and the San Francisco *Examiner.* [3]

Letters written after the nomination by prominent Demo-

[1] July 10, 13, 1868.

[2] July 10, 1868. In New York *World,* July 13, 1868.

[3] McCabe, *Seymour and Blair* (New York, 1868), pp. 273-280 for further newspaper endorsements.

246

crats show on the whole a favorable response. Alexander
H. Stephens thought well of the nomination.[4] Burr of the
Hartford *Times* wrote Welles on July 14 that he thought
Seymour would win. He was certain that he would carry
Connecticut. Although possibly weaker than Hancock or
Doolittle, Seymour was stronger than Chase.[5] Francis P.
Blair, Sr., father of the Vice-Presidential candidate, although
disappointed that " Frank " was not placed at the head of the
ticket, wrote to Tilden on July 15, that he believed the action
of the Convention wise.[6] Frederick A. Aiken, who endorsed
Seymour enthusiastically, advised him to let Vallandigham
know that he was working for " a sure and certain reward,"
in order to hold that temperamental Ohioan to the ticket.[7]
Hiram Ketchum, of New York, who had been favorable to
Chase, wrote Seymour on July 24 that while he would lose
many votes which might have gone to Chase, he would gain
more by the advantage of having a united party behind him.[8]

Gideon Welles did not consider the nomination a fortunate one. Seymour, he entered in his diary on the day it was
made (July 9), had intellect but not courage. " His party-
ism predominates over patriotism." [9] But Welles gave his
support to the ticket, Thomas Ewing, Sr., was also chilly
toward the nomination. It " will give rise to a very sharp
contest with an uncertain result." [10] On September 2 he
would publicly endorse Seymour.[11] His son General Ewing

4 To J. B. Cohen, July 17, 1868. *Stephens Papers*, Library of Congress.

5 *Welles Papers*, Library of Congress, vol. 65.

6 *Tilden Letters*, vol. i, pp. 240-241.

7 July 21, 1868. *Seymour Papers*, Albany.

8 *Seymour Papers*, New York Historical Society, Library, Box 4.

9 *Diary*, vol. iii, p. 398.

10 To Hugh Ewing, July 11, 1868. *T. Ewing Papers*, Library of
Congress, vol. 19, Type copy.

11 Utica *Observer*, Sept. 11, 1868; Memphis *Avalanche*, Sept. 12, 1868.

spoke at a ratification meeting held in Washington on July 18.[12] Former Attorney-General Henry Stanbery, on September 26 spoke for the Democratic ticket at Lancaster, Ohio.[13] General Lew Wallace was a supporter of the Democratic ticket. " He is doing all he can here, and feels alive to your interest." [14] A veteran of many political campaigns, and a member of Andrew Jackson's " Kitchen Cabinet," Amos Kendall, in spite of his great age raised his voice in favor of Seymour; on August 20 he wrote a letter of endorsement to be read at a Democratic rally.[15]

Most of the dissatisfaction with the Democratic ticket came from the West. The Illinois Democrats were not pleased by Seymour's selection, but accepted the ticket as the platform had a Greenback plank.[16] Party leaders in Indiana threatened to bolt the ticket, and were even said to be in favor of a third party nomination. Similar reports came from Columbus, Ohio.[17] The Cincinnati *West and South.* stated that Seymour lacked the mind and character to rally the Democratic masses " in these evil days." [18] On August 1, however, the *West and South* was ready to support anyone, even Seymour, to beat Grant. A German editor from Ohio wrote Seymour on July 20 that the German Democrats were opposed to him, the reason being that they considered Seymour pledged to Chase.[19]

[12] Albany *Argus,* July 21, 1868.

[13] New York *Herald,* Sept. 30, 1868.

[14] R. N. Freeman to H. S., *Seymour Papers,* New York Historical Society Library.

[15] *National Intelligencer,* August 21, 1868.

[16] Cole, *Era of the Civil War* (Springfield, 1918), p. 441.

[17] Cincinnati *Commercial,* July 11, 1868.

[18] July 11, 1868.

[19] L. B. de la Court, editor *Hamilton National Zeitung, Seymour Papers,* Albany.

The Republican press hailed these signs of Democratic dissatisfaction with glee. The New York *Tribune's* Washington correspondent said the Democrats were disgusted with the nominations and that the general verdict was that the Convention blundered.[20] The *Nation* reported the Democrat press generally as lacking in enthusiasm,[21] while the *Independent* said that the only portion of the Democracy who were pleased was the " rebel wing." [22]

There was considerable speculation as to what the defeated candidates for the nomination would say about Seymour. On July 17, in a speech in Virginia Pendleton endorsed the ticket, pronouncing Seymour the foremost statesman of the day.[23] In a message read at a Democratic ratification meeting in Washington on July 18, Pendleton promised he would be found at Seymour's side, in the thickest of the fight.[24] But later in the campaign, Gideon Welles recorded in his diary that " the course and speeches of Pendleton make it clear that he is a disappointed and intriguing man, and that he does not take his disappointment kindly." [25]

Hendricks cordially endorsed his successful rival. A Washington friend wrote to Seymour on July 16, enclosing the " timely, full and cordial " acceptance of Seymour's nomination by Hendricks. On July 27 Hendricks transmitted to Seymour, through a friend, twenty copies of a speech in which he endorsed the ticket.[26] Shortly after the convention Tilden sent van Buren to Washington to line up the friends of Johnson, Chase, Hendricks and Hancock. Unfortunately

[20] July 10, 1868.
[21] July 16, 1868.
[22] July 23, 1868.
[23] Albany *Argus*, July 18, 1868.
[24] *McPherson Scrap Book*, Library of Congress, vol. ii, p. 92.
[25] September 4, 1868, vol. iii, p. 430.
[26] *Seymour Papers*, Albany.

van Buren made a most unfavorable impression.   One R. W.
Latham wrote that he " is a very fine gentleman but don't suit
that kind of business."   Whatever van Buren's shortcom-
ings, he found that only Hendricks had " behaved like a
gentleman," while Hancock was like " an overgrown spoiled
baby who had lost his sugar plum." [27]   The New York
Tribune reported that when Hancock received the news of
the nomination of Seymour he angrily denounced Seymour
for his trickery, and blamed him for his failure to receive
the nomination.[28]   When in July Hancock received a letter
from S. T. Glover, calling his attention to reports that he
was dissatisfied with the nomination and asking him to state
his position, he replied that if he were to hesitate in cordially
supporting the party ticket " I should not only falsify my
own record, but commit a crime against my country." [29]
The *Nation* commented that this letter did not indicate that
the Democratic ticket was going to have in General Hancock
a very ardent supporter.[30]   In this Godkin proved correct.
Hancock did not take an active part in the campaign, even
when the Democratic leaders attempted to prod him.   In
October Tilden wrote to him, enclosing a note from Seymour.
Hancock in reply excused himself for his inactivity by stating
that an old wound had been troubling him, and that as soon
as he was able to do so he would be obliged to attend a military court of inquiry.   Moreover, he had always believed
that army officers should not take part in political campaigns.
" Still, the crisis is of such vital moment that I might probably have acted differently. . . . But neither time nor health
permit me to act." [31]   The Springfield *Republican* referred

[27] Latham to " Mr. Wood," July 20, 1868. *Seymour Papers*, Albany.

[28] July 30, 1868.

[29] New York *Herald*, July 28, 1868; Utica *Observer*, July 30, 1868;
Mrs. Hancock's *Reminiscences*, p. 138.

[30] August 6, 1868.   [31] *Tilden Letters*, vol. i, pp. 240-250.

to Hancock's " terrible " wound, which " has never kept him from doing anything which he has wanted very much to do." [32]

General McClellan who was still abroad when the nominations were made, took an equally unsatisfactory stand. On August 4 he wrote from St. Maurice that he would be very glad to see Seymour President. He had feared that Chase might be chosen. He did not like the financial plank. [33] But when McClellan returned to the United States about October 1, it was rumored that he would support Grant. This belief was strengthened by the fact that the Common Council of New York city, which had at first talked of giving him a public reception, let the matter drop, " probably hearing that his sympathies were not with the Democratic party." [34] Although he did not come out for Grant, McClellan did not enlist as an active worker for Seymour. On October 3 he refused an invitation to preside or to take part in a Democratic rally to be held in New York on October 5. In his letter of refusal McClellan announced his determination to take no active part in politics. He spoke very highly of Grant, but objected to the Radical policy as a " continuation of strife." As a private citizen, he intended to vote for Seymour. [35] It was also reported that McClellan had refused a request from Seymour that he campaign in Pennsylvania for the Democrats. [36] His letter of October 3 may be taken at its face value. In this, his position was quite similar to that of General Hancock.

[32] October 8, 1868.

[33] To Prince, *McClellan Papers*, Library of Congress, vol. 93.

[34] London *Daily News*, October 16, 1868.

[35] New York *Times*, October 6; New York *Herald*, October 7, 1868.

[36] Cincinnati *Commercial*, October 5, 1868. *Tilden Letters*, vol. i, p. 249.

2. RECEPTION BY THE REPUBLICANS

The reaction of the Republicans to the nomination of Seymour was generally a feeling that he could be easily defeated. On July 9, the day of the nomination, Carl Schurz wrote to Horace Greeley that the Democratic nominee was a " most excellent subject for dissection, and I would like to do something in that line on the stump." He asked Greeley for material on Seymour's public statements.[37] In his Reminiscences Schurz refers to Seymour as weak and amiable, while the platform of the Democrats " stopped but little short of advocating violence " to undo the reconstruction acts.[38]

Governor Hayes of Ohio recorded in his diary the belief that Seymour had been chosen because of his identification with the " Peace " Democracy. On July 14 he wrote to his uncle, " Yes, Hurrah for Seymour and Blair! The thing is a wet blanket here to our Democrats. The prospect has certainly improved for us." [39] General Sherman wrote to his wife, on July 11, that it would be dangerous to commit the government to the Democratic ticket. " Seymour was a pure copperhead during the war. Still I shall do or say nothing in public." [40]

Prominent among those former Democrats who had drifted towards the Republicans was Edwards Pierrepont, of New York, a sachem in the Tammany Society. He was a confidant of another former Democrat—the late Secretary of War, Edwin Stanton. On July 12, Pierrepont wrote Stanton that he didn't think any " war " Democrats would support Seymour and Blair. Pierrepont would as soon vote for Davis and Lee. If the Democrats won, the rebels need no longer mourn about the " lost cause." [41]

[37] Greeley Papers, New York Public Library, Manuscript Division.
[38] Vol. iii, p. 286.
[39] Hayes Diary and Letters, vol. iii, pp. 53-54.
[40] Sherman Home Letters, pp. 377-378.
[41] Stanton Papers, Library of Congress, vol. 31.

Two prominent New Yorkers, both Conservative Republicans, were in Europe at the time of the nomination. Thurlow Weed, the close friend of Secretary Seward, wrote from Southampton on July 18 that the result of the Democratic convention disappointed him. If he had a thousand votes, they would all be cast for Grant.[42] John A. Dix had been Conservative enough to be suggested as a Democratic candidate. But he wrote from Paris, where he was American Minister, that Seymour, a gentleman of respectable talents, was without a single qualification for the Presidency. He saw but one hope for the country, the election of Grant.[43] Seymour wrote to a friend that he was glad Dix wrote as he did. He wanted him to show his true character. " There was in the minds of our people a linkering faith in him which did mischief." [44] Another Conservative Republican, Charles Francis Adams, who was relieved as American minister to England by Reverdy Johnson in 1868, and returned to the United States in June voted for Grant.[45]

The attitude of the Republican press was the same as that of the leaders, although some of the newspapers admitted that Seymour was personally very able. The New York *Commercial Advertiser* said that Seymour was not to be beaten by being called a copperhead; that he was the most popular man in the Democratic party.[46] The Boston *Journal* considered him a man of unblemished personal reputation.[47] For the most part, the Republican papers of New York could

[42] Cincinnati *Commercial*, July 30, 1868.

[43] New York *Herald*, September 23; Albany *Argus*, September 24, 1868.

[44] To H. S. Randall, October 5, 1868. New York Historical Society Library, Miscellaneous Manuscript.

[45] Adams, *C. F. Adams* (Boston, 1900), pp. 377-378.

[46] In Utica *Observer*, July 16, 1868.

[47] In New York *World*, July 12, 1868.

see little merit in Seymour, or little chance for his election. The *Herald* preferred Grant. The Democratic Convention, it stated on July 10, had by its action decided that Grant will be the next President. The next day the *Herald* referred to Seymour as the " embodiment of copperheadism," and held that his nomination meant that the Democracy was determined to renounce none of their old heresies. The *Times* said that the Democratic ticket and platform " inspire no apprehension of success," and would disgust the non-partisan voters.[48]

Bryant's *Evening Post* pronounced the work of the Convention a failure, and Seymour a local politician, doomed to failure.[49] He was a man of unsteady purposes, who as President would keep the country in turmoil.[50] A month later Bryant expressed the fear that Seymour, as President, would be controlled by Vallandigham, Pendleton and Blair.[51] The *Tribune* announced that if the Democratic Convention had deliberately attempted to secure a candidate who would be least likely to win Republican votes and decrease Republican opposition, it " could not have hit the mark more exactly." [52] On July 13, the *Tribune* repeated the yarn about Seymour's alleged treasonable correspondence with the Confederate agents in Canada. Three days later it said that when Seymour stated in the Convention on July 8 that he could not with " honor " be the candidate, " he gave us a text of more than usual meaning." [53] On July 25 Greeley listed his charges again Seymour under six heads: He had been op-

[48] July 10, 1868.
[49] July 10, 1868.
[50] July 18, 1868.
[51] August 21, 1868.
[52] July 10, 1868.
[53] July 16, 1868.

posed to resisting secession by force; he had said during the war, that if the Union could only be maintained by abolishing slavery, it should be given up; his support of the Union during the war as Governor of New York, had been grudging; and finally, he had opposed the draft. Dana's *Sun* considered that Seymour was a fair representative of the average sentiment of his party.[54]

Outside of New York the Republican press on the whole took the same attitude as the *Tribune*. The Springfield *Republican* spoke of Seymour as a nullifier since 1861, and a natural coward.[55] This paper was one of many journals that attacked Seymour for his action in calling the draft rioters of 1863 "My Friends." The *Republican* said that the trouble was not that he had called the draft rioters his friends, but that they were his friends and knew it.[56] The point was one labored by the Republicans during the campaign from front page, from stump, and even from pulpit. This was unfair. The actual fact was that Seymour, called into service by the failure of the local Republican authorities to maintain order, had attempted to placate the mob rather than further antagonize it. It might have been a heroic gesture for him to shout defiance to the mob, and get shot for his pains, but that would not have saved lives and property from further depredations. In an interview with the New York *Sun,* Seymour expressed surprise that the Republicans should charge him with inciting a riot in 1863. He said that the purpose of his remarks at the time were to keep down the passions of the people and urge submission to the law. He was willing to see the incident thoroughly discussed in the campaign. He reminded his interviewer that when he ad-

[54] In New York *World,* July 12, 1868.

[55] July 11, 1868.

[56] August 3, 1868.

dressed the mob, on July 4, the troops were away, and he could only temporize with them in a friendly way.[57]

The Republican weeklies were not less critical of the Democratic ticket than the daily press. *Leslie's Weekly* referred to Seymour as a " poor, paltering politician," [58] while *Harper's Weekly* considered him " a plausible politician, an unscrupulous partisan," and " the obsequious servant of the only aristocratic class in this country," evidently referring to his friendships among the New York bankers.[59] The *Nation* spoke of the assured success of the Republican ticket, and said that the Republicans in Congress would not feel so much anxiety to adjourn and take the stump as they would have felt had Chase, Hancock or Hendricks been chosen by the Democrats.[60] Later in the campaign, the *Nation* admitted that Seymour had many advantages over Grant as a candidate from the point of view of his ability to appeal to the public. Seymour had magnetism. He was able to assume an interest in the small affairs of others, and he could put on an air of dignity " which strange as it may seem, is worth more to a public man in America than in any other country of the world." Moreover, Seymour had " tears within easy reach." [61]

One extraordinary feature of the Republican attack deserves special mention. The party press did not wait long to revive the story that there was a taint of hereditary insanity in Seymour's family. Bryant's *Evening Post* began it in the East, on July 13, rather indirectly, by an editorial entitled, " A danger to provide against." In this article, on the position of the country should the President become insane, Sey-

[57] In Cincinnati *Commercial*, July 27, 1868.
[58] October 3, 1868.
[59] July 25, 1868.
[60] July 16, 1868.
[61] September 24, 1868.

mour's name was not mentioned, but attention was called to Grant's unusual mental stability. The *Evening Post* asks for legislation to guard against the danger of an insane President. In the same issue articles from Western papers were quoted which made the direct statement that Seymour was liable to insanity, as he was, according to the Chicago *Tribune,* " of that delicate organism that his whole life has been one of painful anxiety. Mental disorganization is hereditary in his family, and to escape it has been the grand object of all his plans." The Sandusky *Register* thought it particularly cruel in the Democratic Convention " to force the Presidential nomination onto a gentleman who has a taint of hereditary insanity, and then to couple him with one of the Blairs, whose society through the campaign would develop lunacy in the sanest of men."

The New York *Times* said : " There is a very grave danger, in the case of the possibility of the election of Mr. Seymour, that the Vice-President would be called upon to serve. . . . Who that knows Blair's nature, or has read his revolutionary letter, but would be alarmed for the country in such a contingency? " [62] The *Evening Post* followed with some of the alleged " inside facts " of the case. Seymour had assured his friends " that his family were afflicted with a hereditary insanity, which threatens him also; and which he can only hope to escape by avoiding excitement and severe labor." The *Evening Post* also alleged that when Seymour's name was first mentioned in the National Convention itself, he told his friends the " true " reason why he felt bound in honor to decline. It was believed that both Tilden and S. E. Church were informed of Seymour's position and expressly approved it. The Democratic ticket, concluded the *Post,* " means Blair for President." [63] This same report had been

[62] July 14, 1868.
[63] July 14, 1868.

mentioned just before the Convention by the New York
correspondent of the Cincinnati *Commercial,* who thought
that the suspicion that Seymour was really manoeuvering for
the nomination " has been somewhat allayed by the information that he dare not risk the great excitement of a Presidential race because of a hereditary taint of insanity." Seymour's father was alleged to have died by his own hand.[64]
The New York *Tribune,* on July 16, echoed the general
charge, and the *Independent* on July 16, stated : " Seymour is
not without painful apprehension of a stealthily approaching
insanity, which is creeping like a shadow into his brain."

The attacks on Seymour's sanity were resented by the
New York *World,* in an editorial on July 16, " The Last
Radical Canard." The Albany *Argus* came to his defense,
stating that the only connection or relation of Seymour who
had ever been insane was his brother-in-law, and that insanity does not pass to relatives simply by marriage.[65] Another
brother-in-law, the eminent Roscoe Conkling, denied the report of insanity in the Seymour blood. On July 20 Josiah
T. Miller, a cousin of Seymour, wrote from Seneca Falls
that the candidate " is a man of excellent health, and pos-
essed of a vigorous constitution. Uniformly temperate in
his habits, and of the purest morals, he has no seeds of disease
in his system, and his devotion to outdoor pursuits has developed an unusually fine physique." [66] Miller praised the
Seymour stock, but made no reference to a brother-in-law of
the Governor, alleged to be of unsound mind.

The attacks on Seymour were heartless and purely malicious, without a word of truth in them. Nevertheless, the
fables grew in an astonishing fashion. The alleged insanity

[64] Cincinnati *Commercial,* July 3, 1868; also Godkin, July 17, to London
Daily News, July 28, 1868.

[65] Cited by Godkin, *op. cit.*

[66] *National Intelligencer,* August 24, 1868.

and suicide of Henry Seymour, father of the Democratic nominee, were described in detail by a Utica letter, dated July 23, to the Cincinnati *Commercial*. In this letter it was alleged that when Horatio had grown up and graduated from Hamilton College, his father " grew dejected, suffering from a cerebral affection, and among his delusions was one that he had lost all his property. He went out gunning one day, returned disconsolate, and putting the muzzle of the gun to his heart, he touched the trigger with his foot." [67] The Cincinnati *Gazette* charged that Henry Seymour became subject to fits of mental aberration " shortly after the exposure of some of his malpractices as Canal Commissioner of New York," and that in one of these fits he blew his brains out. It added that Governor Seymour's brother likewise died a maniac suicide, and the Governor himself " has been constantly warned by his family and physician to avoid all harassing mental cares and great excitement, as almost inevitably tending to develop the same trait." Once Seymour had been removed to Minnesota, and there kept in seclusion for several months, on the suggestion of his physician. The *Gazette* concluded that " to elect the Democratic candidate is to . . . make General Frank Blair President of the United States." [68] Alexander Long, of Cincinnati, according to the Cincinnati *West and South* for August 29, said that Seymour had told a prominent New York politician that reasons why he could not take a nomination included the fact that " in a few weeks he expected to see his brother consigned to a lunatic asylum, and that the condition of his own health was such as to forbid his becoming a candidate." [69]

Seymour very properly took no public notice of these at-

[67] August 1, 1868.

[68] In Springfield *Republican*, August 25, 1868.

[69] In Cincinnati *Commercial*, August 31, 1868; New York *Times*, September 4, 1868.

tacks, but Long's story so aroused his indignation that he asked Chase, who knew Long, to " call off the dogs." [70]   Perhaps the best answer to these attacks was made by Vallandigham on July 28, when he stated " if he is ' insane ' as little creatures with false malicious tongues insinuate, I would that the same method were in the madness of all other public men." [71]

These attacks on Seymour's insanity grew less frequent as the campaign progressed.   It was impossible to prove them, as they were without foundation.   But the lie having been planted in the mind of the voters, the party press turned its guns on more exposed positions of the Democracy.

3. SEYMOUR'S POSITION

Something should be said of Seymour's general position while these attacks upon him were developing.   His genuine reluctance to embark upon the campaign had been shown in his remarks to the committee of the Convention which formally informed him of his nomination.   He said the honor was unsought and unexpected, and that he was now excluded by his nomination.   He had been caught up by the tide that was moving the country on to a great political change, " and I find myself unable to resist its pressure."   The platform was in accord with his views and he would strive to put its principles into effect.[72]

Two points in this short speech merit attention.   It shows that Seymour felt that the dignity of a Presidential candidate precluded him from actively campaigning in his own behalf.   This attitude he maintained until near the close of the cam-

[70] Seymour to van Buren, Sept. 8, New York Historical Society Library, Box 4, *Seymour Papers*. Van Buren to Chase, Oct. 7, 1868. Historical Society Pennsylvania Library, *Chase Papers*.

[71] Speech, Dayton, Ohio. In Cincinnati *Commercial*, July 29, 1868.

[72] *Public Record*, pp. 341-342.

paign when the growing strength of his opponents led him to yield to the desire of his friends that he make a speaking tour. Seymour's endorsement of the platform was unequivocal, but one may be permitted to wonder what mental reservations he made as to the financial planks. As a candidate of the Convention, he had two choices. He could decline to run or accept the nomination and the platform with it. Any other course would have caused an explosion within the party.

On July 30 Seymour wrote to Tilden a long letter in which he dealt with the problems of campaign organization, but made no mention of the possibility of his declining the nomination.[73] Evidently by this time he had decided to go through with it, in spite of his personal reluctance.

On July 24, Seymour wrote to a friend, C. M. Ingersoll of New Haven, that while he was gratified by the kindness of his friends " they have plunged me into a sea of trouble." He was uncertain of the results of the campaign but, now that he was in the fight, he would do the best he could. This letter was printed by Republican papers in September with much gusto.[74] The Utica *Observer* remarked that its publication indicated a wanton disregard of the properties by the Republicans. " Governor Seymour never wrote a letter which he feared might see the light." The *Observer* quoted the New Haven *Register* to the effect that the letter was undoubtedly stolen from Mr. Ingersoll's private papers and turned over to Greeley of the *Tribune,* who refused to tell how he obtained it or return it.[75] The Cincinnati *Commercial* of July 27 printed a report of an interview with Seymour in which he was quoted as saying that he was confident of his election but would personally prefer defeat.

[73] *Tilden Letters*, vol. i, pp. 242-243.

[74] New York *Tribune*, September 4, 1868; New York *Herald*, Sept. 7, 1868.

[75] September 10, 1868.

In the letter of acceptance written from Utica on August 4, Seymour reiterated his support of the platform, but did not discuss it. He attacked the Congressional reconstruction plan; and he pointed out that a Democratic victory would not produce sudden or violent changes, for the Republicans would continue in control of the Senate, but the extreme measures of the Republicans would be checked. This point answered the Republican charges, inspired by Blair's " Brodhead letter," that the election of the Democratic ticket would result in a violent overturn of the government established in the South by Congress. Referring to the enthusiasm with which the Democratic position had been received, he admitted that this approval would, perhaps, have been more marked " had any others of those named [before the Convention] been selected." He paid a tribute to the Conservative masses and the veterans, and closed with an expression of confidence in victory.[76] Rhodes says that the letter showed Seymour's position to be one of studied moderation, and that it made a strong appeal to disgruntled Republicans by proving that no revolution would follow Democratic success.[77] The receipt of this letter by the press corresponded generally with the attitude taken towards his nomination. The Utica *Observer* said that the letter would increase the pride of Democrats in their standard bearer.[78]

The *Independent* printed a letter from the negro leader Frederick Douglass on Seymour's acceptance. Douglass referred to the letter as " smooth as oil and as fair seeming as hypocrisy itself, containing every disposition to deceive but without the ability." It was " cunning and cowardly." [79]

[76] *Official Proceedings*, Democratic National Convention, pp. 176-179.

[77] *United States*, vol. vi, p. 192.

[78] August 5, 1868.

[79] August 20, 1868.

The *Nation* called the letter a " crafty document," which was Seymour " at full length and with all his faces." The absence of any reference to the financial or suffrage issues was particularly noted.[80] Godkin reported to his London paper that the letter could be read by Greenbacker and bondholder with equal satisfaction and that it illustrated Seymour's marked ability to say nothing in words that may mean anything.[81]

The day the letter of acceptance was published (August 4) Seymour wrote an illuminating communication to Senator Doolittle. He told Doolittle that his nomination had thrown him into confusion and upset all his plans. He had put off his letter of acceptance until the last moment, " with a vague idea that in some way the political program might be changed." He has been astonished by the uprising of the people in favor of the Democracy. " I find I must go on with the work." The reaction against the Radicals had become so deep and strong that " we must teach moderation " which he has done in his letter of acceptance.[82] A week later he sent another friend a letter which did not show excessive confidence in his victory. " Our only course is to get all the strength we can. If we come short of carrying the Presidential ticket we shall gain States and Congressmen. We may not be able to overturn the Republicans now but we shall make good progress in that direction." [83]

Seymour showed more confidence when he wrote Tilden on August 17 that the letters he received from all sections were equally optimistic. " This uniformity of word and facts means a great deal. It foretells a political change." [84]

---

[80] August 13, 1868.

[81] New York, August 8, London *Daily News*, August 20, 1868.

[82] *Magazine of History*, vol. xvii, pp. 58-59.

[83] To Philip Phillips, *Phillips Papers*, Library of Congress.

[84] *Tilden Letters*, vol. i, p. 244.

But as late in the campaign as October 5 he confided to a friend that he was reproaching himself each day " that I suffered myself to be driven from my purpose not to be a candidate for any office." [85]

All in all, it is clear that Seymour accepted the nomination with reluctance, and entered the campaign with considerable misgivings which were only temporarily allayed by the enthusiasm shown around him.   Seymour later considered that his acceptance of the nomination was the worst mistake of his life.[86]

3. THE VICE PRESIDENTIAL CANDIDATE

The attitude of the Democratic press towards the nomination of Gen. Frank Blair for Vice-President was on the whole, and at first, favorable.   But a number of papers, especially the New York *World,* lost their enthusiasm for him as the campaign progressed.   Among the journals which hailed Blair's nomination with approval were the Cincinnati *Enquirer,* Rochester *Union,* Providence *Herald,* Buffalo *Courier,* Boston *Post, National Intelligencer,* Utica *Observer* and the Trenton *American.*[87]

Among individuals Gideon Welles held that Blair was " bold, resolute and determined," with " sagacity as well as will " and with more courage than Seymour.   He was the " most of a man on either ticket." [88]   Senator Doolittle referred to him approvingly as among " the foremost of the War Republicans in council and in the field while the war lasted " and for that reason likely to attract War Democrats to the ticket.[89]   It is interesting to note that Blair's father,

[85] To H. S. Randall, New York Historical Society Library, Misc. Mss.

[86] Conversation with Mr. Wall, New York Historical Society Library, who cited Mrs. Charles Fairchild, niece of Seymour.

[87] New York *World,* July 12, 13, 1868.

[88] *Diary,* vol. iii, pp. 389, 408, 450.

[89] To O. H. Ostrader, July 13, Democratic Speaker's Handbook.

in a letter to Tilden, admitted that " Frank is a mighty small young Hickory " but " the best that we can now command." [90]

On June 30, as we have seen, Blair stated his attitude towards reconstruction in a letter to Colonel James O. Brodhead of Missouri, in which he said that the President should refuse to enforce the reconstruction acts and should " compel the army to undo its usurpations at the South."

This position at once aroused a storm of discussion, which continued until November. The New York *World* said on July 12 that Blair's letter on " the working of negro suffrage by grace of the sword " struck a chord which will " ring out in tremendous response from millions of hearts throughout the North and West." The next day, however, the *World* minimized the chances of Blair ever putting his theory into actual operation, pointing out that as Vice-President he would have little real power. It added that judging from the Republican terror of Blair, Seymour, as President, would be safe from impeachment or assassination. This position indicated the gingerly handling of Blair's candidacy by the *World,* which became more and more marked as the campaign progressed. For example, on September 22 the *World* adopted a defensive tone, stating that the Democratic party was no more bound by Blair's declarations, made before his nomination, than it was bound by similar declarations by Seymour. " The platform, and not anybody's antecedent private utterances, embodies the policy of the Democratic party." This was in answer to the Republican assertion that the nomination of Blair placed the Democracy on record as upholding the doctrine of the Brodhead letter.

The Brodhead letter was not disavowed by all the Democratic journals, however. The Charleston *Mercury* said that the platform of the party squarely accorded with the letter, which was " the legitimate and actual expounding of the plat-

[90] *Tilden Letters*, vol. i, pp. 240-241, July 15, 1868.

form." [91]　Some Northern papers took a similar attitude. The Washington *Express* said the letter had the approval of every intelligent man of the Democratic party, and wished that " our opponents may attack it, and the oftener the better." [92]　The *Express* considered it " the keynote of the music under which the Democrats will march to certain victory," and prophesied that in the event of a Democratic success the negro governments would suddenly collapse. [93]

Among individuals, Gideon Welles wrote in his diary, quite correctly, that Blair's letter stated his policy and the underlying principle of the campaign, which the Republicans would force the Democrats to accept or reject.　His nomination after this letter committed the party to his views. [94] Horatio Seymour was informed by an editor of Appleton, Wis., that Blair personally, and his letter in particular, excited violent denunciation in Wisconsin, with " the Democrats generally talking the worst." [95]　A North Carolina delegate to the national convention, Boyden, deserted the party because of the Brodhead letter.　He was quoted by Godkin in September as saying that Blair used no disguise.　" There is no talk here of a decision of the Supreme Court—no talk of a repeal of the Reconstruction Acts; but the Supreme Executive is first to expound those laws, declare them unconstitutional, null and void, and then send the army to enforce his decision at the front of the bayonet." [96]

In August, General Blair was stationed in the West. From Fort Saunders he wrote two letters in which he at-

[91] In Springfield *Republican*, August 4, 1868.

[92] August 6, 1868.

[93] August 7, 1868.

[94] July 9, 1868, vol. iii, pp. 398-399.

[95] July 14, 1868.　*Seymour Papers*, New York Historical Society Library, Box 4.

[96] London *Daily News*, October 3, 1868.

tempted to clear himself of the charge of being a revolutionist. On August 18, he referred to the statement which had been published in a Georgia Republican paper that Grant had said, " Let us have peace," while Blair had said, " Let us have war." He had never said any such thing. On the contrary, his policy alone could give peace. Grant's peace was to be achieved through the power of the military, and through actual war on the principles of the government.[97] On August 24 Blair added that the " vital principle " of the reconstruction acts had been held void by the Supreme Court in the Mulligan and Cummings cases. " The truth is that the Radicals are the real revolutionists." [98] The New York *Herald* further reported that Blair had written to a friend: " Everywhere I find the people in advance of their leaders. Only the politicians are intimidated by Radical threats. My business throughout this canvass will be to tell the truth, without fear or favor, regardless of myself or the party." [99]

The New York *Tribune* was prominent among those journals which affixed the title of " revolutionist " to Blair. Democracy, the *Tribune,* insisted, meant Revolution and Repudiation—the Brodhead letter and the greenback plank.[100] The New York *Evening Post* considered Blair's nomination " an act of startling boldness," if not of desperation. His election would be popular approval of his desire for bloody war. " It would be the adoption by the United States of a government by assassination and violence, instead of government by law." [101] The *Evening Post* spoke of him as a very

[97] To Col. R. A. Alston, Atlanta, Washington *Express*, Sept. 2, 1868, and elsewhere.

[98] To James Howes, Lafayette, Indiana, Cincinnati *Commercial*, Oct. 18, 1868; New York *Herald*, Oct. 21, 1868.

[99] August 24, 1868.

[100] July 16, 1868, for example.

[101] July 15, 1868.

different man from Seymour. Blair was unscrupulous, un-
hesitating, ambitious, determined and self-willed—" precisely
the timber from which revolutionists are made." [102]

One charge against Blair—that of excessive drinking—
seems to have some foundation. Gideon Welles, in his diary
for October 10, recorded that he feared that Blair was becoming a hard drinker. Blair, unlike Grant, who loved drink
for its own sake, was " convivial, social and given to a
spree. [103] Burr wrote to Welles on July 14 that Blair had
failed in an effort to speak at Bristol, Rhode Island, and Hartford, Connecticut, due to lack of sleep, and because he had
been drinking. [104] The *Nation* on July 23 reported that
Blair's " bill for two days at a Hartford hotel was—board
$10.00, lemons and whiskey $65.00, total $75.00." The Des
Moines *Register,* in August charged that Blair was grossly
intoxicated at a speaking appointment at Hamburg, Missouri.
The Chicago *Republican* asked, " is a habitual drunkard fit
for the high, honorable and responsible position of Vice-
President, with the Presidency in contingency? " [105]

The *Nation* attributed Blair's nomination to the desire of
the Democrats to have a Western soldier on the ticket, and
Blair was one of the few Western Generals with a creditable
war record who was not a supporter of Grant. In spite of
his war record, however, Blair was " one of the most utterly
uninfluential men in this country," due to his political vag-
aries. He brought no strength to the ticket, but would repel
many voters. [106] Godkin reported to his London paper, on
September 24, that Seymour recognized the damage being

[102] August 21, 1868.

[103] Manuscript Diary, *Welles Papers,* Library of Congress omitted
from published *Diary.*

[104] *Welles Papers,* Library of Congress, vol. 65.

[105] October 24, 1868.

[106] July 23, 1868.

done to the party by Blair, and the doubt which his nomination for Vice-President threw upon the result of the election.[107]

George William Curtis on July 30 wrote that in spite of professions of conservatism, the Democrats nominated for Vice-President one " who declares for a forcible overthrow of the reconstruction already established." The triumph of the Democratic ticket would show that the country regretted the success of the war " and desires to prove Wade Hampton's words to be true,—that the Rebellion will yet triumph." [108] Carl Schurz felt in the same way. In his Reminiscences he recalled that the " furious utterances of the fiery Frank Blair " in 1868, " sounded like the wild cry of a madman bent upon stirring up another revolution, while the people wanted peace. The Democrats were evidently riding for a fall." [109]

Blair wrote his letter of acceptance July 13, four days after his nomination. He endorsed the platform in toto, but did not think it necessary to reiterate his opinions upon questions separating the parties. He denounced the Republicans for their violation of Constitutional and individual liberties. He answered the charge that he was a revolutionist by saying " Those who seek to restore the Constitution by executing the will of the people condemning the reconstruction acts . . . are denounced as revolutionists. . . . It is revolutionary to execute the will of the people! It is revolutionary to execute the judgment of the Supreme Court! It is revolutionary in the President to keep inviolate his oath to sustain the Constitution! The appeal to the ballot is not war or revolution—it is the only road to peace." [110]

[107] London *Daily News*, October 7, 1868.

[108] *McPherson Scrap Book*, Library of Congress, vol. i, p. 106.

[109] Vol. iii, p. 286.

[110] *Official Proceedings*, Democratic National Convention, pp. 180-181.

A demagogue Frank Blair most decidedly was not. Every public statement of Blair during the campaign stressed the issue he raised in the Brodhead letter, that the reconstruction acts were unconstitutional and should not be enforced by the President. The consistency with which he stuck to his guns was one reason why in some Democratic circles a fear arose that his downright position was harmful to the ticket, and led to a public demand for his withdrawal as a candidate. Blair was made of sterner stuff than the timorous politicians who were frightened by his position. He had to wait eight years for his vindication, but in 1877 the remaining carpet-bagger governments in the South fell as he said they would fall, following a withdrawal of support by the President and the army.

But though Blair was an honest, brave man, there is some question as to his political sagacity. Conditions in 1868 were not the same as in 1876. The strategy indicated for the Democracy in 1868 was to take advantage of Republican discontent with Congress, and to go before the people with a moderate platform and a ticket calculated to appeal to War Democrats and Conservative Republicans. This strategy was not followed, with disastrous results. But having selected Blair, the party should have followed his example, and stuck to its guns, taking the offensive on all fronts, and not retiring to a position of explanation and excuse.

5. THE ATTITUDE OF JOHNSON AND THE CHIEF JUSTICE

As soon as the Convention adjourned the Democrats became anxious about the position Chase would take towards the ticket. The " Executive Committee " which had worked for Chase in the Democratic Convention was reported to have met on the evening of Seymour's nomination and resolved to support the Republican ticket,[111] but a week later the *World*

[111] New York *Tribune*, July 11, 1868.

printed a letter from a member of the committee denying this. On the contrary, he wrote, its members cheerfully and heartily endorsed the Democratic ticket.

Chase insisted in his correspondence during the campaign that he must be considered neutral—for although a Democrat in sentiment, he did not like the Democratic platform and was especially opposed to General Blair because of his " Brodhead letter " doctrine. To correspondents who asked him for advice, he refused to take sides, saying that he did not himself know how he would vote, if at all. He was unable to vote for Blair and was unwilling to vote for Grant.[112] Late in the campaign the New York *Herald's* Washington correspondent quoted Chase as denying that he had endorsed Grant, and as saying that he thought it due his official position to stand aloof.[113]

The Democrats were eager to obtain a word of approval from him. He was assured that the purity of his intentions as a candidate for the nomination were recognized and honored, and that support of the party nominees in 1868 would assure his nomination and election in 1872.[114] Prominent among those who urged Chase to support Seymour and Blair was his friend van Buren who on July 24 appealed to him not to throw away his new-made Democratic friends. He suggested that Chase support the Democratic ticket and, in the event of its success, leave the Supreme Court and become the inevitable leader of the party.[115] On August 26 van

[112] Letters of July 11, August 24, Sept. 30, Oct. 1 and 29, *Chase Papers*, Library of Congress; August 9, *Chase Papers*, Historical Society of Pennsylvania Library.

[113] October 10, 1868.

[114] J. H. Gilmer to Chase, July 20, in *West and South*, August 15; H. W. Williard to Chase, July 24; J. Lyons, July 24; *Chase Papers*, Library of Congress, vol. 101.

[115] *Chase Papers*, Historical Society Pennsylvania Library.

Buren compared Chase's position with that of General Jackson.   The people failed to get him in 1824, but the leaders had to give way in 1828.[116]   Van Buren took particular pains to assure Chase that Seymour was sincere in his desire to avoid the nomination and in his desire that Chase be selected. Seymour also made public his high opinion of Chase.   In an interview, he spoke " of the great influence the Chief Justice might wield hereafter by placing the government on a firmer basis." [117]

Towards Seymour personally, Chase had a friendly feeling that was exhibited by his correspondence.   He was confident that Seymour would have preferred a very different platform,[118] and declared that he was as much better than the platform as Blair was worse.[119]   He wrote to van Buren that he desired to vote for Seymour, but he could not swallow the reconstruction doctrines of Blair.[120]   Chase also informed a Nebraska friend that he preferred Seymour personally to Grant, but liked the Republican platform better than the Democratic.[121]   He did not hold Seymour responsible for the result of the Convention; " I believe he was sincere throughout." [122]

Chase's attitude towards the failure of the Convention to name him, indeed, was philosophical.   " God disposes of all things—Man only proposes," he wrote on July 14.[123]   The

---

[116] *Ibid.*

[117] Interview, August 20 in Washington *Express*, August 26, 1868.

[118] To J. G. Jones, July 11, *Chase Papers*, Library of Congress, Letter Book 8.

[119] To H. Barney, August 9, *ibid.*

[120] *Seymour Papers*, New York Historical Society Library, Box 4.

[121] To L. C. Jewitt, August 24, 1868, *Chase Papers*, Library of Congress, ser. 2, vol. iii.

[122] To John Paul, September 1, 1868, *ibid.*

[123] To Hamilton Smith, July 14, 1868, *ibid.*, Letter Box 8.

next day he wrote that he was glad he failed to receive the nomination. " It would have been my duty to accept, but I should have been obliged to put my own construction on the platform, and the position would have been far from comfortable." [124] He similarly told Archbishop Purcell of Rhode Island that he preferred his judicial post to the Presidency; [125] and on October 14 he wrote his old friend Charles D. Cleveland that he had wanted no nomination except on a platform he could endorse, and that he had " never ceased to be thankful that it was not offered to me with the platform which was actually adopted." [126]

Some time about the middle of July Chase gave a statement of his relation to the Democratic Convention to his secretary, Schuckers, which with other documents was printed in a leaflet called, " Mr. Chase's Views," bearing the date of August 1, 1868. Just what was the purpose of this leaflet is not clear. Chase was not seeking a third party nomination, and his letters show him scrupulous in maintaining a position of political neutrality. It was probably for distribution among Chase's friends with the idea of justifying himself, or clearing his record of the charges that had been made against him in connection with his candidacy. No mention was made of it in the journals of the day.

The New York *Herald* had been Chase's most ardent and consistent supporter for the nomination. It was disconsolate over its failure to achieve his nomination, and continued to believe that Chase was favored by a majority of the thinking men of the party.[127] Chase appreciated the efforts of the *Herald* in his behalf, as is shown by a letter he wrote to Bennett on July 10. " Your advocacy of my nomination

[124] To Rev. Dr. Nadal, *ibid.*
[125] *Ibid.*
[126] *Chase Papers*, Historical Society Pennsylvania Library, Box 15.
[127] Stebbins, *op. cit.*, p. 344, cites New York *Herald*, July 10, 11, 1868.

. . . was, as I know very well, prompted by no personal consideration," but was due to " your wishes for the welfare of the country.   If you did not accomplish your main object, you called out a magnificent expression of public sentiment and pushed your movement to the very gates of victory." [128]

There was some pressure brought to bear upon Seymour to induce him to refuse the nomination after the Convention had acted.   The Washington correspondent of the New York *Herald* stated the situation in the capital in a dispatch of July 11.   The suggestions from conservatives that Seymour be replaced by Chase seemed to be gaining ground.   With Seymour out of the way, the vacancy would be filled by the National Democratic Committee which would nominate Chase with Blair or some one else for Vice-President, and call upon the States to ratify the change in State conventions which it was hoped would be completed by the middle of August.   " This movement is not confined to mere talk, but measures have already been adopted towards carrying it into effect." [129]

Among those who wished Seymour to decline in order that Chase might be substituted in his place, none was so active or urgent as Alexander Long.   On July 14 he wrote to Seymour, prophesying his defeat and urging him to allow Chase, whose election would be certain, to take his place at the head of the Democratic ticket.   He sent a copy of this letter to Schuckers.   Pendleton and Washington McLean, Long said, refused to have anything to do with inducing Seymour to withdraw.   Long told Schuckers that it had been charged in Cincinnati that McLean and others of the Ohio delegation received a large sum of money for bringing about Seymour's nomination.   Seymour, Long wrote, is weak, timid and eas-

[128] *Chase Papers*, Library of Congress, Letter Book 8.
[129] July 14, 1868.

ily wrought upon, "and should be." [130]   On July 23 Long
wrote to a Philadelphia friend that the Germans of the Northwest were anxious for Chase to be a candidate, and that he
still had hopes that Seymour would decline.   "If we get one
week more at him he must get out of the way. . . ." [131]

Rumours of a third party movement, with Chase as its
nominee, began almost immediately after the Democratic
nominations. [132]   It was reported and denied that the President was in favor of this move. [133]   These rumours also
denied the willingness of Chase to head a third ticket, and
mentioned a proposed Conservative convention, to be held
at Pittsburgh or Cincinnati on August 15. [134]   The *Nation*
remarked that in spite of Chase's "moral downfall," a second
nomination in opposition to Grant was unlikely, for it would
be tantamount to defeat, and a "confession of imbecility"
which even the Democrats would not be likely to make, even
though, as Godkin wrote to his London paper, Chase "really
seems ready to accept a nomination from anybody on any
platform." [135]

Among individuals, Charles G. Halpine was prominent
among the third party advocates.   On July 11 he wrote to
Chase that the "disgust" at the treachery of Tammany Hall
was widespread and asked him if he would consent to run. [136]
A few days later he was reported as preparing to take part in

[130] *Chase Papers*, Historical Society Pennsylvania Library, Box 23.

[131] *Ibid.*, p. 1 missing.

[132] New York *Herald*, July 12, Chicago *Republican*, July 13, New York
Tribune, July 14, 1868.

[133] Chicago *Republican*, July 13, Washington *Express*, July 14, Utica
Observer, July 15, New York *Tribune*, July 16, *Nation*, July 16, 1868.

[134] Washington *Express, op. cit.*, Cincinnati *Commercial*, July 13, Utica
Observer, July 15, New York *Tribune*, July 16, *Nation*, July 16, 1868.

[135] July 15, to London *Daily News*, July 28, 1868; *Nation*, July 16, 1868.

[136] Oberholtzer, *United States*, vol. ii, p. 183n.

a third party organization to nominate Chase.[137]   Whatever
action Halpine may have had in mind was terminated by his
death, on August 3.   He died from an overdose of chloro-
form, taken to relieve pain.[138]   Chase's reply to Halpine, as
well as others was the same—" It is impossible for me to
consent to any further use of my name " in connection with
the national election, or any new political movements.[139]

But Chase's friends were by no means so considerate of
Seymour as he was.   Three men who were supporters of the
Chief Justice attacked the Democratic leader vigorously—
Col. William Brown of Nicolasville, Kentucky, in a speech
on August 20, Henry Reed of the Cincinnati *Enquirer,* who
wrote in the *West and South,* and Alexander Long, who was
quoted at length by Reed in an article on August 29.

Brown's speech was before the Grant Club of Frankfort,
Kentucky.   He traced the Chase movement, before and during the Democratic Convention, and quoted from letters to
him from Chase, in an effort to show that Chase did not
wish to lead an anti-Grant movement.   Brown stated that
Chase expected the election of Grant, and that the friends of
Chase should support Grant.   Brown denounced Seymour as
" weak, nervous and cowardly," and his cowardice was responsible for the failure to select Chase as the nominee.   The
Cincinnati *Commercial* referred to this speech as Brown's
" powerful appeal to all progressive Democrats " to support
Grant.   The New York *Evening Post* said that if Brown
were right " no one can justly blame Mr. Chase for consenting to the movement in his favor." [140]

[137] Cincinnati *Commercial,* July 18, 1868.

[138] Washington *Express,* August 3, 1868.

[139] Letters, July 13, 16, 17, *Chase Papers,* Library of Congress, Letter
Book 8.

[140] Cincinnati *Commercial,* August 24; New York *Herald,* August 26;
New York *Evening Post,* August 26, 1868.

On September 2, Chase wrote to Brown. He regretted Brown's quotations from what Chase had said and written, and in part questioned their accuracy. He asked him not to print anything else from his letters without his permission. As for Seymour, Chase was sure that Brown's speech was intended to be entirely fair towards him, " but is it not somewhat too deprecatory in tone? Justice to him is a duty for us." [141]

Another attack on Seymour was published in the *West and South* for August 29. It was written by Henry Reed, who until August had been connected with Washington McLean's Cincinnati *Enquirer*.[142] He had contributed articles to the *West and South* during the spring favoring Chase's nomination. Reed described the maneuvers in the Convention leading to the nomination of Seymour, which he called " the coup de thimblerig." He quoted at length from a statement by Alexander Long which placed Seymour in a very bad light. Reed said that Seymour was " either weak or dishonest, and that his conduct owed its origin either to treachery or imbecility is so palpable as to forbid denial." [143]

Seymour did not permit these attacks to go without rebuke. On September 8 he wrote to van Buren that " I am constantly subjected to the most indecent attacks from the friends of Mr. Chase and in putting out their untruths they claim to speak as his active supporters. It certainly begins to look as if he was a consenting witness to their assaults." Chase should " call off the dogs," and " is at least in honor bound to discountenance the conduct of his friends." [144] Van Buren wrote to Chase concerning the attacks on Seymour,

[141] Warden, *op. cit.*, pp. 712-713; *Chase Papers*, Library of Congress, Letter Book 8.

[142] Cincinnati *Commercial*, August 2, 1868.

[143] *West and South*, August 29, 1868; New York *Herald*, Sept. 6, 1868.

[144] *Seymour Papers*, New York Historical Society Library, Box 4.

and Seymour's indignation at them.   Chase replied that " I neither share nor countenance any representations derogatory to Governor Seymour."   He believed Seymour to be " an accomplished statesman, an upright citizen and in all his private relations, irreproachable.   That he accepted the nomination under the circumstances, is, I think, to be regretted; but is not to be censured." [145]

It can be said that Chase's attitude towards the two tickets and platforms in the field was one of personal friendliness for Seymour, strong objection to Blair, and opposition to the reconstruction plank in the Democratic platform; while on the Republican side he did not care for Grant personally, but admired his " let us have peace " sentiment, and preferred the Republican to the Democratic positions on the Southern States, although he distrusted the program of the Radical Congress.   He held himself neutral during the campaign.

President Johnson was disappointed by his failure to receive the Democratic nomination, and was not favorably disposed towards Seymour.   He complained to Welles that Seymour had not lifted a finger to sustain the administration throughout the three years' struggle, and that he and his friends had been wholly ignored by the Democracy.[146]   Press reports from Washington stated that the President was " entirely disgusted," and that he did not conceal his chagrin.[147] The Washington correspondent of the New York *Herald* reported that the President would be likely to give his support to Seymour.[148]

The President's dissatisfaction with the Democratic nominees was reported to Tilden, by J. D. Hoover of the Democratic Congressional Committee, on July 15.   Hoover in an

[145] Van Buren to Seymour, September 24, 1868, *ibid.*

[146] *Diary*, vol. iii, p. 403, July 11, 1868.

[147] Albany *Argus*, July 11, 1868; Chicago *Republican*, July 13, 1868.

[148] July 14, 1868.

interview found the President antagonistic because of Seymour's alleged hostile position toward him and the administration.   A Seymour ratification meeting was to be held on
July 18 at Washington, and Hoover asked Tilden to come
and see the President in order to obtain his participation in
the meeting.[149]   Tilden did not go to Washington himself,
but sent van Buren to sound out the President as well as
Hendricks, Hancock, and other leaders whose attitude was
important.

Van Buren on July 18 found Johnson " not only cross but
implacable," and convinced that Seymour was personally unfriendly to him and had wished to see him removed by the
court of impeachment.   The President " seems to want some
deference.   When asked what he is going to do about the
ticket, he replied, ' What is Mr. Seymour going to do towards
the administration? ' "   Johnson said he would not come out
for Seymour and Blair if serenaded by the ratification meeting that evening, so they left him alone.[150]

That Seymour was concerned over the President's attitude
towards him is shown by a letter to Senator Doolittle on
August 4, in which he said that the President " is surrounded
by men very hostile to me, and he has been misled as to my
views and feelings." [151]   During the summer Seymour made
some attempt to influence the President's appointments.   He
wrote Johnson a number of times, recommending various
individuals for positions.[152]   As the campaign advanced, it
became more and more evident that the President would
openly support the Democratic ticket.

On August 25 Seymour was told by Johnson's friend Philo

[149] *Seymour Papers*, Albany.

[150] July 20, 1868, *Seymour Papers*, Albany.

[151] *Magazine of Hstory*, vol. xvii, p. 59.

[152] July 29, Sept. 24, *Johnson Papers*, Library of Congress, vols. 142,
145, 146.   C. Welch to Seymour, August 10, *Seymour Papers*, Albany.

Durfee that the President would give him all the support in his power. Durfee referred to a letter he had just received from the President.[153]

But Johnson decided to support the Democrats only after assuring himself of Seymour's attitude towards himself. His friend John F. Coyle, editor of the *National Intelligencer,* had an interview with Seymour and Tilden in August, and reported the result to the President. Coyle was positive in his assurances that Seymour held the President in high respect and admiration, and if elected, would be glad to accept Johnson's advice. Seymour had been earnest in expressing the hope that Johnson's " services would not be lost to the country in the future; " in other words, he offered an appointment to Johnson, if he should be elected. As for the allegation that Seymour desired Johnson's removal, Seymour had in fact " sought an opportunity to express his sympathy with you " during the impeachment trial, and in his speech at Albany on March 11 had denounced the course of the Radical Senators. Of Tilden Coyle reported that his " active sympathy with you in all your trials has been undisguised." [154]

Johnson's correspondence in July contained a number of suggestions that he lead a third ticket. H. R. Lieberman, President of the " Andrew Johnson Veteran Volunteer Club," wrote to the President on July 13 that the soldiers were not satisfied with the Democratic nominations, and that a third party, headed by Johnson or Chase would sweep the country. " If something is not done at once the soldiers and sailors will support that traitor Grant." [155] A Philadelphia correspondent told the President that he had written to Chase, on behalf of a large group in Philadelphia, asking the Chief Justice to come out for Johnson as a third party candidate,

153 *Seymour Papers*, New York Historical Society Library, Box 4.

154 August 20, 1868. *Johnson Papers*, Library of Congress, vol. 144.

155 *Johnson Papers*, Library of Congress, vol. 142.

on a high tariff, greenback and equal suffrage platform.[156] No replies of the President to these suggestions have been seen. Unlike Chase, when Johnson had nothing to say, he said nothing. That he ever seriously considered the proposal that he run on a third ticket is extremely doubtful. The evidence on this point is lacking.

With President Johnson finally committed to the support of the Democratic ticket, the party leaders began to consult him on the problems of the campaign. On August 28, Tilden wrote asking his advice about the action of the party in Tennessee. On September 4, he asked Johnson to approve leaves of absence for Democratic Generals in order that they might campaign in Maine. In this letter Johnson was told that Seymour recognized " as we all do," his devoted patriotism in " dealing with the present situation of our country." [157] On September 4 Sanford E. Church of New York came to Washington for a series of conferences with the President on the political situation. Church told Welles that his interview on September 5 was very satisfactory, and Welles noted that " there is a strong desire to bring the administration into the support of Seymour and Blair. Hitherto but little has been done in this direction." [158]

In September the President showed evidence that he would take a more active part in the canvas. On the 21st he wrote to John Quincy Adams, thanking Adams for his letter accepting the Democratic nomination of Massachusetts. Adams had stated the issue clearly—the Constitution versus the Congress. On the 23d Adams replied to the President. " My grandfather used to predict that when the great slavery struggle which he saw impending closed, there must come a great constitutional party or anarchy, and today it seems to

[156] Lewis Cooper, July 16, 1868, *ibid*.

[157] *Johnson Papers*, Library of Congress, vols. 144, 145. " Confidential."

[158] *Diary*, vol. iii, pp. 429-430.

me high time for calm and patriotic men to be gathering around the organic law." [159]

On October 22 Johnson took the most outspoken position in favor of Seymour that he assumed during the campaign. The drift towards the Republicans had become so great that Seymour was prevailed upon to make a speaking tour in the North and Northwest. Johnson sent him a telegram of encouragement, which was published.

I see it announced in the papers of this morning that you will enter the Presidential canvass in person. I trust this may be so, as the present position of public affairs justifies and demands it. It is hoped and believed by your friends that all enemies of constitutional government, whether secret or avowed will not be spared; and their arbitrary and unjust usurpations, together with their wasteful, profligate and corrupt uses of the peoples' treasure will be signally exposed and rebuked. The mass of the people should be aroused and warned against the encroachments of the despotic power now ready to enter the very gates of the citadel of liberty. I trust you may speak with an inspired tongue, and that your voice may penetrate every just and patriotic heart throughout the land. Let the living principles of a violated Constitution be proclaimed and restored, that peace, prosperity and fraternal feeling may return to a divided and oppressed nation.

Andrew Johnson.[160]

The position of President Johnson during the campaign was peculiar. He was undoubtedly snubbed by the Democratic National Convention, and indeed, had received little support from the Democracy since the failure of the Democratic-Conservative movement of 1866. Now that the Democrats wanted his influence, especially in the matter of patronage which might affect the election, they were solicitous

[159] *Johnson Papers*, Library of Congress, vol. 145.

[160] *Johnson Papers*, Library of Congress, Telegrams sent. New York *World*, Oct. 24, 1868.

in their wishes for his welfare. Should he ignore them, as they had ignored him, or should he lend his aid for the larger purpose of defeating his enemies the Radicals, and more particularly his personal enemy General Grant? After some hesitation, Johnson raised his voice for Seymour, but there is little evidence that he made political removals in order to injure the Republican ticket.

The position of the members of Johnson's cabinet towards the two parties was divided. For the most part, they took little active part in the campaign whatever their sympathies.

Secretary of State Seward had little liking for either candidate, and took no part in the campaign until October 31st, when he spoke half-heartedly for the Republican ticket, and included in his remarks praise for the President, Generals Hancock, and McClellan, and other Conservative Democrats.[161] Seward's hesitancy in supporting the Republican ticket was noted by the party press, but he was not censured, because of his long record of party service. Secretary McCulloch was dissatisfied with the Democratic candidates and platform, especially the greenback plank, and he would have preferred the nomination of Chase.[162] However, he considered that the reconstruction issue overshadowed all others, and on that issue he agreed with the Democrats;[163] and assisted the Democrats with the patronage at his disposal.[164]

Secretary of War Schofield, the newest addition to Johnson's Cabinet, was friendly to his old commander Grant, but

[161] Welles, *Diary*, vol. iii, p. 401, July 10, 1868; Chicago *Republican*, Nov. 1, 1868. Seward spoke at his home town, Auburn, N. Y.

[162] Welles, *Diary*, July 10, 1868, vol. iii, p. 401.

[163] Philo Durfee to Seymour, August 31, *Seymour Papers*, New York Historical Society Library, Box 4; New York *Herald*, August 31, New York *Evening Post*, Sept. 3, 1868.

[164] McCulloch to Pres. Johnson, Sept. 19, *Johnson Papers*, Library of Congress, vol. 145, Springfield *Republican*, September 16, 1868.

took no part in the campaign.[165]　Attorney-General Evarts took no active part in the contest, although the New York *Times* labeled him the most distinctive Republican in the Cabinet.[166]　The *National Intelligencer* and the New York *Herald* referred to him as a Grant supporter, while the *Tribune* commented on his remaining aloof from the contest.[167]　Postmaster-General Randall was another who did not take kindly to Seymour's candidacy, and was variously reported to favor both parties.[168]　On July 26 Seymour was informed that while Randall, who was opposed to Grant and the Radical control in Congress, was dissatisfied at the result of the Democratic National Convention, yet an overture from Seymour would secure his cooperation.[169]　On August 25 it was suggested to Seymour that Randall might get for the Democrats a share of the contributions levied upon clerks in the New York post office for political purposes.[170]　The New York *Tribune* stated that Randall " manages with indifferent success to ride two horses at the same time." [171]　Whatever opinions he held, he was not active for either ticket.

Secretary Welles was the most outspoken supporter of the Democratic ticket in the Cabinet.　He was not pleased with the nominations or the platform, as we have seen, but supported Seymour as the only course open to opponents of Radicalism.[172]　Welles took his support into the open on Oc-

[165] New York *Herald*, Sept. 28, August 18, 1868.　New York *Tribune*, Sept. 4, 1868.

[166] September 28, 1868.

[167] August 13, 18, September 4, 1868.

[168] Philadelphia *Evening Star*, July 28, New York *Herald*, August 18, 31, New York *World*, August 30, 1868.

[169] C. A. Eldrige, *Seymour Papers*, New York Historical Society Library.

[170] C. J. Palmer, *Seymour Papers*, Albany.

[171] September 4, 1868.

[172] *Diary*, vol. iii, p. 405, July 17, 1868.

tober 3, when he wrote a letter to be read at a Democratic meeting in New York city. He said he would rejoice in the defeat of the Republicans, and in the triumph of those " who are striving for a restoration of the Union." [173] Secretary Browning, according to Welles, viewed the Democratic nomination very much as did McCulloch.[174] He was generally reported as opposed to the Republican ticket, although not active in behalf of the Democrats.[175]

Viewing the Cabinet as a whole, it can be said that the Democrats could hardly expect much active support from its members, although the general sentiment was unfavorable to Grant.

It is a matter of some interest that such men as Welles, McCulloch and Browning, in spite of their disappointment with the action of the Democratic National Conention, should desire the defeat of the Republican ticket. The Republican party had covered much ground since 1865, when such old Lincoln supporters had drifted away from it.

[173] *National Intelligencer*, October 7, 1868.

[174] *Diary*, vol. iii, p. 401, July 10, 1868.

[175] New York *Herald*, August 18, 31; New York *Tribune*, September 4; New York *Times*, September 28, 1868.

CHAPTER XI

The Campaign

I. THE ISSUES

Just as there was greater unanimity as to the candidate among the Republicans than among the Democrats, so the Republicans came nearer to presenting a " united front " on the issues before the country.

The lack of unity among the Democrats on the problems of the day was aptly described by the Springfield *Republican* on September 16. " Will the historian be able to tell what the Democratic party did advocate in this election? A pretty body of material he will have to digest. . . ." The *Republican* mentioned Chase's platform, a hard money, equal rights document; Seymour's speech before the National Convention in which he opposed the greenback idea; Blair's Brodhead letter; Seymour's letter of acceptance; the eloquence of the Southern fire-eaters; General Hampton's account of the reconstruction plank, and the fraternal addresses of the Southern Democrats to the negroes. " What wonder, he will say, that a party thus constituted miserably failed and great was the fall of it."

The New York *Evening Post* on September 28, chided the Democrats for failing to offer a programme of their own, saying that they found fault with the Republicans but offered no indication of their own course if successful. The platforms gave no light, and Blair's Brodhead letter seemed to the *Post* the only certain guide to a correct understanding of Democratic policy. The Chicago *Republican* thought that the Democrats, to have any hope for success, should unite on a more promising issue than that of bold revolution only.[1]   Leslie's Weekly said that there was no vital principle of union among the Democrats, and that their national platform was nowhere accepted as a whole.[2]

The reconstruction issue in its various forms was that which produced the strongest feelings and upon which the Democrats showed the greatest tendency to give ground when attacked.   The preëminence of the reconstruction issue was generally recognized by the Democrats at the beginning of the summer campaign, although there was a tendency to push it into the background during the latter part of the contest.   On July 14 the New York World defined as the primary issue of the campaign the unconstitutionality of the reconstruction acts, and as the secondary issue the financial problems before the country.

The Republican press agreed that a Democratic victory would mean the elimination of the reconstruction laws and an end to negro suffrage.   The New York Times, among others, had so stated before the Democratic convention,[3] and following the nominations, the Republican press was vociferous in charging that " Democracy is Revolution." [4]   If a Democratic victory would not mean revolution, what would it mean? asked the New York Tribune.   The Democrats were willing to take the responsibility of revolution, even unto war, charged the Tribune,[5] while the Nation considered that the party lines of 1860-1861 had been drawn. The fundamental issue was the power of the Federal government.[6]

[1] August 24, 1868.
[2] October 10, 1868.
[3] May 28, 1868.
[4] Chicago Republican, July 24, 1868.
[5] August 1, 1868.
[6] August 6, 1868.

The Fourteenth Amendment, which sought to rivet on the South the essential features of the Radical reconstruction policy, was subjected to attack from the Democrats, not only because of the partisan advantage it sought to give to the Republicans, but also because it was considered a flagrant invasion of State sovereignty.

An extreme though logical statement of the Democratic position was published in the Democratic St. Louis *Republican* in July. The *Republican* declared the ratification of the Fourteenth Amendment by the Southern States null and void, and predicted that if the Democratic party should win it would be so determined.[7] The New York *Herald* on July 24 deplored the tendency of some Democratic newspapers to make the Fourteenth Amendment the issue. As an issue in the State elections of 1866, it remarked, that Amendment gave the Republicans their heavy two-thirds vote in both houses of Congress; and it drew a distinction between the reconstruction acts and the amendments to the Constitution. The Democrats could sweep the reconstruction acts away and welcome. "But it is otherwise with what the war has written in the Constitution."[8] The *Herald* chided the party for being stout defenders of the Constitution, while refusing to recognize a part of it. " What Constitution? The ' Constitution as it was ' or the Constitution as it is? . . . What says Mr. Seymour? "[9]

The financial issues were subordinated to the " Revolution " issue by the Republicans, in spite of all efforts of the Democrats. Schouler correctly states the greenback question did not figure greatly in the contest which followed Seymour's nomination.[10]

[7] In New York *Evening Post*, July 28, 1868.

[8] August 17, 1868.

[9] August 25, 1868.

[10] *United States*, vol. vii, p. 125.

Seymour's position here was difficult. He was opposed to the "Ohio Idea," yet he endorsed the party platform without reservation. As Stanwood states, it was never seriously believed that he was in favor of the Greenback idea.[11] The *Nation* on July 23 thought that his opposition to "repudiation" would result in chilling the enthusiasm of the Western Democrats. The lack of unity among the Democrats on the financial issue was pointed out by the New York *Evening Post* on September 26. The Democratic platform stated the 5/20 bonds should be paid in money worth 70 cents on the dollar. "We hàve asked repeatedly whether the paper money is to be raised by taxing the people or by printing it. Leading Democrats differ in their answers. Some say by taxation, some by printing."

Divergent positions on finance were taken by Massachusetts Democrats in September. Where the New York Convention adopted a platform which called for the taxation of government bonds, one currency for all, and the payment of government bonds in legal tenders, except where gold was specified,[12] the Massachusetts platform demanded a *restoration* of gold and silver as the only legal tenders, and said nothing of bond taxation or the payment of bonds in greenbacks. The *Nation,* commenting on the Massachusetts platform on September 10, said there was little in it, except the endorsement of Seymour and Blair, that any Republican need object to.

The Democratic candidate for Governor of Massachusetts, John Quincy Adams, was even more outspoken on the financial issue than his State Convention. In his letter accepting the nomination (September 14) he frankly stated his disagreement with the Democratic national platform on this subject.

[11] *Presidency*, vol. i, p. 327.
[12] *American Annual Cyclopedia*, 1868, pp. 459-460.

The financial issue was not treated by the National Convention in New York in a manner which satisfied my judgment. By providing for a payment of the bonds, known as the 5/20's, by surplus revenue alone, thus ignoring what seems to me the valuable part of Mr. Pendleton's plan, a withdrawal of the issues of the National Banks, the Democratic party appeared to commit themselves to an indefinite extension of the intolerable nuisance of an irredeemable paper currency. I am too much of a Democrat to regard any such prospect with patience. I believe in hard money, and there I hold myself to be a true Jacksonian Democrat.

But he considered the reconstruction issue of greater importance than the financial one, and this determined his allegiance to the Democracy.[13]

Charges that the Democrats proposed to repudiate the National debt altogether, that they proposed to pay the Confederate debt, and that they proposed to pay slave holders for their emancipated slaves, were made by the more radical Republican journals. Among the Democratic journals, the weekly *West and South* frankly favored out-right repudiation of the nation's obligations,[14] but it was virtually alone in this position. The Springfield *Republican* stated on July 11 that "already we hear it proclaimed by Southern Democrats that they will secure a new issue of bonds to pay for the property lost by them in the war, and who will say that they will not succeed in everything, if once they are allowed to triumph?" The Washington *National Republican* and *Republican* both declared that the Southerners had been promised everything they wanted after a Democratic victory, and that the assumption of the rebel debt would be one of the first things asked for, in spite of the Fourteenth Amendment.

As a vote catcher, the greenback position of the Demo-

[13] Cincinnati *Commercial*, September 23, 1868.
[14] July 11, 1868.

cratic party was of dubious value. As stated by the New York *Herald* on August 16, the issue was popular " and the Democrats have got the whip hand of the Republicans on the issue. Still, neither party is entirely united on the question." The *Herald* believed that in the struggle between gold and greenbacks within the Democratic party, greenbacks would win. Stanwood states that on the greenback issue the Republicans " lost some votes of a certain class," but " they gained many others which were better worth having, even if they did not count any more." [15]

Closely related to the Greenback issue was the charge that the Republicans were wasteful in their expenditure of public money. The Democratic position took a number of forms. They charged that Republican extravagance was responsible for high taxes, resulting in the impairment of business and the failure of the greenbacks to reach par with gold. They added that the enormous sums spent by the Federal government were largely an incident of the Congressional reconstruction policy. The Southern policy was " the root of the whole evil," said Tilden in September.[16] Elect Seymour, end military expenses in the South, and taxes would be reduced and the greenbacks would increase in value. The Democrats also charged that a prolific cause of expense was the corruption among radical office holders. This connection between the greenback issue and extravagance was seized upon by many Democratic spokesmen, including Seymour, Tilden [17] and others of the " hard money " New York group, as a way out of the inconsistent position in which they had been placed by the Democratic planks on finance.

Other issues discussed during the campaign included the

[15] *Presidency*, vol. i, p. 327.

[16] *Tilden Writings*, vol. i, p. 422.

[17] E. g. Speech, September 24, 1868. *Writings*, vol. i, p. 422; Letter in New York *World*, October 12, 1868, *ibid.*, p. 453.

position of labor and the public land policy. On the first, a favorite point made by the Democrats was that the depreciated currency and high taxes which accompanied Republican rule were more oppressive to the laboring man than the capitalist. The Republicans retorted that the greenback policy of the Democratic platform would upset industry and deprive labor of employment. The Democrats made a bid for labor support by picturing Seymour as a friend of the workingman. The Utica *Observer* on August 18 reprinted a letter by Seymour, written in 1864, in which he acknowledged the right of workers to unite and agitate for the eighthour day and other betterments.

The public land policy of the Federal government, with its system of railroad grants, was not as much an issue in 1868 as some years later, but the Democratic platform attacked the land-grant system and insisted the public lands should be reserved for actual settlers. George W. Julian in a speech in Illinois on August 8 said the Democratic plank was good Republican doctrine, which the Democrats had appropriated. He pointed out that the Homested Act had been passed under Republican auspices after the Democrats had blocked it for many years.[18]

It is interesting to note that relatively little mention was made during the campaign of the business depression which had become troublesome in 1867. While this depression may have had a part in accounting for Democratic gains in 1867, it had little or no adverse effect on the Republicans in 1868, in spite of the fact that its effects still lingered.

2. ORGANIZATION

The Democratic National Committee was composed of one member from each of the thirty-seven States. It met in New York on July 9, after the adjournment of the Con-

[18] Julian, *Speeches on Political Questions* (New York, 1872), pp. 401, 402.

vention. August Belmont was chosen Chairman for another four years, and Frederick O. Prince of Massachusetts was again selected as Secretary and Treasurer. An executive committee of ten was chosen. This included representatives from the various sections: John Forsythe of Mobile, James McCloskey of New Orleans, and John W. Leftwich of Memphis; Frederick O. Prince of Boston and William Converse of Franklin, Conn.; August Belmont of New York and John McGregor of Newark, N. J.; Wilbur F. Storey of Chicago, Isaach E. Eaton of Leavenworth, and John G. Thompson of Columbus, Ohio.

In addition to the National Committee there was the Congressional Executive Committee composed of two Senators, five Representatives and four plain residents of Washington, D. C. The officers were Senator J. R. Doolittle of Wisconsin, Chairman, Representative Samuel J. Randall of Pennsylvania, Secretary, and Representative William H. Barnum of Connecticut, Treasurer. The other members were Senator Charles R. Buckalew of Pennsylvania, and Representatives J. M. Humphrey of New York, Lewis W. Ross of Illinois, and Lyman S. Trimble of Connecticut. Jonah D. Hoover, Charles Mason, General Thomas Ewing, Jr., and Montgomery Blair were the non-Congressional members. Blair was added on July 9. The others had served for some time.[19]

Chairman Belmont, who had served since 1860, was an able man of impeccable private and public character, of high standing as a financier. He was in a large measure responsible for the Democratic party holding together as well as it did during the turbulent eight years of his chairmanship. Unfortunately, there existed considerable prejudice against him because of his wealth and his known opposition

[19] *Official Proceedings*, Democratic National Convention, p. 183, New York *Herald*, July 1, New York *World*, July 2, 1868.

to the greenback plank.   As one of the leading financiers of
the country, he could hardly be expected to adopt Pendleton's " Ohio Idea."   He was preëminently a " hard money "
Democrat.

Largely because of this, Belmont was accused of being
tepid in his desire for Democratic victory.   It was reported
on July 20 that at a private Democratic gathering in New
York three days earlier, several ward politicians accused
Belmont and others of lukewarmness in the cause and a
reluctance to give pecuniary aid.[20]   Whether lukewarm or
not, van Buren wrote Seymour on September 23 that Belmont was not optimistic of success.   " I have a letter from
Belmont.   He is discouraged."   Van Buren added that
Belmont's health would not permit him to be of much use
in the campaign.[21]   Republican newspapers attempted to
cultivate the feeling against Belmont in the Democratic party
when they stated that the selection of the agent of the
Rothschilds, who were large holders of United States government bonds, as the national chairman, was rubbing it
into the Western Democrats.

Belmont was a firm believer in the necessity of keeping the
party ranks unbroken and the organization intact.   On
October 21, he issued as Chairman an appeal to the Democracy not to be discouraged by the Republican successes in
the October elections.   Following this, the condition of his
health made a trip to Europe necessary.   The New York
Sun suggested that he might have left the United States in
order to escape the debacle of his party in November.[22]

Although Seymour did not take an active, public part in
the campaign until near the end, he was no mere figurehead.
His letters show that he was greatly concerned about matters

[20] Cincinnati *Commercial*, July 21, 1868.

[21] *Seymour Papers*, New York Historical Society Library, Box 4.

[22] In Stebbins, *op. cit.*, pp. 384-385.

of party organization. On July 20 he wrote Tilden that he had given much thought to party organization and was convinced that a new course should be taken. The National Committee, due to its nature, should not be counted upon. Vigorous organization was necessary and could be obtained only by putting the young men of the party forward. Two gentlemen, Spencer of New York and Palmer of Wisconsin, had suggested a desirable plan for organization through clubs, and he asked Tilden to see them. Their plan was efficient, and would cost little. Seymour thought it should be entered upon at once, to the exclusion of other plans.[23] In furtherance of this plan, an " Order of the Union Democracy " was organized with headquarters in New York City. Tilden was Chief, Augustus Schell was vice-Chief, and James C. Spencer was Secretary.[24]

On August 4 Seymour wrote Senator Doolittle of Wisconsin, putting the party's interests in Washington in his hands. He suggests that the President should be shown the light. Seymour told Doolittle that as a candidate, no one had a claim on him. " I have not a single promise to redeem, nor have I uttered one word to any man as to my action in case we carry the country. I am therefore free to shape the canvass as shall be deemed best." [25]

On September 26 Seymour wrote Tilden, reviewing the campaign up to that time. He felt that the campaign had become stale and confused. He wanted the party's position presented to the public in a fresh manner, " in a way that will arrest public attention, and in a way that will meet the points urged by our opponents, as we now have need of that position." Seymour also made another organization suggestion.

[23] *Tilden Letters*, vol. i, pp. 242-243.
[24] *Seymour Papers*, Albany.
[25] *Magazine of History*, vol. xvii, pp. 58-59.

Now, every candidate for the Presidency must have a privy
council. There must be a number of men upon whom he can
lean, who will help to shape out before election a line of policy
which will carry the country through its difficulties. Able, influential, and thoughtful men should know now what they can rely
upon in the event of our success. With clear ideas on these points
we can work with more vigor, etc. Would it not be well to have
a meeting of ten or twelve persons who should talk matters over
clear through the coming year? Could not some position be
taken now which will do good in the way of foiling the attacks
of our opponents? Up to this time, with the exception of my
consultations with you and two or three others, I have been isolated
in my position. There are many advantages in this, but it should
not be held too long.[26]

The most important Democratic daily in New York City
was the *World,* edited by Manton Marble. It took a defensive position in the campaign as soon as the Republicans
began to score in their attacks on the Democrats for having
nominated the " Revolutionary " Blair for Vice-President.
In October it had shifted from a position of explanation and
defense to a demand that Blair get off the ticket, even if it
involved replacing the head of the ticket as well. This
attitude brought down upon the *World* the denunciation of
other Democratic papers. As early as July 16 it was criticised to Seymour as " more insipid than dishwater." [27] The
New York *Herald's* position was also the subject of considerable discussion among party leaders. During May and
June it had advocated Chase for the Democratic nomination,
and had given the Democrats much unasked advice. Bennett
was opposed to Seymour, and after the nominations endorsed Grant, although continuing to criticize the Southern
programme of the Republicans.

[26] *Tilden Letters*, vol. i, p. 247.

[27] N. J. Waterbury, *Seymour Papers,* New York Historical Society
Library.

Seymour was told that " matters may be changed with the *Herald* by the right men taking wise action." [28]   On July 15 Francis P. Blair, Sr., wrote Tilden suggesting how Bennett might be won over to the support of the Democratic ticket.   Blair had seen Bennett in New York before and after the nominations.   He was antagonistic to Seymour, but favorably disposed towards Frank Blair, Jr., who was a good friend of Bennett's son.   Blair offered to write for the *Herald* if its support could be obtained.

On August 10 Montgomery Blair notified Tilden that Bennett might be won over by an offer of a diplomatic post.

> . . . Bennett looks to position, and there is no getting him without assurance of it. . . . Chase got his support, I am sure, by promising him this mission if he was elected. . . . If Seymour could support Chase for the Presidency for his doings about impeachment I cannot see why he could not appoint Bennett for helping to save the country.   Seymour ought not, under any circumstances, to be approached on this matter.   But I think we might legitimately hold out hopes to Bennett and keep our promise of support in good faith.[29]

In spite of these plans the *Herald* did not give its support to Seymour, though it was vigorous in its defense of Blair against the attacks of the *World*.

Only one New York paper on the Democratic side showed genuine fighting spirit.   In August " Brick " Pomeroy, the " red hot " and " unterrified " Peace Democrat whose Lacrosse, Wisconsin, *Democrat* had been an ardent champion of Pendleton for the nomination, established his New York *Democrat*.   He announced it as an " out-and-out Democratic daily paper " which (so the *Tribune* reported), he said would " advocate the equality of the States or another war." [30]

[28] *Ibid.*
[29] *Tilden Letters*, vol. i, pp. 245-246.
[30] August 20, 1868.

In the weekly field the Republicans had a big advantage. The *Nation, Harper's Weekly,* the *Independent* and *Leslie's Weekly* all had national circulations and all were strongly Republican. The non-Republican weeklies could not compare with them in prestige or circulation. The best written was the *Round Table,* published in New York. This journal was essentially independent, though with strong Democratic leanings. It opposed Grant, but did not wax enthusiastic over the Democratic ticket. Another New York weekly, the *Day Book,* was unreservedly and even radically Democratic. It was of minor influence. In Cincinnati, the weekly *West and South* matched the papers of Pomeroy. It was an out-and-out State Rights Democratic journal, regarded as the mouthpiece of Alexander Long, and hence favorable to Chase's nomination. It did not take kindly to the Seymour and Blair ticket. State rights, free trade and hard money were its favorite issues.[31]   In September 1868, the *West and South* changed its name to the *Commoner,* but no change in policy was made.

Political parties need money as well as committees and journals. Here again the Republicans had a heavy advantage. Chairman Claflin and Secretary Chandler of the National Committee conducted the war-chest campaign. They were successful in exacting large sums from land-grant railroad promoters, and from leaders in finance and industry who, enriched by the war, were hopeful of future favors. Jay Cooke was most prominent among the Republican " angels " and contributed frequently and heavily.[32]   Others who gave large amounts to the Grant campaign were Vanderbilt, the Astors, A. T. Stewart and Henry Hilton. Never before, records Oberholtzer, had the demands of party managers been so " insolent," and never before was a

[31] Prospectus in issue of December 7, 1867.

[32] Oberholtzer, *Jay Cooke,* vol. ii, pp. 69-71.

candidate placed under such great obligation to men of wealth as was Grant, who was kept in the dark in this particular.[33]   The Democrats had a smaller field from which to draw, but they did their best.   Among the heavy contributors to Seymour's campaign were Chairman Belmont, C. H. McCormick, and Augustus Schell,[34] of New York, and William Corcoran of Washington.

The largest individual contributions to the Democratic cause, at one time, which have been noted were made by a group of eight leaders who gave ten thousand dollars each in August, and one who gave forty thousand dollars in October.   The eight leaders were Tilden, Belmont, Schell, McCormick, George I. Magee, Thomas C. Durant and Charles O'Conor.   Their agreement was dated August 15.[35] The individual who furnished $40,000 was H. T. Helmbold of New York.   His gift was reported in the Springfield *Republican* for October 15 with the comment that Helmbold, a patent medicine advertiser, knew " who his friends are, and where his patrons came from." [36]   Helmbold was prepared to back his choice with the wager of a million dollars, according to a signed notice in the Washington *Express* for October 27.

Levies upon Federal office holders for party purposes were complicated by the political situation in Washington.   With the President a Democrat, or at any rate, leaning heavily in that direction, the Cabinet divided, and Congress controlled by the Republicans, the clerks were exposed to attack on both sides.   The Democrats passed the hat first. On August 31 a circular was distributed to " clerks and

[33] Oberholtzer, *United States,* vol. ii, p. 187.

[34] Schell did not take a very active part in the campaign.   Francis Schell, *Memoir of Augustus Schell* (New York, 1885), p. 20.

[35] *Tilden Letters,* vol. i, p. 245.

[36] Also New York *Tribune,* October 20, 1868.

other employees of the government " signed by Montgomery Blair, Acting Treasurer, and J. D. Hoover, Secretary of the Financial Committee of the Democratic Congressional Committee. This circular was addressed to government employees " who claim to belong to the Democratic and Conservative party, and desire the election of Seymour and Blair, and are willing and desire to contribute their mite to the cause." They were told that every dollar given then would be worth ten given a month later.[37]

The Republican circular, in October, was briefer and spoke with greater authority. It was signed by William Claflin and William E. Chandler, Chairman and Secretary of the Republican National Committee, Senator Morgan of New York, Chairman of the Republican Congressional Committee, and Representative Schenck of Ohio, Chairman of the Republican Congressional Executive Committee. The circular " would suggest a voluntary offering in aid of the work. Whatever amount is contributed will be acceptable and judiciously expended." [38]

Seymour was told on August 25 that the clerks in the New York post office were to be assessed on August 31 by the Republicans one per cent on salaries of $1,000 and one and one-half per cent on larger salaries. It was suggested that Postmaster General Randall should be informed of the circumstance, that he might get a good share of the spoil for the Democrats.[39]

Suggestions for the spending of money for party advantage are never lacking. Perhaps the most audacious plan advanced at this time was that the Washington correspondents be bribed *en masse*. R. W. Latham wrote Tilden on July 13 that these correspondents were " in an organized

[37] Washington *Express*, September 3, 1868.
[38] Washington *Express*, October 21, 1868.
[39] C. J. Palmer, *Seymour Papers*, Albany.

state " and could be controlled for Seymour if $3,000 or $3,500 per month were made available. The Republicans, Latham said, had declined to pay them in cash, " but offer largely in case of success. This don't suit." The money should be distributed through F. P. Stanton, who had been a Chase worker. If Stanton has charge of it " you must succeed." [40]

As the campaign advanced, the hopes of each party were reflected in forecasts of the result. The *Nation* on June 4, predicted an electoral vote in November of 212 for the Republicans and 89 for the Democrats. It conceded New York, Connecticut, California, Oregon, Georgia and Arkansas to the Democrats. On June 23 the *Nation* revised its estimate, and forecast 205 for the Republicans and 99 for the Democrats. On July 14 the New York *Tribune* deprecated too great confidence in Grant's success. Again on August 7 it declared that it did not consider Grant's election certain.

But after the Republican victories in the September and October State elections, there was little talk of over-confidence. The general tone of the Republican press was that it was all over but the shouting.

On April 9, three months before the nomination of Seymour, the New York *World* claimed twelve States, including New York, Pennsylvania, Ohio, and Indiana, for the Democratic nominee. With the Southern States still out in April, 124 votes were necessary to elect. The *World* thought Minnesota, Maine, Nevada, West Virginia and Kansas might also go Democratic. On July 13, after the nomination, the *World* claimed a total of 160 votes. By this time all the Southern States except Texas, Mississippi and Virginia were in, but the *World* did not include any of them in its Democratic column. A note of lack of confi-

[40] *Tilden Letters*, vol. i, p. 240.

dence among the Democrats is also found in the *Washington Express,* which asked on September 26, " Will Seymour and Blair be elected? ' We hope so but we fear not ' is frequently the response in this city from men professing to be for them. . . . As for ourselves, we have no sort of doubt as to the triumphant election of the Democratic nominees."

But following the Republican victories in the October elections, there was little hope left among the Democrats in spite of the rallying cries of the party organizations. The last three weeks of the campaign were a period of supreme Republican confidence, which the election proved to be justified.

Reference has been made to the Democratic charges that Colfax was anti-Catholic and prejudiced against foreign-born citizens. Republicans attempted to discredit the Democracy on the ground that the great mass of Irish Catholics were members of that party. The Chicago *Republican,* commenting on the efforts of Democratic journals to make the Republican party responsible for anti-Catholic tirades, called it a " contemptible Democratic trick." " The [Republican] organization can not be held responsible for sermons which divines may preach from the pulpit." [41]

An example of the anti-Irish outburst from Republican sources appeared in the Chicago *Post,* on September 9.

Teddy O'Flaherty votes. He has not been in the country six months. . . . He has hair on his teeth. He never knew an hour in civilized society. . . . He is a born savage—as brutal a ruffian as an untamed Indian. . . . Breaking heads for opinion's sake is his practice. The born criminal and pauper of the civilized world . . . a wrong, abused and pitiful spectacle of a man . . . pushed straight to hell by that abomination against common sense called the Catholic religion, . . . To compare him with an intelligent freedman would be an insult to the latter. . . . The Irish

[41] July 31, 1868.

fill our prisons, our poor houses. . . . Scratch a convict or a pauper, and the chances are that you tickle the skin of an Irish Catholic.[42]

Some inroads into the New York Irish vote by the Republicans were reported. Godkin wrote the London *Daily News* on October 3 reporting such gains by the Republicans for the first time in the history of the party. The means used were said to be legitimate appeals to old memories of those who fought in the army. An Irish Republican campaign paper with wide circulation was started, and several influential Irishmen took the stump for Grant and Colfax.[43] George Francis Train, Irish agitator, was in a British jail at this time, and some Republican politicians got the bright idea of running him for the pugilistic John Morrissey's seat in Congress, with the hope that if elected the British would free him. All of which would appeal mightily to the Irish voters.[44]

Republican arguments with the Irish were not confined to appeals that they " rally 'round the flag." The *Irish People,* a paper edited by one D. O'Sullivan, supported the Democratic ticket until O'Sullivan received a check for $1,000 from a prominent Republican, whereupon the paper hoisted the names of Grant and Colfax. O'Sullivan then attempted to cash in on his new connection by inducing the New York Republican Committee to circulate his paper for him.[45]

All the Irish Democrats were not in New York. On October 30 the *National Intelligencer* printed an appeal of the disfranchized Irish of the South to their Irish fellow citizens of the North. " We are looking to the success of

---

[42] In Utica *Observer*, September 28, 1868.

[43] London *Daily News*, October 16, 1868.

[44] London *Daily News*, October 16, 1868.

[45] Utica *Observer*, October 19, 1868.

the Democratic candidates . . . to free us from the political bondage and the curse of mongrel rule." This appeal was issued by a group of ten Southern Irishmen from New Orleans, Mobile and Savannah who were visiting the North.

In the field of caricature, the Republicans had the enormous advantage of the pencil of Thomas Nast, whose pictures appeared in *Harper's Weekly,* and who also illustrated some of the campaign books of the humorist David R. Locke (Petroleum V. Nasby) of the Toledo *Blade.*

Nast had ridiculed Chase while the Chief Justice was being considered for the Democratic nomination, but not until the Democratic nominations did he reach the heights of inspiration. Commencing in July, *Harper's Weekly* contained each week one or more attacks on Seymour or his party by this greatest of American caricaturists. Examples of Nast's talent were: " The Lost Cause," showing a former Confederate and a New York Irishman searching with a light; " Out, damned spot ", showing Seymour as Lady Macbeth, attempting to eliminate the spot on his record caused by the New York draft riots of 1863; and a double cartoon, "Matched," picturing Seymour and the draft rioters in comparison with Grant at Vicksburg, both in July 1863.

The Democrats lacked both artist and the organ for the presentation, before a nation-wide audience, of cartoons caricaturing their opponents. Apart from a few pictures of "Butcher" Grant, virtually no Democratic cartoons appeared.

David R. Locke furnished the high spots in campaign humour for the Republicans. Locke wrote with the exaggerated misspelling which passed for humour at the time. He spoke as a Democrat of limited intelligence and culture, whose comments on the campaign revealed the alleged purposes and weaknesses of his party in Republican eyes. In the same vein in which he had attacked President Johnson in the Congressional campaign of 1866 in his letters from

" Confederit X. Roads, Kentucky," he now turned his attention to the Democrats. The principal example of his work in 1868 was " The Impendin Crisis in the Democracy." Locke stated that in the Democratic party " every sole may find rest—in it there is sich a variety . . . uv principle that every man, no matter wat the pekoolyer bent uv his mind . . . may find his rock upon which he may sekoorly rest." The Democratic platform was complete. " There isn't a man in the Yoonited States who cant get out uv it anything he wants." " What a gorjis seeries uv campane mottoes we ken put onto our banners! In Noo York we shel hev ' Seemore and Gold! ' In Ohio ' Blare and Greenbax.' In Kentucky ' Dimokrasy and Repoodiashun! " [46]

3. REPUBLICAN STRATEGY

The Radical element in the Republican party dominated the party counsels during the campaign following the nominations, and the Conservatives tended to be inactive although, as the fight progressed, they began to make themselves heard in support of Grant. Grant's reputation as a Conservative was carefully guarded by the Radicals in an effort to win over doubters. They were aided in this by the passive attitude taken by the General. Realizing he was no stump orator, Grant confined his campaign activities to brief interviews and a few trips to scenes of his pre-war life in Ohio, Illinois, Missouri and Kentucky and, in company with Generals Sherman and Sheridan, to Denver. Although this trip resulted in no speeches, the union of these three heroes of the war was made the subject of much ecstatic oratory by the party workers.[47] During the greater part of the campaign Grant remained in semi-seclusion at his house in Galena. With their candidate playing the part of a

[46] Pp. 3, 11, 15 (Toledo, O., 1868).
[47] Oberholtzer, *United States*, vol. ii, p. 185.

" strong, silent man," the Republicans could ignore the attacks upon him—that he was a soldier and no statesman, that he had been unfaithful to his friend President Johnson and so on—and could concentrate upon an offensive upon the enemy. The campaign may be likened to a prize fight in which one fighter continually forces the attack, never permitting the other to " get set ".

The Republicans organized the country much more thoroughly than the Democrats. Grant's early trade as a tanner was used as an excuse for " tanner " clubs throughout the North. The Democrats were going to be " tanned " in the best Appomattox fashion. Grant's military popularity provided the cue for organizing the " Boys in Blue," who were fighting with banner, cape and torch for the same cause as in '65. Mass meetings were held in numerous cities at which the veterans of the war were invariably given the spotlight. The greatest of these gatherings was a " mass convention " of veterans held at Philadelphia on October 1 and 2, and presided over by the inept General Burnside.[48] The circumstance that the date coincided with the date for voters' registration was not, perhaps, to be regretted by the party managers.[49]

One is struck by the fact that in general those soldiers with the highest war reputations took little active part in the campaign on either side. General Sherman, for example, confined his campaign activities to sending a letter to the Philadelphia mass meeting.[50] Sherman's attitude alarmed the Republicans and his silence was the subject of a special meeting of the Republican National Committee.[51] Other eminent military men who were inarticulate Republicans

---

48 New York *Herald*, October 2, 1868.

49 Washington *Express*, September 30.

50 New York *Herald*, October 2, 1868.

51 Gresham, *Life of W. Q. Gresham* (Chicago, 1919), vol. i, p. 344.

were Thomas, Sheridan and Meade. Still others—Hancock, Franklin, McClellan, Buell, Slocum, McClernand and Rosecrans—were Democrats in sympathy if not in campaign activity.[52]

In spite of the military emphasis the Republicans sought to give the campaign, it is noticeable that the military rallies did not occupy the center of the stage to the extent true in the contest of 1866. The reluctance of the most popular generals to take an active part was probably an important reason.

The Republicans relied upon the note of Grant's acceptance, " Let us have peace," to hold the Conservatives to the party. His magnanimous terms to Lee, his refusal to countenance a violation of the Appomattox parole, and the lengths to which he supported President Johnson until the preceding January were all used as bait for the Conservatives and " War " Democrats. As noted by Schouler who recorded his own impressions, in the minds of many the general direction of the campaign was towards harmony, and great hopes were held that Grant as President would allay the sectional controversy. A dramatization of this hope appeared on the vaudeville stage as a part of the Republican campaign—Grant acting as peacemaker between two quarreling brothers, one in blue and one in gray. Grant did not add to the attacks on the South which disfigured many a Republican speech, and what little he did say was in the direction of reconciliation.[53]

One important advantage possessed by the Republicans in the campaign was the control of Congress.[54] The recon-

[52] E. g. *National Intelligencer*, September 29, 1868.

[53] Schouler, *United States*, vol. vii, p. 126.

[54] 40th Congress, after admission of Southern representatives, except Georgia, Mississippi, Texas and Virginia, was: Senate, 54 Republicans, and 12 Democrats; House, 169 Republicans and 50 Democrats.

struction acts gave the Republicans tremendous assistance in those Southern States which were reorganized under their provisions, but Congress did not limit the party advantage to those States.   The three States still unorganized—Texas, Mississippi and Virginia—were excluded from representation in the Electoral College by a Senate Joint Resolution passed over the President's veto on July 20 by a strict party vote.[55]   A week later Congress adjourned, subject to recall by authority of their own resolution.   A member of each House, Representative Schenck of Ohio and Senator Morgan of N. Y., were designated as watch-dogs with the authority to determine whether and when Congress should reassemble during the campaign.[56]   Members of Congress were busy stumping their States and districts, but the Southern Republicans wanted Congress to remain on the job as a sort of emergency squad to pass new proscriptive acts if the Democrats showed signs of carrying their States.   Godkin thought that the Republicans would carry North Carolina and South Carolina in any event, but if the other States were to be carried for Grant he did not think it desirable that Congress should leave things as they stood until the December session.[57]   The Wasington *Chronicle* stated in August that " up to the present writing nothing has transpired to make us feel that our friends in the South will be safe or comfortable in the absence of Congress."   The judgment of the Southern Republicans seemed to be unanimous in favor of a special session.[58]

Congress reassembled on September 21 to compare notes on the campaign, but hardly more than a quorum was present.   The result of the national election was considered to be

[55] *American Annual Cyclopedia*, 1868, pp. 194-195.

[56] Washington *Express*, August 27, 1868, from Washington *Chronicle*.

[57] New York, July 24, London *Daily News*, August 8, 1868.

[58] Washington *Express*, August 27, 1868.

so much in doubt that the body adjourned to meet again on October 16, the Friday following the State elections in Pennsylvania, Ohio and Indiana. Had the Republicans lost the " October States " the majority was prepared to adopt some revolutionary measure to check the rising spirit of " disloyalty " in the North. But Republican victories made any such measures unnecessary and Congress adjourned to reassemble after the next danger spot — the November election. Had the Democrats carried the day, it is possible that the Republicans majority would have busied itself in devising some plan to dispose of Seymour as Tilden was disposed of eight years later.[59]

Godkin, referring to the September meeting, wrote in his London letter that " the mere assembling of Congress has always of late been found to have a very quieting effect on Southern tongues; and it is not improbable that, from now till November, we shall have a great abatement in the violence of the Hamptons, Forrests and others." [60]

The campaign seemed to lack spirit on both sides during July and much of August. This was probably due to Republican over-confidence on one hand and to the disrupting effect of the Democratic Convention struggle on the other. But as the September and October elections approached, both sides began to show increased activity — the Republicans advancing to the attack and the Democrats strengthening their defenses. The failure of the Democrats to take the offensive was due to a number of factors—the lack of agreement on the financial issues, the nervousness aroused in the timid by Blair's bold statements and a desire to conciliate the Conservatives. Whatever the reasons, the Republicans took full advantage of it and attacked on all fronts.

[59] DeWitt, *The Impeachment and Trial of Andrew Johnson* (New York, 1903), pp. 602-603; Oberholtzer, *United States*, vol. ii, p. 197.

[60] New York, September 19, London *Daily News*, October 3, 1868.

The Democracy was charged with Johnson's alleged misdeeds and was taunted with cowardice for having refused to nominate him.   It was accused of having a revolutionary purpose and Blair and the Southerners were attacked as murderers and the fomenters of a second civil war.   The Democrats of the East were labeled repudiationists, while the fact that Belmont headed the National Committee gave the Western orators the chance to charge the Democracy with being a tool of the Rothschilds.   With much wringing of the " bloody shirt " and much torchlight enthusiasm, the Republicans hailed the approach of the balloting.

The South furnished the Republicans with a storehouse of ammunition whence came " Southern outrages," revivals of the " Lost Cause," disloyalty " in many forms and other missiles for Republican ordnance.

4. THE CAMPAIGN IN THE SOUTH

A distinctive feature of the campaign of 1868 was the activity of many former Confederate leaders on one side, and the vigorous waving of the " bloody shirt " on the other. Few of the Southern generals figured in the political campaign.   Of those who did, Forrest of Tennessee and Hampton of South Carolina were the most prominent, both in reputation and in political activity.   But Southern civilian leaders, such as Hill and Toombs of Georgia and Vance of North Carolina raised their voices in the campaign.   Oberholtzer says this activity by the Southern leaders in behalf of the Democratic ticket was more effective than the speeches of the Republican orators in furthering the election of Grant. Nothing they said was allowed to escape Northern readers.[61]

On July 23, 1868, the *Nation* remarked that the most prominent feature of the campaign thus far was " the increasing boldness and prominence of the Southern Demo-

---

[61] *United States*, vol. ii, p. 188.

cratic politicians. They are exhibiting all the indiscretion which spoiled their game in 1865." It rejoiced over their activity. "The Southern politicians seem to possess the art, in the highest perfection, of ruining their own cause." Godkin also wrote his London paper on August 15 that the mere appearance in the political arena of such men as Toombs, Cobb and Forrest was of more service to the Republicans than all the orators and literature they could make use of.[62]

The Chicago *Republican,* commenting on the statements of Southern leaders, which it chose to consider as fomenting a new revolution, asked: "Do the Southern leaders mean it?" The *Republican* exclaimed, "Sure as there is a sun in high heaven, war is intended—war to the knife, the knife to the hilt, the hilt to the heart." [63] *Harper's Weekly,* more moderately, stated that the earnest conviction of the Southerners like Wade Hampton made the campaign a simple one: Grant and Peace, or Blair and Revolution.[64]

What were some of these incendiary statements the former Confederates were charged with making? Hampton was accused of saying that the Confederate flag had been preserved, and that he would some day use it to rally his old comrades in arms. This Hampton denied at Columbia, S. C., on August 7. What he really said was that the Confederate flag was furled, "to be buried in the grace of our lost cause." [65] Zebulon Vance of North Carolina was reported to have said that "what the Confederacy fought for would be won by Seymour and Blair." [66] Benjamin H. Hill of Georgia, in a speech at New York to the Young Men's

[62] London *Daily News,* August 31, 1868.

[63] September 8, 1868.

[64] October 3, 1868.

[65] *McPherson Scrap Book,* vol. vi, p. 9 (Library of Congress).

[66] New York *Evening Post,* September 30, 1868.

Democratic Union, declared that no matter who was elected President, the Southern States, each for itself, " will quietly, peacefully, but firmly take charge of and regulate their own internal domestic affairs in their own way, subject only to the Constitution."   Hill wanted to know if Grant, as President, would send troops to the South to regulate their affairs in an unconstitutional manner.[67]

Robert Toombs of Georgia was reported to have said on July 23 that in the event of Democratic victory, the " so-called Governors and legislatures which have been established in our midst shall at once be made vacate.   The Convention at New York appointed Frank Blair especially to oust them." [68]   *Harper's Weekly* early in September printed a collection of expressions by Southerners.   Howell Cobb was quoted as saying that the reconstruction acts were void and that the " grinning skeletons " in control of the Southern States would be ousted if Seymour and Blair were victorious. Albert Pike of Arkansas had written in the Memphis *Appeal:* " The South is our land, the North is a foreign and hostile realm. . . . The day will come when the South will be independent."

The Southern leaders were in a peculiar position.   If they voiced their real affection for the Lost Cause and detestation of the Radical Republicans, their remarks were sure to be interpreted as calling for a new uprising.   If they talked peace and moderation (as most of them did), the Republican accounts of their remarks were interlined with things they did not say.   Under the circumstances, they had better have kept quiet, but this they did not do.   And some of the former Confederate Brigadiers continued to slip a " Rebel Yell " from time to time into their speeches.

[67] Hill, *Senator Benjamin H. Hill* (Atlanta, 1891), p. 330.   Speech on October 6, 1868.

[68] New York *Tribune*, August 1, 1868.

The Democratic leaders in the North were not blind to the damage that was done their cause by the actual or imaginary speeches of the Southerners. Hampton was told to forget about the " Lost Cause " in his speeches.[69] The New York *World* labeled his speeches " silly," and the Charleston *Mercury* and the Richmond *Whig* criticised him for " showing our hand too soon." [70] Tilden realized the importance of not arousing Northern feeling by intemperate acts or utterances on the part of Southerners. On August 28 he wrote to President Johnson asking his advice on the situation in Tennessee. " All friends of the Democratic party are deeply interested in seeing that no opportunity be given for any attempts on the part of the present ruling power in Tennessee to revive the old antagonism of any portion of our Northern people. The greatest moderation, prudence, and forbearance should under all circumstances be practiced by all who love their country and hope to see it restored." [71]

Benjamin H. Hill, whose New York speech on October 6 has been referred to, was one of a group of Southerners, including Cobb, Vance, and John B. Gordon, who came North during the campaign to explain the real attitude of the South. Their efforts were not encouraged by Northern Democrats, as it concluded that their appearance would not aid the Democratic cause.[72] Deprived of a rostrum, Hill turned to the press and wrote letters to the New York *Times* and *Herald* emphasizing the moderation of the Southerners.[73] The Cincinnati *Commercial,* commenting on their absence from the platform, wanted to know the reason. " Would it be disagreeable to have Messrs. Cobb and Hill

[69] Spencer to Seymour, Aug. 1, 1868. *Seymour Papers,* Albany.

[70] *Nation,* August 6, 1868.

[71] *Johnson Papers,* Library of Congress, vol. 144.

[72] Pearce, *Benjamin H. Hill* (Chicago, 1928), pp. 191-192.

[73] *Times,* Oct. 9, 11, 12 ; *Herald,* October 3, 8, 1868.

tell the Northen people plainly what construction is put upon the Tammany platform down South?" [74]

General Rosecrans was alive to the danger arising from uncensored statements by the former Confederates. On August 5 he wrote with considerable agitation to Seymour because "hotheaded talking rebels" in New York "boast that if the Democrats win they will have everything their own way and get pay for their negroes yet." [75] Rosecrans decided to do something about it. In August he went to White Sulphur Springs with the idea of conferring with prominent former Confederates, and to obtain from them assurance which would "satisfy every Northern mind" that the Southerners were loyal. [76] Here he wrote a public letter to General Lee, in which he asked Lee and other Southern Generals who were willing to act with him to give "a written expression of views that can be followed by a concurrence of action." The statement should "pledge the people of the South to a chivalrous and magnanimous devotion to restoring peace and prosperity to our common country. I want to carry that pledge high above the level of party politics—to the late officers and soldiers of the Union Army." Rosecrans was confident such a pledge would meet with a response so warm that the "rainbow of peace" would appear in a political sky "now black with clouds and impending storm." [77]

General Lee and thirty others from ten Southern States signed a letter in accordance with General Rosecrans' request. They admitted that slavery and secession were settled by the war and the South had sincerely returned to

[74] October 9, 1868.

[75] *Seymour Papers*, New York Historical Society Library.

[76] Washington *Express*, August 29, 1931.

[77] New York *Times*, September 5, 1868. (White Sulphur Springs, August 26, 1868.)

its old allegiance. The Southerners had a kindly feeling for the negroes. Both whites and blacks in the South were necessary for each other's welfare. But they were opposed to giving political control to the negroes, who were not qualified to use political authority. The South wanted peace, self-government, and relief from misrule. Among the signers of this document were Beauregard and Stephens.

This was the only part taken by Lee in the political campaign, and it would have been as well if he had taken none. The letter had little or no effect upon the situation. Godkin's comment was typical. He wrote that " it will simply exasperate the Republicans at the North, and will not help the Democrats. . . . Lee's letter will therefore be received simply as another attempt to throw dust in Northern eyes. . . ." [78] *Harper's Weekly* took advantage of Lee's appearance to attack him. His whole career " shows him to be one of the weakest of men," and his " treachery to the government was not less contemptible than odious." [79]

Mention has been made of the willingness of some of the Southern leaders to accept a qualified form of negro suffrage. A serious effort was made to get the colored voters into the Democratic ranks, with some slight success. The New York *Herald* on August 12 stated that the Southern politicians seemed at last to appreciate the importance of the part the negro was to play in the Presidential election. Colored Democratic clubs were being formed, and addresses by colored Democrats were being distributed. The purpose of the whites, the *Herald* stated, was to instill in the mind of the negro the fact that his best friend is his white neighbor. The next day the *Herald* reported a stampede of the negroes from the Republicans to the Democrats. " The negroes begin to see that the radicals have cheated them." A possi-

[78] New York, August 29, London *Daily News*, September 14, 1868.
[79] September 19, 1868.

bility existed that Grant might lose the entire South through a defection of negro voters.[80]   The New York *Evening Post* declared that the movement to convert the negroes to the Democracy " is really getting to be of first rate importance; " that it was more than a joke, and that the Republicans had better watch the South carefully, or their dusky brethren would be whisked out from under their noses.

Godkin reported to his London paper on August 19 that the Southerners were laboring hard with the negroes, and were using a combination of persuasion and intimidation. A large number of negroes, in Mississippi for instance, had been won over. " I must do the Southerners the justice to say, however, that they hold out no false hopes as to the suffrage." [81]

Wade Hampton of South Carolina was the leading Southern advocate of a qualified suffrage for the negroes.   Hampton declared in August: " it will not do to say the negro has no right to vote, for, right or wrong, he will vote in this next election, and his vote may turn the scale.   Let us meet this as a practical question, and seek . . . to work good for ourselves." [82]   In October he wrote that he had advocated qualified negro suffrage for over a year.[83]   He represented one of three points of view which prevailed among the South Carolina Democrats.   Former Governor James L. Orr represented the small group of whites who were willing to coöperate with the Republicans, while Benjamin F. Perry represented the other extreme—those who insisted on uncompromising opposition to the Republicans, and were opposed to negro suffrage in any form.[84]

[80] August 13, 1868.

[81] London *Daily News*, September 3, 1868.

[82] Memphis *Avalanche*, August 18, 1868.

[83] Utica *Observer*, October 22, 1868, from Charleston *Daily News*, October 21, 1868.

[84] Taylor, *Negro in South Carolina* (Washington, 1924), p. 186.

In August the Democratic Executive Committee of South Carolina issued an address to the negroes of the State, in which they attempted to show that the Southern Democrats were their real friends and reproached them for the numerous disorders into which they had been led by political excitement.[85] The whites reminded the negroes that while the negro was not necessary for them, " we think you will find it very difficult to do without us; " and added a warning that the disturbances in which the negroes had taken part, led by unscrupulous white men, were hurrying them into a war between the races.[86] The comment of the New York *Tribune* was, " If this is the best the Democrats of Charleston have to say for themselves, they had better set their houses in order, for the day of their departure is at hand." [87]

Further action by the South Carolina Democrats to placate the negroes was taken in October, when the State Central Executive Club adopted a resolution in favor of qualified negro suffrage.[88]

In Georgia the Democrats took similar action. On September 26 the Democratic State Committee issued an address urging the whites to allow the negroes to vote without molestation, as under the law as it existed the negroes had the right to vote.[89] In October the same committee resolved that it accepted the existing status of the negro, and would protect him in his right to vote.[90] The Democracy of Arkansas, it was reported to the New York *World,* " have

[85] *American Annual Cyclopedia,* 1868, p. 699.

[86] *McPherson Scrap Book,* Library of Congress, vol. vi, pp. 9-11.

[87] Sept. 1, 1868.

[88] McPherson, *op. cit.,* vol. ii, p. 159, item dated Columbia, S. C., October 16, 1868.

[89] *American Annual Cyclopedia,* 1868, p. 317.

[90] New York *Tribune,* October 17, 1868.

stripped for the fight, throwing away all opposition to negro suffrage." They proposed to attack the Republicans with their own weapon, the negro ballot.[91] A Democratic State Convention held at New Orleans on September 30, to choose Democratic electors, resolved that the Democracy of Louisiana would protect the negro in his legal rights, including suffrage. They called for a fair election.[92] On October 29 a committee representing the Democratic clubs of New Orleans adopted a resolution guaranteeing every voter, without reference to race, color or politics, full protection in voting.[93]

As Godkin wrote, the Democrats used persuasion and threats to bring the negroes to their support. Benjamin Hill at Augusta, Georgia, on August 21, urged the negroes to support their real friends, the Southern whites, and promised that if the Democracy was successful, the wages of negroes would be increased fifty per cent by Christmas.[94] Barbecues were given for negro voters. It was reported that before a barbecue at La Grange, Ark., the Democrats posted the following notice: " Come one! Come all! Both white and black! As the infamous lie is in circulation that the meats for colored persons will be poisoned, we nail that Radical tack to the counter by offering choice of tables to our colored friends, or we will divide places with them." [95] Southern Democrats, within four years of the war, were willing to sit down and eat with their former slaves!

There was unquestionably some intimidation of negro voters by threats of physical violence, but this was disavowed by official party action in the States where it existed or was threatened. Another form of intimidation, equally effective,

[91] Little Rock, August 25, Cincinnati *Commercial*, Sept. 21, 1868.

[92] *American Annual Cyclopedia*, 1868, pp. 437-438.

[93] Springfield *Republican*, October 30, 1868.

[94] Pearce, *Hill*, pp. 183-185.

[95] *Harper's Weekly*, September 12, 1868.

was the boycott. As stated by Hampton, on July 25: "Those negroes who are not for us are against us, and if they cast their destiny with the radicals, to them and not to us must they look for support. Of course all present contracts should be kept in good faith, but let us not employ in the future anyone, white or black, who gives his aid to the Republican party." [96] A Democratic club in Columbia, S. C., in carrying out this programme, resolved that no member " shall employ, rent lands to, or patronize any radical, after the present contracts shall have expired." They will not hire any itinerant negroes who could not show they were members of some Democratic association. [97] Similar action was taken by other Democratic organizations in other States. [98] A Louisiana paper, the *Planter's Banner,* enjoined the Democrats to say to the negroes on election day, " Choose today whether you take the Southern white man or the carpetbagger for your future friend. If you choose the men who have been raising the devil in this Parish since the war, look for no more favors from us." [99]

Republican comment on this form of pressure put to the negroes by the Democrats was biting. The Washington *National Republican* said that the Democracy was openly declaring " they will starve a large class of people—it being in their power to do so—unless these men will . . . submit to be driven to the polls like so many dumb driven cattle." [100] *Harper's Weekly* referred to the " system of certificates

[96] Cincinnati *Commercial*, July 30, 1868; New York *Evening Post*, August 10, 1868.

[97] New York *Evening Post*, August 8, 1868. Citing Columbia, S. C. Phoenix.

[98] Cincinnati *Commercial*, November 2, 1868.

[99] Warmouth, *War, Politics and Reconstruction* (New York, 1930), p. 70.

[100] August 15, 1868.

which decrees starvation against any colored laborer who cannot prove his Democracy," together with the aroused "rebel spirit" and terrorism, as placing "the alarming situation of the Southern States beyond question." [101]

While the Southern Democrats showed a disposition to make overtures to the negroes, their attitude towards the white Republicans was bitter. Social ostracism, was the treatment they should receive, according to Benjamin Hill. "Drive them from your society, forsake them in their business, and brand them like Cain, to be fugitives and vagabonds upon the face of the earth." [102] Howell Cobb was reported to have said of the white Southern Republicans: "Upon them there should be no mercy. They have dishonored themselves and sought to dishonor you. Anathematize them. Drive them from the pale of social and political society. Leave them to wallow in their own filth and mire." [103] Hampton was equally outspoken when speaking of the scalawags. "There are no words in the English language to express the bitter contempt entertained by me for these renegades and traitors." [104] An example of a denunciation of white Republicans by a Democratic party organization was a circular issued by the Democratic Central Committee of Louisiana. The Democrats were urged to withdraw all countenance, association and patronage from the carpetbaggers, and to "thwart every effort they may make to maintain a business and social foothold among you." [105]

There was undoubtedly considerable violence connected

[101] September 12, 1868.

[102] Speech, August 21, Augusta. *McPherson Scrap Book*, Library of Congress, vol. vi, p. 34.

[103] New York *Tribune*, August 1, 1868.

[104] *Nation*, August 27, 1868.

[105] Warmouth, *op. cit.*, p. 66.

with the campaign in the South. Its amount was exaggerated by Northern Republican newspapers and stump speakers with the purpose of discrediting the Democrats. The Republicans failed to point out that such violent occurrences as did take place were usually the result of provocative acts on both sides. The Democrats charged, with some truth, that the aggressiveness of the negroes, which they claimed brought about conflict, was due to direct incitement by white Republicans, who wished to create the impression of a reign of terror.

The Ku Klux Klan was extending its operations, and was referred to by Republicans as a revival of rebellion and as an organization for mass murder. But one is struck, when reading Northern Republican papers, by the comparative scarcity of references to the Klan as compared with a year or two later. In June the New York *Times* reported that the Southern States were as orderly as the North, and that there was no more reason for Federal troops in one section than in the other.[106]

One of the most discussed riots during the campaign was a conflict at Camilla, Ga., on September 19. Here a large band of armed negroes collided with a sheriff's posse, and eight or nine negroes were killed and many wounded, while several whites were injured.[107] The Republicans charged a deliberate slaughter, while the Democrats declared that the incident was a conflict between the forces of law and order on one side, and a law-defying mob on the other.[108] This riot, properly understood, said Benjamin Hill in a letter to the New York *Times,* " will exhibit to the Northern people more clearly than a thousand speeches could, the exact reason why the Southern whites are, at present, un-

[106] June 28, 1868.
[107] Account in *American Annual Cyclopedia*, 1868, p. 316.
[108] Utica *Observer*, September 23, 1868.

willing to extend universal, indiscriminate suffrage to the negroes." [109]

On September 26, as a result of this conflict, the Democratic Executive Committee of Georgia issued an address disclaiming all intention to use violence. The Democrats were asked to endure extreme provocation rather than retaliate in a violent manner upon the negroes.[110] The *Nation* professed to believe that affairs like the Camilla riot could be stopped by the Democratic leaders in New York. That they had not done so was inexplicable, unless it was that they did not really care for Seymour's election, but wanted only control of New York.[111]

Lousisiana was also the scene of a number of outbreaks. On September 28, in St. Landry parish, a melee occurred in which it was reported that one hundred negroes, one white Republican, and one white Democrat were killed, and a large number wounded. Three thousand Democrats were said to have taken part. In spite of the fact that this affair was much larger than the Camilla riot, it received less attention in the Northern press. A local Democratic paper, *Planter's Banner,* on October 10, commented: "We hear nothing from St. Landry. The negroes all over the Parish have been disarmed, and have gone to work briskly. Their loyal league clubs have been broken up, the scalawags have turned Democrats, and the carpetbaggers have been run off. . . . St. Landry is quiet for the first time since the war." The *Planter's Banner* reported the people generally were well satisfied with the result of the riot. Their only regret was that the carpetbaggers escaped.[112] A smaller affair took place in Franklin, Louisiana, on October 17. A scalawag

[109] New York *Times,* September 25, 1868.

[110] *American Annual Cyclopedia,* 1868, p. 317.

[111] September 24, 1868.

[112] Warmouth, *op. cit.,* pp. 67-68.

and a carpetbagger were killed, with the result that the negroes settled down quietly and most of them began to " show a disposition to vote the Democratic Ticket, and live on friendly terms " with their white neighbors.[113]

The trouble in Louisiana, according to the Springfield *Republican,* " prove what we apprehended, that the rebel Democrats, on slight pretense, created a reign of terror among Republicans," with the purpose of carrying the State for the Democratic ticket.[114] Governor Warmouth records that the violence practised by the Democrats in Louisiana at the November election forced the legislature to pass registration and election acts to protect the Republicans at future elections.[115]

South Carolina had its share of political violence. On August 31 Governor Scott issued a proclamation stating that he had information that armed and disciplined organizations had been formed in the interest of the Democratic party. He called for their disbanding. The charge was denied by the State Democratic Committee, which declared their party relied upon the ballot, and eschewed all forms of violence.[116] On September 14 the legislature passed an act to establish a State police force in order to suppress insurrection.[117] Next month the South Carolina Democratic Committee issued an address calling upon all Democrats to forego the use of violence, and to protect the negroes in their legal rights. On October twenty-nine Governor Scott reciprocated with a proclamation which stated that the Democratic address had " quieted the apprehensions and conciliated the respect and goodwill of their political opponents." He earn-

[113] *Ibid.,* p. 69. *Planter's Banner,* October 31, 1868.
[114] November 3, 1868.
[115] Warmouth, *op. cit.,* pp. 153-154.
[116] *American Annual Cyclopedia,* 1868, p. 699.
[117] *Ibid.,* p. 700.

estly invoked the coöperation of his fellow Republicans in following a pacific policy.[118]

Now and then a Southern newspaper escaped control. On September 1, the Tuscaloosa *Independent Monitor* published a woodcut showing a scalawag and a carpetbagger playing stellar roles at a " necktie party." The carpetbagger's carpet bag was plainly marked " Ohio ". The reader was informed " the above cut represents the fate in store for these great pests of Southern society—the carpetbagger and the scalawag—if found in Dixie's land after the break of day on the 4th of March next." [119] The Montgomery *Mail* on September 26 feared the *Monitor's* illustration would be good for a loss of five or ten thousand votes from those who would otherwise have voted the Democratic ticket. " It may lose us Ohio, and, in that event, will lose us the election. . . . It is a terrible thing." [120] Two days after the appearance of the *Monitor's* drawing the Alabama State Democratic Executive Committee adopted resolutions denying any responsibility for intemperate expressions by any newspaper or individual. The Alabama Democracy were a party of law and order, and disapproved the excesses of the Tuscaloosa *Monitor*.[121]

The Mississippi Democrats, on August 11, likewise denounced all forms of violence, and denied that the people of Mississippi desired a renewal of " those scenes of insubordination and bloodshed which have so recently passed." [122]

The situation in Texas, the Chicago *Republican* reported on October 30, was one of " demonaic lawlessness " caused by the " Ku Klux Democracy." In whole counties not a

[118] Springfield *Republican*, October 30, 1868.
[119] In Cincinnati *Commercial*, September 19, 1868.
[120] *Ibid.*, Oct. 6, 1868.
[121] *Ibid.*, Sept. 28, 1868 from Cincinnati *Enquirer*, September 25, 1868.
[122] *McPherson Scrap Book*, Library of Congress, vol. vi, p. 55.

single Republican was tolerated. The Republicans had been driven forth as if they were wild beasts " which to destroy was a solemn duty." The New York *Tribune,* on September 5, printed a Little Rock despatch to the effect that actual war existed in Arkansas. Some counties were in open rebellion, with the civil authorities powerless and the Democratic speakers and press advising the murder of carpetbaggers. " Blair's letter has done much to produce this condition of things."

Conditions in North Carolina were more peaceful. Van Buren reported to Seymour, after a talk with ex-governor Jonathan Worth, that the North Carolina whites " have a horror of anything like trouble or collision " and that if the Democrats failed to carry the State it would be chiefly from this dread. The Democrats expected to receive part of the negro vote.[123] In July it was proposed in the House at Washington to send arms to the South to arm the Republicans against the Ku Klux. It was a North Carolina scalawag, Boyden,[124] who protested. " We cannot afford to fight each other. Keep away your arms. . . . If we need anything in the way of arms send us the Army of the United States; but do not arm neighbor against neighbor." [125]

In Tennessee the situation held the possibility of trouble. Governor Brownlow was detested by the Democrats. The Ku Klux were especially strong, and the Governor threatened to call out the militia to oppose them. The answer of the Democrats to this suggestion was frank. The Nashville *Banner* said that if the Radicals were determined upon relentless warfare, with no quarter, " so let it be. If nothing but war will suffice, then let it come—war to the knife,

[123] New York Historical Society Library, Miscellaneous Manuscripts, Van Buren.

[124] London *Daily News,* October 3. (New York, September 19, 1868.)

[125] New York *Herald,* July 25, 1868.

and the knife to the hilt, and damned be he who first cries:
' Hold! Enough!' " [126]   General Forrest in an interview pre-
dicted a conflict if the militia were called out to suppress the
Ku Klux.   Forrest, incidentally, denied membership in the
Klan,[127] although he was a high official in that organization.
The Chicago *Republican* saw great danger in the situation.
The Ku Klux were " a living dangerous reality " which
meant mischief, and was a standing menace to the Union.
It might " be employed to terrible advantage " even in the
capture of Chicago! [128]

On July 20 a joint resolution passed Congress excluding
from the Electoral College the vote of those states not yet
readmitted under the reconstruction Acts.   The States were
Virginia, Mississippi and Texas.   In addition to these, the
vote of Georgia was challenged, after the election, because
her legislature, with a Democratic majority on September 3,
had expelled its negro members and replaced them with
whites, on the ground that negro suffrage did not include
negro office-holding.[129]

The exclusion of the three unreconstructed States from
the Electoral College was not accepted by the Democrats
without a protest.   As an officeholder said of Virginia, that
State " is still the State of Virginia, and her electoral vote
must be counted.   Should it be cast for Grant it would be
counted by this Radical party. . . . Should it be cast for
Seymour and Blair, by the Eternal it shall be counted." [130]
Pendleton was reported to have written on August 21 to a

[126] In Chicago *Republican*, July 18, 1868.

[127] Cincinnati *Commercial*, September 3, 1868.

[128] September 4, 1868.

[129] Schouler, *United States*, vol. vii, p. 174n.; *American Annual Cyclo-pedia*, 1868, p. 313.

[130] *Harper's Weekly*, Sept. 5, 1868.   G. C. Smith, Gov. Montana Territory.

friend in Texas " about your being allowed to vote, be not alarmed; we shall see that Texas is represented. Vote by all means." [131] The Republican press commented angrily upon this letter until Pendleton pronounced it a forgery.

It was proposed in Mississippi that the three excluded States proceed to choose Presidential electors in the usual way, in defiance of Congress, and offer these votes for counting. If with the aid of these votes Seymour should be elected, and defeated without them, they should " fight for their rights." [132] The New York *Tribune* said it was clear that the rebels meant to take possession of the government, by fair means or foul. " They would a little prefer to succeed by violence, so that the result would be equally certain." Godkin said the scheme to count the excluded votes was silly and would never be carried out. [133] President Johnson, on October 6, issued an order to all army officers in which he quoted the provisions of the Constitution relating to the election of the President and the laws forbidding military and naval officers to obstruct such elections. The Springfield *Republican* considered the order a rebuke for General Reynolds, in command in Texas, who had forbidden the citizens to hold an election for Presidential electors. [134]

In addition to the outright exclusion of the votes of these States by Congress, the Republican State governments in the other Southern States imposed " test oaths " which excluded a large number of white voters. This also aroused a protest.

On July 14 the Chicago *Republican* stated that the " noteworthy part of the campaign development so far, is, that the disfranchised classes at the South expect to vote at the

[131] Washington *Express*, September 25, 1868.
[132] New York *Tribune*, Sept. 12, 1868.
[133] New York, September 24, London *Daily News*, October 7, 1868.
[134] October 13, 1868.

Presidential election . . . provided they can get the mass of the Democratic party North to back them up in this intention." Wade Hampton said at a Democratic ratification meeting in New York that relief to the South could come only if the Northern Democrats would pledge themselves to see that a fair election would be held—that the white people of the South should vote. He asked the Northerners to promise that if they did vote, the votes would be counted, and " if there is a majority of the white votes that you will place Seymour and Blair in the White House in spite of all the bayonets that shall be brought against them." [135]   The Democratic Executive Committee in South Carolina issued a statement supporting this stand.

The Republican legislatures in some of the Southern States proposed at first to cast the vote of their States for Presidential electors, but finally decided (except in Florida) to provide for a popular vote.   In Alabama the bill providing for the election contained a provision punishing by fine and imprisonment any attempt to challenge a vote.   The Springfield *Republican* commented that " No State's vote is wanted for Grant and Colfax through the aid of such means as this suggests are to be introduced." [136]   The Washington *Express*, referring to Republican plans for capturing the Southern electoral vote, said that " The ingenuity in the way of civil despotism has been exhausted.   What then, does this new movement mean?   It means war!" [137]

An interesting feature of the Southern campaign was the visit of John Quincy Adams, Democratic nominee for Governor of Massachusetts, to South Carolina in October. On September 22 Wade Hampton sent Adams an invitation. On the 28th Adams accepted the invitation, modestly under-

[135] *Harper's Weekly*, August 1, 1868.
[136] October 8, 1868.
[137] August 19, 1868.

estimating his political importance. " I represent nothing in
Massachusetts, but a comparatively small and very unimport-
ant minority, and am regarded as hardly less objectionable,
though far more insignificant than yourselves by the
majority." He emphasized his Conservative position, and
while criticising the reconstruction policy, was very moderate in his view as to how the situation should be met. Adams
warned the Southerners that " if the Democrtic party is
defeated in their canvass, it is because the people fear its
success would jeopardize the substantial results of the war.
. . . For my own part, I think it would be very difficult to
get rid of any of the logical and legitimate results of the war,
if we tried ever so hard, but still our people are very sensitive
on that point." [138] The *Nation* considered Adams' reply to
Hampton " an exceedingly sensible letter, which was modest,
straightforward, and " devoid of the blubber with which the
views of ' standard bearers ' are usually encumbered." [139]

Adams spoke three times in South Carolina, in Charleston
on October 9, Columbia on October 12, and at Charleston
again on October 16. He did not appear under false colors.
In his first speech at Charleston he gave his political record
as a Freesoiler, a supporter of Lincoln, the War, and emancipation. At the end of the war he " believed that the time
had come to say to the South, you shall at once be readmitted." Let the negroes vote if they wish, he said. He
believed in equal, not universal suffrage. He recommended
to the South Carolinians the Massachusetts qualifications for
voting: Six months' residence, a tax, and literacy. " I believe that the white people of the South will soon be willing
to stand on this platform. Many of them agree to it even
now." [140] His speech at Columbia on the 12th was in the

[138] New York *Herald*, October 13, 1868.
[139] October 15, 1868.
[140] *McPherson Scrap Book*, Library of Congress, vol. vi, pp. 14-15.

same tenor. The New York *Tribune* remarked that it showed an aptitude for public affairs, and that " He said a great many fine things, to which ' therefore vote for Seymour and Blair! ' was but a limping corollary." [141]   The Springfield *Republican* likewise considered the Columbia speech Adams' ablest effort. It exhibited an admirable temper and practical wisdom, and should do much " to give him a place among the statesmen of the country in the happy times when war and reconstruction shall alike be things of the past." " This young gentleman has a way of telling unpleasant truths to Southern fire-eaters, which is almost amusingly like his grandfather." [142]   The comment by Southern papers was equally cordial. The Charleston *Mercury* considered the whole Columbia speech excellent in tone and temper, adding that its frankness was not its least valuable feature; while the Richmond *Dispatch* likewise approved his honest and wise advice to the South.[143]

Adams' speech at Charleston, on October 16, was even more outspoken than his previous addresses. " I am an opponent of General Grant, but I would speak kindly of him, and I do believe that he is an upright, honorable man, who will try, if elected, to do his best, not for a party only, but for the whole people of the country." In his opinion, "You, the people of South Carolina have got to concede equal rights to the people of your State as freely as we concede them to the people of our State, before cordiality between the States can again be restored." Concerning the negro vagrancy laws Adams said, " once for all, that idea must be abandoned. It will not do. We are not going to have slavery or any of its details or results." [144]

[141] October 19, 1868.

[142] October 15, 1868.

[143] In Cincinnati *Commercial*, October 19, 1868.

[144] New York *World*, October 21, 1868; *McPherson Scrap Book*, Library of Congress, vol. vi, pp. 19-20.

Adams was invited to speak at Macon, Ga., but was unable to accept, and upon his return to Massachusetts replied to that effect. He called upon the Southerners to be good losers. " You must try frankly and cheerfully to meet like men the fate you dared like men to invoke. If our people cannot suddenly renew their shattered confidence or dare not grasp your outstretched hand, why take it coldly as a part of your penalty, and set yourselves to extort a fresh faith, and compel us from sheer admiration of your pluck to grasp your hand unobserved." [145]

Adams' Southern tour served a twofold purpose. It gave the Southerners a first-hand idea of the position of the Conservative Northern Democrats, and exercised a restraining influence on their tendency to use the " Rebel Yell " as a view-halloo while chasing carpetbaggers and negroes. On the other hand, the North was made aware, through the cordial reception of the man and his words, that the Southerners did not all have spiked tails and horns, and that they could listen to counsels of moderation without uncoiling ropes and stoking up the fires under tar pots. This was the interpretation placed upon the visit by even the New York *Tribune.*[146]

5. THE SEPTEMBER AND OCTOBER ELECTIONS

A number of State elections were held in Northern States in September and October,[147] and the results in each case were carefully scanned for evidence of what was to be expected in November. These elections were as follows:

[145] *McPherson Scrap Book*, Library of Congress, vol. vi, p. 40, from Macon, Georgia *Telegraph*, November 1, 1868.

[146] October 19, 1868.

[147] Election figures from *American Annual Cyclopedia*, 1868; *Tribune Almanac*, 1869; *World Almanac*, 1869; *Democratic Almanac*, 1869; McPherson, *Reconstruction*.

Date	State	Principal office to be filled	Candidates and percentage of votes Republican		Democrat	
Sept. 1	Vt.	Governor	J. B. Page	73.6%	J. L. Edwards	26.4%
" 8	Calif.	Members of Congress (3)	1 elected	49.6	2 elected	50.4
" 14	Maine	Governor	J. L. Chamberlain	57.7	E. F. Pillsbury	42.3
Oct. 6	Nebrs.	Governor	David Butler	58.4	J. R. Porter	42.6
" 13	Pa.	Auditor General	J. F. Hartranft	50.7	C. E. Boyle	49.3
" 13	Ind.	Governor	Conrad Baker	50.1	T. A. Hendricks	49.9
" 13	Ohio	Secretary of State	I. R. Sherwood	51.7	Th. Hubbard	48.3
" 13	Iowa	Secretary of State	Edw. Wright	61.9	Hemer	38.1
" 22	W. Va.	Governor	W. E. Stevenson	55.8	J. M. Camden	44.2

With the exception of California the Republicans carried every one of these States, as the table shows.

The Democrats had no chance of carrying Vermont, but because it was the first of the State elections, they made a determined effort to cut down the Republican majority. Though they sent good speakers and spent money liberally, the Republicans carried the State by an increased majority.[148] The interest which this canvass aroused in the State is shown by the total vote cast. In 1867 the Republicans carried Vermont with a majority of 10,000 in a total vote of 43,000. In 1868 they carried it by a majority of 17,000 in a total vote of nearly 58,000. The Republican percentage was about the same in each year—73.3% in 1867 and 73.6% in 1868. These figures represented a decline from the figure for 1866 —75.1%. The Republicans hailed his success as a sign that the skids were being placed under Seymour and Blair, and pointed to the greatly increased Republican majority. The New York *Tribune* considered it a decisive victory which showed that work would bring success, as the vigorous efforts of the Democrats were met in the proper spirit.[149]

[148] Alexander, *Political History of New York*, vol. iii, p. 205.
[149] September 2, 1868.

Godkin called it a brilliant triumph which was due to the wild talk of the Southern orators, who were being implored by the northern Democratic managers to keep still.[150]   The Conservative New York *Herald* withheld interpretation until Maine should be heard from, but agreed that the Southern fire-eaters were responsible for the increased Republican majority.[151]

As a matter of plain figures, the Vermont election showed two facts—first, that the people of the State were keenly interested, and second, that the relative strength of the parties was almost precisely the same as a year before.

The next State election was a Democratic success.   California elected its three members of Congress on September eighth.   The total vote cast for the three seats was 54,548 for the Democrats, or 50.4%, and 53,873 or 49.6% for the Republicans.   The Democrats elected two of the three candidates.   This represented a decrease of about two per cent compared with the election for a Supreme Court justice in 1867, when the Democratic candidate received 52.2% of the votes cast.   The Democratic candidate for Governor of California in 1867, with three parties in the field, received fifty-four per cent of the total votes cast.   These figures indicate that the Democrats in California were losing ground, although they still had a majority.   The majority disappeared in November, when Grant carried the State by about 500 votes, or with 50.2%.

The election in Maine was held on September 14.   The chief position to be filled was Governor, with E. F. Pillsbury, Democrat, running against the Republican incumbent, J. L. Chamberlain.   This was the third successive year these men had been opposing candidates for the position.   With the

[150] New York, September 2, London *Daily News*, September 18, 1868.
[151] September 2, 1868.

personal element the same, the shifting of the voters takes on a wider significance than otherwise. In 1866 Pillsbury received 37.8% of the votes cast, in 1867 44.4% and in 1868 42.3%. Thus the very minor shift towards the Republicans shown in Vermont two weeks before, was emphasized and increased in Maine. The total vote cast (131,000) was greater than the year before (103,000), and was even larger than the vote in Maine the following November (113,000). In November Seymour received 41.7% of the total.

The Republican press hailed the victory as decisive evidence of the coming nationwide defeat of the Democrats. The Republican majority of 20,000 in Maine was a part of "the great tidal wave of public honesty" sweeping over the country, according to the New York *Tribune*.[152] The *Nation* said the result made Pennsylvania safe for the Republicans in October. Maine and Vermont "have decided the contest in favor of General Grant."[153] *Harper's Weekly* declared that the result showed the Democratic reaction of 1867 was spent.[154]

The Democrats, however, argued that the result showed chiefly an increased vote on either side, and that the Republican majority was less than 1866. The unusually large Democratic vote of 1867 was explained by the presence of the prohibitory liquor law issue in the campaign that year. Many Republicans had voted the Democratic ticket in 1867 on that one issue.[155] Gideon Welles was very pessimistic over the Maine election. It confirmed his impression that "Seymour's name is unfortunate and likely to prove disastrous."[156] The prospect for Democratic victory in

[152] September 15, 1868.

[153] September 17, 24, 1868.

[154] October 3, 1868.

[155] New York, September 16, London *Daily News*, September 28, 1868.

[156] *Diary*, vol. iii, p. 436, September 15, 1868.

November, Welles entered in his diary, is very remote.[157]
The Democrats committed a serious error in sending Pendle-
ton into the State. He made no converts, and aroused the
Republicans to extra efforts.[158]

The next State election was Nebraska's, on October 6.
Nebraska was admitted in 1867, with the Republicans in
control at the time of admission and organization of the first
State government. This control they maintained. The
Republican candidate for Governor, David Butler, received
8,679 votes or 58.4% of the total, and the Democrat, J. R.
Porter, received 6,188, or 41.6%. Seymour's percentage
in November was 36.5%.

On October 13 four States were to hold State elections,
Pennsylvania, Indiana, Ohio and Iowa, the importance of
which was realized by both Republicans and Democrats.
Iowa was conceded to the Republicans, but the Democrats
made valiant efforts to win in the other three, as they felt
that the verdict in these States would be decisive.

Carl Schurz's attitude was typical of the more thoughtful
Republicans. He wrote his wife that if the Republicans
should carry Indiana and Pennsylvania, " we shall be quite
certain of the result in the Presidential election. If we fail
in that, the whole business will be doubtful. The signs of
the times are indeed favorable, but the results of the spring
elections taught us not to place too much confidence in
appearances." [159]

The Democrats were hopeful, and in some cases optimistic.
Montgomery Blair told Welles that the Democrats would
carry Indiana and Ohio and probably Pennsylvania. Welles
hoped " he may not be mistaken, yet I candidly confess I
have no confidence of such a result in either State." On

[157] *Ibid.*, p. 438, September 17, 1865.
[158] *Ibid.*, p. 439, September 18, 1868.
[159] Schurz, *Intimate Letters*, p. 440.

October 12 he thought " The Democratic leaders have very skillfully knocked out their own brains, or my impressions are wrong." Welles confessed that he had no heart in the campaign after the nomination of Seymour and Blair, though he kept this to himself.[160]

Pennsylvania in 1868 was a doubtful State, and the Democrats were fully aware of its importance. Seymour's correspondence included letters calling on him to act vigorously in order to carry the State. Sanford E. Church wrote to him on September 19: " Pennsylvania is the battle ground and we must carry it." [161] The candidate was urged to make speeches in the State,[162] and was informed that money was necessary for a Democratic victory. His friend, George L. Miller of the Omaha *Herald,* wrote him on September 18 that his advice was " to purchase a verdict " in Pennsylvania, Indiana and Ohio.[163] From Pennsylvania came word that the Republicans would carry the State unless more money were made available. "Votes must be had, money will bring them and nothing else will." With $10,000 the writer could increase the vote of the party by twelve thousand, and " in such a manner as to defy an army of detectives and legislative investigations." [164]

Less frank in describing the use of the money required was Montgomery Blair, who wrote to his friend William W. Corcoran the banker, asking him to assist in raising funds for the Democratic campaign in Pennsylvania. He claimed the Republicans were raising money by the hundred thousand, and that it was to be applied by Blaine, who was the operating briber in Maine.[165]

[160] *Diary,* vol. iii, pp. 440, 451, September 21, October 10, 1868.

[161] *Seymour Papers,* Albany.

[162] T. C. Field, New York. *Seymour Papers,* New York Historical Society Library, Box 4.

[163] *Seymour Papers,* Albany.

[164] D. S. Rook, September 13, 1868, *ibid.*

[165] *Corcoran Papers,* Library of Congress, vol. xv.

Both parties charged bribery and fraudulent voting. The Soldiers and Sailors Convention, called by the Republicans to meet at Philadelphia on October 1 and 2, had for one of its purposes, according to Democratic State Chairman William W. Wallace, the illegal registration of visiting soldiers, in order that these names could be fraudulently voted in the election. He called attention to the fact that registration of voters took place in Philadelphia on the same days the Convention was to meet.[166] The Republicans made numerous charges that the Democrats planned to use fraudulently naturalized aliens, repeaters and other illegal practices in the Pennsylvania election. It was alleged that Philadelphia would be the scene of most of this rascality.

The New York *Evening Post* stated the frauds planned " have been proved, by unquestionable evidence, to be systematic and extensive." It was charged that the Democratic Supreme Court Justice, Sharswood, who had been elected the year before had issued over five thousand naturalization papers within two weeks. Seven hundred and twenty were issued in one day.[167] On October 8 the *Evening Post* printed a letter from a Justice of the Supreme Court of Pennsylvania protesting against the frauds for which Judge Sharswood was responsible. He charged that naturalization papers were issued to applicants even when the judge was not on the bench.[168]

The use of " repeaters " and " colonized " voters by the Democrats were freely charged. The *Nation* on October 8 stated that a prize fight scheduled to be held outside of Philadelphia on election day had been postponed until the 15th by agreement with Democratic managers who paid $200 in order that some one or two hundred reliable " repeaters " would not be out of the city on election day.

[166] Washington *Express*, Sept. 30, 1868.
[167] October 5, 1868.
[168] Justice J. M. Read to Chief Justice Thompson.

John Russell Young of the New York *Tribune* staff sent word to Philadelphia on October 12 that from 3,000 to 5,000 " repeaters " had left New York City for Philadelphia that day in order to vote in the Philadelphia election.[169]

In the Ohio contest a great deal of interest was centered around Vallandigham's effort to return to Congress. His opponent was the Republican incumbent, Gen. Robert Schenck. This interest, which at times seemed to receive a monopoly of political news from Ohio, arose from Vallandigham's war record and from the fact that the chief State office to be filled was only that of Secretary of State.

Vallandigham at first refused to run, but at the very end he permitted his name to be used and was nominated.[170] This last-minute acceptance caused some ill-feeling in his district, as a number of men entered the contest for the nomination on the understanding that Vallandigham would not seek it. A document was issued by disgruntled Democrats of the district which gave the reasons why he should be defeated. It was charged that Vallandigham had gone to the National Convention to defeat Pendleton; that he was in the " conspiracy " to nominate Chase; that he had declared he would not run for Congress and had become a candidate after two of his friends had entered the race. The New York *Herald* printed this document with the comment, " It looks as if the Schenck radicals had a finger in the pie." [171]

An interesting sidelight of this contest in Ohio was the reply of General Schenck to the charge that he had lost $15,000 at faro. Schenck, it will be remembered, was the man who in Grant's administration as Minister to Great Britain was reported to have taught London how to play poker. To the faro charge he replied " I have never played

---

[169] Philadelphia *Evening Star*, October 12, 1868.

[170] J. L. Vallandigham, *Vallandigham*, pp. 425-427.

[171] August 28, 1868.

a dollar or a cent on faro or any such game." [172] Schenck attacked Vallandigham during the campaign as being "the chief sachem in the Democratic wigwam" who had dictated the nomination and the platform of the Democracy.[173]

The Republicans charged the Ohio Democrats with plans to carry the election by fraud. On September 28 the New York *Evening Post* reported that a large sum had been sent to Dayton from New York City to be used in Vallandigham's campaign. The plan was to import from Kentucky and the strongly Democratic Fifth Ohio district enough illegal voters to elect Vallandigham.[174] The *Nation* on October 8 stated as a well-known fact that Vallandigham had "colonized" his district with illegal voters. Evidence on charges such as the above is virtually impossible to obtain. Perhaps the best reply the Democrats could have made after the election would have been to point to the vote cast—Vallandigham 15,818, Schenck 16,293.[175]

In Indiana the Democrats appear to have been hopeful. The popular Senator Hendricks was running for Governor against Conrad Baker. On August 1 Seymour was assured that Indiana was safe,[176] although on the 10th he was asked for $25,000 for use in Indiana. The request was endorsed by Senator Hendricks, he was told.[177] On August 31 Hendricks wrote to Seymour, "Our prospects are cheering in those parts of the State which I have visited. . . . If we can hold our present position we will carry the State." [178] The Republicans recognized the likelihood of a Democratic

[172] New York *Times*, Sept. 5, 1868.

[173] *Ibid.*

[174] September 22, 1868.

[175] Vallandigham, *op. cit.*, p. 430.

[176] N. E. Payne, *Seymour Papers*, Albany.

[177] A. Jones to N. E. Payne, sent to Seymour, *ibid.*

[178] *Ibid.*

victory.[179]　As for Iowa, the campaign there attracted little national attention due to the closer contests in the other three States.

When the votes were counted it was found that the Republicans had carried all four States by larger majorities than in the preceding election, although the Democratic vote was also larger. In Pennsylvania, where the Republican National Committee had spent $40,000, J. T. Hartranft defeated C. E. Boyle for Auditor General by 331,416 to 321,739, or 50.7% to 49.3%. The Democratic vote was 54,000 above that in 1867. The Democrats elected their candidate for mayor of Philadelphia. The vote in Philadelphia was 60,808 to 60,633. In Ohio I. R. Sherwood defeated Thomas Hubbard for Secretary of State 267,065 to 249,682 or 51.7% to 48.3%. The Democratic vote was 9,000 above that in 1867.

In Indiana, to which the Republican National Committee had sent $50,000, Baker defeated Hendricks for Governor by the close margin of 171,575 to 170,617 or 50.1% to 49.9%. There was no statewide election in Indiana in 1867. Hendricks' vote was 15,000 greater than the party vote in 1866. In Iowa Edward Wright defeated Hemer, the Democrat, by 120,265 to 74,461, or 61.9% to 38.1%. Hemer received nearly 16,000 more votes than his party polled in 1867.

The New York *Herald* considered that the October elections settled the question. " Grant will be President by an overwhelming vote." [180]　The loss of Pennsylvania was the death blow to Seymour. Godkin reported to his London readers that the Republican victories took all the excitement out of the canvass. Grant's election was made certain and in addition the question of paying the National bonds in

[179] Gresham, *Gresham*, vol. i, p. 345; *Nation*, October 8, 1868.

[180] October 14, 1868.

greenbacks was disposed of.[181] The *Nation,* speaking of
the " colonization " frauds in Indiana, said that Republican
gerrymanders in that State were in part to blame, as they
set the Democrats " an example of sharp practice." [182] The
Democrats had their own obtuseness and wickedness to thank
for their defeat.[183]

For the most part the Democratic papers put the best face
on the situation possible, although the New York *World*
and some others showed signs of panic. The Utica
Observer's optimism seems a little forced, but that paper
insisted the Democrats had no cause to be disheartened. A
change of a single vote in each school district, it remarked,
would change the result in the States which had just voted.
Although our " gains, everywhere, are encouraging," the
Observer admitted that the returns did not indicate such a
sweeping Democratic victory as would have made the result
of the November elections certain. With all the appliances
of force and fraud the Republicans were able to claim only
bare majorities in the States absolutely necessary to secure
Grant's election. The *Observer* stated that the Democrats
could spare either Ohio or Pennsylvania, and still win, and
" with Illinois on our side we can spare both. But we shall
lose neither." " Close up the columns, and forward to
victory," called the *Observer*.[184]

A sample of the note of despair which crept into some
Democratic journals as a result of the election was the wail
of the Charleston *Courier*. " The measure of our cup is
almost fully to overflowing. We may not be permitted to
look for any ray of brightness from the North." [185]

[181] London *Daily News*, October 26, 1868, New York, October 14.
[182] October 15, 1868.
[183] October 22, 1868.
[184] October 14, 15, 1868.
[185] In New York *Herald*, October 18, 1868.

The Democratic State Committee of Ohio issued an address on October 19, which did not pretend " to deny that the result of the recent elections were injurious to the best interests of the country," but declared that there was nothing in the results " to justify despondence or excuse any relaxation of the efforts of the Democracy." The Committee recalled that in 1864 the Democrats polled 18,000 more votes in November than in October, and stated that the party had carried ten thousand votes over the preceding election. The Democrats were implored to keep on working until the last hour on election day in November.[186]

Seymour's confidence, according to a report in the New York *Times* on October 18, was shaken. In commenting on the Republican victories, he was reported to have said: " Well, sir, the Democracy cannot hold me responsible. I persistently and repeatedly declined the nomination." Probably Seymour did not make this ungracious remark, but that it expressed his sentiments is likely enough. The following note, probably by his nephew Henry S. Miller, is in the Seymour papers in New York. " After the Pennsylvania elections of 1868 I went up to see him. Said he, ' Henry, how do you like being beaten? ' He was just as cool as you are now. Said I, ' I don't know that you are beaten! ' 'Oh, yes, we are beaten; we may save the State of New York, but that is all we can do.' "[187]

An old warhorse of the Jacksonian Democracy, Amos Kendall, was an interested observer of the Republican victories. He wrote to William Corcoran, the banker, on October 14, " I fear the elections of yesterday have in the main gone radical, but the Democratic Party are developing a strength which cannot fail to modify the future policy of the government."[188]

[186] *American Annual Cyclopedia*, 1868, p. 604.
[187] *Seymour Papers*, New York Historical Society Library.
[188] *Corcoran Papers*, Library of Congress, vol. xv.

Yet Gideon Welles seems to have plucked up courage in spite of the defeats. On October 27 he entered in his diary that " the spirit of the people who are opposed to Radicalism seems unbroken. Defeat in the great States has not disheartened them. A few men, anxious for office, have fallen away, but not one honest man has wavered, so far as I know, yet many will not vote for Seymour." [189] His friend Burr, of Hartford, feared that the voters who had been " on the fence," would vote for Grant as a result of the October elections, and he was not confident of victory in Connecticut.[190] Another veteran of the party's battles, Thomas Ewing, Sr., of Ohio, wrote to his son on October 18, that the elections settled the question of the Presidency in favor of Grant, and also showed that though the Republicans had disgusted the country by their reckless violence, the Democrats " threw back into the hands of the radicals the prestige which they had cast away." If the Democrats had chosen a conservative national ticket, they would have carried the October States.[191]

One other State election was held before the November election. On October 22 West Virginia elected a Republican, W. E. Stevenson, Governor by 26,935 votes to 22,218 for his Democratic opponent, J. M. Camden.

[189] Vol. iii, p. 462, October 27, 1868.

[190] To Welles, November 1, 1868. *Welles Papers*, Library of Congress, vol. 65.

[191] *Thomas Ewing Papers*, Library of Congress, vol. xix.

CHAPTER XII

DEMOCRATIC DESPONDENCY: THE VOTES ARE CAST

1. THE PROPOSALS TO CHANGE THE DEMOCRATIC TICKET

IN some Democratic circles the failure to make a better showing in the " October States " created so much of a panic that a last minute change of candidates was at once proposed. While this suggestion occurred to various leaders, the proposal by the *World* on October 15 received the greatest attention. There is evidence that the friends of President Johnson and Chief Justice Chase looked with some favor upon the proposed change in candidates, as possibly giving to them at the last minute the chance they failed to receive in the Democratic National Convention.

An early intimation that Democrats failure in the October elections might call for drastic action was mentioned by Francis P. Blair, Sr., on October 8. The veteran wrote to Senator Doolittle " Whatever the results next Tuesday may bring, our friends most deeply concerned in their personal and political destinies must, they think, have counsel from the North. I am desired to invoke our wisest and most trusted friends to come to Washington and consult of the course then to be taken. Pray come to my son's [Montgomery's] house on the 17th instant. I write other notes to bring together a council of friends who will say nothing of the contemplated meeting." [1]

One explanation of the meeting is suggested by a letter from Blair, Sr., to Tilden on October 19, in which he says that

[1] *J. R. Doolittle Papers*, Library of Congress, 1860-1887.

344

the movement to change the ticket was entered into by Seward and Chase to replace Seymour by Chase. Some rumour of this was perhaps in the air as early as October 8, and hence the meeting called by Blair to forestall it. In his letter to Tilden, Blair denounced both Seward and Chase. The union of the two to control the Democratic party, if successful, " would bring not only defeat, but eternal disgrace on the Democracy." [2] Montgomery Blair in the Washington *Evening Star* [3] supported the theory that Seward was behind the movement. Seward, he thought, influenced the President in opposition to the interests of Seymour. Blair charged that Seward felt himself politically dead if either Seymour or Grant should win. Under Johnson, Chase or Hancock he would still have a future.

That a change in the ticket was considered before the October election results were known was stated by the New York *Herald*.[4] " It seems a movement, having for its object the withdrawal of Seymour and Blair, was commenced here a few days before the election by certain gentlemen who foresaw defeat in Pennsylvania, Ohio and perhaps Indiana. . . . I am told the same policy was discussed last week in New York, and perhaps the scheme . . . originated in that city and was only further considered here."

Another explanation of the origin of the proposal of the *World* that the ticket be changed was given in the New York *Herald* for October 30. On October 14, the day after the election, according to this account, S. L. M. Barlow of New York wrote to Montgomery Blair, suggesting a change, but Blair refused to take part in the movement. Seward's name was linked with the proposal, his participation not being " out of any friendship for the Democracy." The *Nation*

[2] *Tilden Letters*, vol. i, pp. 198-199. Dated 1865 in error.

[3] In New York *Times*, October 20, 1868.

[4] October 16, 1868.

(October 22) declared that the thought " was first conceived by Mr. Washington McLean and some of the other Pendleton leaders in Ohio." It also suggested " that all hope of electing their Presidential candidates having been lost, our Democratic politicians in New York resolved to take some means of impressing the New York rank and file with the necessity of trading Seymour votes for Republican votes for Hoffman and assemblymen." The New York *Sun* stated that one effect of the movement in New York would be that " no senseless notion of fidelity to candidates who cannot be elected will now prevent the Democracy from making regular exchanges in favor of candidates who can be." When the politicians of New York understand this they will praise the *World* as heartily as they now condemn it.[5]

A more elaborate explanation was given by the New York *Evening Telegram*. Just after the Maine election Barlow of New York and others asked Seymour if he would withdraw in favor of Chase or Johnson if the Democrats lost the October elections. They claimed to represent the National Committee in asking this question. Seymour was said to have given a written reply, disclaiming any personal desire for the Presidency, and leaving himself in the hands of his friends as to his action in the contingency mentioned. With this document, Barlow opened negotiations with John H. Coyle in Washington and Washington McLean in Cincinnati, offering to pledge support to the nomination of Pendleton in 1872, if the Western Democracy would agree to the contemplated change in the ticket. Coyle agreed, but the Pendleton supporters held back until October 12 or 13, when they telegraphed the Democratic leaders in New York that they were ready for the change. But Frank Blair refused to withdraw. The *World* then undertook to drive Blair from the field, and the conspirators also opened fire in Wash-

[5] In New York *Tribune*, October 20, 1868.

ington and the West with a declaration that the present Democratic ticket was hopelessly defeated, and nothing could save the party but a change of front.[6]

Some features of this explanation were borne out by the action of the *National Intelligencer* (Coyle's paper) and the Cincinnati *Enquirer* (McLean's paper) in supporting the *World's* suggestion. But the absence of any material support for the *World* among the party leaders in New York indicates that the explanation is not wholly accurate. Mayor Hoffman, for example, denied the movement had the support of the party leaders, and stated it was made without their knowledge.[7]

That the feeling that Seymour should give way became articulate in Executive circles in Washington is shown by an entry in the diary of Secretary Welles for Wednesday, October 14. With the results of the elections known, Welles called on the President, who told him that " Randall called just before I did and was feeling very blue, and when he left said he would telegraph Tilden to get Seymour out of the way. It was pretty evident, the President said, that the present ticket could have little hope." Welles commented that Johnson was not displeased with the turn things were taking, and had hopes that attention might yet be turned on himself. " But his intimacy with and support of Seward forecloses, if nothing else would, any such a movement. On that rock he split." [8]

The mention of Chase's name in connection with suggestions that the ticket be changed was not without some foundation. On September 10 Alexander Long wrote to Chase that Vallandigham, then a candidate for Congress had decided to withdraw if the Democrats lost Maine on September 14

[6] In Cincinnati *Commercial*, October 21, 1868 (New York, October 20).

[7] New York *Herald*, October 21, 1868.

[8] Vol. iii, pp. 453-454.

by more than 18,000. Long had asked Vallandigham if, in the event of his withdrawal, he would not " unite with a few discreet friends " and see Governor Seymour, with a view of inducing Seymour to withdraw in Chase's favor if the Democrats should fail to carry either Pennsylvania, Ohio or Indiana in the October elections. Vallindigham entertained the proposal favorably.[9]

Van Buren was also in touch with the situation. On October 8 Chase wrote him that in no contingency, " as it seems to me, can any change of front be made, nor indeed, is any change desirable." [10]

On October 15 the storm burst about the ticket. The most telling blow came from the New York *World,* in an editorial on " The Youthful, Indomitable Democracy." The *World* began by congratulating the party for doing so well in the October elections, considering that it was proclaimed dead by the Republicans only two or three years ago. " But our gains were not as great as the party desired and deserved." The party would have triumphed but for two things, the absence of either of which would have given victory—the military popularity of Grant and the perversions of General Blair's position. The slander about the position of Blair and some of the Southern leaders " has repelled more than votes enough to have turned the balance in our favor." The *World* called for the removal or neutralization of the influences barring the party from success. If the party had made mistakes these should be admitted and corrected now, rather than four years later. " If there is any impediment to success which can yet be removed by noble daring, or self-sacrificing virtue, or a bold stroke of policy, now is the hour for action! "—"The capacity of a few men to form a great resolution, may shape

[9] *Chase Papers*, Historical Society of Pennsylvania Library.
[10] *Chase Papers*, Library of Congress, Letter Book B.

the destiny of the country." This rather ambiguous appeal to the party contained no direct call for the resignation of Seymour. Blair was the cause of the trouble. The "few men" referred to were evidently the Democratic National Committee, which the *World* virtually asks to meet and make the necessary changes in the ticket. The *World* was supported in its position by the Washington *National Intelligencer,* which on October 16 reprinted the *World's* editorial of the 15th, and added its own endorsement.

The Republican papers of New York City naturally held that the *World's* proposal was the counsel of extremity. The *Evening Post* (October 15) thought that Seymour and Blair were impediments to Democratic success, but the platform was a greater one. The Democrats "have nothing to lose in the present campaign, for all is already lost." The New York *Times* (October 16) did not doubt the failure of the *World's* proposal, for " it arrays itself against the vital, governing forces of the Democracy." The *Herald* (October 17) thought that " no more suicidal policy could be suggested by the worst enemy of the Democracy," and added " What sane man would consent to stand in the breach at the eleventh hour?" The *Tribune* (October 16) was surprised that the *World,* hitherto an ardent Seymour supporter, should succumb to pressure. Seymour, added the *Tribune,* was more dangerous than Blair to the Democratic party. The Springfield *Republican* (October 17) commented on the demoralization of the Democratic party. " All this is delicious reading to Republicans."

The consternation among the Democratic leaders in Washington as a result of the *World's* proposal was given by a despatch to the *Times.* " The Democratic managers here anticipated such a move, and have been at work since yesterday to see what they could do. But all is confusion. . . . Some want Chase, some want Hendricks, some want Hancock, and still others curse the *World* and its friends for their cowardice." [11]

Gideon Welles in his diary for October 15 gives some insight into the situation and his own views in it. " Seymour is doomed to defeat, and at this late day a rally for another can hardly be made, if attempted." Although there had been a good deal of talk of throwing aside the ticket, " this talk is idle." It might not be difficult, since the last elections, to persuade Seymour to withdraw, but the substitution of Chase would not make the ticket stronger. " The talk about the President means nothing. There is no intention to make him the candidate. . . . I am sorry he listens to it." On the 16th Welles expressed his preference for Hancock or Doolittle, if a change was to be made, although he felt that a " change of front at this late day would be a pretty certain percursor of defeat." [12]

While the Democrat pot was boiling so merrily, Chief Justice Chase was in correspondence with his friend Alexander Long, who wrote from Cincinnati on the 15th, " Confidential," that he was sending his law partner (George F. Hoeffer) to Washington to consult Chase on matters not suitable for telegraphing. " The demand among the Democrats for the withdrawal of Seymour and Blair and the substitution of yourself with Franklin, Ewing or some one else is universal." Blair, in Cincinnati, admitted all was lost and would cheerfully withdraw, according to Long. The Ohio Democratic State Central Committee had been called together by telegraph to meet in Columbus on October 16. Long expected the Committee to demand a change in the ticket and the nomination of Chase, and he urged Chase to accept the nomination without hesitation. " Your success will be tri-

[11] October 16, 1868.
[12] Vol. iii, pp. 454-455, 458.

umphant and one of the grandest achievements ever accomplished in popular government." [13]

The suggestion of the *World* was not permitted to go unrebuked by those Democrats who were not stricken with panic. Belmont, Tilden and Augustus Schell met it with the statement to J. D. Hoover of the Washington Congressional Committee on October 15: " No authority or possibility to change front. All our friends consider it totally impracticable and equivalent to disbanding our forces. We in New York are not panic-stricken." [14] The Washington correspondent of the Boston *Post* stated that the article in the *Intelligencer* on October 16 was written before the reception of the telegram from Tilden, Belmont and Schell. If advance copies had not already been given out to radical correspondents it would have been suppressed.[15] The espousal of the *World's* suggestion by the *National Intelligencer* on October 16 " produced a storm of indignation among the Democrats here who, without exception, ridiculed the nonsense of the New York *World*." No one was louder in denouncing the folly of the *World* than President Johnson, " who laughs at the crowings of the Radicals " and " professes today strong confidences in the election of Seymour and Blair." [16] The New York *Tribune* also stated that President Johnson thought the proposal injurious and ill timed, nor had he intimated a wish to replace Seymour.[17]

Hancock was unwilling to have anything to do with the movement, and he earnestly dissuaded the movers in it from pressing it further.[18] He was reported to have said that the

13 New York Historical Society Library, Misc. Mss. Long.
14 New York *Herald*, October 17 (Washington, October 16, 1868).
15 In Utica *Observer*, October 19, 1868.
16 Albany *Argus*, October 19.
17 October 19, 1868.
18 New York *Herald*, October 17.

defeat of the party was certain, whatever it might do.   Gen-
enral Rosecrans was quoted to the effect that it was too late
for a change in front.[19]   The report was very general that
Chase refused to listen to the suggestion that he replace Seymour.   The Washington correspondent of the Cincinnati
Commercial October 17 reported Chase as saying that " he
looked upon the talk about a change of candidates as a temp-
est without wind or water. . . . He was not seeking a candidacy for the Presidency and did not desire it."   The Boston
Post's correspondent said that Chase " expressed his astonishment that anyone pretending to have a particle of political
sagacity should be guilty of the folly exhibited in the columns
of the New York *World*." [20]

Few Democratic newspapers followed the lead of the
World.   Opposition to the suggestion was prompt and general.   The Washington *Evening Express* of October 16
wanted to know why " we are called on at this time to surrender. . . . Now is the time for a renewed, vigorous charge
all along the line."   The Rochester *Union* proclaimed that
" The Democracy with one voice indignantly reject the evil
counsel of the *World,* and the Utica *Observer* echoed with
" Form the lines closer, men.   Yield no particle of hope." [21]

The Memphis *Avalanche* denounced the suggestion of the
World as all bosh.   " The Democratic party is pledged to
party leaders."   The Newark *Journal* spoke of the *World* as
" a noted skirmisher rather than a regular soldier," which
" is about to unfurl the white flag in the presence of the
enemy." [22]   Perhaps the bitterest denunciation of the *World*
came from the New York *Democrat,* Brick Pomeroy's paper.
" Traitor, fool, renegade, tool of a wicked power; uncover

[19] Cincinnati *Commercial*, October 17, 1868.

[20] In Albany *Argus*, October 19, 1868.

[21] Albany *Argus*, October 19, 1868.

[22] In New York *Times*, October 18, 1868.

your head, take off your shoes, for the place where thou dost stand is holy ground. Your fire will die out, but the bush of Democracy will live for pilgrims to rest under the shade thereof, after turning aside to spit on your graves!" [23] The Albany *Argus* (October 19) referring to the *World's* proposal said " The Democracy of the Nation repels the suggestion of a capitulation or retreat." Other papers opposed to the suggested change in the ticket were the New York *Evening Express,* Louisville *Courier,* Macon (Ga.) *Telegraph,* Detroit *Fress Press,* Nashville *Union and American,* Harrisburg *Patriot,* Buffalo *Courier* and the Rochester *Union.*

While this agitation was occurring in the press, the position taken towards it by the candidates—Seymour and Blair —was of great public interest. The chief target of the *World's* attacks was Blair. He announced his willingness to retire in a speech at St. Louis on the evening of October 16, " Whenever by so doing I can add one vote to the strength of the Democracy." He was " ready to make any sacrifice." Referring to a report that both he and Seymour had signified their intention to decline in favor of some other candidates, Blair said " both candidates will always be ready to lay down their candidacy when it can no longer be of service to the Democratic party." Blair announced his determination not to abandon the field " in one sense at least I mean to bear my share of the battle; whether in the ranks or as an officer will depend on the wishes of the Democratic party." [24] Both Seymour and Blair were reported to have telegraphed to the Executive Committee that they were willing to act for the best interests of the party.[25] Before making the speech at St. Louis on the 16th, the latter wrote to his father asking Tilden and the senior Blair to judge what action he should

[23] New York *Tribune,* October 20, 1868.

[24] New York *Herald,* October 18; Utica *Observer,* October 19, 1868.

[25] Cincinnati *Commercial,* October 18, 1868.

take.   Blair, Sr., wrote to Tilden on October 29 asking that, if any change in the ticket was contemplated, he telegraph him and he would come to see him.[26]   Tilden wired on the 20th " without contemplating any change, I should be glad to consult with you." [27]

The opposition of Belmont and his Committee to the proposal of the *World* was unrelenting.   In addition to the telegram to J. D. Hoover of the Washington Committee, Belmont, Tilden and Schell telegraphed to W. F. Storey, the Democratic National Committeeman from Illinois, on October 17, in reply to a query, that the suggested change " was wholly unauthorized and unknown to National Democratic Executive Committee or any member thereof."   It was branded as absurd and as having been received by the masses of the party with astonishment, derision and indignation.   An optimistic estimate of the October elections followed.   " We came nearer to our expectations than Republicans to theirs," and continued effort by the Democracy would be crowned with success.[28]

On Saturday, October 17, at Utica, a conference took place between Seymour and some members of the National Executive Committee, at which Seymour said that any changes which should be made must include his withdrawal; that he was nominated against his wishes, and it would be a relief for him if another name were substituted for his own.   The Committee replied that no change had been contemplated and that, in their judgment, nothing could be so injurious to the Democratic cause as a change of candidates.[29]   The sponsors of the movement wanted Belmont to call the full membership of the Democratic National Executive Committee together to

[26] *Tilden Letters*, vol. i, p. 198 (date given in error as 1865).

[27] *Ibid.*, p. 251.

[28] *Tilden Letters*, vol. i, p. 251.

[29] Utica *Observer*, October 19, 1868; also New York *Herald* and *World*.

consider the *World's* proposal. This Belmont did not do, and for his lack of action was denounced by those favoring the movement.[30]

As the situation continued serious, with the *World* and the *National Intelligencer* reiterating the suggestion that a change in the ticket be made, and Republican papers reporting with enthusiasm the quarrels among the Democrats, it became evident that some action should be taken by the Chairman of the Democratic National Committee. Accordingly, on October 20, Belmont issued from New York an " Address to the Conservatives Voters of the United States." No direct reference was made to the discussion over the change in the ticket, and on the contrary the unity of the party was declared to be perfect. The Republican accusation that the Democrats intended revolution and defiance of established order was denied and denounced. " The ballot box and the supreme will of the American people are the only means of redress to which we look." Horatio Seymour was extolled as a patriot devoted to the Union and " a man equally beloved for the purity of his private character and honored for his public virtues." The record of the Republican party for the past four years was attacked, and the South was promised a return to Constitutional government, with peace and union, if the Democrats should be victorious. The financial issue was disposed of by promising economy in government, an equitable system of taxation, and a development of the country's resources, to place Federal finances on a solid and stable footing and to pave the way for a gradual and safe return to specie payment. The address concluded: " Our ranks are unbroken: our courage is unabated. Once more to the breach and this time victory! " [31]

[30] Baltimore *Commercial*, October 17, in *National Intelligencer*, October 19, 1868; Baltimore *Sun* in Washington *Express*, October 19, 1868.

[31] *Belmont Letters, etc.*, pp. 188-190.

The *National Intelligencer* was not satisfied with the address, but continued to call for a meeting of the National Executive Committee to place before the people Chase, Hancock, Johnson or Hendricks in place of Seymour.[32]

The leadership of the party was severely criticised as a result of the agitation for a change in the ticket. With more effective management, it was felt, such a demand would have been discussed and settled in party council, without allowing the whole agitation to be carried on in the public prints, to the delight and comfort of the Republicans. Chairman Belmont was attacked on the ground that he allowed more than thirty days to elapse after the nominations before he consulted with Seymour. It was charged that when he did get in touch with Seymour, " it was done with a demand that Mr. Seymour should promise to permit Wall Street to name the Secretary of the Treasury in case of his election. This impertinent and disgraceful demand was promptly and forcibly repelled by Mr. Seymour. Hence the *World* and Wall Street have been since that time continually plotting for his defeat." This story gives some indication of the distrust in which the New York leadership of the party was held in other sections. A more intelligerent criticism of the guidance of the party was contained in the *Round Table* which declared that Seymour's chances of winning had disappeared, and that the Democratic leadership was largely to blame:

We do not speak of Mr. Seymour, who had perhaps had less to do with the management of the canvass than any other prominent man of his party. We do speak of those who have pulled wires, handled pursestrings, and concocted ideas for the organization. Undoubtedly the ablest conceivable efforts might not have succeeded, although we think they would have done so.[33]

[32] October 22, 1868.
[33] October 17, 1868.

The New York *Herald* on October 19 reported that Democratic politicians in Washington were "abusing Belmont soundly for his alleged ineptness, and charged him with even worse, for they say he has sold out to the enemy and that his continued refusal to summon the ticket together is explainable on that theory." This attitude is that of those opposed to his refusal to approve the change in candidates. The question may well be raised, however, to what extent was the agitation due to the failure of Belmont's leadership? It is hard to see how he could have acted differently, once the proposal got into print, and it is equally hard to see how he could have prevented a public discussion of a suggestion that had occurred to so many. As has been shown, the *World* was not the only source of the proposal. It is possible that closer relations between the National Committee and the party press might have kept the newspapers from airing the troubles of the party to the extent they did. That is only conjecture. It is also possible that an appeal to the voters, stressing party unity and confidence in the ticket, issued immediately upon the publication of the *World's* suggestion, might have taken the edge off that proposal. But again that is conjecture.

On October 20 Chairman Tilden of the New York State Committee issued an address corresponding to the national address of Belmont. Here again no reference was made to the suggestion by the *World*. After comparing the Democratic vote in October with that of 1866, the address stated: "You have driven the Republicans to the baggage wagons. You have almost routed them. Fellow Democrats! Is this a moment for doubt as to what you ought to do?" [34]

On October 30 a Democratic Convention of the Eastern District of Rhode Island adopted a resolution disapproving of the suggested change in candidates, declaring the entire

[34] *McPherson Scrap Book,* Library of Congress, vol. ii, p. 22.

satisfaction of the Convention with Seymour and Blair, and pledging them hearty support.   The Democratic State Committee of Connecticut also issued an address denouncing all proposals for a change in candidates, and ending " Cowards may go to the rear.   The Old Guard steps forward firmly to the front." [35]

The interpretation given by the Republican press to the movement to replace the Democratic ticket indicated plainly the folly of the Democrats in washing their party linen in full view of the enemy.   The *Tribune* gleefully announced that the Democracy was disintegrating and that " suave qui peut " was now the cry of their ranks.   The Springfield *Republican* said that the proposal emphasized the extent and meaning of the Republican victories in October.   *Harper's Weekly* called the proposal of the *World* " the crowning folly of an extremely foolish newspaper," and said that as the country rejected the policy of the Democratic party in the elections, an effort was beng made to renounce the policy. The Chicago *Republican* thought the object of the movement was not victory in November, but to form an organization including all elements of opposition to the Republican party, and which shall " turn its back upon the dead issues of the past."   The failure of the movement, according to Godkin, was due to the fact that it was produced too late.   " The only result of the *World's* outburst was to satisfy the public that the Democratic politicians themselves had given up the game as lost. . . .   There is perhaps now plenty of bitter repentance in the Democratic ranks for not having nominated Chase." [36]

A conservative view of the situation was offered by John Quincy Adams in a conversation on the train while returning from his South Carolina trip.   Adams shrewdly remarked " It is now too late to change the candidates.   The election

[35] Washington *Express*, October 24, 1868.
[36] New York, October 29; London *Daily News*, November 10, 1868.

of General Grant is inevitable, and such a movement would materially damage the interests of the Democracy." He did not believe that Chase could ever have defeated Grant, and said that he certainly could not do so if made the nominee so late in the campaign. Adams blamed the Democratic platform more than the candidates for the impending defeat of the party. The Democracy, he asserted, should have gone before the country on one issue—reconstruction.[37]

2. SEYMOUR'S SPEAKING TRIP IN OCTOBER

Reference has been made to Seymour's reluctance to take an active personal part in the campaign. He felt that stump speaking by a candidate for the presidency was incompatible with the dignity attached to the nomination. Seymour's position on this point was reënforced by the refusal of his rival, Grant, to take the rostrum. But the advantages of this situation all lay with the Republicans, for Grant lacked ability in public speaking, while Seymour was one of the most effective orators in his party.

Seymour's wishes were generally respected until the campaign in Pennsylvania became keen, when he was requested by various leaders to speak in that State. Among these were William Wallace, Pennsylvania Chairman, and William Cassidy, editor of the Albany *Argus*.[38] Seymour did not accede to these requests, and the October elections passed without his appearance on a political platform. Up to October 13 the only speeches he made were non-political addresses at Albany and at the Saratoga Agricultural fair. In these speeches he made no reference to the issues of the day, and at Saratoga confined himself to eulogizing farm life and discussing the every day problems of the farmer.[39]

[37] New York *World*, October 21, 1868.

[38] *Seymour Papers*, Albany.

[39] Utica *Observer*, September 10, 11, 1868.

The Republican gains in October, and the resulting signs of panic in certain Democratic quarters, were probably the reasons why Seymour abandoned this passive attitude and agreed to take the stump actively. When he did so, he did so completely, and made a tour which extended as far west as Chicago.

The New York *World* announced on October 20 that Seymour would break his silence, and would open his personal campaign in Buffalo on October 22. Seymour's home paper, the Utica *Observer,* was enthusiastic over the tour Seymour was to make. "Our Chieftain Leads the Host" was its heading for an article which stated that in the crisis Seymour had risen above personal considerations. "He is moved by no ambition: he is deterred by no obloquy. Now, as ever, he meets the emergency of the hour and treads the road that duty points." [40]

It was the announcement that Seymour was to take the stump which drew from President Johnson his most active contribution to the Democratic campaign—his wire to Seymour expressing the hope that the tour would result in victory.

At the same time that Seymour went West, Blair came East, and spoke at Tammany Hall on October 27. The *World's* hostile attitude toward Blair was reflected in its reception of his speech, which it attempted to "soft pedal" while the *Herald* defended him for his frankness. [41]

Seymour left Utica on his tour on October 21, [42] accompanied by Francis Kernan. The trip lasted until the day before the election, November 2, when he returned to Utica. He spoke at Syracuse and Rochester, October 21; Buffalo,

[40] October 21, 1868.

[41] Stebbins, *op. cit.,* p. 384.

[42] Details of tour from Utica *Observer,* New York *World* and *Public Record.*

October 22; Cleveland, October 23; Chicago, October 24; Indianapolis, October 26; Columbus, October 27; Pittsburg, October 28; Harrisburg and Reading, October 29; Philadelphia, October 30; and Wilkesbarre, October 31. He returned to Utica by way of New York City. On various parts of his tour the local Democratic leaders joined him briefly, and he delivered many short talks at small cities and towns along his way.

In his speeches Seymour emphasized the conservative character of the Democratic programme, and decried all proposals for changing existing conditions by means other than the usual processes of law. He attacked the Republicans for their extravagance, and maintained that this lay at the root of the currency difficulties. He denounced the Republican attacks on the Supreme Court and the President as unconstitutional. The Radical reconstruction policy was oppressive to the South, and should be abandoned, but only by orderly and lawful means. Seymour proclaimed that his party stood for a return to orderly, peaceable constitutional government, with the States equal before the Federal government and with civil authority supreme over military authority. He tended to ignore the greenback and suffrage issues.

In short, he made clear his opinion that the Republicans, not the Democrats, were the revolutionists and the violators of the Constitution. A vote for him would be a vote for a return to Constitutional Federalism, and a Democratic victory would heal the wounds of the war, which had been kept inflamed by the Republican policy.

The Springfield *Republican* considered the tour a failure, and criticised the Democrats for not standing up squarely to the programme which was marked out by the platform and the nominations.[43] This was the position taken generally

[43] October 30, 1868.

by the Republican press. But after the votes were in, Seymour was assured by Church that his trip had been of great service. " It saved us in this State, and put the party in excellent condition. It was a great advantage to you personally, as you came out of the fight with flying colors." [44]

3. THE VOTES ARE CAST

On November 3, the highest hopes of the Republicans were realized, and Grant was elected by 214 electoral votes to 80 for Seymour.[45] The popular vote was 3,012,833 for Grant and 2,703,249 for Seymour; or in percentages, 52.71% and 47.29%. Seymour carried only Delaware, Georgia, Kentucky, Louisiana, Maryland, New Jersey, New York and Oregon. If the former Confederate States (except Virginia, Mississippi and Texas, which did not vote, and Florida, whose electors were chosen by the legislature) are taken as a unit we find that they gave Grant 401,199, or 48.3% and Seymour 429,840, or 51.7%. Seymour received a majority of the popular vote in the South and at the same time the electoral vote from only two of these States; the reason for this lay in the large Democratic majority in the two states carried, Georgia and Louisiana. Taking the non-Confederate, or " loyal " States as a unit, we find that Grant received 2,611,634 or 53.5%, and Seymour 2,273,400 or 46.5%. This figure may be compared with the percentage of the total vote cast for McClellan in 1864—44.1%; a gain for the Democrats in 1868 of nearly 2.5%. Dividing the North into sections we get the following percentages for 1868:

[44] November 16, 1868, *Seymour Papers*, Albany.

[45] Election figures from *American Annual Cyclopedia*, 1868; Stanwood, *Presidency*, vol. i, p. 328, McPherson, *Reconstruction*; and *Tribune, Democratic* and *World Almanac*, 1869. See Appendix A and C.

Section	Grant	Seymour
New England	63.1	36.9
Middle States	50.5	49.5
Loyal Slave	41.1	58.9
Middle West	54.6	45.4
Trans-Mississippi	63.9	36.1
Far West	50.6	49.4
Total	53.5	46.5

A significant fact about Seymour's vote is that it ran consistently behind the State Democratic vote, whether cast in October or November. Grant ran ahead of the State tickets in every Northern State but one. In Delaware Grant received ten votes less than the Republican Congressional candidate, and Seymour received nineteen votes more than the Democrat running for Congress. Taking the North (or rather those States, North, West, and Border which were never in the Confederacy) as a whole, we find that the Democratic State tickets (or Congressional in some instances) polled 48.1% of the vote cast, compared with Seymour's 46.5%.

It is interesting to speculate as to the result, if Seymour could have carried the " solid South " as was done by Democratic candidates from 1880 on. Grant received 52 Southern votes, including Missouri as a Southern State. Twenty-three electoral votes were not cast—those of Mississippi, Texas and Virginia. Adding these 75 votes to Seymour's 80 gives 155. Subtracting the 52 votes from Grant's 214 gives 162. Therefore, the Democrats could not justly say that Grant was elected through the operation of the reconstruction acts.

In members of Congress, the Democrats made a slight gain; instead of fifty representatives in the Fortieth Congress (elected in 1866), they had sixty-one in the Forty-First. The number of Democratic Senators in the new Congress decreased by two, however. Senators Dixon of Connecticut,

Buckalew of Pennsylvania, Patterson of Tennessee, and Doolittle of Wisconsin were replaced by Republicans. Thomas F. Bayard succeeded James A. Bayard as one of the Democratic Senators from Delaware. Willard Saulsbury, Democrat, held over. Besides Bayard, William T. Hamilton of Maryland, John P. Stockton of New Jersey and Eugene Casserly of California were new Democrats in the Senate. The total in the Fortieth Congress was 12. In the Forty-First it was 10.

The changes in the lower House were:

State	*Fortieth Congress*		*Forty-First Congress*	
	Republicans	*Democrats*	*Republicans*	*Democrats*
Connecticut	1	3	3	1
New York	20	11	18	13
New Jersey	3	2	2	3
Maryland	1	4	0	5
Tennessee	7	1	8	0
Ohio	16	3	13	6
Indiana	8	3	7	4
Illinois	11	3	10	4
Missouri	8	1	6	3
Minnesota	2	0	1	1
Oregon	1	0	0	1
Alabama	6	0	5	1

It is interesting to note that apart from the reconstructed South (where conditions were abnormal) the members of the lower houses of the State legislatures varied as follows: [46]

1864	1747 Republicans	593 Democrats
1865	1793 "	658 "
1866	1848 "	659 "
1867	1761 "	1125 "
1868	1889 "	996 "

The negro suffrage issue appeared in three states in the

[46] These figures, noted from the *Annual Cyclopedia* and the almanacs, are probably not precise, but they are approximately complete for the 26 non-Confederate States.

form of proposals to put negro suffrage in the State Constitutions. The proposal was defeated in Missouri (74,053 to 55,236) and carried in Minnesota. The Democrats claimed that the result was obtained by trickery.[47] In Nevada the Constitutional change was made by the legislature, which as elected in 1868 was Republican by a large majority in both houses. "White" was struck from the State Constitution by a vote of nearly two to one.[48]

Republican charges of fraud against the Democrats in the few States they did carry were general, but the situation in New York City [49] was the one most widely aired. Attention was attracted to New York by the fact that Seymour carried the State by exactly ten thousand votes. Charges and counter-charges of fraud in the coming election were freely made in New York City for some weeks before the balloting.[50] Following Seymour's victory, a Congressional investigation was demanded by the Union League Club of New York City,[51] and a select committee was appointed by the House of Representatives to look into the facts. The report of the committee accused the Democrats of "every known crime against the elective franchise." [52]

The unusual fact that Seymour had exactly 10,000 votes more than Grant gave rise to a charge that this result was obtained fraudulently in order to save bets the Democrats

[47] *American Annual Cyclopedia*, 1868, p. 505.

[48] *Ibid.*, p. 533.

[49] For general discussion, see Alexander, *op. cit.*, chapter 15, Stebbins, *op. cit.*, chapter 14, Myers, *Tammany Hall* (New York, 1917), p. 217 and following.

[50] For example, New York *Tribune*, October 22, New York *World*, October 30, New York *Evening Post*, November 2, *Nation*, October 29.

[51] New York *Evening Post*, November 6, 1868.

[52] 40th Congress, vol. iii, *Session House Reports*, nos. 31, 40 (paged consecutively), p. 4. Also *Senate Miscellaneous Documents*, no. 4.

had made upon their majority.[53]   But the official tabulation
of the votes gave this precise result by comparing the votes
received by a single Democratic elector and a single Republican elector, each at the head of the list.   A comparison of
the thirty-two other electors on each side gives a variation in
one case as high as 94 votes.[54]   Moreover, if Tweed padded
the city vote to overcome the up-state votes as was charged,[55]
how did it happen than he hit the mark by exactly 10,000
votes when his information about the up-state results was
wired to him before the actual counting?   This tabulation
up-state in most instances would not have been in the hands
of Democrats exclusively or even largely.   The districts were
Republican.   With the city vote padded to overcome an ap-
proximate lead, in order for the count to come out exactly at
any predetermined figure, it would have been necessary to
" adjust " the up-state vote in accordance with the inflated
city vote.   This was obviously impossible.

It was freely charged before the election that Seymour was
to be " knifed " in order to make Hoffman's victory certain.
At first glance, the fact that Hoffman received some 10,000
more votes than Seymour would tend to suggest that trading
had taken place.   On the other hand, Seymour ran behind his
ticket in every Northern State but one (Delaware).   That
he should fall behind Hoffman by 10,000 in the largest State
in the Union was not suspicious—it was only consistent.   It
is possible that some trading took place, but it is not likely
that it was extensive or that it was done on a large scale or
in an organized manner.

While New York City received the spotlight in connection
with the charges of fraud in the election, it was not the only

[53] E. g. Curtis, *Republican Party*, vol. i, p. 509.

[54] Official canvass in Utica *Observer*, extra, no date, in Library of
Congress.

[55] New York *Evening Post*, November 3, 1868.

State which the Republicans alleged was won by the Democrats through the use of illegal methods. The *Nation* on November 12 charged that Georgia and Louisiana were carried by " organized assassination," and that New Jersey as well as New York was gained by fraud. Allegations of fraud were also made in connection with the bare Democratic majority of 165 in Oregon. In this instance it was charged that voters were brought in from the Idaho and Montana regions.[56]

When the Senate came to count the electoral vote in February, objection was made to that of Georgia on the grounds that the State had not fully complied with the Reconstruction Acts; that the electors of the State had not met to cast their vote on the proper day; and that the election in Georgia had not been fairly conducted. After a hectic discussion, the Senate voted 28 to 25 to count Georgia's vote, and the House voted 150 to 41 not to count it. The vote was formally announced as 80 for Seymour with Georgia and 71 for Seymour without Georgia, Grant being elected in either case.[57]

[56] Woodward, *Political Parties in Oregon* (Portland, 1913), p. 264.
[57] Stanwood, *Presidency*, vol. i, p. 331.

CHAPTER XIII

Conclusion

THERE remains for consideration the reason for the victory of Grant and its significance. The general impression—that Grant's victory was a "walk-over" and that the Democrats had no chance—is not accurate.

Burgess summarized the election by saying—

If the electorate of the South had been as in 1860, or probably as it was in the years of the Johnson governments, Seymour and Blair would have triumphed. As it was, but for the greenback plank in the Democratic platform and the indiscretions of General Blair they might have triumphed. That is to say, if the reconstruction policy of Congress had been the sole issue, it is quite possible that the Republicans would have lost the election; even with the most popular man in the North their standard bearer.[1]

Schouler, writing from his personal impressions and recollections of the contest, stressed the hopes for pacification which were centered in Grant as a major factor in his success. He made "no effort to bolster Union animosity against the South, like many of his party leaders, but his attitude was pacific and reconciling, and this was what the people wanted. His expression "Let us have peace" was the real platform upon which he won. To such a platform the North stood ready to commit itself; and ex-Confederates, too, trusted in the magnanimity of their conqueror. The campaign was in the general direction of harmony.[2]

Rhodes stated the victory of Grant was not so over-

[1] *Reconstruction and the Constitution*, pp. 212-213.
[2] *United States*, vol. vii, pp. 126, 126n.

whelming as the electoral count seemed to indicate. Had Seymour carried the " solid South " of 1880-1892, he would have been elected. This last statement, as we have seen, was incorrect. Rhodes sums up the campaign by saying that the strongest factors in Republican success were the immense personal popularity of Grant and the adroit use made by the Republicans of Southern " outrages " and unrest. He thinks that Seymour could have made a closer fight had he been permitted to make his own platform and choose his own running mate, " but no combination of circumstances could have beaten Grant." [3]

Stanwood also gives the conventional view—that Grant was unbeatable. The campaign was one-sided, though interesting; Grant's fame and high regard in which he was held " did not allow the result to be doubtful," although there were already some " notworthy defections " from the Republican party on account of the radical Southern policy.[4]

Henry Minor, in his party history, asserts that Seymour received some 300,000 majority of the white voters of the country while the 650,000 negro voters went Republican.[5] As a general statement, this is probably true. An appreciable minority of the Southern negroes voted with their former masters, though it would be difficult to fix a percentage. Ten per cent would be a liberal estimate. But the general thesis—that a majority of the white men of the country favored the Democratic party in 1868—is true, and is worth emphasizing. Reviewing the figures, a total vote of 5,716,000 was cast, of which Grant received 3,012,000 and Seymour 2,703,000. Assuming that there were 500,000 negro votes cast and that Grant received 450,000 (Grant received 402,000 Southern votes, predominantly black) and

[3] *United States*, vol. vi, pp. 195-196.
[4] *History of the Presidency*, vol. i, pp. 326-327.
[5] *Story of the Democratic Party*, p. 301.

Seymour 50,000, we find the white vote would be Republican, 2,562,000, and Democratic, 2,653,000. This, of course, is a very rough estimate.

All in all, it can be said that the Republican popular majority in 1868 was dependent upon negro suffrage, and this was probably true in most of the Presidential elections between the Civil and Spanish Wars.

The response of the Republican press to Grant's victory was what one would expect. The New York *Times* [6] said that Tammany had destroyed all chance of Democratic success when it dictated the platform and candidates in the New York Convention. The *Evening Post* [7] thought the result showed a popular determination that the Republican Congress should not be coerced. The New York *Sun* said Grant's victory would cause the waves of passion and violence in the South to subside. [8] The Springfield *Republican* held that the result was a popular triumph for Grant, and did not carry approval of the general policy of Congress. The Republicans won in spite of that policy. The *Republican* was glad that the heavy party majority in the House of Representatives had been reduced. As for the Democratic party, as a " disloyal " organization, it was dead and gone and " even its name is likely to perish."

The *Nation* [9] expected the Democrats to be able to furnish the country with a decent opposition, for the developments of the last month of the campaign indicated the existence of " a large body of persons who are sensible of the folly which has marked the course of the party during the last year or two." *Harper's Weekly* [10] said the canvass turned on Blair,

[6] November 5, 1868.

[7] November 4, 1868.

[8] November 4, 1868.

[9] November 5, 1868.

[10] November 7, 1868.

" because he is the positive point " and represented the real Democratic purpose and policy. *Leslie's Weekly* [11] pronounced the Democratic party dead and gone. The reason for its defeat was that the Democrats had tried to roll back the years and reopen the conflicts settled by the war.

James G. Blaine in a speech in the House on December 10 stated that the election just passed would prove to have been "the last in which the lately rebellious section, even if it could be wholly controlled by rebels, will have sufficient power in the electoral vote of the country to make it the object either of hope or of fear on the part of political organizations striving for the government of the nation." [12]

The New York *Herald,* still interested in what might have been, said on November 5 that its favorite, Chief Justice Chase, might have won if he had been the Democratic nominee.[13] The *World* on the other hand considered the movement for Chase in every way unfortunate, and a contributing cause of Seymour's defeat. Seymour's refusal to permit his name to be used before the Convention proved fatal to him in November, for if he had been a candidate the Chase movement would have been headed off, the Pendleton movement would not have developed, Blair would not have been placed on the ticket, and Seymour would have defeated Grant. Seymour, apart from this mistake, was the wisest and most sagacious of the Democratic leaders.[14]

Chase's opinion of the result was remarkable. On November 6 he wrote to Gerrit Smith, " Well, the election is over. I believe the result is the best for the country, though I could not bring myself to make a choice. Any-

[11] November 7, 1868.
[12] Stanwood, *Blaine* (Boston, 1905), pp. 99-100.
[13] In Stebbins, *op. cit.,* p. 403.
[14] November 5, 1868 (Boston, 1905).

thing certainly is better than Blair and revolution." [15]   This
letter is very illuminating.   It shows first that Chase did
not vote for Seymour after all, and that he swallowed hook,
line and sinker the Republican ranting about Blair.

Welles recorded in his diary that Grant's victory did not
surprise him.   There had been mismanagement and weakness on the part of the Democratic leaders, if nothing worse.
The New York Democratic capitalists, deprived of Chase,
were willing to see Seymour defeated.   " Pendleton and his
friends have acted like disappointed partisans, very stupidly
for themselves, very badly for the country, as if they were
afraid something might happen to hereafter defeat him." [16]
President Johnson was reported in the Philadelphia *Evening
Star* to be in ill humour with Grant's election.   It was
rumoured that he was considering resigning in order to forestall Grant by giving Wade control of the patronage and the
Cabinet for three months. [17]

The semi-Democratic *Round Table* said that Seymour's
weaknesses had been two.   He was bitterly hated by the
Republicans and had injured his position as a candidate by
refusing to run until the last minute.   The *Round Table*
thought that a victory in the October elections, which would
have been possible with a change of 10,000 votes, would
have given the Democrats the victory in November.   Grant
would not be the servant of the Radicals, according to this
journal.   He would crush out corruption, and would reform the civil service.   He was, in point of fact, a Democrat, and would prove to be a conservative President.   The
Radicals could be expected to break with him in a little
while. [18]

---

[15] *Chase Papers*, Library of Congress.
[16] Vol. iii, p. 464, November 17, 1868.
[17] November 10, 1868.
[18] October 31, November 7, 28, 1868.

Seymour's correspondence during the period following the election is interesting. The Pennsylvania leader, Heister Clymer, wrote him on November 5 praising him for his gallant fight. He called attention to the fact that, even if he had been elected, his hands would have been tied with a Republican Congress. Clymer credited Seymour with keeping the party intact after the disastrous October elections.[19]

On November 25 Pendleton wrote Seymour in an effort to moderate the recriminations which were disturbing Democratic harmony. He referred to the discussion among the Democrats as profitless, unjust, and offensive. " After election grumblings, embracing retrospect and prophecy, fault-findings and threats seem to be essential to some minds." In spite of the grumblings, " the tone and organization and discipline of the party in Ohio is entirely unbroken." [20] Pendleton invited Seymour to visit Cincinnati.

After reflection, Seymour reached the opinion that his defeat was due in large measure to the greenback plank in the Democratic platform. More than a year after the election he wrote George L. Miller of Omaha that the platform in 1868 was held by the public to threaten an unsettling of the financial situation.

The first great need of a great business community is certainty and security. . . . The idea of paying bonds in greenbacks was popular at first sight but when men looked into it they found it was started by men who meant to make greenbacks very cheap and thus unsettle prices. Instead of looking to a return to the standard of the world, we were charged with the purpose of putting out to sea and sailing away from land. This alarmed not only the bond holders but all creditors and business men. It was like Satan's flight into Chaos.[21]

[19] *Seymour Papers*, New York Historical Society Library, Box 4.
[20] *Seymour Papers*, New York Historical Society Library.
[21] *Ibid.*

By some observers Grant's election was held to show that
the people repudiated the greenback idea.   The *Round Table*
stated that the election " seems to have extinguished the
doctrine that our public bonds are payable in greenbacks."
Of the four prominent supporters of this doctrine in both
parties " Stevens is dead, Mr. Pendleton is silenced and
Senator Sherman is muzzled.   The irrepressible Butler alone
can raise a voice in its favor." [22]   Blaine in Congress on
December 10 stated that " the election of Grant has settled
the financial question." [23]   Bearing out Seymour's position
is the fact that towards the end of the campaign there was
a strong movement among business men to defeat the
Democrats.[24]

But Schouler and Rhodes are in agreement that the greenback issue did not figure greatly in the campaign.   Rhodes
points out that New York and New Jersey, hard money
States, went for Seymour with the greenback platform, while
Ohio and Indiana where the " Ohio Idea" had greatest
popularity went for Grant.[25]   And it is interesting to note,
in this connection, that in the nine States from Ohio to
Kansas, and north to Canada, Seymour received 43.8% of
the total vote cast while his percentage for the entire North
was 46.5% and for the entire nation 47.3%.

Summing up the election as a whole, it may be said that
the victory of the Republicans was to have been expected,
and that their victory was more pronounced because of the
errors of their opponents.   The Republicans entered the
campaign with tremendous advantages.   They had the
prestige of a victory won in a patriotic war against treason-

[22] November 28, 1868.

[23] Stanwood, *Blaine*, p. 100.

[24] Stanwood, *Presidency*, vol. i, p. 327.

[25] Schouler, *United States*, vol. vii, p. 125; Rhodes, *United States*, vol.
vi, p. 196.

able rebellion—as they considered it. The Republican organization was complete and had the assurance that goes with repeated successes. For eight years the party had dominated the political landscape in the " loyal " North. To this was added, through the operation of the Reconstruction Acts, a commanding position in the South. They had carried the war, politically as well as in a military sense, into the enemy's country. The machinery of the national government was in their hands so far as overwhelming Congressional majorities could give it to them, and the State governments—except for New York, Connecticut, Delaware, Maryland, Kentucky and Oregon—were under their control in varying degrees of completeness.

The State elections of 1867 and of the spring of 1868 had indicated that a reaction was under way against the Republicans. In order to counteract this tendency, the Republicans selected General Grant as their national standard bearer. Grant lacked qualities of statesmanship, and was innocent of any pronounced political views, but these weaknesses were as nothing when balanced against his tremendous personal popularity as the conqueror of the South. The death of Lincoln nearly four years before had left Grant the great surviving hero of the war. His candidacy was of major importance to the Republicans. His record emphasized the fact that the party which had nominated him had " saved the union," while his reputation for magnanimity and moderation appealed to those moderate Republicans who were restless under Radical Republican control.

The party which " saved the union " should rule it. Although more than three years had passed since Appomattox, the passions of the war had not died down. Indeed the Republicans in their quarrel with the President, and in the national and State elections of 1866 and 1867, had not allowed the war feeling to subside but had " waved the bloody shirt " with great effectiveness, and the same tactics were used successfully in the Presidential contest.

The Democrats were thus faced with a stupendous task. What little chance they might have had of ending Republican control was thrown away by their own mistakes.

The Democratic platform contained two major errors. The reconstruction plank antagonized the moderates, and this error was accentuated by the nomination of Blair, the author of the " Brodhead Letter," for Vice-President. The financial planks aroused the fears of the business interests of the country.

The nomination of Seymour was a mistake, as he realized. In spite of his excellent public and private character, he was easily identified in the Northern mind with the Democratic opposition to the war. What chances he may have had were decreased by the fact that he was nominated at the last minute and in a manner which excited suspicion, either that his selection was the result of a " deal " in the Convention or that it had been determined upon long before the meeting of the Convention. Neither of these suppositions were true, but Seymour's sincerity and that of the New York party leaders generally were attacked during the campaign with telling results.

Had the Democrats nominated General Hancock with a conservative Western civilian, such as Senator Hendricks, as his running mate, the party would have made a better showing in the election. With this ticket it is possible that the Democrats would have carried Pennsylvania, Indiana, and even Ohio, in the October elections. It is certain that, with Hancock and Hendricks at the head of the party, no such demoralizing move as that of the *World* in October would have been made. On the other hand, Hancock aroused little enthusiasm among the " Peace " element in the Democracy, although he would have been more acceptable than Seymour to the " greenback " element.

Another error, perhaps inevitable, was the part played by the Southern leaders in the campaign. It was natural that the leaders of the Southern whites should speak out during the contest but the result was bad in its effect on Northern opinion. The Southerners could have little hopes of influencing the national result and their statements were easily misrepresented by the Republicans.

But the Democratic party was not in a position to avoid errors. The party had been disrupted by the war, and the divisions had persisted and been added to. War and Peace Democrats, Northern and Southern Democrats and, more recently, Greenback and Gold Democrats represented lines of party cleavage which continued party defeat had done little to eliminate. To unite these elements was a herculean task which the party managers were unable to accomplish in 1868.

Considering everything, the Democrats did remarkably well. The party was reorganized while under fire, and succeeded in polling a majority of the white voters of the country. Furthermore, the Democrats had forced their opponents to put aside their statesmen, actively identified with Republican doctrines, and nominate the military hero of the war. These facts indicate the vitality of the underlying principles of the Democracy, and the existence of widespread discontent with the Radical Republican program.

While it is probable that Hancock and Hendricks would have received a heavier popular vote than Seymour and Blair, it is unlikely that they would have defeated Grant and Colfax. Because of the large Democratic minorities in Northern States which they could not hope to carry (Illinois and Michigan for example) and the Republican hold on the South, it would have taken more than a popular majority for the Democrats to have carried the electoral college. Sixteen of the Democrat electors came from the South. Had the Democrats carried the October elections in Pennsylvania, Indiana and Ohio, it is likely that Congress would have acted to prevent the possibility of any Southern States supporting the Democratic ticket. If this situation had existed, it is possible that Hancock would have carried in November: Pennsylvania (26), Ohio (21), Indiana (13), Connecticut (6), and California (5), in addition to those Northern States carried by Seymour. This would have given Hancock seventy-one more Northern votes, but Grant, under this supposition, would have carried Georgia and Louisiana, thus subtracting sixteen votes from Hancock. This would have given Hancock a total of 135 electoral votes, leaving Grant still with 159. The above changes in the Northern States would have been accomplished if a change of less than five per cent had taken place in their vote.

Victory for the Democrats, with the addition of the seventy-one Northern electoral votes, would have been possible only if they had held Georgia and Louisiana. In this case, the totals would have been: Democratic 151—Republican 143. The vote of Georgia, it will be recalled, was disputed by Congress when the electoral votes were counted. If the vote of Georgia had been decisive, would the Democrats have acquiesced in the refusal of the Republican Congress to count it for their candidate? It is fortunate indeed that this question did not come up.

It is clear that the Democratic party in 1868 was not in the position of last-ditch extremity to which many writers assign it. The above analysis of the election shows that the party made a good fight, under heavy odds, and that with better leadership the party would have contended with their opponents on almost equal terms. Coming between the war election of 1864 and the Greeley debacle of 1872, the strength of the Democracy in 1868 has not been generally recognized. From the point of view of the Republican party, the chief significance of the campaign was that the Republican forces, under Radical domination, saw in the situation in the South an opportunity to perpetuate its power, and therefore vigorously " waved the bloody shirt " in the North. The Northern Republican leaders expected to build up a Southern Republican following that would make the party really national. Eight years of misrule by their Southern allies were necessary before the mass of Northern Republicans abandoned this hope. Eight years were to elapse before " Let us have peace " became a reality rather than a campaign slogan.

APPENDIX A

PERCENTAGES OF DEMOCRATIC VOTE IN NORTHERN STATES, 1864-1868

Section	1864 State	1864 Presid.	1865 State	1866 State	1867 State	1868 State	1868 Presid.
New England......	37.2	36.5	33.7	36.3	43.2	39.4	36.9
Middle States......	49.8	49.3	47.7	48.8	52.2	50.7	49.5
Loyal Slave.	49.8	46.1	45.8	58.8	60.8	62.6	58.9
Middle West	43.6	43.3	43.5	44.2	47.7	46.5	45.4
Trans-Mississippi...	37.3	37.3	40.9	37.1	40.3	38.9	36.1
Far West	41.1	41.8	43.7	46.9	53.2	50.3	49.4
Total North ...	44.3	44.1	44.0	45.4	49.5	48.1	46.5

Computed from data in:

Annual Cyclopedia, 1865-1868.

Almanacs—*Tribune*, 1866-1869.
        Democratic, 1866-1869.
        World, 1868-1869.

McPherson, *History of Reconstruction*.

Stanwood, *History of the Presidency*, vol. i.

381

APPENDIX B

Summary of the Ballots for President in the Democratic National Convention, New York City, July 7, 8, 9, 1868

Candidates	Ballots 1	2	3	4	5	6	7	8	9	10	11	12	13	14	15	16	17	18	19	20	21	22[1]	22[2]
Horatio Seymour, N. Y.	....	....	....	9	....	....	....	....	....	....	....	....	....	....	....	....	....	....	....	....	....	22	*317
Geo. H. Pendleton, Ohio	105	104	119½	118½	122	122½	137½	*156½	144	147½	144½	145½	134½	130	129½	107½	70½	56½	....	....	....	....	....
Th. A. Hendricks, Ind.	2½	2	9½	11½	19½	30	39½	75	80½	82½	88	89	81	84½	82½	70½	80	87	107½	121	132	*145½	....
W. S. Hancock, Pa.	33½	40½	45½	43½	46	47	42½	28	34½	34½	32½	30	48½	56	79½	113½	137½	*144½	135½	142½	135½	103½	....
Andrew Johnson, Tenn.	*65	52	34½	32	24	21	12½	6	5½	6	5½	4½	4½	....	5½	5½	6	10	....	....	5	4	....
S. E. Church, N. Y.	*34	33	33	33	33	33	33	....	....	....	....	....	....	....	....	....	....	....	....	....	....	....	....
Asa Packer, Pa.	26	26	26	26	27	27	26	26	26½	*27½	26	26	26	26	....	....	....	....	22	....	....	....	....
Jas. E. English, Conn.	16	12½	7½	7½	7	6	6	6	6	....	....	....	....	....	....	....	....	....	6	16	19	7	....
Joel Parker, N. J.	13	*15½	13	13	13	13	7	7	7	7	7	7	7	7	7	7	7	3½	....	....	....	....	....
S. J. Field, Calif.	....	....	....	....	....	....	....	....	....	....	....	....	....	....	....	....	....	....	*15	9	8	....	....
J. R. Doolittle, Wisc.	13	12½	12	12	*15	12	12	12	12	12	12½	12½	13	13	12	12	12	12	12	12	12	4	....
F. P. Blair, Jr., Mo.	½	10½	4½	2	9½	5	½	½	½	½	½	½	½	....	....	....	....	....	*13½	13	....	....	....
Reverdy Johnson, Md.	8½	8	*11	8	....	....	....	....	....	....	....	....	....	....	....	....	....	....	....	....	....	....	....
Th. H. Seymour, Conn.	....	....	....	....	....	....	....	....	....	....	....	....	....	....	....	....	....	....	*4	2	....	....	....
S. P. Chase, Ohio	....	....	....	....	....	....	....	....	....	....	....	½	½	....	....	....	½	½	½	....	*4	....	....
J. T. Hoffman, N. Y.	....	....	....	....	....	....	....	....	....	....	....	....	....	....	....	....	*3	3	....	....	½	....	....
Thomas Ewing, Jr., Kans.	....	½	*1	1	....	....	....	....	....	....	....	....	....	....	....	....	....	....	....	....	....	....	....
G. B. McClellan, N. J.	....	....	....	....	....	....	....	....	....	....	....	*1	....	....	....	....	....	....	....	....	½	....	....
J. Q. Adams, Mass.	....	....	....	....	1	....	....	....	....	....	....	....	....	....	....	....	....	....	....	....	....	....	....
Franklin Pierce, N. H.	....	....	....	....	....	....	....	....	....	....	....	....	1	....	....	....	....	....	....	....	....	....	....

* indicates highest vote received by each candidate.

Names given in order of highest vote received throughout the balloting.

Ballots 1 – 6, July 7
     7 – 18, July 8
     19 – 22, July 9 Two roll calls on the 22nd ballot.

Notes on ballots.

Ballot 1. Church, N. Y. 33. Johnson, all but 4 from Southern States.

    4. Seymour, N. C. 9.

    5. J. Q. Adams, S. C. 1.

    6. Recess after fifth ballot.

    7. Hendricks presented. Indiana, Henricks 9½, Pendleton 3½.

    8. New York, Church to Hendricks. 33 votes.

   12. Chase, California ½; McClellan, Tennessee 1.

   13. Thirty-minute recess after 12th ballot. Pierce, Tennessee 1.

   15. Pennsylvania, Packer to Hancock, 26 votes.

   17. Illinois, Pendleton 8½, Hendricks 7.

   18. Adjournment defeated after 17th ballot. Illinois, Hendricks 16. Adjournment because of quarrel in Illinois delegation.

   19. Pendleton withdrawn before 19th ballot. Blair and Field presented.

   20. Fifteen-minute recess following 19th ballot.

   21. Chase, Massachusetts 4.

   22. Attempt to adjourn to St. Louis defeated after 21st ballot. Seymour, Ohio 21, Tennessee 1, on first roll call. Presented by McCook of Ohio.

   22. (Second roll call) Seymour unanimously nominated, in spite of efforts to decline.

Adapted from table in *Official Proceedings*, p. 174.

APPENDIX C

The Presidential Election of 1868

State	Electoral Vote		Popular Vote		Majorities	
	Grant	Seymour	Grant	Seymour	Grant	Seymour
Alabama	8	....	76,366	72,086	4,280	
Arkansas	5	....	22,152	19,078	3,074	
California..........	5	....	54,592	54,078	514	
Connecticut	6	....	50,641	47,600	3,041	
Delaware	......	3	7,623	10,980	....	3,357
Florida	3	....	See note			
Georgia............	......	9	57,134	102,822	....	45,688
Illinois	16	....	250,293	199,143	51,150	
Indiana............	13	....	176,552	166,980	9,572	
Iowa	8	....	120,399	74,040	46,359	
Kansas	3	....	31,049	14,019	17,030	
Kentucky..........	......	11	39,566	115,889	....	76,323
Louisiana..........	......	7	33,263	80,225	....	46,962
Maine	7	....	70,426	42,396	28,030	
Maryland	......	7	30,438	62,357	....	31,919
Massachusetts	12	... .	136,477	59,408	77,069	
Michigan	8	....	128,550	97,069	31,418	
Minnesota	4	....	43,542	28,072	15,470	
Missouri	11	....	85,671	59,788	25,883	
Nebraska	3	....	9,729	5,439	4,290	
Nevada............	3	....	6,480	5,218	1,262	
New Hampshire	5	....	38,191	31,224	6,967	
New Jersey	......	7	80,121	83,001	....	2,880
New York..........	......	33	419,883	429,883	....	10,000
North Carolina	9	....	96,226	84,090	12,136	
Ohio	21	....	280,128	238,700	41,428	
Oregon	......	3	10,961	11,125	....	164
Pennsylvania	26	....	342,280	313,382	28,898	
Rhode Island	4	....	12,993	6,548	6,444	
South Carolina	6	....	62,301	45,237	17,064	
Tennessee..........	10	....	56,757	26,311	30,446	
Vermont	5	....	44,167	12,045	32,122	
West Virginia	5	....	29,025	20,306	8,719	
Wisconsin	8	....	108,857	84,710	24,147	
Total.......	214	80	3,012,833	2,703,249	309,584	

The electoral vote of Florida was cast by the State Legislature.

No election was held in Mississippi, Texas or Virginia.

From *American Annual Cyclopedia*, 1868, p. 753; Stanwood, *History of the Presidency*, vol. i, p. 328.

BIBLIOGRAPHY

I. Biographical Material

BIOGRAPHIES

Most Important

Cook, Thomas M. and Knox, Thomas W., *The Public Record (etc.) of Horatio Seymour.* New York, I. W. England, 1868.

Oberholtzer, Ellis P., *Jay Cooke, Financier of the Civil War.* Philadelphia, George W. Jacobs, 1907. Two vols.

Schuckers, J. W., *The Life and Public Services of Salmon Portland Chase.* New York, D. Appleton, 1874.

Vallandigham, James L., *A Life of Clement L. Vallandigham.* Baltimore, Turnbull Bros., 1872.

Warden, Robert B., *An Account of the Private Life and Public Service of Salmon Portland Chase.* Cincinnati, Wilstach, Baldwin & Co., 1874.

Others

Adams, Charles Francis, *Charles Francis Adams.* Boston, Houghton-Mifflin, 1900 (American Statesmen Series, John T. Morse, Jr., Editor).

Adams, James Truslow, *The Adams Family.* New York, The Literary Guild, 1930.

Bancroft, Frederic, *The Life of William H. Seward.* New York, Harper & Bros., 1900. Two vols.

Barnes, Thurlow Weed, *Memoir of Thurlow Weed.* Boston, Houghton-Mifflin, 1884 (Vol. II of the Life of Thurlow Weed, by T. W. Barnes and Harriet A. Weed).

Bigelow, John, *The Life of Samuel J. Tilden.* New York, Harper & Bros., 1895. Two vols.

Bloss, G. M. D., *Life and Speeches of George H. Pendleton.* Cincinnati, Miami Printing and Publishing Co., 1868.

Carroll, Howard, *Life of Horatio Seymour.* (Typed copy in Seymour Papers, New Historical Society Library. 81 pages. Also in New York *Times*, August 18, 1879.)

Clarke, Grace Julian, *George W. Julian.* Indianapolis, Indiana Historical Commission, 1923.

Cook, Theodore P., *The Biography and Public Services of the Hon. Samuel J. Tilden.* New York and Chicago, H. S. Goodspeed & Co., 1884.

Croly, David G., *Seymour and Blair. Their Lives and Services.* New York, Richardson & Co., 1868.

Eckenrode, Hamilton James, *Rutherford B. Hayes, Statesman of Reunion.* New York, Dood, Mead & Co., 1930 (American Political Leaders, Allan Nevins, Editor).

Ewing, James Rees, *Public Services of Jacob Dolson Cox*, Washington, Neale Pub. Co., 1902. (Ph. D. thesis, Johns Hopkins University.)

Foulke, William Dudley, *Life of Oliver P. Morton.* Indianapolis, Bowen, Merrill, 1899. Two vols.

Gresham, Mathilda, *Life of Walter Quintin Gresham.* Chicago, Rand-McNally, 1919. Two vols.

Hancock, (Mrs.) Almira, *Reminiscences of Winfield Scott Hancock, by His Wife.* New York, Charles L. Webster, 1887.

Hart, Albert B., *Life of S. P. Chase.* Boston, Houghton, Mifflin, 1899 (American Statesmen Series, John T. Morse, Jr., Editor).

Hill, Benjamin H., Jr., *Senator Benjamin H. Hill of Georgia, His Life, Speeches and Writings.* Atlanta, H. C. Hudgins & Co., 1891.

Ingersoll, L. D., *Life of Horace Greeley.* Chicago, Union Pub. Co., 1873.

McCabe, James D., *The Life and Public Services of Horatio Seymour . . . [and] Francis P. Blair, Jr.* New York, United States Pub. Co., 1868.

McLaughlin, James Fairfax, *Tilden Memorabilia, A Series of Historical Letters.* New York, National Printing Co., 1880.

Merriam, George S., *The Life and Times of Samuel Bowles.* New York, Century Co., 1885. Two vols.

Milton, George Fort, *The Age of Hate, Andrew Johnson and Reconstruction.* New York, Coward McCann, 1930.

Ogden, Rollo, *Life and Letters of Edwin Lawrence Godkin.* New York, Macmillan, 1907. Two vols.

Paine, Albert Bigelow, *Th. Nast, His Period and His Pictures.* New York, Macmillan, 1904.

Pearce, Haywood Jefferson, *Benjamin II. Hill, Secession and Reconstruction.* Chicago, University of Chicago Press, 1928.

Pike, James S., *Chief Justice Chase.* New York, Powers, Macgovern & Slipper, 1873 (pamphlet, 18 pages).

Schell, Francis, *Memoir of the Hon. Augustus Schell.* New York, privately printed, 1885.

Seward, Frederick W., *Seward at Washington as Senator and Secretary of State.* New York, Derby & Miller, 1891.

Stanwood, Edward, *James G. Blaine.* Boston, Houghton, Mifflin Co., 1905 (American Statesmen Series, John T. Morse, Jr., Editor).

Stryker, Lloyd Paul, *Andrew Johnson. A Study in Courage.* New York, Macmillan, 1929.

Walker, Francis A., *General Hancock*. New York, D. Appleton, 1895 (Great Commanders Series).

Wall, A. J., *A Sketch of the Life of Horatio Seymour 1810-1886*. New York, privately printed, 1929.

Williams, C. R., *Rutherford Birchard Hayes*. Boston, Houghton-Mifflin, 1914. Two vols.

Wilson, James Harrison, *The Life of Charles A. Dana*. New York, Harper & Bros., 1907.

Winston, Robert W., *Andrew Johnson, Plebeian and Patriot*. New York, Henry Holt, 1928.

——, *A Biographical Review of the Military and Civil Services of Major General W. S. Hancock*. n. p. 1868 (pamphlet, 8 pages).

——, *Civil Record of Major General Hancock, during his Administration in Louisiana and Texas*. n. p. 1880.

AUTOBIOGRAPHIES, DIARIES, REMINISCENCES, ETC.

Most Important

Blaine, James G., *Twenty Years of Congress*. Norwich, Conn., Henry Bill Pub. Co., 1886. Two vols.

McCulloch, Hugh, *Men and Measures of Half a Century*. New York, Charles Scribner's Sons, 1888.

Piatt, Donn, *Memories of the Men Who Saved the Nation*. New York, Bedford, Clarke & Co., 1887.

Welles, Gideon, *The Diary of*. Boston, Houghton, Mifflin, 1911. Three vols. (John T. Morse, Jr., Editor.)

Others

Butler, Benjamin F., *Butler's Book*. Boston, A. M. Thayer, 1892.

Cox, Samuel Sullivan, *Three Decades of Federal Legislation, 1855-1885*. Providence, J. A. & R. A. Reid, 1885.

Forney, John W., *Anecdotes of Public Men*. New York, Harper & Bros., 1873, 1881. Two vols.

Julian, George W., *Political Recollections, 1840 to 1872*. Chicago, Jansen, McClurg & Co., 1884.

Poore, Benn : Perley, *Perley's Reminiscences of Sixty Years in the National Metropolis*. Philadelphia, Hubbard Bros., 1886. Two vols.

Reagan, John H., *Memories, with Special Reference to Secession and the Civil War*. New York, The Neale Pub. Co., 1906.

Schurz, Carl, The Reminiscences of. New York, McClure & Co., 1907-1908. Three vols.

Warmouth, Henry Clay, *War, Politics and Reconstruction*. Stormy Days in Louisiana. New York, Macmillan, 1930.

Watterson, Henry, *Marse Henry, An Autobiography*. New York, Doran, 1919. Two vols.

Weed, Thurlow, Autobiography of. Boston, Houghton, Mifflin, 1883 (Harriet H. Weed, Editor, volume one of *The Life of Thurlow Weed*, by T. W. Barnes and H. A. Weed).

COLLECTED LETTERS, SPEECHES, WRITINGS, ETC.

Most Important

Bigelow, John (editor), *Letters and Literary Memories of Samuel J. Tilden.* New York, Harper & Bros., 1885. Two vols.

Howe, M. A. De Wolfe (editor), *Home Letters of General Sherman.* New York, Charles Scribner's Sons, 1909.

Schurz, Carl, Intimate Letters of, 1841-1869. In Wisconsin Historical Society Publications, vol. xxx, 1928.

Williams, C. R. (editor), *Diary and Letters of Rutherford Birchard Hayes.* Columbus, Ohio State Archaeological and Historical Society, 1924. Five vols.

Others

Belmont, August, *Letters, Speeches and Addresses.* Privately printed, 1890.

Bigelow, John (editor), *Writings and Speeches of Samuel J. Tilden.* New York, Harper & Bros., 1885. Two vols.

Chase, Samuel P., Letters of. In American Historical Association, *Annual Report*, 1902, vol. ii.

Hamilton, J. G. de R., *Correspondence of Jonathan Worth.* Raleigh, North Carolina Historical Commission, 1909. Two vols.

Julian, George W., *Speeches on Political Questions.* New York, Hind & Houghton, 1872.

Seward, William H., The Works of. Boston, Houghton, Mifflin, 1884 G. E. Baker, editor). Five vols.

Thorndike, R. S., *The Sherman Letters.* New York, Scribner's, 1894.

MANUSCRIPT COLLECTIONS

The Library of Congress (Washington, D. C.)

Most Important

The Papers of:

    Salmon P. Chase.
    Andrew Johnson.
    Gideon Welles, including the Manuscript Diary.

Others

    William Allen.
    P. G. T. Beauregard.
    Jeremiah S. Black.
    William W. Corcoran.

James R. Doolittle.
Thomas Ewing.
George B. McClellan.
Franklin Pierce.
John Sherman.
William T. Sherman.
Edwin M. Stanton.
Alexander H. Stephens.
John C. Underwood.

Historical Society of Pennsylvania, Library (Philadelphia)

The Papers of Salmon P. Chase.

Dreer Collection, Letters of American Lawyers (only a few items).

New York Historical Society, Library (New York City)

Papers of Horatio Seymour.
Miscellaneous manuscripts.

New York State Library, Manuscripts Division (Albany)

Papers of Horatio Seymour.

New York City Public Library, Manuscripts Division

Gideon Welles Papers.
Horace Greeley Papers.

II. General and Special Studies (Secondary)

Most Important

Alexander, D. A. S., *Political History of New York*. New York, Henry Holt, 1909. Four vols.

Bowers, Claude G., *The Tragic Era. The Revolution after Lincoln.* Boston, Houghton, Mifflin, 1929.

Dewey, Davis Rich, *Financial History of the United States*. New York, Longmans, Green & Co., 1924. (Ninth edition.)

Oberholtzer, Ellis P., *A History of the United States Since the Civil War*. New York, Macmillan, in progress. Four vols.

Rhodes, James Ford, *History of the United States*. New York, Macmillan, 1906. Seven vols.

Stebbins, Homer A., *Political History of New York, 1865-1869.* New York, 1913 (Ph. D. thesis, Columbia University).

Others

Barclay, Thomas M., *The Liberal Republican Movement in Missouri, 1865-1871*, Columbia, Missouri, State Historical Society, 1926 (Ph. D. thesis, Columbia University).

Beale, Howard K., *The Critical Year, A Study of Andrew Johnson and Reconstruction.* New York, Harcourt Brace, 1930.

Belmont, Perry, *National Isolation an Illusion, etc.* New York, G. P. Putnam's Sons, 1925.

Burgess, John W., *Reconstruction and the Constitution, 1866-1876.* New York, Charles Scribner's Sons, 1902 (The American History Series).

Cole, Arthur C., *Illinois—The Era of the Civil War, 1848-1870.* Springfield, Illinois Centennial Commission, 1919. (Vol. III of Centennial History of Illinois.)

Curtis, Francis, *The Republican Party, 1854-1904.* New York, Putnam's, 1904. Two vols.

De Witt, David M., *The Impeachment and Trial of Andrew Johnson.* New York, Macmillan, 1903.

Dilla, Harriet M., *The Politics of Michigan* (1865-1878). New York, 1912 (Ph. D. thesis, Columbia University).

Dunning, William A., *Reconstruction, Political and Economic.* New York, Harper & Bros., 1907. (The American Nation Series, A. B. Hart, editor.)

Fleming, Walter L., *The Sequel to Appomattox.* A Chronicle of the Reunion of the States. New Haven, Yale University Press, 1921 (Chronicles of America, Allen Johnson, editor).

Fulton, Chandos, *The History of the Democratic Party from Thomas Jefferson to Grover Cleveland.* New York, P. F. Collier, 1892.

Hickok, *The Negro in Ohio, 1802-1870.* Cleveland, 1926. (Ph. D. thesis, Western Reserve University).

Knapp, Charles Merriam, *New Jersey Politics During the Period of the Civil War and Reconstruction.* Geneva, New York, W. F. Humphrey, 1924 (Ph. D. thesis, Columbia University).

Minor, Henry, *The Story of the Democratic Party.* New York, Macmillan, 1928.

Myers, Gustavus, *History of Tammany Hall.* New York, Boni & Liveright, 1917.

Porter, George A., *Ohio Politics during the Civil War Period.* New York, 1911. (Ph. D. thesis, Columbia University.)

Powell, T. E., *The Democratic Party in the State of Ohio.* Ohio Publishing Co., 1913. Two vols.

Quillin, Frank U., *The Color Line in Ohio.* Ann Arbor, George Wahr, 1913. (Ph. D. thesis, University of Michigan.)

Ryan, D. J. and Randall, E. O., *History of Ohio.* New York, Century Historical Co., 1912. Five vols.

Schouler, James, *History of the United States.* New York, Dodd, Mead & Co., 1913. Seven vols.

Shipley, Max Leroy, *The Greenback Issue in the Old Northwest* (*1865-1880*). Urbana, Ill., 1930 (abstract of Ph. D. thesis, Univ. of Ill.).

Smith, Theodore Clarke, *Political Reconstruction, 1865-1885.* (Chapter 20 of Vol. VII of the Cambridge Modern History, New York, Macmillan, 1903).

Stanwood, Edward, *History of the Presidency.* Boston, Houghton, Mifflin, 1898.

Taussig, Frank W., *The History of the Present Tariff, 1860-1883.* New York, G. P. Putnam's Sons, 1885.

Taylor, Abrutheus Ambush, *The Negro in South Carolina During the Reconstruction.* Washington, D. C., Association for the Study of Negro Life and History, 1924.

Thomson, A. M., *A Political History of Wisconsin.* Milwaukee, E. G. Williams, 1900.

Ware, Edith E., *Political Opinion in Massachusetts During the Civil War and Reconstruction.* New York, 1916. (Ph. D. thesis, Columbia University.)

Wilson, W. L., *The National Democratic Party.* Baltimore, H. L. Harvey & Co., 1888.

Wilson, Woodrow, *Division and Reunion, 1829-1889.* New York, Longmans, Green & Co., 1894. (Epochs of American History.)

Woodward, Walter Carleton, *The Rise and Early History of Political Parties in Oregon.* Portland, J. K. Gill Co., 1913. (Ph. D. thesis, University of California.)

III. Contemporary

Breen, Matthew P., *Thirty Years of New York Politics Up to Date.* New York, The Author, 1899.

Carey, Mathew, *The Democratic Speakers Handbook.* Cincinnati, Miami Printing and Publishing Co., 1868 (Augustus R. Cazanran, pseud.).

Dicksinson, Anna E., *What Answer?* Boston, Ticknor & Fields, 1868.

Gillet, Ranson H., *Democracy in the United States.* New York, D. Appleton, 1868.

Hiatt, James H., *The Voters' Text Book, etc.* Indianapolis, Asher, Adams & Higgins, 1868.

Hume, John F., *The Abolitionists, etc.* New York, G. P. Putnam's Sons, 1905.

Locke, David R., *Ekkoes from Kentucky.* Boston, Lee & Shepard, 1868. (Petroleum V. Nasby, pseud.).

——, *The Impendin Crisis uv the Dimocracy.* Toledo, Ohio, Miller, Locke & Co., 1868 (Petroleum V. Nasby, pseud.).

IV. CONTEMPORARY POLITICAL PAMPHLETS

Five bound volumes of pamphlets in New York City Public Library

Ephemera, 1865-1868.
Financial, United States, 1862-1869.
Pamphlets, 1865-1872.
United States History, 1866-1869.
United States History after 1866.

Individual pamphlets. (Included in above in many cases)

Blair, Francis P., Speech, Indianapolis, September 23, 1868.

von Bort, P. H., *General Grant and the Jews.* New York, 1868.

The Democracy, and Its Policy: Speeches, G. S. Boutwell, Thaddeus Stevens and General Schenck, House of Representatives. July 11, 1868. Washington, D. C. Union Republican Congressional Committee, 1868.

Democratic Falsehoods Exposed. *Facts for the People.* Washington, D. C., 1868.

An Epitaph: *In Memory of the Democratic Party—The Soldiers' Friend,* 1868. A " Broadside."

Lunt, George, Jr., *Letters to a Hunker Democrat,* 1868.

Massachusetts and South Carolina. Correspondence between J. Q. Adams and Wade Hampton. Speech of J. Q. Adams. Columbia, S. C., October 12, 1868.

Miller, George L., Address at Unveiling of Bust of Horatio Seymour, Utica, 1899. (In New York Historical Society Library.)

The Path to Conservative Triumph, New York, 1868.

Peace of War. Speeches of Senators Morton, Stewart and Nye. United States Senate, July 9 and 10, 1868.

Pendleton, George H., Speech, Bangor, Maine, August 20, 1868.

——, Speech, Milwaukee, Wisconsin, November 2, 1867.

Principles of the Democratic Party. Speech of John A. Logan, House of Representatives, July 16, 1868. Washington, D. C., Union Republican Congressional Committee, 1868.

Record of the Democratic Convention. Treason and Democracy, Washington, D. C. Union Republican Congressional Committee, 1868.

Horatio Seymour—The War Record of a Peace Democrat. Washington, D. C. Union Republican Congressional Committee, 1868.

Seymour, Horatio and Tilden, Samuel J., Speeches at New York State Democratic Convention, Albany, March 11, 1868. New York *World* Tracts, no. 1, 1868.

Seward, William H., Speech, Auburn, New York, October 31, 1868. Washington, D. C., Philip & Solomons, 1868.

V. MAGAZINE ARTICLES, PROCEEDINGS OF SOCIETIES, ETC.

American Historical Association, *Annual Report 1902*, vol. ii, pp. 514-522. Letters of S. P. Chase.

American Historical Review, January, 1930, pp. 276-294. Howard K. Beale, " The Tariff and Reconstruction."

Americana (American Historical Magazine), vol. ii (1907), pp. 151-172. Edwin S. Todd, " The Presidential Election of 1868." Vol. iv (1909), pp. 332-335, vol. viii (1913), pp. 220-223, 518-522. Duane Mowry, contributor, " Letters of James R. Doolittle."

Annals of Iowa, 3rd ser., vol. xii, pp. 618-619. John Brigham, " Henry Clay Dean's Correspondence with Horace Greeley," 1867.

The Magazine of History, vol. xvii (1913), pp. 56-64. Duane Mowry, contributor, " Selections from the Correspondence of James R. Doolittle."

Michigan Political Science Association. *Publication*, vol. iii, no. 1 (1898). Mary Joice Adams, " The History of Suffrage in Michigan."

Mississippi Valley Historical Review, vol. xi, no. 4 (1925). R. C. McGrane, " Ohio and the Greenback Movement."

North American Review, vol. cv (July, 1867), p. 280: " Letter of Hugh McCulloch."

Vol. cvii (July, 1868), pp. 167-186: Adams S. Hill, " The Chicago Convention."

Vol. cvii (October, 1868), pp. 445-465: George B. Woods, " The New York Convention."

Ohio Archaeological and Historical Quarterly, vol. xv (1906), pp. 313-341: Joseph B. Foraker, " Salmon P. Chase."

Vol. xxxvii (1928), pp. 220-427: Clifford H. Moore, " Ohio in National Politics," 1865-1896.

Oregon Historical Society Quarterly, vol. ii, no. 4 (1901). William D. Fenton, " Political History of Oregon, 1865-1876."

South Atlantic Quarterly, vol. xxvi (1927), pp. 404-416. Marguerite Hall Albjerg, " The New York Press and Andrew Johnson," (Ph. D. thesis, University of Wisconsin).

Southern History Association, *Publications*, vol. ix (1905), p. 26; vol. xi (1908), pp. 94-105. Duane Mowry, contributor, " Doolittle Correspondence."

Trinity College Historical Society Publications, vol. vii (1907), pp. 17-31. " Selections from the Correspondence of Bedford Brown, 1859-1868."

Wisconsin Historical Society *Proceedings* (1911), pp. 60-76. Evarts B. Greene, " Some Aspects of Politics in the Middle West, 1860-1872."

VI. GOVERNMENT AND PARTY DOCUMENTS

Congressional Globe

Report on New York Election Frauds. House Documents no. 31, February 23, 1869; no. 41, March 1, 1869. Third Session, Fortieth Congress.

Democratic National Convention. *Official Proceedings*, Boston, Rockwell and Rollins, 1868.

Republican National Convention. *Official Proceedings*. Chicago *Evening Journal*, 1868.

VII. ANNUALS AND REFERENCE WORKS

American Annual Cyclopedia. New York, Appleton, 1865, 1866, 1867, 1868,

The American Year Book and Register, 1868. In the *American Journal of Education,* vol. xviii (1869).

Almanacs. New York *Tribune,* 1866-1869, inc.

New York *World,* 1868-1869.

Democratic, 1866-1869, inc.

Biographical Directory of the American Congress, 1774-1927. Washington, Government Printing Office, 1928.

Cyclopedia of Political Science. New York, Charles E. Merrill, 1893. Three vols., John J. Laylor, editor. Vol. i, article by Alexander Johnston on "Democratic-Republican Party." Vol. iii, article by Alexander Johnston on "Reconstruction."

McPherson, Edward, *The Political History of the United States of America during the Period of Reconstruction, 1865-1870.* Washington, Solomons & Chapman, 1875. (Reprinted and added to, from McPherson's Political Handbooks, 1865-1870.)

VIII. JOURNALS AND NEWSPAPERS CONSULTED

Weekly Magazines

Harper's Weekly (New York, Republican).

The Independent (New York, Republican).

Frank Leslie's Illustrated Newspaper (New York, Republican).

The Nation (New York, Republican).

The Round Table (New York, Independent).

The West and South (Cincinnati, Democratic).

Newspapers

New York City

Evening Post (W. C. Bryant, Republican).

Herald (J. G. Bennett, Independent).

Sun (C. A. Dana, Republican).

Times (H. J. Raymond, Republican).

Tribune (Horace Greeley, Republican).

World (Manton Marble, Democratic).

Washington, D. C.

National Intelligencer (John F. Coyle, Democratic).
Express (J. D. Hoover, Democratic).
National Republican (Republican).

Philadelphia, Pa.

Evening Star (Independent).

Chicago, Illinois

Republican (Republican).
Times (Wilbur Storey, Democratic) weekly edition only seen.

Cincinnati, Ohio

Commercial (Murat Halstead, Republican).

Springfield, Mass.

Republican (S. K. Bowles, Republican).

Albany, N. Y.

Argus (William Cassidy, Democratic).

Utica, N. Y.

Observer (Democratic).

Memphis, Tennessee

Avalanche (Democratic).

London, England

Daily News (for letters of E. L. Godkin, from New York).

Newspaper clippings, no names or dates, in six scrapbooks of Edward McPherson, in Library of Congress.

IX. Works Consulted but not Cited

Abbot, Lyman, *Henry Ward Beecher.*
Badeau, Adam, *Grant in Peace.*
Barnes, William H., *History of the 39th Congress.*
——, *History of the 40th Congress.*
Bauchar, R., *Rise and Fall of Political Parties in the United States.*
Beecher, Henry Ward, *Selections from His Writings.*
Bingham, Johnson, *James Harlan.*
Boutwell, George S., Reminiscences of.
Chadsey, Charles E., *The Struggle Between President Johnson and Congress.*
Cooper, T. V. and Fenton, H. T., *American Politics.*
Cullom, Shelby M., *Fifty Years.*
Depew, Chauncey M., *My Memories of Eighty Years.*

Dix, Morgan, *Memoirs of John A. Dix.*
Fessenden, Francis: *Life and Public Service of William Pitt Fessenden.*
Ford, John, *Life and Public Service of A. H. Green.*
Foraker, Joseph B., *Notes of A Busy Life.*
Galbreath, Charles G., *History of Ohio.*
Godkin, E. L., *Reflections and Comments.*
Godwin, Parke, *A Biography of William Cullen Bryant.*
Gordy, J. P., *History of Political Parties in the United States.*
Greeley, Horace, *Recollections.*
———, *Record on Amnesty and Reconstruction.*
Hamilton, Peter J., *The Reconstruction Period.*
Haynes, Fred E., *Third Party Movements Since the Civil War.*
Hibben, Paxton, *Henry Ward Beecher.*
Hollister, O. J., *Life of Colfax.*
Kent, Frank R., *The Democratic Party.*
Lowell, James Russell, *Political Essays.*
McCarthy, Charles H., *Lincoln's Plan of Reconstruction.*
McClure, Alexander K., *Recollections of Half-Century.*
Maverick, August, *Life of Henry J. Raymond.*
Olbrich, Emil: *The Development of Sentiment on Negro Suffrage to 1860.*
Palmer, John M., Personal Recollections of.
Patton, Jacob H., *The Democratic Party.*
Platt, Thomas C., *Autobiography.*
Robinson, E. E., *Evolution of American Political Parties.*
Ross, Earle D., *The Liberal Republican Movement.*
Sherman, John, *Recollections.*
Slater, Walter, *Life of James W. Grimes.*
Steiner, Bernard C., *Life of Reverdy Johnson.*
Stephens, Alexander H., *Constitutional View of the War Between the States.*
Taylor, Richard, *Destruction and Reconstruction.*
White, Horace, *Life of Lyman Trumbull.*
Wilson, Henry, *History of the Reconstruction Measure.*
———, *Rise and Fall of the Slave Power in America.*

INDEX

397